Richard E. Flathman

Richard E. Flathman's work is innovative in its focus on language both as a way to help comprehend the meaning and significance of central political concepts as well as a way to understand the importance of opacity and unintelligibility. His books and essays illuminate and defend a distinctive conception of what he calls virtuosity or willful liberalism that advocates robust notions of pluralism, individuality, and political freedom.

The editor has focused on work in three key areas:

Equality, Authority, Rights, and Philosophy as Therapy
The first selections focus on key political ideas and how Wittgenstein's understanding of language can help untangle puzzles associated with those ideas. What results from a careful attention to meaning are not merely reports on usage, but a defence of particular understandings of equality, authority, and rights.

Situating and Disciplining Freedom
These readings illustrate Flathman's preeminence as a theorist of political freedom. He defends a view of freedom as negative, situated, and elemental. Against critics and defenders, he uses Wittgenstein's view of language to argue in support of a freedom that is social and rule-bound. Drawing on the work of Nietzsche he argues in his later work that control and discipline are not merely compatible, but necessary for freedom of agency.

Opacity, Liberalism, and Individuality
These selections explore the limits of meaning and the role of unintelligibility in supporting pluralism, individuality, and willful liberalism. Part of this enterprise entails drawing on perspectives and thinkers beyond the liberal canon. The final essay sets out Flathman's broader conception of the relationship between doing the history of political theory and doing political theory.

P.E. Digeser is Professor of Political Science at the University of California, Santa Barbara. She is the author of *Our Politics, Our Selves?* (1996), *Political Forgiveness* (2001), and *Friendship Reconsidered: What it Means and How it Matters to Politics* (2016).

Routledge Innovators in Political Theory
Edited by Terrell Carver
University of Bristol
and
Samuel A. Chambers
The Johns Hopkins University

Routledge Innovators in Political Theory focuses on leading contemporary thinkers in political theory, highlighting the major innovations in their thought that have reshaped the field. Each volume collects both published and unpublished texts, and combines them with an interview with the thinker. The editorial introduction articulates the innovator's key contributions in relation to political theory, and contextualises the writer's work. Volumes in the series will be required reading for both students and scholars of twenty-first century politics.

1 **William E. Connolly**
Democracy, pluralism and political theory
Edited by Samuel A. Chambers and Terrell Carver

2 **Carole Pateman**
Democracy, feminism, welfare
Edited by Terrell Carver and Samuel A. Chambers

3 **Michael J. Shapiro**
Discourse, culture and violence
Edited by Terrell Carver and Samuel A. Chambers

4 **Chantal Mouffe**
Hegemony, radical democracy, and the political
Edited by James Martin

5 **Ernesto Laclau**
Post-Marxism, populism, and critique
Edited by David Howarth

6 **George Kateb**
Dignity, morality, individuality
Edited by John Seery

7 **Hanna Fenichel Pitkin**
Politics, justice, action
Edited by Dean Mathiowetz

8 **Richard E. Flathman**
Situated concepts, virtuosity liberalism and opalescent individuality
Edited by P.E. Digeser

Richard E. Flathman
Situated concepts, virtuosity liberalism and opalescent individuality

Edited by P.E. Digeser

LONDON AND NEW YORK

First published 2017
by Routledge
2 Park Square, Milton Park, Abingdon, Oxon OX14 4RN

and by Routledge
711 Third Avenue, New York, NY 10017

Routledge is an imprint of the Taylor & Francis Group, an informa business

© 2017 P.E. Digeser and Richard E. Flathman

The right of P.E. Digeser to be identified as author of the editorial matter, and of the individual authors as authors of their contributions, has been asserted by them in accordance with sections 77 and 78 of the Copyright, Designs and Patents Act 1988.

All rights reserved. No part of this book may be reprinted or reproduced or utilised in any form or by any electronic, mechanical, or other means, now known or hereafter invented, including photocopying and recording, or in any information storage or retrieval system, without permission in writing from the publishers.

Trademark notice: Product or corporate names may be trademarks or registered trademarks, and are used only for identification and explanation without intent to infringe.

British Library Cataloguing in Publication Data
A catalogue record for this book is available from the British Library

Library of Congress Cataloging in Publication Data
A catalog record for this book has been requested

ISBN: 978-1-138-85280-8 (hbk)
ISBN: 978-1-315-72326-6 (ebk)

Typeset in Times New Roman
by Wearset Ltd, Boldon, Tyne and Wear

Contents

Acknowledgments	vii
Introduction P.E. DIGESER	1

PART I
Equality, authority, rights, and philosophy as therapy 11

1 Equality and generalization, a formal analysis (1967) 13

2 Wittgenstein's philosophy of language and political and social philosophy (1973) 23

3 Authority and the "surrender" of individual judgment (1980) 32

4 Liberalism and authority (1989) 42

5 The theory of rights and the practice of abortion (1989) 55

PART II
Situating and disciplining freedom 85

6 Kinds of freedom (1987) 87

7 Is the positive theory of freedom a theory of freedom? (1987) 98

8 Situating freedom (1987) 116

vi *Contents*

9 Control, resistance, and freedom (2003)   141

PART III
Opacity, liberalism, and individuality   157

10 Individuality, plurality, and liberalism (1992)   159

11 Of liberty, authority and power (1993)   182

12 Strains in and around liberal theory: an overview from a
strong voluntarist perspective (1998)   203

13 Here and now, there and then, always and everywhere:
reflections concerning political theory and the study/
writing of political thought (2006)   217

An interview with Richard E. Flathman   238

Index   248

Acknowledgments

On September 6, 2015, Richard E. Flathman died at the age of 81. An ardent defender of individuality, a keen analyst of freedom, and an unabashed liberal, he was the George Armstrong Kelly Professor of Political Science, emeritus at the Johns Hopkins University.

We are grateful to the following publishers and journals for permission to reprint the chapters in this collection:

University of Chicago Press for Chapter 3 "Authority and the 'Surrender' of Political Judgment" in *The Practice of Political Authority* (Chicago), 1980, pp. 90–91 and pp. 100–108. Chapter 6 "Kinds of Freedom" in *The Philosophy and Politics of Freedom* (Chicago), 1987, pp. 15–24 and pp. 323–325. Chapter 7 "Is the Positive Theory of Freedom a Theory of Freedom?" in *The Philosophy and Politics of Freedom* (Chicago), 1987, pp. 87–109 and pp. 330–332. Chapter 8 "Situating Freedom" in *The Philosophy and Politics of Freedom* (Chicago), 1987, pp. 114–116 and pp. 120–147 and pp. 332–333.

Cornell University Press for Chapter 4 "Liberalism and Authority" in *Toward a Liberalism* (Ithaca), 1989, pp. 48–64. Chapter 5 "The Theory of Rights and the Practice of Abortion" in *Toward a Liberalism* (Ithaca), 1989, pp. 168–205. Chapter 10 "Individuality, Plurality, and Liberalism" in *Willful Liberalism* (Ithaca), 1992, pp. 83–84 and pp. 92–119.

Routledge for Chapter 9 "Control, Resistance, and Freedom" in *Freedom and Its Conditions* (New York), 2003, pp. 82–99.

Sage for Chapter 11 "Of Liberty, Authority and Power" in *Thomas Hobbes: Skepticism, Individuality and Chastened Politics* (Newbury Park), 1993, pp. 103–127.

University of Minnesota Press for Chapter 12 "Strains in and Around Liberal Theory" in *Reflections of a Would-Be Anarchist* (Minneapolis), 1998, pp. 3–11 and pp. 12–16 and pp. 166–167.

Cambridge University Press for Chapter 13 "Here and Now, There and Then, Always and Everywhere: Reflections Concerning Political Theory and the Study/Writing of Political Thought" in David Armitage, ed., *British Political Thought in History, Literature and Theory, 1500–1800* (Cambridge), 2006, pp. 254–277.

Atherton Press for Chapter 1 "Equality and Generalization: A Formal Analysis" in J. Roland Pennock and John W. Chapman, eds., *Nomos IX* (New York), 1967, pp. 38–51.

viii *Acknowledgments*

Macmillan for Chapter 2 "Wittgenstein's Philosophy of Language and Political and Social Philosophy" in *Concepts in Social and Political Philosophy* (New York), 1973, pp. 30–38.

Every effort has been made to contact copyright holders for their permission to reprint material in this book. The publishers would be grateful to hear from any copyright holder who is not here acknowledged and will undertake to rectify any errors or omissions in future editions of this book.

Introduction

P.E. Digeser

Richard E. Flathman has been called "the most authentic Hobbesian of our time" and "the most idiosyncratic and the least classifiable" of contemporary theorists (Tuck 2002: 228; Levy 2006: 23). For many years, he was best known for his numerous book-length treatments of central concepts in political philosophy. In that body of work, he "played what is perhaps the dominant role in introducing what was once called 'analytic political philosophy' into political theory" (Wertheimer 1990: 181). His later work carves out a view of liberalism that is less state-centric, more sympathetic to pluralism and less dependent on conceptions of the reasonable and the rational. In addition, he has come to be known as a proponent of self-enacted individuality that celebrates the sometimes opaque and opalescent character of the individual. Flathman argues that we sometimes cannot fathom one another, but we also possess a kaleidoscopic, many-hued interiority that can, on occasion, be comprehended by ourselves and others. Both of these attributes are important sources of individuality and pluralism. Flathman has shown himself to be a keen analyst of political ideas, a prominent therapist of philosophical conundrums, a skeptic of state institutions and authority, and a fierce defender of individuality and freedom.

This introduction will highlight three innovations of Flathman's work. The first involves his contribution to understanding the meaning of key political ideas, as well as the limits of meaningful understanding. As a theorist of meaning and of the limits of meaning (or what he sometimes calls "unmeaning"), Flathman presents an account of how to engage in political theory and be responsive to others. A second innovation carves out a place for the "willful" in a theoretical world that tends to be dominated by the rational and the reasonable. This theoretical contribution undergirds a liberalism that differs from liberalisms that rest on the rational and the reasonable. A third innovation involves Flathman's understanding and defense of individuality. His approach to individuality expresses an anti-perfectionist perfectionism that he argues is central to the liberal ideal. What makes it an anti-perfectionism is that his position does not endorse some kind of substantive specification for the shape of that enacted self (Flathman 2006). It is not a position that sees a natural or identifiable goal toward which all human being are or should be drawn. Yet, it is still a perfectionism insofar as it endorses a distinction between an attained and unattained

2   *Introduction*

self: between what we are and what we could make ourselves into. This third innovation draws liberalism into literatures and questions that it has sought to evade and avoid, moving it beyond its traditional state-centric focus. The following takes up each of these innovations in turn.

A theorist of meaning and unmeaning

As with a number of thinkers in the middle of the twentieth century (e.g., J. L. Austin, John Searle, Norman Malcolm, Elizabeth Anscombe. H. L. A. Hart and Hanna Pitkin), Flathman's work from the 1960s into the 1980s was greatly influenced by Ludwig Wittgenstein's notion that it is only in and through language that understanding is possible. The "linguistic turn" in the first half of the last century pushed political philosophy beyond the metaphysically-based claims of prior political thinkers, the value-neutrality of empirically or scientifically grounded political science, and the grand narratives offered by many historically-driven theoretical accounts. Inoculated against appeals to nature, essences, timeless truths, and an ultimate universal or collective good, Flathman argued that understanding the world, ourselves, our interactions, and our institutions could be achieved through close attention to language and how it was and is being used.

Flathman's work, however, is not entirely free of a set of deeper commitments. By taking on such Wittgenstinean notions that meaning is in use and that language is composed of public, rule-governed practices, Flathman was able to analyze and explore the meaning and value of a number of central political concepts. Even if there is a prodigious diversity to our language and "[s]ome aspects of human affairs are … more difficult of access than others … 'everything lies open to view'" (Flathman 1973: 38). During this time, in addition to setting aside the conventional wisdom within political science for how to approach and study politics, Flathman also resisted various approaches to the human condition that simply shut down the possibility of reaching intersubjectively meaningful, normatively significant conclusions about basic political concepts and ideas. Logical positivism (of the sort advanced by A. J. Ayer (1946) and Charles Stevenson (1944)) and the predominance of behaviorialism in political science (see, for example, the work of David Easton (1953), Heinz Eulau (1969), and Glendon Schubert (1958)), led some to believe that moral and ethical assessments are either meaningless or nothing more than emotional utterances—expressions of impulses and feelings that carry no intersubjective weight or value. Political theory's reputation may have hit its lowest point in Robert Dahl's 1958 book review of Bertrand de Jouvenel's *Sovereignty: An Inquiry into the Political Good*. Dahl wrote:

> Bertrand de Jouvenel is one of a very small group of writers in our own time who make a serious effort to develop political theory in the grand style. In the English-speaking world, where so many of the interesting political problems have been solved (at least superficially), political theory is dead. In the Communist countries it is imprisoned. Elsewhere it is moribund.
>
> (Dahl 1958: 89)

Introduction 3

Still others believed (and continue to believe) that unless language is grounded in something more than our historically contingent conventions, practices, and norms, we would fall into a kind of global unintelligibility (see, for example, the work of Leo Strauss (1965) or Alasdair MacIntyre (2001)). If the view of language and meaning suggested by Wittgenstein is plausible then all such positions are, at their heart, incoherent. Nevertheless, Flathman's later work suggests that positions that talked of mutual unintelligibility did point to something important, something that he later came to embrace.

If we focus on Flathman as a theorist of meaning, it is important to note that his careful explorations of central political ideas such as the public interest, equality, obligation, rights, property, authority, freedom, liberalism, pluralism, civil disobedience, individuality, citizenship, legitimacy, education, policing and the rule of law were not simply reports on these terms as they were being used. Among other things, what becomes "open to view" once we closely examine ordinary language is that there are better and worse accounts of our ideas and concepts. For example, as a prominent theorist of authority, Flathman argues that the character of language and rule-following has implications for disputes that have dogged our understanding of the term. It is commonplace in debates over the meaning of authority for thinkers to argue that if authority requires anything, it must require a surrender of judgment on the part of those who are being commanded to carry out the orders, decrees, laws, or directives being issued by the authority. In contrast, as he discusses in the selections on authority in this volume, Flathman argues that by examining what it means to follow a rule and what must be the case in order for a practice of authority to exist, we see that the idea that authority cannot demand the surrender of judgment. As a rule-governed and rule-generating practice, authority requires that its participants must exercise judgment in order to understand the law and determine its applicability and scope. Nevertheless, even if the exercise of judgment is constitutive of the practice of authority, it remains the case that authority "abbreviates and truncates the processes of reflection and judgment through which agreement develops among free human beings" (Flathman 1989: 64). The larger set of authoritative norms and beliefs that supports a practice of authority (what he calls the authoritative) simultaneously opens the practice to reason-giving even as particular authorities may refuse to give reasons for their actions.

Another illustration of how his conceptual work moves beyond a mere report of use can be found in Part II of this volume, where Flathman analyzes the meaning and value of freedom. In the confrontation between the proponents of negative freedom and the supporters of positive freedom, Flathman begins with a five-fold distinction between types of freedom (1987). More significantly, he argues that that the central competing positions on freedom are both correct and incorrect. Defenders of negative freedom are correct in thinking that political freedom should be understood in terms of the absence of external impediments, but incorrect to the extent that they subscribe to an unsituated, private self and fail to distinguish mere movement from action. In contrast, defenders of positive freedom are correct in arguing that human agency and hence freedom require

4   *Introduction*

sociality, but incorrect in claiming that this means having to define political freedom in terms of virtue or the general will. The positive freedom position goes wrong by associating unfreedom with heteronomous or unvirtuous action. For if the vicious were unfree how could they be responsible for their actions? The negative freedom position goes wrong by failing to see that the self was deeply enmeshed in rule-governed practices. Drawing on the work of Wittgenstein, Flathman argues that freedom must be situated—a term that he uses as shorthand for the idea that it is inseparable from publicly shared, mutually meaningful language. Our freedom can be evaluated only if we see ourselves as much more than deeply privatized entities who are enslaved by whims and passions. This understanding of freedom is later deepened and amended in Flathman's engagement with Foucault and Nietzsche, and in his subsequent analysis of the role of discipline and the ideal of individuality.

In *Willful Liberalism* (1992), Flathman notes that he first read Wittgenstein as "theorizing the enablement of meaning." It was through that reading that much of his conceptual work was conducted. But by the 1990s, he came to believe that "this reading overlooks and suppressed a great deal." As he now understands him, "Wittgenstein is as much a theorist of unmeaning and the limitations and disablement of meaning as of their opposites. Or rather, by virtue of being a great theorist of the one he is a theorist of both" (1992: 6 n. 2). In many respects, it is this realization that moves Flathman beyond the conventionalism of his earlier work on political concepts. What is meaningless is "parasitic" on the meaningful. More surprising is his claim that the meaningful provides us a way to not only identify, but also to value the meaningless (Flathman 1992: 73–74). Despite (or because of) a system of languages in which "everything is open to view," we have the possibility for languages and practices that are "indeterminate, opalescent, opaque, and occluded" (1992: 97). Opacity is itself lodged in the conditions of understanding (and not a return to or an endorsement of a notion of a private language which both Wittgenstein and Flathman reject). If this is true, then opacity accompanies our attempts at mutual and self-understanding. This conclusion is joined with the notions of individuality and pluralism that come to dominate his later writing.

If, in his earlier work, Flathman resists the claims of those who denied intelligibility to our normative and ethical language, his more recent work resists those who argue that our language renders the world and ourselves transparent and intelligible. Perhaps the ideals of clarity and understanding as voiced by such distinct theorists as Socrates, Descartes, Hegel, Habermas and Taylor are not always and everywhere ideals. These thinkers see opacity and occlusion as "defects to be remedied where possible, deficiencies that should be regretted where they cannot be eliminated" (Flathman 1992: 108). In responding to these positions, Flathman argues that language operates in such a way that opacities, partial understandings, misunderstandings and not knowing whether we understand—as well as combinations of certainty and uncertainty—are all possible. Moreover, he regards opacity as sometimes an advantage, bolstering robust notions of individuality and pluralism. It can perform this role because opacity makes it difficult for others to manipulate and control what they cannot fully understand. We are often an enigma to ourselves and to others and these are not such bad things. Most would accept the idea that we sometimes fail to understand one another and some would argue that we cannot but fail to understand one another in various ways. Flathman's argument is closer to the latter position, with the addition that this failure should be "protected, welcomed, and even cultivated" (1992: 113) because of its potential to protect and cultivate individualities and pluralities.

Like Wittgenstein, Flathman is a theorist of both meaning and unmeaning. To render mutual intelligibility impossible would be to render unintelligibility unintelligible. We are neither entirely transparent nor entirely opaque to one another. In many cases, we are intelligible in certain respects and a mystery in others. For example, it is quite possible to understand what someone else believes without understanding why they believe what they do: liberals in the United States may understand the propositional meaning of the claims that guns are necessary for freedom, that climate change is unrelated to human activity, and that President Obama is not an American citizen, without understanding how certain conservatives can believe these propositions. Alternatively, US conservatives can understand the meaning of the propositions that safe and legal abortions are a right, gay marriage is consonant with the idea of marriage, and that health insurance is a human right without understanding how liberals could believe those things. Examples of this sort can be found across religious beliefs, cultural practices, and historical time period.[1] But just as, if not more, disturbing, this opacity may also extend to one's own self. "Know thyself" is at best a partial achievement or a brief abatement of mystery. At the interpersonal level, the possibility for mutual opacity throws a wrench into any political project that seeks to employ reason, argument, persuasion, or even authoritative commands to secure universal agreement, community, harmony, and unity. This perspective places Flathman at odds not only with Straussians, communitarians, Marxists, discourse theorists, and natural law theorists, but also with powerful liberalisms that pursue stability and agreement through reason and transparency: Rawlsians, utilitarians, libertarians, and defenders of deliberative democracy. The territory that Flathman has sought to claim is what he calls willful liberalism.

The rational, the reasonable, and the willful

One way to understand willful liberalism is to contrast it with liberalisms that are focused on the idea of the reasonable in contrast to the rational. The rational as deployed by rational choice theory and certain forms of utilitarianism presupposes a single, unified agent pursuing its own ends and interests (Rawls 2005: 50). In contrast, the reasonable entails no more than a willingness to propose and honor fair terms of cooperation and rests on a desire to "be able to justify our actions to others on grounds they could not reasonably reject" (Rawls 2005: 49, 50 n. 2). For liberalisms, such as Rawls's, which place great weight on the reasonable, what appears rational can be unreasonable and hence unacceptable. The rational does not disappear, but it is checked by the idea of the reasonable.

6 *Introduction*

Reasonable liberalisms can also push back against positions that are influenced by romanticism, post-structuralism, and agonism. These other theories may see rationality as a trap and the drive to agreement, system, and unity has itself a kind of failing or a cover for the exercise of power. In contrast, the reasonable is seen as providing a way for diverse individuals to be bound to principles that govern the basic institutional arrangements of society. By being reasonable, reasonable liberals argue that we can construct rules and norms to which we can agree and abide by.

Just as the reasonable does not do away with the rational, Flathman's conception of the willful does not dispose of the reasonable (or the rational for that matter). Nothing in his argument suggests that the rational and the reasonable lack meaning or cannot be deployed in ways that enhance the quality of human life. They are not, however, the only (language) games in town, and they do not necessarily deliver the goods that their proponents claim. In particular, Flathman argues that focusing on the reasonable and the rational can lead liberalism to truncate or betray its highest commitments to pluralism and individuality. For example, Rawls defends pluralism, but only if it is a reasonable pluralism. In other words, for Rawls, we need not tolerate positions that we do not find reasonable in the sense discussed above. Toleration always has its limits and in the predominant strains of liberalism something that is seen as unreasonable is unlikely to be tolerated let alone valued or celebrated. To be open to an unreasonable pluralism—that is, a pluralism that was potentially open to both reasonable and unreasonable beliefs, actions and individuals, is to move into a territory that is largely occupied by non- and even anti-liberal thinkers—for example, Friedrich Nietzsche, William James, and Michel Foucault. But into that territory Flathman believes liberalism must go.

At this point, Flathman's claims regarding opacity support his skepticism toward liberal aspirations to secure a reasonable order. Those claims suggest that, on occasion, it may be impossible to satisfy the desire to justify our actions and beliefs to ourselves, let alone to others. He writes, "Rather than Reason [willful liberalism's] chief emblem is Will construed as largely or at least finally mysterious" (Flathman 1998: 13). Flathman's call for a willful liberalism is meant to defend a more robust pluralism, one that is celebratory of differences, idiosyncrasies and idiolects (i.e., the distinctive linguistic patterns peculiar to particular people) that we may not even understand. It is a liberalism that is committed to "that extreme but inspiring form of pluralism that is the cultivation and celebration of individuality" (Flathman 1998: 41). What falls outside the reasonable need not be something to be feared, rejected, or merely tolerated. At the very least, willful liberalism is focused on how individuals can see themselves and others. It is more a project of ethos formation and less one of generating institutional arrangements. Willful liberalism is about a certain generosity of spirit that goes beyond toleration and the respect for rights. It is a liberalism of virtuosity that rests on the spirit of liberality and magnanimity.

Individuality

Flathman's willful liberalism is also an "individuality-affirming" liberalism (Flathman 1994: 680). What does he mean by individuality, and how can it be affirmed within liberal theory? While the writers that Flathman most admires talk of self-made individuality (Montaigne), free-spiritedness (Nietzsche), and "imagined forms of individuality" (Hampshire), he tends to settle on an Oakeshottian conception of self-enacted individuality. Flathman understands Oakeshott's conception of self-enactment to include work on one's own desires and sentiments as well as acting in ways that express and secure them. The internal work is frequently difficult, because self-enactment entails a self-overcoming that is rarely easy. However, such self-overcoming may bring into being a plurality of "selves each of whom enacts herself in distinctive ways" while satisfying the distinctive moralities of self-enactment and self-disclosure (2005: 129). As in the case of opacity, it is just such a plurality which liberalism should celebrate and foster.

In contrast to other understandings of individuality, Flathman's ideal is meant to be open-ended in its conceptualization. Once again, drawing on Oakeshott (1975), Flathman sees it as adverbial: self-enacted individuality rests less on a defined set of actions or substantive ideals and more on a particular style of how to approach one's life and the world. As such, Flathman's conception of individuality is an anti-perfectionist perfectionism that forgoes attributing a specific content to individuality. As he notes in the interview that concludes this volume, it is also a form of individuality that can be characterized as opalescent, a term that conveys a sense of "interiority but also communicativity." In addition, it is not a conception of the self that is able to transcend its social circumstances (as we saw above, for Flathman the self is always "situated") or requires arriving at a unique vision or way of acting in the world that is totally new. The internal work on oneself does not necessitate seeing the self as an internal helmsman with a clear view of everything that is going on within its domain. Instead, Flathman's notion of the self is one that is itself plural, a many-in-one or what he also calls a self that is "for and against itself" (2003: 7). In this environment, self-enactment requires either resisting already given feelings and desires or making a positive commitment to choose certain motivations over others. In either case, the endorsement of certain sentiments over others is not meant to be understood as vanquishing parts of oneself that do not fit or fully illuminating every nook and cranny of the self. Self-enacted individuality is not modeled on conquest.

Alternatively, self-enacted individuality is not a letting-go or self-indulgence (1992: 211). To engage in self-enactment requires an element of discipline. Hence it is an achievement and not an inevitability. Moreover, it is an achievement that is (and perhaps should be) never fully complete. Once one has attended to one's character one cannot simply slap one's hands together and say, "Well, now that I've done that, what's next?" However much the vista from a given outcropping is enjoyed, the shaping of one's character is always a work in progress. Affirming self-enacted individuality means affirming and protecting the

8 *Introduction*

pluralism that is the inevitable result of self-enactment. What does this affirmation mean for liberalism?

In Flathman's view, the affirmation of self-enacted individuality extends the literatures, problems, and purposes of liberal theory beyond traditional understandings of liberalism. As discussed in the essay, "Strains in and Around Liberal Theory" (included in this collection), Flathman's view of liberalism appropriates some impulses from existing liberalisms while rejecting others. For example, Flathman notes that much of liberal theory is state-centric. It sees itself as addressing a set of questions regarding how best to secure liberty through limited, accountable government. Within this state-centric project, one of these liberalisms—what Flathman calls virtue liberalism—sees institutions (including the state) as securing those goals by cultivating a particular form of subjectivity (e.g., the autonomous individual, the civic-minded citizen, the reasonable person). Although there is a sense in which Flathman's self-enacted individuality suggests a virtue liberalism, he thoroughly rejects the ideal of a unitary perfectionism that is in the service of institutional stability and efficacy or is itself a goal or project of the state.

Another of these liberalisms—what Flathman calls agency liberalism—emphasizes desire and pluralism, gives primacy to negative liberty, argues against projects that mold characters or engage in soulcraft, and tries to find ways to minimize the intrusiveness of the state. Flathman is far more comfortable with agency liberalism (1998: 13). Consequently, he has

> considerable sympathy for the Hobbesian idea that the primary aim of politics should be to sustain a *modus vivendi* among competing and conflicting groups that in politics we ought to resist the temptation to attempt to transform ourselves or others into different and better people.
>
> (1994: 682)

But Flathman is also strongly attracted to anarchism's abandonment of the state. Although he is not an anarchist, he does see anarchism as inoculating him against "the too ready, the insufficiently skeptical and cautious acceptance of the institution of government" (1998: 83).

Flathman's agential and anarcho-sympathic, individuality-affirming liberalism would appear to land him on the shores of libertarianism. When his views approach that destination, however, he tacks away. As he mentions in the interview and in Chapter 12, libertarianism leads to a dreary emphasis on economic matters—to making a living as opposed to making a life. Moreover, while libertarians may be correct in thinking that the state should not be in the business of making us into different and better people, their approach is still state-centric, because they focus their efforts on divesting the state (along with a variety of other institutions) of its heavy interest in crafting selves (1996: 733). There is a sense that Flathman has little or no confidence that such divestment will ever happen. Instead, he argues that "it follows (for me) that we must be prepared to resist ... [the state] as necessary and possible and that, more generally we must

Introduction 9

attempt to sustain toward it what Nietzsche called a 'pathos of distance'" (1996: 733). This is not a complete abandonment of the state and its institutions (as if that were a real option). Rather it is a distancing or willful alienation from the state whatever its form or shape. For example, Flathman makes clear in the interview that he does not have much confidence that a turn toward democracy would be an improvement. The state (whoever happens to be in control) is not me, and who I am will not be found in the state and its operations. Sustaining that distance requires a struggle against those political projects that seek to brand upon us a particular form of subjectivity.

Can Flathman triangulate a liberalism that is between the state and its absence? Part of his answer is that liberalism need not be restricted to what the state should and should not do (Flathman 1994: 683). There are other, perhaps just as pressing, matters to be considered and understood. This perspective comes to the fore when he rejects a collectivist/democratic vision of politics, a vision in which everyone is involved in the democratic process that secures the equal capacity of all to participate. He writes:

> An alternative might be to cultivate in a fashion at once several and collected (Oakeshott, Nietzsche) an "ethos, [a] bearing ... [a] style" that mutually and in that sense universalistically cherishes ideals, but that particularly says with Nietzsche "my ideal is mine (and yours is yours) and you can't have it."
>
> (1996: 734)

Instead of a state-centric liberalism, he affirms a willful, individuality-centric liberalism.

Flathman's writings in the past four decades have disclosed contributions and innovations to political thought that may themselves be understood as the result of self-enacted individuality. They are situated in an intellectual context that he has wrestled with, rejected, appreciated, and redeployed in the effort find his own voice. In so doing he has imagined a willful liberalism of character, opalescent features of self-enacted individuality, the virtuosity of self-reliance, the limits of reason and reasonableness, the opacities that we encounter in ourselves and others, and the pluralities enabled and maintained by these features of human experience. Flathman is a theorist of meaning and unmeaning whose own style of thought and theory have furthered our understanding of the conventions, rules, concepts, ideas, and ideals that constitute our form of life.

Note

1 But even this explanation is "too neat." In Chapter 10, Flathman's discussion of Wittgenstein's comments on opacity present the possibility that in some circumstances we may not be able to say whether the parties understand one another or not. In Flathman's terms, the array of possible approaches to the notion of understanding is itself quite complex.

10   *Introduction*

References

Ayer, A.J. 1946 [1936]. *Language, Truth and Logic*, 2nd edn. London: Gollancz.

Dahl, Robert A. 1958. "Political Theory: Truth and Consequences." *World Politics* 11: 89–102.

Easton, David. 1953. *The Political System: An Inquiry into the State of Political Science*. New York: Alfred A. Knopf.

Eulau, Heinz. 1969. *Behavioralism in Political Science*. New York: Atherton Press.

Flathman, Richard E. 1973. "Introduction" to *Concepts in Social and Political Philosophy*, ed. Richard E. Flathman. New York: Macmillan.

Flathman, Richard E. 1987. *The Philosophy and Politics of Freedom*. Chicago: University of Chicago Press.

Flathman, Richard E. 1989. *Toward a Liberalism*. New York: Cornell University Press.

Flathman, Richard E. 1992. *Willful Liberalism: Voluntarism and Individuality in Political Theory and Practice*. Ithaca: Cornell University Press.

Flathman, Richard E. 1994. "Liberalism: From Unicity to Plurality and on to Singularity." *Social Research* 61: 671–686.

Flathman, Richard E. 1996. Review of Wendy Brown, *States of Injury: Power and Freedom in Late Modernity*. *Political Theory* 24: 728–734.

Flathman, Richard E. 1998. *Reflections of a Would-Be Anarchist: Ideals and Institutions of Liberalism*. Minneapolis: University of Minnesota Press.

Flathman, Richard E. 2003. *Freedom and Its Conditions*. New York: Routledge.

Flathman, Richard E. 2005. *Pluralism and Liberal Democracy*. Baltimore: Johns Hopkins University Press.

Flathman, Richard E. 2006. "Perfectionism without Perfection: Cavell, Montaigne, and the Conditions of Morals and Politics." In *The Claim to Community*, ed. Andrew Norris. Stanford: Stanford University Press.

Levy, Jacob T. 2006. "It Usually Begins with Isaiah Berlin." *The Good Society* 15: 23–26.

MacIntyre, Alasdair. 2001. *Dependent Rational Animals: Why Human Beings Need the Virtues*. Chicago: Open Court.

Oakeshott, Michael. 1975. *On Human Conduct*. Oxford: Oxford University Press.

Rawls, John. 2005. *Political Liberalism: Expanded Edition*. New York: Columbia University Press.

Schubert, Glendon A. 1958. "The Study of Judicial Decision-Making as an Aspect of Political Behavior." *American Political Science Review* 52: 1007–10025.

Stevenson, Charles L. 1944. *Ethics and Language*. Hartford: Yale University Press.

Strauss, Leo. 1965. *Natural Right and History*. Chicago: University of Chicago Press.

Tuck, Richard. 2002. "Flathman's Hobbes." In *Skepticism, Individuality and Freedom: The Reluctant Liberalism of Richard Flathman*, ed. Bonnie Honig and David R. Mapel. Minneapolis: University of Minnesota Press.

Wertheimer, Alan. 1990. Review of Richard E. Flathman, *Toward a Liberalism*. *Political Theory* 18: 180–184.

Part I

Equality, authority, rights, and philosophy as therapy

1 Equality and generalization, a formal analysis (1967)

To treat people equally is to treat them in the same way. To treat people in the same way is to treat them according to a rule. "Equally" is defined in the *Oxford English Dictionary* to mean "According to one and the same rule." Philosophers, aware of this relationship, have attempted to explicate and refine the notion of equality through the notion of general rule or generalization. Historically, the salient names in this connection are Rousseau and Kant. Many contemporary philosophers have concerned themselves with generalization, but few have applied their conclusions to "equality." The purpose of the present chapter is to analyze the concept of equality in the light of recent discussions of generalization. I will argue that the concept of equality can be explicated in terms of generalization, and that to do so shows that as normative concepts both equality and generalization are of derivative significance. These conclusions will lead to suggestions concerning the importance of utilitarian considerations in morals.

I

Recent work in ethics or meta-ethics has been concerned to identify and provide formalized statements of the principles and rules that operate, if only in a concealed manner, in moral discourse. The concept of generalization has been the object of substantial attention in these respects, and we now have several analyses of what has been called the Generalization or Universalizability Principle (hereafter GP). Professor Marcus Singer, who has made the most detailed study of the topic, states GP in the form we will adopt for the purposes of this chapter: "What is right (or wrong) for one person must be right (or wrong) for every relevantly similar person in relevantly similar circumstances."[1] According to this formulation, if X is right for A, it must be right for B, C, D,… N unless A or his circumstances is different from B, C, D,… N or their circumstances in a manner justifying making an exception of A. There is, it would appear, a presumption in favor of equal treatment of all persons and any departure from that rule must be justified.

One feature of GP, its "formal" or "neutral" character, requires immediate attention. Before the universal principle that GP expresses can be applied to a problem, two particular premises must be established. The first is of the form:

14   *Equality, authority, rights, and philosophy*

"This X is right for this A"; the second: "This B is, vis-à-vis this A, a relevantly similar person in relevantly similar circumstances." GP states a relationship between these premises; it does not tell us how to establish them in any instance. Until they have been established, GP, although valid as an abstract principle, has no application. GP does one thing: When it has been established that X is right for A and that A and B are relevantly similar, the principle requires that it be wrong for A to act or be treated differently from B. Hence GP is formal or neutral in the sense that, taken alone, it does not prescribe the proper content of any decision. Clearly, then, the crucial problems are those involved in establishing the particular premises in specific cases. Those problems, and the question of GP's utility once those problems have been resolved, will be our primary concern. We will also give attention to an argument that a substantive doctrine of equality is concealed by the ostensibly formal or neutral character of GP.

II

It will facilitate the analysis to use a real controversy concerning equality as a source of examples and illustrations. The recent United States Supreme Court decisions concerning apportionment in state legislatures, the "one-man, one-vote" decisions, are well suited to this purpose.[2] In the Court's view, the question before it in the Reynolds case was whether the Equal Protection clause[3] permits a state to employ a system of apportionment in which the representatives of some districts represent substantially fewer citizens than the representatives of other districts. Although insisting that "mathematical exactitude" is neither desirable nor practicable as a standard for determining the adequacy of a plan, the majority nevertheless found that Equal Protection "requires that a state make an honest and good faith effort to construct districts in both houses of its legislature as nearly of equal population as practicable."

In terms of GP, the issue can be restated as follows: "Is it constitutional for A (the citizens of legislative district A′ in state Q′) to have X (number of citizens per representative) if B, C, D,... N (the citizens of legislative districts B′, C′, D′,... N′ in state Q′) do not have X (have Y, a larger or smaller number of citizens per representative)? Under GP the answer could be, for example, "Yes, if X is right for A and if vis-à-vis B, C, D,... N, A is (the class of A consists of) relevantly different persons in relevantly different circumstances. [*sic*] The decision, in other words, would seem to turn on establishing the two premises we have identified. We will try to show, however, that what appears to be two tasks is in fact one—establishing the rightness of X.

Many of the arguments of Warren's opinion, by contrast, suggest that in matters of apportionment "right" and the kind of equality demanded by the equal population rule are equivalent; they collapse the first premise of GP into the second. Much of his opinion is designed to show that various differences among citizens such as class, economic status, place of residence, and other characteristics, although alleged to justify differences in treatment, are irrelevant to apportionment. The assumption seems to be that "equal" in the Constitution

Equality and generalization 15

establishes a presumption that the equal population rule is right (constitutional), and the task is less to defend that presumption than to show that the conditions required for its application (relevant similarity of all citizens) are satisfied. If challenges to the relevant similarity of all citizens can be met, the question of "right" (constitutionality) will be answered. In common with many egalitarian arguments, in other words, Warren treats equality as a sufficient normative principle. To clarify the logic of this argument we will examine some of the key contentions that Warren offers to support his conclusion.[4]

Warren's aim is to support the conclusion that all citizens should be treated according to the rule, "Equal representatives for equal population." To do so he asserts: "With respect to the allocation of legislative representation, all voters as citizens of the State stand in the same relation."[5] Presumably this means that there are no differences among citizens or their situations that would significantly affect their opportunity to participate effectively in or the manner in which they are affected by the system of representation. But the empirical proposition crucial to Warren's argument is highly doubtful. A citizen's relation to the system of representation, his opportunity to participate in and benefit from that process, can be affected by such factors as the predominant interest pattern in his district, whether his party affiliation is that of a majority or a minority party, difficulties of communication with political and governmental centers, informal political tradition, size (in area) of districts, and perhaps others. By adopting the equal population rule Warren *makes it* true that all citizens "stand in the same relation" to the system in the respect required by that rule. But they may stand in very different relations to the system in other respects.

It is of course possible that Warren could justify rejecting these other differences. Indeed it is certain that some of the above-mentioned factors would have to be ignored, especially in establishing constitutional requirements concerning the conditions of participation. It would be difficult and perhaps undesirable to refine those requirements to take account of all of the differences that have been alleged to be relevant.[6] But this possibility, although relevant to whether Warren's conclusion could be defended, does not support the logic of the argument by which the conclusion is reached.

More particularly, it does not support the assumption that "right" (constitutionality) and "equal" can be equivalent, that establishing the second premise of GP will establish the first premise as well. If the premise that all citizens "stand in the same relation" with regard to representation is not literally true in all respects that affect representation, then treating them according to a rule based on that premise will mean that there will be respects in which they will be treated differently (unequally). In opting for the equal population rule, Warren treats all citizens equally in the respect required by that rule. But in doing so he accepts inequalities with regard, for example, to size (in area) of electoral districts, distance from governmental centers, and perhaps others. Once again, he might be entirely justified in so doing. But his justification cannot be in terms of equality. For he has, if only tacitly, chosen between equalities. He has preferred the equality of the equal population rule to the equality of, say, size of electoral districts.[7]

16 *Equality, authority, rights, and philosophy*

Inasmuch as he is choosing between competing equalities, he has, again if only tacitly, turned to some principle other than equality to make that choice, that is, to decide what is right. "Right" and "equality" are not equivalent; equality is not an independent or a sufficient normative principle.

These considerations can be generalized. They suggest that "right" and "equality" could be equivalent, that establishing the second premise of GP would also establish the first, only if the decision-maker was not faced with the kind of choice Warren had to make. This choice, however, can be avoided only if all those involved in or affected by a decision are similar persons in similar situations in *all* respects that might affect the results of the decision. Given the diversity of men and their situations, it is difficult to believe that such decisions are a regular occurrence—especially in politics where we are typically concerned with very large numbers. Hence questions arise about the significance of the principle of equality.

It might be useful to restate the foregoing argument in terms closer to those used in our preliminary discussion of GP. When GP is applied to a concrete issue, it serves to raise a comparative question—whether X is right for A *and* for B, C, D,... N. The foregoing argument supports our earlier contention that this comparative question cannot be answered until we have determined whether X is right for A. Warren's argument, and all arguments that treat equality as a sufficient standard of right, suggests that X can sometimes be right for A *because* A and B, C, D,... N are treated in a like manner. But this argument either begs the question of the first premise of GP—"Is X right for A?"—or simply restates it for B, C, D,... N and A. The question whether X is right for A must be independent of GP. It is not a comparative question (that is, not in the sense of GP or equality; it may be comparative in the sense of comparing the merits of alternative policies or actions) and it cannot be answered by a comparative formula or rule. If we treat A wrongly, it will not help to say that we have treated him the same as B, C, D,... N.

The same is true of B, C, D,... N. The rightness or wrongness of giving X to B, C, D,... N could turn on a relationship of equality or inequality between B, C, D,... N and A only in the circumstances specified above. (Even in those circumstances questions of ethical naturalism might arise.) Treating them equally in one respect will usually involve treating them unequally in another, possibly more important, respect. If we treat B, C, D,... N badly, it will not help that we have treated B, C, D,... N and A alike. To decide the rightness or wrongness of X for B, C, D,... N, we must repeat for the latter those steps taken to determine whether X was right or wrong for A.

Our reason for contending that establishing the first premise of GP is the main task should now be clear. For the procedure just described establishes the second as well as the first premise. It tells us whether B, C, D,... N are, vis-à-vis A, relevantly similar persons in relevantly similar circumstances. Our purpose is to discover whether X is right or wrong for both A and B, C, D,... N; and, by hypothesis, we have now done so. What could be more relevant than that the same policy is right or wrong for both? Indeed, what other proper answer could there be to the question of whether they are relevantly similar? The second premise of GP, in short, is properly established through the same procedures as the first, by determining the rightness or wrongness of applying X to B, C, D,... N. If that determination accords with the result obtained in making the same decision with regard to applying X to A, then A and B, C, D,... N are relevantly similar persons in relevantly similar circumstances and what is right or wrong for B, C, D,... N must (logically) be right or wrong for A. If the results of the two determinations differ, A and B, C, D,... N are not relevantly similar—and what is right for A is not right for B, C, D,... N.

GP demands a certain relationship between A and B, C, D,... N; but that relationship is a logically necessary relationship between the results obtained by the application of tests that are independent of GP. The moment we lose sight of this fact we are in danger of mistreating a person, or class of persons, on the irrelevant grounds that he, or it, is receiving the same treatment as others.

III

It might be contended that the foregoing analysis fails to consider certain dimensions and characteristics peculiar to equality questions. We have dissolved equality questions into a series of right–wrong questions connected in a *post hoc*, formal manner. At the least, it might be alleged, this analysis ignores prominent aspects of moral and political thought and practice.

The objection is justified in that one aspect of equality questions is partially masked by the foregoing discussion. The difficulty in the above account is its apparent suggestion that judgments about the rightness or wrongness of X for A are *entirely* independent of, and cannot be upset by, concern with B, C, D,... N. There are cases in which this is obviously not true. If A and B, C, D,... N are part of the same moral or legal system, giving X to A might have consequences for B, C, D,... N, consequences that must be considered in deciding whether it is right to give X to A. In the cases discussed thus far, we have assumed we had accounted for the impact of X on both (all) parties or classes; but there are other types of cases to be considered. Hence the foregoing discussion is incomplete; it needs to be supplemented by an enumeration and further analysis of the combinations that logically can arise under GP. Although this will involve some repetition of earlier arguments, it should summarize the results of those arguments and show what must be added to them in order to handle the objection before us.

We will continue to assume that X is right for A taken alone (that is, without considering the impact on B, C, D,... N, of giving X to A). Holding this constant, there are two basic types of situations (A and B) and six types of cases (A. 1–3 and B. 1–3) that can arise under GP.

Situation A.: If X is not right for B, C, D,... N, A and B, C, D,... N are not relevantly similar, and what is right for A is, by hypothesis, not right for B, C, D,... N.

Hence: A.1. To treat A and B, C, D,... N alike would be to treat unlike cases alike and would violate GP.

18 *Equality, authority, rights, and philosophy*

This is the standard type of case in which GP is violated. The Reynolds decision illustrates the point nicely. The Court holds that the equal population rule is the "controlling criterion" under the Equal Protection Clause. All citizens must be treated equally in the respect indicated by that rule. A.1. shows that this rule can be a requirement only if it would not be wrong to treat B, C, D,... N in this way. Critics of the decision hold that this condition is not satisfied in some states, that use of the equal population rule will lead to results of the A.1. type. To insist that all citizens be treated equally in this respect might involve treating them unequally in respects more important to the citizens in question and to the system.

To apply the equal population rule to Colorado, for example, might require that citizens of area D', an isolated mountain district with unique interests, be placed in a legislative district (D) which is uniquely large in terms of area, which poses very difficult transportation and communication problems, in which the overwhelming majority of the population have interests and political affiliations (for example, party) markedly at variance with those of the citizenry in D', and in which the citizens of D' share no mechanisms and channels of informal political activity with the other citizens of D. If these conditions do not obtain in other districts of the state, or, as posited, for other citizens in D, the citizenry of D', although treated equally in terms of the equal population rule, are treated unequally in other respects. Hence to impose the equal population rule upon them would be to treat unlike cases alike. More important, it might be to treat unlike cases alike in a manner that results in treating some groups well and other groups badly.

To treat A and B, C, D,... N differently in situation A, for example to give X to A but not to B, C, D,... N, might appear to be acceptable under GP. But this is one of the situations prompting the objection that the present analysis ignores distinctive aspects of equality questions. Before we can decide whether it is right to give X to A but not to B, C, D,... N, we must decide whether it would be right not to give X to B, C, D,... N when one of the conditions is that we are giving X to A. Although we have posited that it would be wrong to give X to B, C, D,... N, we do not yet know whether it would be wrong to treat B, C, D,... N in the proposed manner, that is, subjecting them to whatever effects would result from giving X to A.

This case (A.2.) is not covered by A.1.; it is an entirely different case and an entirely different problem. But the principle employed to decide A.1. must be used to decide A.2. (and A.3.) as well. We can decide A.2. only by asking whether it is wrong to treat B, C, D,... N in this manner.

Hence: A.2. If the policy of giving X to A but not to B, C, D,... N is not wrong for B, C, D,... N, a permissible classification has been made and it is right to give X to A.

A.2. is the paradigm case of the permissible classification, and a great deal of governmental action falls under it.

A.3. If giving X to A but not to B, C, D,... N wrongs B, C, D,... N, the classification is not permissible and the policy must be abandoned. Note that it is not the mere fact that A and B, C, D,... N are treated differently (unequally) that renders X obnoxious. Or rather, there is only one sense of "unequal" in which this is true, namely that one is treated well and the other badly. They are also treated unequally in many respects under A.2., which is unobjectionable. Again, we can decide only by looking at the effects of the policy for B, C, D,... N.

A.2. and A.3. are common in government. A.2. allows a degree of flexibility that is essential if government is to act widely but with discrimination. And the search for A.2.'s sometimes leads to A.3.'s instead. It would be undesirable to tax those with incomes under 5,000 dollars at 90 percent, but it would also be undesirable if we were thereby prevented from taxing multimillionaires at that rate. It would be wrong to conscript men over sixty years of age, but it might be disastrous if we were thereby prevented from drafting men under twenty-six. For another illustration, consider the problem in Reynolds. Strict adherence to the equal population rule renders it impossible for cases of type A.2. to arise in the area of apportionment. Because the rule is satisfied only if everyone in the system is treated equally in this particular respect, the rule must be right for everyone or for no one.

Situation B.: If X is right for B, C, D,... N, A and B, C, D,... N are relevantly similar persons in relevantly similar circumstances, and what is right for A must be right for B, C, D,... N.

Hence: B.1. If X is applied to A and to B, C, D,... N, it does not violate GP. If Warren's argument is tenable, the equal population rule falls under this heading. Notice that this is the one and only case in which that rule is consistent with GP as it has been interpreted here.

B.2. If the policy of giving X to A but not to B, C, D,... N does not wrong B, C, D,... N, a permissible classification has been made and GP is not violated.

This is another situation that prompts an objection to the analysis. But the fact that B.2. is not fully covered by B.1. does not upset the above analysis or indicate that it cannot take account of the distinctive features of equality questions. B.2. is a different policy from B.1., and it must be evaluated independently. But nothing in the analysis prevents us from noticing and evaluating the fact that giving X to A has consequences for B, C, D,... N despite the fact that B, C, D,... N are not given X.

B.2. is perhaps the most interesting result with regard to equality. The argument is that the fact that X is right for both A and B, C, D,... N does not require that it be wrong to give X to A but not to B, C, D,... N. To prove that giving X is right is not to prove that withholding it is wrong. To show that it would be wrong to withhold X from B, C, D,... N while giving it to A would require a demonstration that the results of withholding X from B, C, D,... N, under these circumstances, would be wrong.

Consider the following hypothetical case. School districts A and B would both benefit from receiving X dollars of state aid. State resources are sufficiently great to give X to A and B without hampering other programs, but A has a large population of educationally deprived children and B does not. It would be right to give X to both A and B and to give X to A and not to B would be to treat them

20 *Equality, authority, rights, and philosophy*

unequally in one important respect. But if we are right about B.2., to do the latter would not be wrong. The inequality would not lead to bad results for B and hence it would be based upon a permissible classification.

This point is at the heart of the present argument. "Equally" means "according to one and the same rule." Whenever we treat according to a rule, we will be treating equally in respect to that rule. Clearly then, the crucial question will be "according to what rule should we treat people in this case?" The principle of equality will rarely answer this question because ordinarily we must choose between equalities. If we choose to treat A and B equally in respect to educational achievement, we will treat them unequally in respect to the size of the grant awarded. This must be defended in terms of the relative importance of equal educational achievement as against equal grants of money. To dramatize the example, let us consider whether we could justify giving a larger grant to B despite the fact that B is already ahead of A in terms of educational achievement. To justify such a policy we would have to find another rule that we regard as more important than either size of grant or educational achievement. Let us say that the national defense would be served by concentrating the bulk of our resources in B. If our rule was "maximize contributions to the national defense," we could properly say that A and B had been treated equally if B received a larger grant, unequally if A and B received an identical grant. Hence one could not object to the rule on the ground that it violated the principle of equality. One could only object that the kind of equality served by the rule was less important than other kinds of equality that might have been served in the same situation. Such an objection would involve an appeal from equality to some other principle.[8]

B.3. If to refuse to give X to B, C, D,... N while giving it to A wrongs B, C, D,... N, GP is violated and the policy must be abandoned.

The problem in *Reynolds* is instructive concerning B.2. and B.3. If B.2. would be unobjectionable under GP, the equal population rule would not be a requirement in situations of this type. It would be acceptable to follow the rule in such cases, but it would not be wrong to depart from it. If Colorado employed the equal population rule in most of its legislative districts, there would be no *prima facie* bar to departure from that rule in dealing with cases such as our hypothetical D'. Special treatment for D', regardless of how great the departure from the equal population rule, would be condemned only if it could be shown that it wronged non-D's. If, say, all non-D's, by every measure other than the equal population rule, were receiving effective representation, special treatment of D' would no more be a problem than the special treatment we accord to some people virtually every time government acts. For the rule to be a requirement, all departures from it must fall under B.3. This is the position that defenders of a strict "one-man, one-vote" rule, or any comparable egalitarian rule, must defend.

These cases, allowing for recombination among the situations and types, exhaust the logical possibilities under GP. Although they complicate the earlier analysis, none of them upsets that analysis. If correct, the analysis shows that GP, or equality, is not a sufficient criterion of a justifiable decision. We must decide whether policies are right or wrong, good or bad; since we will rarely, if ever, be able to treat equally in one respect without treating unequally in others, to equate "right" with "equal" and "wrong" with "unequal" produces the logically absurd result that our decisions must be both right and wrong. This absurdity is avoided by using a criterion other than equality to choose between competing equalities. GP states a logical relationship between the results obtained through use of such a criterion. Hence the analysis indicates that equality is a significant normative criterion only in a *derivative* sense.

Notes

1 Marcus Singer, *Generalization in Ethics*, New York: Alfred A. Knopf, 1961, pp. 19–20; alternative formulations are presented on pp. 5 and 31. There is a very extensive critical literature concerning Singer's book, and I have profited substantially from it. It would be impracticable to cite that literature here, but mention should be made of Alan Gewirth's "The Generalization Principle," *Philosophical Review*, Vol. 73 (April, 1964), p. 229, in which the reader will find arguments similar in important respects to some of those presented here.
2 The leading case is *Reynolds* v. *Sims*, 377 U.S. 533 (1964). A series of companion cases follows immediately in the same volume. I would like to emphasize that it is not the purpose of this chapter to present an evaluation of the Court's decisions in these cases. The arguments of the chapter would be relevant to such an evaluation, and in it critical statements will be made concerning Chief Justice Warren's argument in the Reynolds case. But the purpose of these remarks will be to question the logic of the argument by which the conclusion is reached, not the conclusion itself. A competent evaluation of the latter would require a much wider investigation than I have undertaken. Also, because I am using the cases purely for illustrative purposes, I have not scrupled to ignore complexities in the Court's reasoning, which would lead beyond present purposes. It is my belief that the following interpretation of Warren's argument can be defended in terms of the text of his opinion, but I have not attempted to defend it here.
3 Article 14, Section 1.
4 Inasmuch as Warren is interpreting a Constitution to which he must be faithful, it might be thought misleading or worse to say that *he* "treats equality" as a sufficient principle. The Constitution, it might be alleged, established the principle and Warren is required to accept it in his role as judge. If the content of "equal" in "equal protection" were entirely clear, this argument would be persuasive. We will try to adduce logical considerations to show that it is not, and hence that the language used above is appropriate.
5 *Reynolds* v. *Sims*, 565. The sentence ends "regardless of where they live." But in the course of the opinion Warren makes the same contention for all differences alleged to be relevant (there is something of an exception for existing political subdivisions) and hence it is not a distortion to broaden the passage by omitting the restriction.
6 To assume difficulty or undesirability too readily, however, is to risk assuming away the issues concerning proper apportionment. It is instructive in this connection to consider the British practice, a practice that has gone to great lengths in adapting to some of the differences mentioned above. The British have evidently found this practicable, and they have rejected the conclusion that the numerical equality for which Warren opts will provide a base from which the citizen can overcome all other inequalities. For a general account of British practices see Vincent E. Starzinger, "The British Pattern of Apportionment," *The Virginia Quarterly Review*, Vol. 41 (Summer 1965), pp. 321ff.

22 *Equality, authority, rights, and philosophy*

7 Here again (cf. note 4 above) it might be argued that Warren did not "choose" between equalities but read the Constitution as *requiring* the equal population rule. Leaving aside general issues concerning the difficulty of interpreting the Constitution, the foregoing argument is intended to show that it is logically impossible for the words of the document, taken alone, to require this finding. Perhaps the usual materials of constitutional interpretation, previous court decisions, intent of the Framers, etc., support Warren's finding. Inasmuch as our concern is not constitutional law but the logic of "equality," this fact, if it is a fact, is of little relevance here and does not affect the above argument.

8 It has been suggested that this example strains ordinary usage; that "equally" would be used in connection with the effects of the policy on A and B, not its effects on the country at large. One response to this objection would be that the argument considers the effects of the policy on A and B in what Rousseau would call their corporate capacities. Both are members of the system; the system is affected in a particular manner; and hence both, as members, are affected in the same way. It is my view that much public policy is justified, and can only be justified, in this way. But this response concedes more than is necessary to the objection. "According to one and the same rule" is a standard meaning of "equally" and the above argument is in conformity with it. The objection that the argument strains usage could be sustained only if another interpretation of "equally" could be sustained. My suspicion is that an exchange on this point would show not that the argument strains ordinary usage of "equally" but that it departs from widespread conceptions as to which kinds of equality are most important.

2 Wittgenstein's philosophy of language and political and social philosophy (1973)

Wittgenstein presented a very restricted view of the objectives of philosophy and indeed the achievements open to philosophers. Philosophy is a purely descriptive activity, and what it describes is the obvious, what everyone knows; it should not generalize, explain, or even advance theses, and although criticism and reform are possible, they are no part of the philosopher's task. Philosophy is a therapeutic enterprise. Its aim is to help others to escape from the sort of confusions and muddles that result from inattention to language and its place in human affairs. To these ends it might clarify the use of concepts such as "authority," "obligation," and "rights" but it would do so not to teach us something we do not know about these concepts – because we already know everything there is to know about them – but to clear up difficulties that we have gotten into by reminding us of things we know but to which we are not paying sufficient attention.[1]

In one respect our discussion of Wittgenstein is been an argument that his own philosophical practice does not conform to his preachments about what philosophy should do. The arguments we have been examining constitute a highly general account or analysis of language and meaning. Of course this account insists upon the great diversity of language games and makes no attempt to reduce that diversity or to explain it in terms of some single or very small number of quintessential factors. But the argument that language is diverse and irreducible is itself a kind of generalization, and the account contains numerous other contentions of equal generality.

For immediate purposes the two most important of these contentions are the discussions of "right," "true," and "know" in connection with the critique of the possibility of a private language and the closely connected arguments about rules, language games, and the relationships between the latter and what people do. To begin with the first discussion, recall Wittgenstein's argument that public language eliminates the difficulty with "E," the difficulty that a person using "E" would have nothing independent of his memory against which to test his use and hence could not know that he was actually using it in the correct manner. Unlike private language, in short, public language allows of such notions as a correct and incorrect, sensible and nonsensical use of concepts and in many cases allows certainty as to whether a concept has been used correctly or nonsensically.

24 *Equality, authority, rights, and philosophy*

This claim on Wittgenstein's part is essential to his view of philosophy as therapeutic. The notion of doing therapy presupposes the possibility of distinguishing between healthy and unhealthy, normal and abnormal, correct and incorrect. If there were no established, shared criteria by which to judge whether a particular use of language is sensible rather than nonsensical, there would be no grounds on which to claim that there has been confusion, misuse, and so forth, and no grounds on which to claim that therapy has been administered and a cure actually effected. Moreover, Wittgenstein's claim that "I know I am in pain" is nonsensical, that the grammars of talk about sense perception and talk about physical objects are different, or any one of the myriad of other claims he advances in his work, are claims not only that *he* knows that this is so, but that what he knows is (even if they could not say it on their own) known to be so by any speaker of the language. It is for this reason that he believes he need do, indeed can do, no more to support his claims than "assemble reminders" of how the concepts are in fact used by any speaker playing the language game or games in which they figure. Although there is a great diversity of language games and much variation in the manner in which they are played, knowing how to play them involves, at least very often, knowing rules that hold "not just once" and not just for one person, but for everyone who plays this particular game wherever and whenever they play it. In these respects, such claims as " 'I know I am in pain' is nonsensical" are put forward as truths of an entire generality, truths that hold from speaker to speaker and from one instance of playing the game or games in question to another. In short, Wittgenstein's contention that philosophy *can* be therapeutic rests upon, presupposes, the possibility of identifying recognizably true generalizations about language. And in his own practice of philosophical therapy he advanced a large number of such generalizations and claimed that they are true.

If such generalizations about language are possible, the question arises as to the purpose or purposes of identifying and advancing them, the uses to which advancing them might profitably be put. Wittgenstein argues that philosophy is and should be no more than therapeutic. This is in effect an argument that the only useful purpose that could be served by advancing such generalizations would be to help us escape from muddles and confusions that we have gotten into by not attending to what we as speakers of the language know about it. (And it seems that it is primarily, though not exclusively, philosophers who get into such muddles – and this because they attempt to use concepts outside of the language games that are their natural homes.) One can readily agree that this is a valid and an important purpose, a valid and important reason for making the sort of investigations that Wittgenstein made. Numerous writers have agreed that, as it is sometimes expressed, philosophy is a "second-order" discipline or activity. It does not itself attempt to teach us about our lives and the world. Insofar as it presents statements about these subjects, they are no more than reminders of what we already know. The task of improving our knowledge of ourselves and the world falls to the various sciences and social sciences. The philosopher's task is to examine the manner in which physicists, biochemists, sociologists, and so forth, use concepts in framing, interpreting, and reporting the results of their "first-order" investigations, to help them avoid or escape from muddles, confusions, fruitless or confounded perplexities – "hangups" is the vernacular suggested by the notion of therapy – that result from misuse of the concepts they employ. Thus political and social philosophy would be a critical examination of the language of political science, sociology, anthropology. Because many of the concepts used by political and other social scientists also figure in political and social life, political and social philosophy might also contribute to clarity concerning the language of politics and social interaction. Its objectives, however, remain therapeutic; it aims to remove and avoid obstacles to an understanding of politics and society, not to supply such an understanding.[2]

To repeat, performing such therapy depends on its being possible to *know* the correct and incorrect uses of whatever concepts are in question. Wittgenstein's philosophy of language provides reasons for thinking that this condition can be satisfied. (It is not the only extant set of reasons for thinking that this condition can be satisfied. Many of the writers who have taken the view that philosophy is a second-order activity have based their position on understandings of language very different from Wittgenstein's.) But in providing reasons for thinking that a therapeutic philosophy is possible, his philosophy of language also provides reasons for thinking that philosophy, particularly political and social philosophy, can legitimately aspire to further, in some respects more ambitious, objectives and accomplishments. To make this entirely explicit we need only combine the proposition that we can *know* the proper use of concepts with Wittgenstein's argument that the "*speaking* of a language is part of an activity,"[3] that acting is at the bottom of the language game. On this view knowledge of the use of language is also knowledge of actions and activities. Understanding an activity involves understanding, being able to use, the concepts that figure in that activity; understanding concepts involves understanding the activities in which those concepts are used. Thus Wittgenstein's claim that it is possible for philosophers to perform conceptual therapy is also the claim that philosophers can know about, can understand, the human activities of which concepts are an integral part.

Now it is not to be thought that these last remarks are somehow a working out of implications in Wittgenstein's thought of which he himself was not aware or that they are in conflict with Wittgenstein's own understanding of his position. The integral relationship between and inseparability of language, meaning, and action are among the most central, the most important arguments Wittgenstein advanced. It would be altogether wrong to suggest that Wittgenstein thought the therapy performed by philosophy is insignificant or trivial, that it is concerned, in the phrase so often encountered among superficial critics, with "words" or "mere words." The confusions with which philosophical therapy is concerned, in Wittgenstein's words,

> have the character of *depth*. They are deep disquietudes; their roots are as deep in us as the forms of our language and their significance is as great as

26 *Equality, authority, rights, and philosophy*

the importance of our language. – Let us ask ourselves: why do we feel a grammatical joke to be *deep*? (And that is what the depth of philosophy is.)[4]

Granting the importance of philosophical therapy, however, we must nevertheless ask why philosophy should *restrict itself* to providing therapy. If philosophers can know enough about concepts and the activities of which they are part to clear up confusions and misconceptions, what is to prevent them, what is there against, their instructing us about our concepts and activities before the confusions develop, for purposes having no definite connection with confusions. Why should they not advance the sort of accounts of men and then activities that political and social philosophers have been putting forward from classical antiquity to the present? More specifically, if political and social philosophers can know the correct use of concepts such as "rights" and "obligation," "equality" and "justice," "liberty" and "authority," and hence can achieve a well-grounded understanding of the activities of which these concepts are an integral part, why should they not put their knowledge to more than therapeutic uses?

The discussions that form the bulk of this volume[5] indicate that many thinkers influenced directly or indirectly by Wittgenstein have decided that they can and should do so. Many of those discussions are indeed intended (among other things) to clear up confusions and misconceptions to which previous writers have fallen victim. But most of the discussions that follow (and a much larger literature that is addressed to the same kinds of issues) proceed at least in part by analyzing the uses of concepts; most of the analysts represented argue, or at least tacitly assume, that in analyzing the uses of concepts they are also analyzing the political and social activities, practices, and arrangements of which the concepts in question are part, and few if any of them think of their enterprise as nothing more than therapeutic in character and purpose. As we argued at the outset, this literature, most of which would be impossible to understand apart from the direct or indirect influence of Wittgenstein's work in the philosophy of language, should be viewed as a continuation, on the basis of a new set of philosophical premises, of the long tradition of political and social philosophy, a tradition that aims to enlighten us concerning the political and social dimensions of our lives.

On what grounds, then, did Wittgenstein criticize previous attempts to prosecute this enterprise and why did he reject it for himself? Does the work presented in this book properly stand condemned by the very philosopher to whom it owes many of the premises from which it proceeds?[6] Wittgenstein says, "If one tried to advance *theses* in philosophy, it would never be possible to question them, because everyone would agree to them."[7] And again: "in philosophy we do not draw conclusions. 'But it must be like this!' is not a philosophical proposition. Philosophy only states what everyone admits."[8] Assuming that Wittgenstein is not using "theses" and "conclusions" in some special way, there is no doubt that the philosophical writings presented here do what Wittgenstein says philosophy as he understands it does not, even cannot, do. Hence it seems that he would have to say that the writings presented here are not, properly speaking, philosophy. And the reasons he gives for his view at least appear to be consistent with the account he presents of language and meaning. Language is a part of our lives. It is what it is because we do what we do with it. The meaning of a concept is the use to which it is put by those who speak the language – by us. Since language *is* what people do with it, it must be the case that everyone (who speaks the language in question) knows what it is. Thus if philosophical theses and conclusions are about language (and if they are correct), it seems that everyone would indeed admit, would indeed agree, to them. Philosophical theses and conclusions would either be truisms or be false. Rather than advancing theses or conclusions thereof, philosophy only assembles reminders for particular purposes, that is, *reminds* people of what they already know but are neglecting.[9]

But does the argument (thesis?) that language is what people do with it require or even support the conclusion that all true theses about it must be redundant truisms?[10] This is in fact an immensely complicated question and much contemporary work in the philosophy of language is concerned with it.[11] We cannot go into the technical questions in detail but we can notice a distinction or two which cast serious doubts on Wittgenstein's view as we understand it.

First, there is the now familiar distinction between knowing how to do something and knowing what one does in doing that which one knows how to do. It is a truism that people who speak a language know how to speak it (though of course they make occasional mistakes of various kinds). But it hardly follows that everyone who knows how to speak is therefore able to give an explicit and orderly account of the rules they follow, the techniques they apply in speaking. To take a simple example, most (but not all) native speakers of English, French, and other natural languages do not regularly make mistakes with the person, number, or tense of verbs. And when they do make a mistake they will readily agree to the correction. It is by no means the case, however, that every native speaker can perform, unaided, even such simple analytic tasks as giving the conjugation of a verb or parsing a sentence (to say nothing of the more complex analyses of grammarians and linguists). They know how to use the language but they cannot give an account of what they do when they use it. If only because this is so, there are obvious utilities in having specialists who study how people speak and put together orderly and systematic accounts of what their performances consist of. There may be a sense in which the accounts they give are truistic, but they are by no means redundant or insignificant. If this is true of matters of lower school grammar, it is the more obvious and the more important as regards the sophisticated distinctions, classifications, and explanations of the linguistically oriented philosopher. Perhaps it is true that competent speakers of English would not say, "I know I am in pain," but how many of them could analyze this feature of their linguistic (non)behavior as Wittgenstein did?

The importance of this point is magnified when we attend to the fact that speaking and acting are interwoven. There is a large number of speakers who know how to use concepts such as rights, justice, obligation, and equality – who know their way about in the activities in which these concepts figure. If this were not the case there would be no concepts and activities for political philosophers to analyze. But if anyone thinks that accounts of these concepts and activities

28 *Equality, authority, rights, and philosophy*

can only be truistic or obviously false, let them give such an account and see whether everyone will admit to it.

Wittgenstein's argument that speakers of a language know how to use the concepts and know their way about in activities, far from posing a problem for or a barrier to a conceptually oriented (or any other) political philosophy, is the basis on which such political philosophy is built. The problem Wittgenstein poses is not that the theses of political philosophy will be truistic and redundant, rather it is that such a political philosophy is likely to be very complicated and difficult to do. We must take seriously Wittgenstein's insistence on the prodigious diversity of uses to which language is put, the endless variety of language games in which it figures, the techniques, purposes, and fine shades of behavior that differentiate one language game and its concepts from another. Saying what people (including ourselves) do who know how to engage in these activities will often be a matter of great difficulty and complexity.[12] Political philosophers who are themselves speakers of the language and participants in the activities they are analyzing will know how to use the concepts and otherwise to engage in the activities. Thus in their role as political philosophers they can as it were observe their own conduct and that of fellow participants and thereby obtain what we can just as well call the evidence on which to base an account of the activity. Owing to the very detail and complexity this evidence is likely to have, putting it together into an account that is both tolerably accurate and yet contributive to the goals of political philosophy will be difficult.

Perhaps we can put the matter as follows: We can think of Wittgenstein's philosophy of language as providing epistemological premises and even a method for political and social philosophy and social science, particularly for a political and social philosophy that addresses itself to the political and social life in which the philosophers and social scientists are themselves participants. The chief premises of the epistemology are that language games are constituted by what the participants do (know how to do) and that this knowledge is necessarily shared among the participants. The "method" consists of examining what people (ergo everyone) do (does) when they do what they know how to do, that is, an examination of the rules accepted and followed, the techniques employed, the objectives and purposes pursued, and the fine shades of behavior characteristic of playing the language game. The obvious problem with the epistemology and the method is that they generate "data" that is likely to be so abundant, complex, and subtle as to be unmanageable.

There are also further problems, problems that have been more widely canvassed than the one just discussed. Not everyone participates in all language games, and not everyone who does participate does so in all aspects of the game. If it is by virtue of playing a language game that one knows how to use the concepts of that game, and if knowing how is the basis of knowing what, then it would seem to follow that only participants in a game could philosophize or do social science concerning that game. If so, the quest for generality, for a comprehensive account or understanding of political and social life, a quest that has been prominent in both philosophy and much social science, might have to be abandoned.

Two general comments should be made before we conclude. First, to say that the diversity and complexity of language games is a problem for political and social philosophy is to make certain assumptions about the character and objectives of such philosophizing. The Wittgensteinian perspective teaches us to think of political philosophy as itself a distinct language game or perhaps family of such games that must be understood in its own right. We cannot conclude that the "difficulties" we mentioned are truly difficulties for political philosophy without examining this game – its concepts, questions, categories of analysis, and so on. A detailed examination of these matters is obviously impossible here. But few would argue that political philosophy has aimed at or should aim at a re-enactment of political life as experienced by participants. Thus the impossibility of such a re-enactment is not itself a difficulty for political philosophy. Yet all concerned would agree that there is some sense in which political philosophy is about political life, that it properly aims, among other things, to abstract from, generalize over, and assess politics as perpetuated and experienced by participants, not simply to ignore the latter. Whatever the particulars of one's judgment as to what this "some sense" should be (and it is a matter of great controversy), the complexity and diversity Wittgenstein stresses is going to complicate the task of political philosophy. But then why should anyone think that the enterprise of political philosophy would be anything other than complicated? If Wittgenstein teaches us something about the ways in which and why is complicated, he does a great service. But he does another service as well, He gives us grounds for thinking that we *know* something about the complexity of political life and hence are in a position to examine the efforts of political philosophers (our own or those of someone else) and make informed and reasoned judgments about their value. Political philosophy at its best will indeed require what most of us have always believed it to require, namely, analytic and synthetic power that are bequeathed to no more than a small number of human beings. But the efforts of such persons concern, are about, something with which, more or less, we are all familiar. For this reason Wittgenstein's teaching can be viewed as an invitation to an active, critical study of political philosophy and political philosophers. I hope that readers of this book will approach the subject in this spirit.

The second point concerns the fact that not everyone participates in all language games and that not all who participate do so to the same degree. If, or to the extent that "knowing how" depends upon participation, it is evident that those who do not participate in a particular activity cannot make the same claims to knowledge as those who do; and this has wide and important implications for conceptually oriented political philosophy or social science. But in working out these implications we must bear in mind at least two other aspects of Wittgenstein's argument as well. The first is his insistence that language is public, not private. The rules purposes, techniques, fine shades of behavior, circumstances, and so forth, involve, are keyed to, matters that are in principle accessible to all. They may be subtle, complicated, and hard for the unexperienced to detect, appreciate, or master. But presumably they have been mastered by the participants; and if the participants could not in principle describe, convey, *teach* them

30 *Equality, authority, rights, and philosophy*

to others, that would prove that they in fact had not mastered them themselves. That is to say that political philosophers can learn about them if they take the trouble – which may indeed be considerable – to do so. Of course, the degree to which they must do so in order to carry forward their enterprise will depend upon the objectives of that enterprise as they understand it. The second point concerns Wittgenstein's remarks about the "common behavior of mankind" that we noted earlier. The common behavior of mankind, he says, "is the system of reference by means of which we interpret an unknown language."[13] This seems to mean that, in fact, whatever the explanation for it may be, there are certain ways of acting that one encounters in many diverse language games among many peoples. This suggests that there are respects in which our experience as human beings provides guidance, makes possible a sense of familiarity, even in situations most of the particulars or distinctive features of which are unfamiliar to us. Familiarity with these ways of acting is by no means a guarantee of under-standing. One human being, Wittgenstein later adds,

> can be a complete enigma to another. We learn this when we come into a strange country which entirely strange traditions; and, what is more, even given a mastery of the country's language We do not *understand* the people. (And not because of not knowing what they are saying to themselves.) We cannot find our feet with them.[14]

But even here, it is important to emphasize, we can at least realize that we do *not* understand them. The understandings afforded by knowledge of the common behavior of mankind, it seems fair to say, are not themselves a sufficient basis for doing political philosophy or social science concerning their activities. But it would seem to provide the possibility of realizing which steps would have to be taken in order to make political philosophy or social science possible. Some aspects of human affairs are indeed more difficult of access than others, but "*everything* lies open to view."[15] Wittgenstein's philosophy of language is very far from encouraging the thought that political philosophy is a simple, uncompli-cated enterprise. But if political philosophy is about, seeks to understand, the political life of man, Wittgenstein gives us excellent grounds for optimism concerning it.

Notes

1 Ludwig Wittgenstein, *Philosophical Investigations*, translated by G. E. M. Anscombe (New York: The Macmillan Company, 1953). Unless otherwise indicated all sub-sequent citations in this introduction are to the *Philosophical Investigations*. Refer-ences to Part I will give the paragraph number only, references to Part II will give "II," the roman subsection of II, and the page. See esp. 80–90, 108–133, 254–255, 309–464, II, xi, p. 206e, II, xii, p. 230e, II, xiv, p. 232e.
2 For a recent and explicit endorsement, of this view of political and social philosophy, see the introduction in Anthony Quinton, ed., *Political Philosophy* (New York: Oxford University Press, 1967).
3 23, italics in original.

Wittgenstein's philosophy of language 31

4 111.
5 Richard E. Flathman, ed., *Concepts in Social and Political Philosophy* (New York: Macmillan, 1973).
6 There is one view that we will mention only to dismiss. It is sometimes suggested that Wittgenstein would reject work such as is presented here because it concerns a type of concept, that is, ethical concepts, that cannot be analyzed. Wittgenstein does say that "our concepts in aesthetics and ethics" have blurred edges and that "if you look for definitions corresponding" to their use you will feel that "anything – and nothing – is right." But this characteristic is hardly unique to aesthetic and ethical concepts, and it is by no means Wittgenstein's view that it prevents us from analyzing them. What he says is, "In such a difficulty always ask yourself: How did we *learn* the meaning of this word ('good' for instance)? From what sort of examples? Then it will be easier for you to see that the word must have a family of meanings" (77). It is no more his view that we cannot analyze *this* family of meanings than that we cannot analyze the meanings of, say, "game."
7 128, italics in original.
8 599.
9 126–127.
10 We may observe in passing that if all true theses are truisms it might be necessary to conclude that most of the "reminders" issued by Wittgenstein himself are thereby shown to be theses, not reminders, and also shown to be false. It is hard to think of any large number of Wittgenstein's reminders to which "everyone" has agreed. As influential as it has been, Wittgenstein's philosophy, like every other important philosophy, is immensely and fundamentally controversial. If his philosophy consists of reminders of what everybody knows, it is difficult to see why this should be the case.
11 See, for example, Stanley Cavell, *Must We Mean What We Say?* esp. I (New York: Charles Scribner's Sons, 1969); Introduction to J. J. Katz and J. A. Fodor, eds., *The Structure of Language* (Englewood Cliffs, N.J.: Prentice-Hall, Inc., 1964); Introduction to Richard Rorty, ed., *The Linguistic Turn* (Chicago: The University of Chicago Press, 1967).
12 Wittgenstein says:

> The use of this word [the word happens to be "reading"] in the ordinary circumstances of our life is of course extremely familiar to us. But the part the word plays in our life, and therewith the language-game in which we employ it, would be difficult to describe even in rough outline.

He then goes on to give a very lengthy description, the point of which, I take it, is to show how hard it is to capture what we do so often and so readily in everyday life (156).
13 206.
14 II, xi, p. 233e.
15 126, italics added.

3 Authority and the "surrender" of individual judgment (1980)

There has been a remarkable coalescence of opinion around the proposition that authority and authority relations involve some species of "surrender of judgment" on the part of those who accept, submit or subscribe to the authority of persons or a set of rules and offices. From anarchist opponents of authority such as William Godwin and Robert Paul Wolff through moderate supporters such as John Rawls and Joseph Raz and on to enthusiasts such as Hobbes, Hannah Arendt, and Michael Oakeshott, a considerable chorus of students have echoed the refrain that the directives that are standard and salient features of practices of authority are to be obeyed by B irrespective of B's judgments of their merits. As Richard B. Friedman puts the matter, B does not and cannot

> make his obedience conditional on his ... personal examination of the thing he is being asked to do. Rather, he accepts as a sufficient condition for following a prescription the fact that it is prescribed by someone acknowledged by him as entitled to rule. The man who accepts authority ... surrender[s] his ... individual judgment ... [in that] he does not insist that reasons be given that he can grasp and that satisfy him, as a condition of his obedience.[1]

Joseph Raz presents a more complex analysis that treats rules with authority as themselves giving B reasons for action that he can grasp and that (should) satisfy him. But Raz nevertheless accepts a notion of surrender of judgment in that he contends that the reasons given by X itself ordinarily exclude consideration of possible competing reasons for action. Indeed he makes this notion of "exclusionary reasons" the defining feature of *in* authority.[2]

Those comparatively few writers who have dissented from this proposition, for example, neo-Thomists such as Yves Simon and rationalists such as Carl Friedrich,[3] have been dismissed as not understanding the difference between authority and authority relations on the one hand, and advice, counsel and reasoned exchange and argumentation on the other.

Because they are so central to the notion of A or X having authority for or over B, the questions that come together under the rubric of "surrender of judgment" are crucial to the analysis of what authority is and is not. They are also at

The *"surrender" of individual judgment*   33

the heart of the normative theory of authority. Numerous writers contend that this feature of *in* authority should be crucial to our judgments concerning its merits as a feature of political life. From Hobbes to Oakeshott, F[ormal]-P[rocedural] theorists have insisted that "surrender of judgment" allows political societies to order and regulate social life in the face of disagreement over substantive issues and the merits of actions and policies. In respect to *an* authority, it has of course frequently been argued that "surrendering" judgment to the wiser, the better informed and the more skillful is good or right (Plato went so far as to make doing so a part of justice) because it leads to true beliefs and correct decisions and actions. Even deeply antiplatonic thinkers, for example utilitarians such as J. S. Mill and especially George Cornewall Lewis, have contended that such "surrender" to *an* authorities is rational because of the great increase in efficiency that it introduces into human affairs.[4] On the other hand, opponents of authority have always argued that this very feature of it necessarily destroys the moral integrity of the B's, thereby rendering all forms of authority intolerable.

In our judgment the normative views just referred to are exaggerations if not outright errors; the salient issues about justifying authority cannot be resolved, positively or negatively, in terms of this alone among its alleged characteristics. But our judgment in this respect depends upon rejecting interpretations of "surrender of judgment" that have been shared among most opponents and proponents of authority; defending the judgment requires an alternative analysis of the place of B's judgments and action on his judgments in the practice of authority. In at least this sense normative questions will be very much before us.

In authority and the exercise of judgment

In the case of *an* authority relations, it is misleading to say that B "surrenders" his judgment to A; rather, B allows his judgment to be influenced by considerations that reach him by the vehicle of A's pronouncements and performances and in the context of the practice of authority. In short, B does *not* surrender his judgment. Rather, he *exercises* his judgment. *An* authority relations are distinguished not by the surrender of judgment on B's part but by the distinctive circumstances under which and the distinctive manner in which B exercises his judgment. The circumstances (given the practice of authority in B's society or subsocial milieu) are that B knows or believes (on the basis of information obtained directly or vicariously) that the quality of A's past performances has demonstrated his superior knowledge or skill concerning a subject matter or activity that interests B or with which B is otherwise involved. B's recognition of A's superiority in this respect provides B with a good reason to (supports his judgment that he should) give distinctively respectful attention to A's pronouncements or performances concerning that subject matter. It also gives B good reason to (supports his judgment that he should) believe, follow the example set by, and so forth A's statements and actions with less critical scrutiny of their merits than B would give to the statements and actions of persons not

34 *Equality, authority, rights, and philosophy*

established (to his satisfaction) as *an* authorities and with less independent examination of the questions or issues involved than he would make if he were presented with the judgments of anyone else concerning them. If B refuses to accord such distinctively respectful attention to A's statements or performances, or if he refuses to accept or to act on those statements or performances with less scrutiny or independent examination than he gives when not presented with established *an* authorities, he rejects A's authority (or, perhaps, rejects the practice of *an* authority) and it becomes impossible for him to maintain an *an* authority relationship with A (or, perhaps, with any A). But the same result ensues if B ceases to make the kinds of judgments we have described. It follows that interpretations which equate good or right action with unqualified and uncritical submission to the beliefs and decisions of some other person are not interpretations of authority relations. Equally, arguments that object to *an* authority relations on the ground that they are destructive of individual autonomy either confuse *an* authority relations with something that they are not and cannot be (for example relations of dominance and submission or the sheer imposition of brute and alien forces) or rest on a conception of autonomy so tender, so virginal, that it could be instantiated only by an exceedingly jealous god. Finally, interpretations that stress the efficiency of participation in *an* authority relationships make a valid point so long as they recognize that the gain is relative or comparative; so long, that is, as they recognize the respects in which B's *qua* B's must continue to exercise critical judgment concerning the statements and performances of those they recognize as A's.

A possible response to the account, likely to be made by F-P theorists of the Oakeshott persuasion, is that, while perhaps accurate enough as an explication of what commonly goes on under the rubric of *an* authority relations, it shows that *an* authority relations are *authority* relations in name only; that *an* authority is categorially distinct from true or genuine, which is to say *in*, authority.

This objection is important at the present juncture because it implies that we cannot draw upon the foregoing analysis of *an* authority relations in order to further understand and assess the "surrender" of judgment in the case of *in* authority relations. If *an* and *in* authority are categorially distinct, characteristics of the former would be no more relevant to understanding the latter than propositions about the population of China.

It is manifestly a fact that the term "authority" is used of *an* authority relations. But if our account of this usage is correct, what is important about it is that the usage brings along with it the differences between the distinctively respectful attention that the B's are liable to give to *an* authorities and the kind of attention we all owe to one another under the norms of polite conduct. However we choose to label it, this is a distinct kind of relationship of considerable importance in human affairs. Given that the relationship is distinct and important, and given that it is commonly called a relationship between authorities and nonauthorities, it is less than clear why the theorist should treat it as anything other than just that.

Working from this premise, we return to *in* authority relations and an attempt to specify further the meaning of "by right" and "rightfully" as they attach to A's

The "surrender" of individual judgment   35

and X's by virtue of their standing in a practice of *in* authority rules. It will be helpful to begin by reconsidering the thesis that *in* authority yields rules to be obeyed, not statements to be believed.

This thesis rests on one of the important points of distinction between *an* and *in* authorities. In the former, A's authority is relational because he has it by virtue of the *recognized* quality of his performances. Joseph Raz to the contrary notwithstanding, in the absence of B's who give such recognition, *an* authority would be impossible.[5] But it is not a feature of *an* authority relations for A to intend that the B's *qua* B's *act* in a certain manner in response to A's performances. Nor does A's continuing as an authority depend on any action on the part of the B's. They may believe his statements, stand in awe of the skill of his performances, and do nothing more. Apparent counterexamples to this account either are spurious or are instances in which a single person both holds an office of *in* authority and is *an* authority on the subject matter dealt with by that office. The "doctor's orders" to patients that are in fact pieces of advice are an example of the former, and professors who require their students to repeat their teachings in order to pass an examination are sometimes (i.e., when the professor is genuinely an authority on his subject matter) examples of the latter.

By contrast, the rules and orders that are the usual devices through which A's exercise their *in* authority are directives intended by the A's to determine the course of action of the B's in a certain respect. If the B's do not understand this, and if they do not ordinarily comply, the authority of the A's will be lost. ("Usual" and "ordinarily" are in the previous two sentences in recognition of qualifications to the points the sentences assert. In addition to directives, *in* authorities issue permissions or powers which the B's are at liberty to use or not as they see fit. And as we argue later, occasional, even quite frequent, noncompliance does not necessarily destroy authority.) Thus it is (roughly) true that *an* authorities issue statements to be believed and not rules or commands to be obeyed. And it is also (roughly) true that *in* authorities issue rules to be obeyed.

Is it also true that *in* authorities do not issue statements to be believed? If so, it would follow that our account of the "surrender" of judgment to *an* authorities is irrelevant to understanding *in* authority relations. If the B's of an *in* authority relationship are not asked to believe anything, then considerations concerning the conditions under which belief is logically possible can hardly be helpful to understanding the role of the B's. Clearly, however, it is false to say that the B's are not asked to believe *anything*. At a minimum they must believe that there is a difference between rules that carry authority and those that do not, and they must believe that *these* rules carry authority. This being true, and it also being true that belief necessarily involves reflection and judgment on the part of the believing (or disbelieving agent), judgment is a necessary part of *in* authority relations.

It might be responded that the foregoing statement, while true, is trivial because it has no bearing on those aspects of *in* authority relations to which the thesis we are now considering (that *in* authority does not require or even solicit belief) is intended to apply. B must believe that A or X has authority, but he is

36 *Equality, authority, rights, and philosophy*

explicitly not expected to believe, in the sense of thinking true, well-founded or justified, the *content* of the statements that A issues or in which X consists. As rules or commands, these statements are not eligible as subjects of belief. To treat them as eligible for belief or disbelief is to make a category mistake in the Rylean sense. As C.W. Cassinelli has put the point in question, A's possessing *in* authority is a circumstance logically entailing beliefs on the part of B's. But his exercise of that authority, in the sense of requiring or prohibiting this or that action of B, is a condition that excludes the relevance (though not the existence) of any and all beliefs (save the belief that the requirement or prohibition carries authority) to the decision whether to comply.[6] B "surrenders judgment," to repeat Friedman's words, in the sense that he

> does not make his obedience *conditional* on his own personal examination and evaluation of the thing he is being asked to do. Rather, he accepts as a sufficient condition for following a prescription that it is prescribed by someone acknowledged by him as entitled to rule. The man who accepts authority ... surrenders[s] his ... individual judgment because he does not insist that reasons be given that he can grasp and that satisfy him, as a condition of his obedience.[7]

The corollary, of course, is that by "rightful" and "by right" it should be understood, not merely that A is entitled to issue the rule, but that he is entitled to do so without giving reasons for it and entitled to have B obey it despite B's not receiving any reasons for doing so beyond those provided by A's authority.

B's relations to *an* authority cannot be assimilated to the sort of respect owed under the rules of polite conduct. Similarly, *in* authority cannot be reduced to the case in which B does what A directs because B's independent examination of the merits of that action has convinced him that it is the best thing for him to do. On these interpretations, the distinction between authority and advice, counsel or even mere expressions of A's opinion evaporates. But this conclusion leaves open the question whether B's relation to *in* authority can be interpreted in a manner analogous to what we found to be yet another mistaken interpretation of *an* authority relations, namely that B has an obligation to believe what A says simply because A, *qua* an A who B recognizes as such, says it. Is the fact that a rule or command carries *in* authority itself a conclusive reason for B *qua* B to have an obligation to conform to the rule or to obey the command?

We argued that the defect in the analogous interpretation of *an* authority is that it destroys a condition of authority as opposed to mere compulsion or dominance—the condition, namely, that B must be in a position to judge the merits of A's pronouncements and performances. It might be argued, however—indeed this is exactly what Friedman and Cassinelli are arguing—that no such requirement obtains in the case of *in* authority. The requirement obtains for *an* authority because of the conceptual connection between that concept and concepts such as "true," "valid," "profound," "correct," and so forth, together with the fact that the latter concepts entail criteria, independent of A's views, by which A's views

The *"surrender" of individual judgment*   37

can be assessed. Because *in* authority has no connection with these or any comparable concepts, it entails no such requirement.

But this is false. Or rather, it could conceivably be true only on an understanding of *in* authority that is objectionable on normative grounds and is probably otherwise untenable.

In fact, of course, persons holding positions of *in* authority regularly act as if their pronouncements are true, wise, or otherwise substantively meritorious. But we can agree with F-P theorists that their position as *in* authorities does not itself entitle them to do so. We can also agree that no single such pronouncement can be shown to lack *in* authority merely (!) because it is not just, right, good, or in conformity with other normative standards. (We return to this last question below.) But there is at least one evaluative concept, or family of evaluative concepts, with which *in* authority pronouncements are necessarily connected. The most familiar member of this family is "valid," and the members of it most commonly employed in the kind of context we are considering are "constitutional" and *"ultra* and *intra vires."* Whatever other tests *in* authority pronouncements might be expected to meet, they must be shown to be valid in the sense of consistent with the "constitution," the *"grundnorm,"* the "rule of recognition," or whatever, that is the source of the authority they are alleged to have.

To state this requirement, of course, is to state a tautology. An A or an X carries *in* authority only if it satisfies this test. Hence the theorists we have been discussing are likely to respond that their arguments encompass this point. But their arguments do not encompass all of the implications of this point for the question of "surrender" of judgment on B's part. The question whether a rule or command is valid is commonly difficult, often vexed. It is intimately connected, moreover, with the often equally vexed question of what actions the A or the X requires of or prohibits to B. The question whether A has authority to issue rule X is often undecidable apart from a determination of the range of actions it implies for B. These questions do not decide themselves. They are decided through the exercise of judgment by parties to the *in* authority relationship.

The interpretation of "surrender of judgment" that we are considering, then, must either deny the importance of these questions or turn their resolution entirely over to the A's. Cassinelli apparently leans to the former alternative.

> The recipient [B] must ... realize that the communication [from A] is an imperative, that the governor does not intend to convince, persuade, or bargain. However, he need not understand precisely what the communication is saying, and he can even misinterpret it to the extent that he believes it to say something which the governor did not at all intend. The governor's exercise of authority is not undermined by obscureness and misunderstanding. The recipient must only be aware that he is being told to do something.[8]

Taken literally, this passage suggests that it does not matter how B (or anyone else?—need A himself understand it?) understands a rule or command. B need understand no more than that he is told to do something—anything whatever.

38   *Equality, authority, rights, and philosophy*

Unfair as it may be to Cassinelli, this parody brings out a main difficulty with "surrender of judgment" in the interpretation presently before us. Given that the A or the X is rarely if ever simply pellucid, simply self-explicating, this interpretation leaves us to choose among the following three alternatives:

1   it does not matter how B understands A or X or what actions he takes or refrains from taking, it matters only that he does *something* and that he does it *because* he knows that X has authority;
2   it matters how X is understood and what B does, but the question of the meaning of X is entirely for the A's, B's role being restricted to accepting their determination without question;
3   B must himself interpret (at least provisionally) X and hence must exercise judgment concerning it.

Alternative 1 is manifestly absurd. It makes the relationship between the rule or command and the content of B's actions purely random. Alternative 2 is that objectionable theory according to which A has unqualified authority to determine the scope of his own authority. Leaving aside normative objections to this view, there is a serious question whether it is, in any form consistent with continued use of "authority," even cogent. At a minimum B must *decide* what to do when faced with A or X. He "must" decide because if he does not do so we would no longer have authority and the action of discharging an obligation, but imposition or compulsion. There is also a question whether authority is sociologically possible on this understanding of the A–B relationship. We have argued that authority needs the support of some array of values and beliefs that has acceptance in the society or association of which it is part. For values and beliefs to give such support, a kind of congruence must be thought to exist between them and the actions and requirements of authority. The initiatives, the leadership, in maintaining such congruence may indeed rest largely with the A's. But the B's must believe that the congruence exists, and this belief requires judgments on B's part.

In reality, then, the only tenable alternative is 3—which is to say that the A–B relationship entails the exercise of at least some kinds of judgment on B's part. "Surrender of judgment" to *in* authority cannot cogently be interpreted in the manner we have been examining.

Can it be cogently interpreted as excluding B's judgments about properties of X's other than their implications for B's conduct and the validity of those implications? Do *in* authority relations as such require B to surrender his judgment concerning the justice, the desirability, the wisdom, and so forth of an A or X? That they do so is the proposition on which F-P interpreters of "surrender of judgment" (whether defenders or critics of *in* authority) have been most insistent. Of course, B may in fact make such judgments. But any such judgments that B makes are purely private; they are not only irrelevant but inappropriate to his public role as a participant in relationships of *in* authority. In respect to that role, B must understand that judgments about the merits of A or X are either irrelevant or vested

The "surrender" of individual judgment 39

exclusively with A. If this point is not sustained, F-P theorists argue, *in* authority evaporates and at most we have counsel, advice, persuasion or argumentation over the merits of courses of action. "Surrender of judgment" in at least this sense is a categorial feature of *in* authority relations.

The first step in interpreting this contention is to emphasize again some of the considerations discussed in chapters 3 and 4 [of *The Practice of Authority*], considerations that call attention to the continuities between questions about the implications and validity of an X and questions about its merits. Without rehearsing those considerations in detail, the minimal and undeniable point is that decisions about validity and implication require judgments concerning intentions and thereby about the pro-attitudes of parties to the relationship. In this respect at least, the A–B relationship excludes unqualified "surrender" of judgment concerning normative issues on B's part.

Can we say more than this? Are there further respects in which normative judgments by B are required by or at least consistent with his role *qua* B? Can, must, B *qua* B make and act upon continuing assessments of X's without thereby denying the authority of the latter or taking his leave from the authority relationship?

We must first set aside the argument that attempts at such judgments involve some species of category mistake—that rules and commands simply do not allow of judgments about their merits. Rules and commands are directives; they prescribe to action. As such they are paradigms of statements susceptible of normative assessment. Of course the person making such assessments must consider the properties distinctive to rules and commands—cannot treat them as mere predictions of how A's or B's will act, or as pieces of advice, requests, and so forth. But if these properties are taken into account, the merits of rules *qua* rules can be assessed. Thus at most the point is that *acting on* judgments about substantive merits is excluded from the role of B. Although any A or X can be described or characterized in a variety of ways, at least some of which invite normative assessment, the only characterization relevant to the conduct of B *qua* B is that the A or the X has the standing of a rule that carries *in* authority. The due process rule, for example, might be characterized as a principle of great importance to legal systems, as an element of natural justice, as a recurrent feature of human arrangements, as a great bulwark of human liberty and dignity, as an unfortunate burden on the police, and no doubt in a variety of other ways, many of which express normative judgments. On the thesis we are considering, however, the sole characterization relevant to the conduct of B *qua* B is that the due process rule carries authority in the jurisdiction of which B is a part.

The availability of a variety of characterizations of the formulations that are X's is part of the reason why B's must exercise the self-discipline that Oakeshott emphasizes so strongly. If the one and only way to characterize the formulation were as an A or an X, then the only alternatives with which persons who are B's would be presented would be to obey or to disobey the A or X. The argument for self-discipline in effect contends that for purposes of action B's confronted with an A or an X must proceed as if B is the only role they play and as if the characterization "an A" or "an X" is the only characterization that they may consider.

40 *Equality, authority, rights, and philosophy*

This is not "implausibly circumspect" (Oakeshott), it is impossibly limiting. There is no such thing as a person who is nothing but a B, and there is no such thing as a formulation that is nothing but an A or an X. In thought and action the several roles that any person plays and the several characterizations of which any formulation allows inevitably coexist and interact in a variety of ways. As important as they are, role conceptions and distinguishing characterizations do not and cannot (if only because they are commonly defined in part by reference one to the other) form hermetically sealed compartments or windowless monads that are or could be altogether isolated from one another.

It is in part for these reasons that human affairs do not present us with pure cases of *in* authority on the F-P model or instantiations of "civil" or "enterprise" associations in unalloyed form. It is largely for this reason that F-P theorists argue, often passionately, for "self-discipline." Arguments for self-discipline would be pointless if the allegedly irrelevant modes of thought and action were not so readily available and so tempting.

But there is a further reason for this circumstance, a reason that casts doubt on any tendency to dismiss the discrepancies between model and practice on metatheoretical grounds. The reason is that actual practice has commonly displayed a widely shared belief, held on normative grounds, that there *ought* to be interpenetration and interaction, that the roles and kinds of characterizations *ought not* to be treated as totally distinct. In its most emphatic form the belief is expressed as the conviction that citizens have a positive *duty* to make continuing assessments of the substantive merits of X's and a positive duty to make action on these assessments an integral part of *in* authority relations.

In principle this duty could be discharged in a manner consistent with the interpretation of "surrender of judgment" characteristic of F-P theorists from Hobbes forward. X's and proposed X's would be assessed for the purpose of deciding whether they should achieve and should retain authority, not whether they should be obeyed as long as they have authority. The B's are not to surrender their judgment as to the merits of X's; they are only to surrender the prerogative of acting on those judgments as long as the X's carry authority. Or more exactly, they are to surrender the prerogative of basing decisions about obedience and disobedience on judgments about merits while continuing to claim that their actions are taken *qua* participants in the practice of *in* authority in question.

Notes

1 Richard B. Friedman, in Richard E. Flathman, ed., *Concepts in Social and Political Philosophy* (New York: Macmillan, 1973), p. 29.
2 See Joseph Raz, *Practical Reason and Norms*; and "On Legitimate Authority," in Richard Bronaugh, ed., *Philosophical Law* (Westport, CT: Greenwood, 1978).
3 See Yves Simon, *A General Theory of Authority* (Notre Dame, IN: Notre Dame University Press, 1962); Carl J. Friedrich, "Authority, Reason and Discretion," in Carl J. Friedrich, ed., *Authority* (Nomos 1) (Cambridge, MA: Harvard University Press, 1958); and *Tradition and Authority* (London: Pall Mall Press, 1972).
4 See esp. George Cornewall Lewis, *An Essay on the Influence of Authority in Matters of Opinion* (London: John W. Parker, 1849). On the views of Lewis, Mill, and the jurist

John Austin, see Richard B. Friedman, in J. B. Schneewind, ed., *Mill: A Collection of Critical Essays* (New York: Doubleday, 1968).

5 Joseph Raz, in Bronaugh, *Philosophical Law*, p. 10. But cf. his account of advice, p. 15.

6 See C. W. Cassinelli, "Political Authority: Its Exercise and Possession," in Anthony de Crespigny and Alan Wertheimer, eds., *Contemporary Political Theory* (New York: Atherton Press, 1970).

7 Friedman, in Flathman, *Concepts in Social and Political Philosophy*, p. 129.

8 Cassinelli, in de Crespigny and Wertheimer, *Contemporary Political Theory*, pp. 77–78.

4 Liberalism and authority (1989)

Discourse about liberalism and authority suffers distracting embarrassments. If the discourse aspires to contemporaneity it may well be accused of necromancy or even necrophilia; liberalism and authority are dead. Nor can it easily take refuge in historicality; one set of eminent authorities avers that liberalism has existed nowhere outside the pages of hopelessly unhistorical "histories" of political thought, another that authority has enjoyed but a fleeting presence in one or two times and places.[1] Should one be so heedless as to persevere with the discourse, the choices would appear to be unattractive: unmasking one's supposed subject matter or perpetuating mythologies.

The bold categoricality of these contentions arouses suspicion of lurking essentialisms. If "liberalism" is dead and "authority" is gone—*sans phrase* as it were—the least we must say is that each of "them" must have lived and been among us in forms pretty definite and well understood. Medical examiners need bodies to pronounce over. Even the proposition that liberalism is a figment would seem to betray certitude about what "it" has been thought to be and confidence that the supposititious entity will elude our most assiduous researches. The Exorcisor needs to know what the ghost was thought to be like and where it was said to lurk.

Uncomfortable with such convenient but almost certainly oversimplifying assumptions, I hope for nothing so dramatic as confirmation or refutation of the sweeping empirical contentions I have mentioned. As suggested, however, the very presuppositions of those contentions encourage the thought that there are subject matters—if only at the level of ideas—available for examination and reflection. Equally important, the uncommon fervor with which the contentions are commonly advanced engenders the suspicion that examining these subject matters may tell us something about our political estate. I will use the terms *liberal* and *authority* without further apology, but I will not make a concerted effort to define *liberalism* or to document the past or present reality of authority. I will be examining a number of ideas that are familiar and, I think, commonly associated with these terms. Insofar as I have a theme it is also familiar, namely, that the deep tension between liberalism and authority, the deep ambivalence of liberals concerning authority, could hardly be otherwise. I hope also to suggest that this is no bad thing; that our political estate is the better for it.

I

Getting this examination under way will require some initial simplifications of my own, especially concerning the tenets of liberalism. Conveniently, Bruce Ackerman's recent book in, but ultimately against, liberal thinking helps us to arrive at a serviceable abbreviation.[2]

1 Human beings are purposive, goal-seeking creatures whose actions and patterns of action cannot be understood apart from their conceptions of good.
2 Conceptions of good and goals of action are irreducibly plural. There are no criteria of good that exclude the possibility of cogent disputation, and application of the available criteria frequently leads to conflicting judgments and conclusions.
3 There is a scarcity of at least some of the goods that human beings seek and of the resources necessary to effective pursuit of those goods.
4 Hence there is certain to be disagreement and competition and very likely to be conflict among human beings.
5 Disagreement, competition, and conflict neither can nor should be eliminated, but conflict must be contained within nondestructive limits.
6 The primary objective of politics is to promote an ordering of human interaction which allows each person the greatest possible freedom to pursue goals compatible with effective constraints on destructive conflict.

These propositions, of course, are neither exclusive to liberalism nor somehow exhaustive of all of the ideas that have ever been claimed for or ascribed to it. Self-designated non- or antiliberals might accept some of them, and some self-denominated liberals would want to alter the formulation of one or more. Certainly numerous contemporary liberals would insist on adding to the list, most particularly by including propositions about equality. But even if the list does not give us the historical gist or the philosophical essence of liberalism, it provides an interrelated set of ideas that engender a distinctive understanding and assessment of authority.

In respect to authority, our initial need is less for a list of tenets than for a set of distinctions. Following with one largish addition, the important account of Richard B. Friedman, we may distinguish among *in* authority, an *authority*, and *the authoritative*.[3] Presidents and police officers are *in* positions of authority. They hold offices that are invested, and that invest their occupants with, authority to promulgate rules and issue commands concerning classes of action, rules, and commands that are binding on all those subject to the jurisdiction of the office. Charles Goren holds no such office and hence possesses no such *in* authority. Rather, by virtue of his exceptional knowledge of and skill at playing the game of bridge, he is *an* authority on that game for numerous persons who play it. To my knowledge, Edmund Hoyle never held any office and is in any case long since deceased. Yet play "according to Hoyle" is *authoritative* for players of poker and numerous other games.

44 *Equality, authority, rights, and philosophy*

In Friedman's view, the distinction between *in* and *an* authority is categorical. Their presuppositions or conditions, the character of relations conducted in terms of them, are not only entirely different but antithetical. *In* authority presupposes disagreement and equality among the parties to the authority relationships; *an* authority assumes consensus (or at least the realistic possibility of achieving it) and inequality. As Thomas Hobbes has taught us to think, *in* authority arises because persons more or less equal in the respects salient in their interactions fall into intractable disagreement over issues that cannot be sidestepped or postponed. To prevent destructive conflict, those persons create an office of authority and agree in advance to abide by all *intra vires* decisions of the occupant of that office. In the colorful language that is commonly employed in this connection, for purposes of action in regard to matters that have been regulated by the authority, they "surrender their judgment" to it. By contrast, *an* authority develops because one person (Able) achieves superiority of wisdom, knowledge, or skill over another (Baker) in respect to matters of interest or importance to both. As with *in* authority, Baker defers to Able. But this deference is based not on the assumption that agreement cannot be reached as to the proper resolution of substantive issues or questions, but on the belief that Able's judgment and actions are likely to be correct, wise, skillful. This belief is grounded in and justified by the quality of Able's previous performances as judged by criteria accepted by Baker. Accordingly, it will be proper for Baker to give up the belief and withdraw the deference if Able's performances deteriorate. Thus *an* authority relations are integrally concerned with the substantive merits of Able's performances. They presume not that there is intractable disagreement between the parties but rather that the parties will agree once Able has discerned and enunciated the truth, displayed the correct technique, and the like. Whatever terminology we choose to employ, *in* and *an* authority are radically different concepts and (if instantiated in practice) phenomena. The tendency to assimilate them has been productive of dangerous confusion. (Later we will see that in Michael Oakeshott's view a closely related confusion has engendered the mistaken belief that the modern state is possessed of the desirable property of *in* authority and, indeed, is responsible for the distinctive evils of modern life.)[4]

No one acquainted with Friedman's acute analysis will deny that there are important differences between *in* and *an* authority. Our discussion of those differences, however, has already displayed at least one important commonality between them. There are others as well and they are material to understanding liberal attitudes toward political authority.

In both *in* and *an* authority Able's performances constitute considerations that are not only relevant to but ordinarily decisive concerning performances on Baker's part. We might say that Able's performances constitute reasons for *this* as opposed to *that* performance by Baker. (Later, however, we will have to give further attention to the notion "a reason for.") Whether this commonality explains or justifies our use of one and the same term, some such deference is rudimentary to both concepts and both relationships.

Liberalism and authority 45

I want to try to understand this common feature by examining the relationships between *in* and *an* authority and what I called the authoritative. Expressions such as "that's according to Hoyle" and "that's not kosher" are used well beyond the confines of card play and dietary practice. As with notions such as "the done thing," "that's not on," and even (though with a harder, not necessarily a sharper, edge) "Christian," "un-American," and their ilk, these notions invoke beliefs and values that the speaker regards as strongly settled and widely shared among the members of her culture, community, or group. Conduct that accords with those beliefs and values is approved "as a matter of course," while actions that deviate from or conflict with them are therefore suspect and in need of explicit and detailed justification. Social scientists refer to such beliefs and values as forming the culture, the mores or folkways, the national character, and so forth of the societies they study. The philosopher Wittgenstein seems to have them in mind in such of his statements as the following: "It is what human beings *say* that is true and false, and they agree on the *language* they use. That is not agreement in opinions but in forms of life." "If language is to be a means of communication there must be agreement not only in definitions but also (queer as this may sound) in judgements."[5]

Attending to such "agreements" helps us to understand features of *an* authority relationships that are otherwise puzzling and perhaps objectionable. If Able's standing as *an* authority depends on the truth, wisdom, and skill of her performances, it appears that Baker must be able to judge those performances. But if Baker is in fact competent to make such judgments, it would seem that Baker has no need for Able's authority; it would seem that there is no work for Able's authority to do. On the other hand, if Baker is incapable of judging Able's performances but nevertheless defers to Able, Baker is deferring not to Able's authority but to Able herself.

These considerations have led Michael Oakeshott to conclude that *an* authority is a bogus, but also an extremely dangerous, notion. Where use of the notion is more than a way of giving cheap compliments to Able, it shows that Baker has become an "individual manqué" who has willingly submitted to a despotism.[6] No one who has worried about the burgeoning role of "experts" in our society will entirely dismiss Oakeshott's view. Understood as a critique of much of what passes for *an* authority relationships his conclusions are disturbing in their perspicacity. Moreover, he helps us to see why *an* authority relationships, especially if viewed from the perspective of liberalism, are inherently unstable. Nevertheless "*an* authority" is more than a frequently encountered misnomer. Nor are genuine *an* authority relations necessarily more dangerous or objectionable than authority relations of other kinds.

Consider the *an* authority of medical doctors—say, Michael deBakey's standing as an authority on heart disease and treatment. Few of deBakey's patients are competent to assess the technical details of his diagnoses, prescriptions, surgical performances. But it does not follow that they *must* choose between caring for themselves and submitting to his personal despotism (of course, they may in fact do either). Other members of the medical and related professions are competent

46 *Equality, authority, rights, and philosophy*

to and have in fact judged his technical performances. His standing as *an* authority is, in part, a result of the fact that such judgments have been made and have generally been favorable. Using Wittgenstein's language, we might say that there is agreement on the opinion that deBakey is exceptionally knowledgeable about and skillful in the treatment of heart problems. As important as it is, however, this is not the main point in the present context. Such agreement in "opinion" is possible only because there is also agreement at levels at once deeper and more general. Among medical practitioners, life scientists, biomedical engineers, and the like, there is substantial agreement on a body of general knowledge about human and other organisms, about various questions of procedure and technique not specific to the heart and its treatment, and so forth. At least some of this knowledge is shared widely in the society. Yet more generally, there is substantial agreement on such questions as the objectives of medicine and on what counts as health and illness, successful and unsuccessful treatment. As parties to an agreement, as sharers in these authoritative beliefs and values, patients have the criteria necessary to a variety of judgments, judgments that, when made and collected, support or fail to support deBakey's standing as *an* authority. The judgments also support (or not) the belief that it is appropriate to accord his decisions and actions distinctively respectful consideration. When we understand that *an* authority is grounded in the authoritative, we see how puzzles concerning it can be resolved and major objections to it parried.

In the light of the tenets of liberalism set out above, the inherent instability of *an* authority relationships results from the very features that make such relationships possible. As the term itself implies, the beliefs and values that make up the authoritative are in part normative in character. Agreement concerning them must therefore be more as opposed to less firm, more as opposed to less widespread; it can never be entirely firm and it is unlikely that it will ever long remain entirely encompassing. Wittgenstein and numerous others have given us powerful reasons for thinking that it is impossible to question all of the elements of the authoritative at once. To put the same point another way, if we could imagine a number of people who lived in spatial proximity but who agreed on nothing, we would have imagined a group of people for whom *an* authority (among other things!) would be impossible. But because (on the liberal view) each and every belief and value is logically subject to dispute, because no element of the authoritative can be logically immune to cogent questioning, the basis of *an* authority relationships must on principle be uncertain. More important, perhaps, from the liberal point of view the relation ought in fact to be kept in something of an uncertain condition. As John Stuart Mill emphasized so forcefully, a society that has ceased to question its most basic values and beliefs has no basis for them, has regressed into a kind of nonage, and is vulnerable to one or another form of despotism.[7]

Liberals treasure knowledge and wisdom; such progress as human societies have made from barbarism to civilization is largely calibrated by the development of these.[8] Moreover, few liberals (certainly not Mill) believe that such progress is possible without divisions of labor and specializations of function that

Liberalism and authority   47

are all but certain to produce *an* authorities and *an* authority relations. Yet the tenets of liberalism positively require suspicion and distrust not only in respect to *an* authorities but of the very suppositions of *an* authority relationships.

The school of thought running from Hobbes to Oakeshott celebrates *in* authority precisely because it breaks the connection between authority and the authoritative and hence is not encumbered by these complications and liabilities. Subscription to an office of *in* authority, so far from assuming or depending on shared beliefs and values, presupposes the absence of any such consensus. Subscribers defer or "surrender judgment" to the decisions of *in* authorities not because they agree with them and not because they are confident that they would agree with those decisions if they possessed the special competence or expertise of those who made them. *In* authority has (is said by these writers to have) nothing whatever to do with Able's knowledge, expertise, or skill, with the content or merits of Able's decisions, and nothing to do with beliefs, values, or opinions held by Baker or the members of Baker's society.

Or rather—the difference is of the utmost consequence—*in* authority has to do with these phenomena in the single respect that the members of the community share the belief that they will be unable to reach agreement on numerous and important of the issues that arise in the course of their interactions with one another. It is this postulate that justifies their common willingness to conform, without regard to content, to the decisions of those invested with authority.

As with Oakeshott's views about *an* authority, this account and assessment of *in* authority has much to be said for it. Moreover, we see below that basic contentions of the Hobbes–Oakeshott theory have great prominence in liberal thinking about authority. I suggest that much of this thinking about authority consists in an attempt to accept those contentions without fully embracing the suppositions on which Oakeshott thinks they depend. Liberals have recognized that favorable judgments of the content of the rules and commands cannot be the only good reason for obeying them, a recognition that informs and is elaborated by their enthusiasm for such notions as the rule of law, government of laws not of men, constitutionalism, and procedural as opposed to substantive due process. Yet liberals have balked at the notion of surrender of judgment and the intimately related view that *in* authority relations should or even could be entirely independent of substantive beliefs and values and judgments derived from them.

On the question of "could," liberals are undoubtedly correct. As important as it is, the distinction between *an* and *in* authority cannot be drawn in the manner Oakeshott (and Friedman) suggests. The relationship between *in* authority and the authoritative is not the same as between *an* authority and the authoritative, but there must be such a relationship.

There are several lines of argument that support this conclusion. In my judgment, the most powerful of these is grounded in Wittgenstein's analysis of language and meaning, particularly his analysis of key notions such as rules, following a rule, and "knowing how to go on." These notions are not only salient in but constitutive of *in* authority on the understanding thereof that we are

48 *Equality, authority, rights, and philosophy*

considering. If Wittgenstein's analysis of them is correct, Oakeshott's understanding of *in* authority is not just mistaken, it is incoherent in crucial respects.

Fortunately, Oakeshott himself has provided us with a closely analogous but shorter route to the same conclusion. Subscription to *in* authority is human conduct. All human conduct is informed by, is incomprehensible apart from, beliefs and values, objectives and purposes, accepted by the agent or actor. Nor are these features difficult to discern in the discussion of authority itself in this tradition. Hobbes was as keen to promote surrender of judgment as any writer previous to Oakeshott. But as the proverbial "every schoolboy" knows, Hobbes urged such surrender *on the ground that, in order that*, we might escape from or avoid that intolerable condition he called the state of war. Oakeshott is much more circumspect, much more parsimonious, in his formulation of the same point. But his *cives* or citizens subscribe to the *in* authority of the state in order to "abate" somewhat the "contingency" that is at once the condition and, if entirely unabated, the deadly enemy of their liberty.[9] A person who cared not for her liberty, or one who did not believe that surrender of judgment to authority is necessary or at least contributive to preserving it, could not maintain subscription to authority. In a society lacking consensus on at least these values and beliefs authority would be what it presently appears to be in places like Lebanon, Haiti, and El Salvador (and what Oakeshott thinks it has been in much of human history), that is, an impossibility. Moreover, "abating contingency" is a portmanteau objective that requires a good deal of elaboration and specification if it is to yield guidance in formulating, applying, and most important for present purposes, in obeying or disobeying the rules and commands issued by *in* authorities. These processes of elaboration and interpretation will of necessity be informed by any number of further, more specific beliefs and values. Where there is no tolerably wide consensus on some number of such further beliefs and values these processes cannot be sustained.

II

In company with such students of authority as Tocqueville and Weber, then, I contend that *in* authority shares with *an* authority dependence on the authoritative. Not every decision and action in a practice of *in* authority must or even could express or congrue with authoritative beliefs and values. But if there are no such beliefs and values, or if practitioners do not find a general and continuing congruence between them and the workings of authority, authority is an impossibility.

Because of this parallel between the two types of authority, the liberal's wariness of *an* authority must extend to *in* authority as well. In the nineteenth century this suspicion was expressed most forcefully in the concern over the tyranny of the majority and the despotism of society over the individual. In our time it presents itself in the antipathy to communitarian thinking, whether emanating from the New Left, Jonesville, the Moral Majority, or even academic political theorists committed to strongly participationist theories of democracy. Celebrating as they

Liberalism and authority   49

tend to do some body of substantive moral and political truths and goods, all of these modes of thought threaten to still critical thinking over the fundaments of social life. The liberal nightmare, instantiated in the waking state by totalitarianism, is the circumstance in which an entire union, embracing action as well as thought, is effected between an encompassing body of uncritically held beliefs and values and the activities of the most powerful bearer of authority, the state.

But liberals have been and remain endlessly ambivalent concerning the authority of the state. As with their closely analogous attitude toward the *an* authority of experts, this ambivalence is rooted in the tenets discussed at the outset and can be expected to continue as long as those several tenets are accepted. The first two of those tenets require skepticism about if not rejection of *in* authority. But there is a standing temptation, at least partly grounded in one or more of the other four tenets, to use *in* authority to contain conflict and in this and other ways to maximize liberty. If liberalism has a history, that history is replete with attempts, never more than partially successful, to reconcile, or at least to achieve a practicable coordination between, these two impulses. In the space that remains I comment on these attempts in the light of the foregoing discussions.

I said in passing that Able's authority provides Baker with a reason for deferring to Able's decisions and judgments. It might well be thought, however, that this claim about, this characterization of, authority relations is precisely what liberalism cannot allow. The notion "a reason for" is difficult to explicate. Most of its uses, however, involve a distinction between the arbitrary and the nonarbitrary. The former often implies subjectively held or merely personal opinion, while the latter suggests evidence and argumentation deserving of interpersonal standing. *A* is a reason for *B* if *A* is correct, true, justified, and the like by virtue of the evidence and argumentation that support it. *A* is not a reason for *B* if it lacks these characteristics. Now, if Able's authority is grounded in the authoritative, and if the authoritative consists in disputable beliefs and values, indeed if it is a condition of Baker's liberty that Baker realizes this and in fact disputes those beliefs and values, then it follows that Able's authority cannot provide Baker with a reason for accepting and/or acting on Able's decisions and judgments.

Oakeshott's treatment of *in* authority can be interpreted as an attempt to solve this problem. It would be oversimplifying and otherwise seriously misleading to categorize Oakeshott as a liberal. But his skepticism about the possibility of true or justified belief concerning the substantive questions of moral and political life ("practical" questions in the language of his *Experience and Its Modes*), while grounded in philosophical convictions different from the skepticism of most liberals, is at least as deep as theirs. And their antipathy to the use of authority to impose such beliefs on those who do not accept them pales by comparison with his. Thus he entirely rejects the notion of *an* authority, seeks to found *in* authority exclusively on procedural considerations, and proposes to restrict its activities to questions about which issues of true and false, correct and incorrect, are not allowed to arise.

50　*Equality, authority, rights, and philosophy*

As already suggested, the generic impulses that move Oakeshott in this regard are also at work in liberal attempts to solve the problem we are considering. The rule of law, constitutionalism, the notion of an office, the rules of procedure characteristic of legislatures, courts, and rational-legal bureaucracies—all of these are intended less to resolve moral and political questions than to put constraints on which questions will be taken up and on the manner in which those that are addressed are debated. Viewed in the light of our discussion of liberalism, they can be interpreted as attempts to give the notion "reason for" a standing as compatible as possible with basic liberal tenets. If we regard "reasons" as propositions that are undoubtedly true, perhaps even that could not be false, then no such reasons are available. But some propositions have better standing than others; some considerations are less subject to dispute than others. If we can ground authority in, constrain its activities by, those propositions and considerations that deservedly enjoy such standing, we will as a practical matter have provided ourselves with reasons for accepting and deferring to authority.

In a number of political societies this project seems to have met with sufficient success to have sustained authority and authority relations over considerable periods and despite a great deal of disagreement at the level of Wittgenstein's "opinion." So far as I can judge, not many Englishmen or Americans think of provisions of the British and the United States constitutions as necessary truths. A preponderance of these two populations nevertheless appears to believe that those provisions are defensible and do accord a deserved legitimacy to the arrangements, institutions, and practices of British and American government. Indeed, the fact that these constitutions are not repositories of immutable truths, and hence that their provisions are subject to discussion, interpretation, and deliberate change, is viewed in many quarters as among their merits.

On this understanding, however, the notion "a reason for" and everything that depends on it has no better than a comparative and a contingent standing. Given other beliefs that for the moment we are choosing not to question, we can say that A is a better reason for X than is B, perhaps that A is the best reason for X which is now known to us. And we can sometimes say that the reasons for X are better than the reasons for Y. But the comparative, contingent, and hence hypothetical character of these judgments leaves them in an unstable, a vulnerable, condition. This circumstance may or may not disquiet citizens, but it is unsettling to many philosophers—including, oddly enough, many philosophers who are also liberals.

Perhaps as a consequence, the ambivalence of liberal philosophers toward authority is rehearsed, in more insistently philosophical terms, as ambivalence concerning tenets basic to their own position. Attempts are made to amend or qualify the idea that conceptions of the good and related axiological conceptions are irreducibly plural. Arguments are sometimes advanced that there are at least some things that must be good; arguments are more frequently advanced that there are some that are not and cannot be.

If liberalism begins in the seventeenth century and if John Locke is a liberal, this ambivalence makes its appearance at the very beginning of the liberal tradition. An

Liberalism and authority   51

empiricist and a nominalist, a voluntarist, contractarian, and believer in negative liberty, Locke nevertheless argued that moral and political good and right are constrained by certain natural rights. Because political authority must be grounded in good and right, authority is also so constrained. The efficacy of these natural rights is of course contingent on their having achieved authoritative standing in this society or that. But their philosophical standing, their standing in reason and as reasons for action, is necessary not contingent. To deny them is to make a discernible, a correctable, error of reasoning: any individual who fails to respect them is thereby convicted of immortality. Any political system that does not conform to them is a tyranny.

The inconsistencies within Locke's thought have delighted his enemies, confounded his friends, and bedeviled his commentators for three centuries. On the face of things, his natural rights are simply dogmatic, representing either residues (in Pareto's sense) of previous natural law and natural right thinking or ad hoc devices adopted to solve or to conceal glaring difficulties in his moral and political thought (an appearance that, for me, natural rights doctrines continue to present—most notably in the work of Robert Nozick).[10] Later writers, however, at least some of whom are insistent in their claim to be liberals, have continued and refined Locke's effort to stabilize or solidify morals and politics by putting philosophical constraints on conceptions of good. The most sophisticated of these attempts, particularly fascinating when compared to the arguments of Oakeshott, take their inspiration from Immanuel Kant (whether legitimately so I will not here venture to say). They reach what appears to be their apogee in the work of Rawls and have attained to a kind of reductio ad absurdum in the recent argument of Bruce Ackerman.

Oakeshott accepts the premises that human action is purposive and that the conceptions of good that inform its purposiveness are irreducibly plural. From these premises he infers that we may not use political or any other kind of authority to limit the diversity, substantively speaking, of thought and action. Individuals pursue their purposes as they see them. If some individuals happen to share a purpose, they may form an association to pursue it in concert. Such associations are founded entirely on the consensus that informs them and properly cease to exist the instant that consensus disappears. Any attempt to maintain such an association by use of authority will explode it in conflict or transform it into a tyranny. As the encompassing political entity, the state cannot hope for consensus on substantive issues. It must rigorously exclude such issues from its concerns and restrict itself to maintaining "civility" in the pursuit of individual and group objectives. Its sole task is to see to it that its members pursue their multifarious purposes within the confines of "adverbial rules" adopted exclusively to minimize (they can never eliminate) conflict of an uncivil variety. Purposiveness and the diversity it engenders are treasured, not banished or even reduced. But they are excluded from politics; they are excluded from interactions involving authority.

Liberals such as Rawls and Ackerman share many of Oakeshott's premises but do not want to accept (all of) the politically restrictive inferences he draws

52 *Equality, authority, rights, and philosophy*

from those premises. As suggested above, they want better to secure the foundations of authority. In part for that reason they are committed to objectives over and above civility. Yet they recognize that there is sharp disagreement concerning those objectives and they are convinced that the objectives will not be achieved if their pursuit is left to individuals and groups lacking public authority. Hence they seek to justify, consistent with the premise that there are no incorrigible axiological truths, the use of authority to attain and maintain goals beyond civility. They need somehow to derive exceptionally powerful normative conclusions from exceptionally weak premises.

Their inventiveness in this enterprise is often a wonder to behold. But they cannot conceal the fact that they are in the impossible position known proverbially as trying to get, or rather claiming to have gotten, blood out of a turnip. A veritable barrage of criticism has shot down the crucial Rawlsian claims. Acceptance of maximin and the difference principle is not rationally compelled for those equipped with the concept of justice, a capacity for instrumental reasoning, and such information as is available on the nether side of the veil of ignorance. It can be said with entire confidence that the same fate awaits Ackerman's astonishing contention that a distribution rule requiring no less than strict arithmetic equality in the division of most resources follows deductively from no more than a skeptical metaethics. If I am correct that these conclusions are not compelled by reason, imposing them by authority would have a decidedly illiberal appearance.

III

Having insinuated my largely favorable judgment of the liberal position into these remarks, it would be fitting for me to say something in defense of that judgment. Happily, competing civilities ordain brevity. I restrict myself to three connected remarks.

Liberals argue that liberty engenders diversity. In a number of its classic formulations this argument relies on empiricist and emotivist assumptions that are something of an embarrassment. I have to recognize that my own attachment to the liberal outlook may be explained by a native distaste not only for the dogmatic but for the evangelical and even the enthusiastic. There are, however, better philosophical foundations for such a position than those provided by Ayer's *Language, Truth and Logic* and its ilk. I can't do much more than drop a name, but I suggest that these better foundations may be found in Wittgenstein, particularly in his discussions of what certainty, agreement, and related notions are not and cannot be, are and can become. These discussions might be called skeptical, but they are only skeptical of mythological, hypostasized notions of certitude which, being unattainable, generate a general and a destructive skepticism with which Wittgenstein has nothing to do. Are certainty, well-founded agreement, justified belief, distinctions between better and worse arguments, possible among free human beings? Properly understood, they are not only possible but humdrum in their homely ordinariness. But they are not given, they are

Liberalism and authority 53

achieved and reachieved, earned and earned anew, through discourse within practices and conventions. They cannot be posited or asserted.[11]

On this understanding, we can say that a good deal of agreement, well-founded judgment, and certainty have been achieved in respect to many features of our politics. This is my second point. I can amplify it just a bit by saying that it explains why Oakeshott's argument about *in* authority works as far as it does and why in this and some other societies the rule of law, constitutionalism, certain basic rights, are quite firmly established. From a stance outside of the tradition that he presumes, Oakeshott's adverbial rules and procedural principles, what for him and for most of us are the canons of civility in politics, would represent highly doubtful conclusions concerning deeply substantive issues. Our agreement in these judgments constitutes the language of our politics. It is a language arrived at and continuously modified through no less than a history of discourse, a history in which we have thought about, as we became able to think in, that language.

It is not inconceivable that this agreement, this language, might be achieved in respect to matters about which there is now no more than a mix of agreement and disagreement in opinion. For example, it might be achieved in respect to those questions of social justice about which Rawls has written with much eloquence. But such certainty as we have achieved or may achieve is not necessary in any of the usual philosophical senses; it is not a deduction from the categorical imperative or a deliverance of God, Nature, or any notional Archimidean Reason.

Thus my third point. Liberals are correct that authority is dangerous. If we understand the grounding of authority in the authoritative and the ways in which it therefore requires rather than excludes the exercise of judgment, we understand how authority relations are possible for us. Nevertheless, by comparison with our other practices, authority abbreviates and truncates the processes of reflection and judgment through which agreement develops among free human beings. It asserts and commands the certainties distinctive to it. The view that we cannot do without such abridgments and that we ought not to do comfortably with them is not the least of liberalism's contribution to our political estate.

Notes

1 The death of liberalism has been announced so often that documenting even the more prominent such assertions would be tedious. The demise of authority is also a recurrently popular theme, but by far the most interesting and important statements are by Michael Oakeshott in *On Human Conduct* (Oxford: Clarendon Press, 1975) and Hannah Arendt, especially in "What Is Authority?" in her *Between Past and Future* (New York: Viking Press, 1961).

2 Bruce Ackerman, *Social Justice and the Liberal State* (New Haven: Yale University Press, 1980).

3 Richard B. Friedman, "On the Concept of Authority in Political Philosophy," in *Concepts in Social and Political Philosophy*, ed. Richard E. Flathman (New York: Macmillan, 1973).

4 Oakeshott, *On Human Conduct*.

54 *Equality, authority, rights, and philosophy*

5 Ludwig Wittgenstein, *Philosophical Investigations*, I, 241, 242 (New York: Macmillan, 1953). I have discussed the notion of the authoritative and other aspects of the present topic at greater length in my *The Practice of Political Authority: Authority and the Authoritative* (Chicago: University of Chicago Press, 1980).

6 Oakeshott, *On Human Conduct*, esp. ch. 2.

7 John Stuart Mill, *On Liberty* (New York: E. P. Dutton, 1951), esp. ch. 2.

8 Some of the complexities and paradoxes in the subject of authority, and perhaps much of the appeal of Oakeshott's and related attacks on it, stem from the well-established tendency to characterize the development of civilization as a movement away from "authority" and relations dominated by "authority." On this conceptualization uncivilized societies (often called "traditional") are organized and dominated by a set of values and beliefs for which there is no basis in evidence or reason but which are treated as "authoritative" in the sense of being immune to question. The history and anthropology that inform uses of this conceptualization are deeply suspect. But insofar as they are correct, no liberal should treat them as histories or anthropologies of authority and authority relations

9 Oakeshott's views about human conduct are presented most systematically in the first essay of *On Human Conduct*. The discussion of *cives* and their subscription is primarily in the second essay. The notion of abating contingency is at p. 74.

10 Robert Nozick, *Anarchy, State, and Utopia* (New York: Basic Books, 1974).

11 Wittgenstein's discussions of these points are most accessible in his *On Certainty* (Oxford: Basil Blackwell, 1969).

5 The theory of rights and the practice of abortion (1989)

Is there a convincing argument for a *right* to abortion on demand? A variety of particular forms of such a right are now legally established in this and a large number of other legal systems, and it is known that these rights have been successfully exercised millions of times. Yet defenders of such a right are not in agreement as to the patterns of reasoning that best support it, and a large number of people continue to believe that abortion itself, and certainly a right to abortion on demand, are utterly indefensible. I hope to contribute to the discussion of this difficult matter by drawing explicitly on aspects of existing theory concerning rights. I will try to show that explicit attention to the idea that there should be a right to abortion on demand serves to clarify controversy over abortion and helps to produce a strong argument in favor of what has become (in an astonishingly short period of time given the centuries of opposition to it) accepted legal and moral practice over much of the globe.

It must be stressed at once that the question "Should there be a right to abortion on demand?" is not equivalent to the question of whether abortion is (ever) morally, legally, or otherwise justified or defensible. True, if abortion could not be justified at all, there could hardly be a justified right to it. But it is possible that abortion could sometimes be justifiable and yet that there would be no adequate justification for according or establishing any rights to have abortions. Abortions might be permitted under certain circumstances but in every case the decision for or against them would be made by some authority. (It could even be the case that abortions were mandatory; which would imply that there was a duty to have one but no right to do so.) Rights are distinctive moral and/or jural entities, and having and exercising, protecting and respecting, violating and infringing on them are distinctive modes of action. It is impossible to derive a sufficient justification for any particular right from the distinctive characteristics of rights as such, but justifications for all particular rights are, tautologically but not trivially, justifications for rights and not something else. Hence such justifications must take the distinguishing characteristics of rights into account.

What is a right?

There are a number of distinct types of rights that will have to be distinguished if we are to make headway with our question about the right to an abortion on

56 *Equality, authority, rights, and philosophy*

demand. There are nevertheless certain generalizations that hold across the major subtypes, and we will begin by discussing them.

We can think of the rights we actually have (as opposed to those that are merely proposed or that we may think we ought to have) as warrants for actions. These warrants are supplied by rules that are established in some society, group, or association. Once established the rules themselves warrant the holders (A's) of the rights they create in taking a certain class or type of action (X) and they place other persons (B's), who can be expected to object to A's doing X, under various kinds of restrictions, prohibitions, or requirements in respect to A's doing X. When A sets to do X and B comes forward to object, A can conclusively establish a kind of propriety for her doing X, and a kind of inapplicability for B's objection, by producing the constitutional provision, statute, court decision, feature of the moral code, and so forth that constitutes the warrant for her claimed right to do X. Such warrants hold against—that is, serve to defeat—a more or less clearly specified range of the known or anticipated objections to A's doing X. Thus to have a right to do X in a particular jurisdiction, community, or group is to have a distinctive degree of assurance, in advance as well as during and after the fact of acting, that doing X will be held to be proper by some criterion possessed of authoritative standing in that jurisdiction or society. Doing X will be held to be correct or blameless despite the fact that members of the society vigorously object to it.

Two features of this account of rights deserve further emphasis. First, when a society or group establishes a right it in effect adopts an official or collective or authoritative position concerning a more or less clearly identified class of actions and objections to that action. It commits itself, in advance of specific instances of the action qua exercises of the right (and hence in advance of knowing the consequences of particular instances of the exercise of the right), to the position that the class of actions will be permitted (and at least to that extent encouraged). The unfolding of experience may convince that this commitment is mistaken and may lead to alteration or repeal of the rule that established the right. But until such time as the rule has been changed, the action will be entitled to protection whenever proposed or taken by a holder of the right. Such commitments, moreover, are all but invariably made in the awareness that the actual exercise of the right will commonly be controversial, that there will be persons who strongly object to A's doing X. If it could be expected that A's doing X would be universally welcomed or at least accepted, there would be no point to establishing a right to do X.

The second feature that deserves emphasis is implicit in the first. The commitment just described is in effect a commitment to accept and to protect the decisions of right holders to do X or not. With rare exceptions that are irrelevant here, to have a right to do X is to be at liberty to do X or not as one sees fit. If A decides that it will be to her advantage to do X, the fact that there is an established right to do X itself warrants her in proceeding to do it. If she chooses to reveal her reasons for doing X and others find them objectionable or even repugnant, they may think badly of her as a person and she may suffer some ill consequences as a result. But

The practice of abortion 57

given that she has a legal right to do X, others cannot properly hold that her doing X was, is, or would be illegal; given that she has a moral right, others cannot hold that it was, is, or would be immoral. The practice of according rights is one of the, probably the, single most dramatic respect in which societies accord autonomy of action to individual agents.

Types of rights

The last sentence will require elaboration when I reach the question of the justification for including the practice of rights among the arrangements and institutions that structure our legal and moral lives. It will also prove to be a crucial consideration in my proposed justification for a right to abortion on demand. But before taking up these matters I must pause to note some significant distinctions among types of rights, distinctions that concern the particulars of the warrants supplied by various rights. Because the distinctions in question are familiar and largely uncontroversial, and because I can barely touch the interesting theoretical questions that arise concerning them, this part of our discussion will be brief.

The all but canonical work here is by Wesley N. Hohfeld.[1] Responding primarily to legal materials (statutes, court opinions, legal commentaries), Hohfeld developed distinctions among four recurrent uses of "a right" and "rights." He drew the distinctions in terms of what he called the "correlates" and the "opposites" of each of the uses. The correlate is the jural attribute that attaches to some B by virtue of A's having a right of a particular type. The opposite applies to A herself and is what the term says, namely, the opposite of having the right that A actually has. (On examination the notion of the opposite of a right commonly proves to be elusive.) In schematic form the four types are as follows (see Table 5.1).

Probably the most familiar of these types is the second, rights in the strict sense. If B validly contracts to pay A \$400 per month for the use of A's apartment, A thereby acquires a right in the strict sense to that payment and B a correlative duty to make the payment. The important point is that there is no such thing as a right of this type without an identifiable B or B's with a specified obligation in respect to that right. In the language used above, the combination of the rules concerning contracts and the fact that some B has entered into a valid contract with some A warrants A in demanding that B pay and (assuming no defeating conditions intervene) puts B under a definite obligation to meet that demand.

Table 5.1 Typology of rights

	Type of right	*Correlate*	*Opposite*
1	liberty	no-right	duty
2	right strict sense	duty	no-right
3	power	liability	disability
4	immunity	disability	liability

58   *Equality, authority, rights, and philosophy*

Both the difficulty and much of the interest of the first type, rights in the sense of liberties, lie in the correlate that Hohfeld dubbed a "no-right." As the category name indicates, if A has a right to X in this sense she has a liberty, is at liberty, to do X. But what exactly does this imply for other persons? Presumably the B's have a duty to respect the right. But of what does respecting the right consist? My own interpretation, which I have elaborated elsewhere,[2] is that B's no-right merely (!) means that she must not contend that it was, is or would be wrong for A to do X. If the liberty is a legal one, B must not contend that A's doing X is illegal; if the X is a moral liberty, B cannot properly contend that A's doing X is morally wrong or blameworthy. Unlike rights in the strict sense, however, A's liberties do not warrant her in demanding, and B's no-rights do not obligate her to perform, any affirmative action to aid or facilitate A's doing X. Indeed the combination of A's liberty and B's no-right does not itself prohibit B from acting in ways that may, as a practical matter, make it difficult or impossible for A to succeed in doing X. To take a familiar example, if A's right to freedom of speech under the United States Constitution is a liberty, B (the Congress, a police officer, an ordinary citizen) may not contend (or act on the contention) that it would be illegal for A to exercise that right. But B need not supply A with a soapbox, a public address system, or time on national television. Indeed A's liberty does not itself prohibit B from beating a bongo drum so that A's speech cannot be heard.[3]

How can rights be justified?

The liberal principle

The bearing of the foregoing on the question of a right to abortion on demand is not far to seek. To accord a right of any sort to abortion on demand would be (is) to provide all those who have that right and who decide they want an abortion with a warrant for having one, a warrant that is established, as conclusive against some specified range of objections against the desire and its satisfaction. If the right is a legal right in the sense of a liberty, according it bars all other persons (in the jurisdiction) from contending that having an abortion (under the conditions included in the definition of the right) is or would be illegal; if a moral liberty, it bars all other persons (in the moral community) from contending that having an abortion (under the conditions included in the definition of the right) is morally wrong or blameworthy. If the right is a legal or a moral right in the strict sense, it would be established that the desire to have, and having, an abortion is not only innocent but imposes some further obligations (for example, to perform the abortion if one is a qualified physician) on assignable B's. To accord a right to abortion on demand, in other words, is not merely to say that there is a reasonable case for abortion, that fair consideration will be given to allowing abortions under certain circumstances, or that others will respond tolerantly, charitably, or sympathetically to persons who wish to have or have had abortions. Rather, it is to put the legal or moral authority of the society or community on the side of those who want abortions and against the objections of those who oppose them.

Quite clearly, it would be impossible to justify according any species of right to abortion without detailed consideration of the characteristics and consequences of abortion itself, of the particular conditions under which the right would obtain, of the type of right under consideration, and (in the case of rights in the strict sense) of the specifics of the obligations that would correlate with the right. As with all rights without exception, sufficient justifications and disjustifications are impossible apart from the particulars of the right in question.

It nevertheless remains the case that all rights are rights; that it is impossible to accord a right to a particular X without according a right. And because a right is a something, not an anything whatever, because rights are characterized by a more or less distinct and identifiable family of characteristics (albeit it would be impossible to state the necessary and sufficient conditions of something counting as a right), there are considerations of a more general nature which bear on the question of whether there should be any rights at all and on the question of whether, given that we know something about a particular X, there should be a *right* to that X.

Among the most prominent of the features characteristic of rights is the extent to which they protect and encourage freedom of action on the part of the individuals (or other agents) who hold them. The most obvious respect in which this is true is the one I have been discussing: in ways that vary according to the right in question, A's desire to act is protected against objections and other forms of resistance thrown up by persons who believe that they, others, or some thing or state of affairs will be disadvantaged or harmed by A's proposed action. This deserves to be regarded as a feature of the logic of the notion of rights. If no restrictions of any kind are placed on any B's, we simply are not dealing with a right.

This characteristic of the logic of a right is surrounded or accompanied by a number of others, one of which might be called the asymmetry between the positions of A and B. It is ordinarily for A to decide whether to exercise her rights or not. Whereas in most cases it is clearly wrong for B to fail to discharge her obligations vis-à-vis A's right, the notion that it is wrong for A not to exercise her rights is not well established. If a second party criticizes A for not exercising rights that A clearly has, A is usually justified in telling that party to mind her own business. A cannot unilaterally determine what rights she has, but her autonomy in deciding what to do with her rights is very great.

A second such feature concerns the rhetoric characteristic of rights discourse, especially the rhetorical style characteristic of the A's. It is not only common but generally thought unexceptionable for A's to claim, maintain, assert, demand, and insist on their rights. And it is seldom taken amiss, often applauded if they do so insistently, forcefully, staunchly, boldly, and even zealously. A right is something to which one is entitled, something one can unabashedly and unapologetically assert against all challenges and challengers.

How can a practice with these characteristics be justified? What assumptions are being accepted in a society that not only sustains such a practice but gives it,

60 *Equality, authority, rights, and philosophy*

as this society has done, an honored place among its institutions and arrangements? It is worth noting in this context that the practice of rights is by no means without its critics. There have been and are societies and cultures that find the self-assertive individualism characteristic of the practice of rights deeply objectionable. Indeed there is a persistent minority in this culture that reacts negatively to the very idea of rights. In most cases this view is associated with yearning for a greater degree of community, fraternity, and similar values in human relations. Persons who espouse it seek fellowship, integration, and cooperation; deep, intense, and intimate ties. And they find the practice of rights antithetical to these values. Rights are said to disaggregate and to fragment. They generate selfishness and competition rather than friendship, love, and a willingness to sacrifice for others and for the community.

A society or culture that sustains and celebrates individual rights has not necessarily rejected all of the values associated with concepts such as community. Its members may believe that there is an important, even a vital place for love, friendship, and fellowship; they may want to sustain relationships to which rights and their exercise are indeed inappropriate. But it is clear that a society or culture will not value the practice of rights as we know it unless it has a strong commitment to some kind of individualism; unless the preponderance of its members believe that free, autonomous individual action is at least one of the chief among their values, a value that social, political, and moral institutions and arrangements ought to honor and to serve.

It will be convenient to give this commitment or value a more explicit formulation and to provide it with a name. The name I propose is "the liberal principle" (LP) and the formula I will employ is as follows:

> It is a prima facie good for individual persons to have and to be in a position to act on and to satisfy interests and desires, objectives, and purposes.

Although it is impossible to derive or defend this principle in anything like adequate detail here, three comments concerning it cannot be avoided.

First, I take it to be a part of our moral (as opposed to our merely genetic or biological) concept of a human being that all human beings in the moral sense (hereafter human persons or simply persons)[4] do have interest and desires, purposes and objective, and are capable of acting on and pursuing them. This feature of the concept shows up in many ways, one of the more dramatic of which is the very special manner in which we expect one another to relate to persons who for some reason have failed fully to develop these characteristics or who have partially lost them. Consider the vastly greater care that is owed to such persons; the concern, solicitude, active helpfulness, and so forth that is expected in respect to them. By contrast, interactions among persons who suffer no such disabilities may appear to be almost reckless in the ways in which they presume that others can, as we sometimes say, "take care of themselves." (Which is part of the reason that persons with partial disabilities are, rightly, sensitive about inappropriate forms of "solicitude" which assume that the partially

The practice of abortion 61

disabled person cannot "take care of herself" in respects in which, in fact, she is perfectly well able to do so.)[5] In short, the interested, purposive character of human persons is ordinarily presupposed or taken for granted. And where this presumption must be qualified in respect to the ability of an individual to act on her interests and desires, other persons are expected to give special attention to fostering and serving them.

These same considerations—and this is the second comment—go some distance toward supporting what is of course the chief moral thrust of LP, namely, that it is prima facie a good thing for persons to be able not just to have and to act on but to satisfy their interests and desires, achieve their purposes and objectives. A related consideration that offers further support concerns what can be called the transitive character of interests, desires, and so forth. All interests and desires are in or for some object or state of affairs, all purposes and objectives make essential reference to a condition or outcome that it is the person's purpose or objective to achieve. Hence to say (1) that persons have interests and desires, objectives and purposes, and (2) that this is a good thing is surely to imply (3) that it is, at least prima facie, a good thing to satisfy the interests and desires and achieve the objectives and purposes. To state (1) and (2) but to deny (3), although not formally a contradiction, is at least to write a recipe for intolerable frustration.

My third comment on LP will bring us closer to its bearing on the justification for rights. As is indicated by the qualifier "prima facie," the principle is not itself a sufficient justification for any action. If accepted, the principle establishes a presumption that individuals ought not to be criticized for or otherwise prevented from having, acting on, and satisfying interests and desires, objectives and purposes. All criticisms, prohibitions, and so forth must be justified in the light of the fact that they prevent or qualify the achievement of a prima facie good. But the presumption that the principle establishes is always subject to defeat. In respect to any action whatever (save the action of denying the principle itself) it may be possible to justify a criticism, a prohibition, or a constraint.

For this reason alone LP will not itself sufficiently justify any right and hence will not sufficiently justify any instance of the practice of rights. Any right, and hence the practice of rights in any instantiation, involves additions to the protection that LP provides for individual actions. It adds the notion that there are some actions that are not simply prima facie good but are conclusively justified against some more or less definite range of objections. And rights in the strict sense add the further protection accorded by the particular obligations they assign to the B's. These additions require defense. They require defense, among other reasons, because they involve restrictions on the very good that LP celebrates. This is most obvious in respect to rights in the strict sense because the obligations that such rights entail serve to prevent the B's from acting on and satisfying those interests, desires, and so forth that prompt them to want to interfere with A's doing X. Thus adherents of LP have reason to be suspicious of the practice of rights and of all particular rights.

62 *Equality, authority, rights, and philosophy*

LP nevertheless provides a plausible foundation for the practice of rights. This is because the principle celebrates that very individualism and freedom of individual action for which rights provide further and more conclusive kinds of protection. (That is, given that there will be rules, laws, and restricting institutions and practices of some sort, the practice of rights celebrates such individualism more explicitly and directly than the other rules and practices with which we are familiar.) A society strongly committed to LP, it is true, will almost certainly be in need of fewer rights than one with a weak commitment to it. This is because its members will already have committed themselves to respect for the kind of individualism that rights protect. But it will also be well prepared for the practice of rights. If it finds that certain modes of individual action are particularly important and yet especially liable to interferences and objections, acceptance of the idea of according those actions the special protection that rights afford will come easily to it.

Can a legal right (liberty) to abortion on demand be justified?

Arguments for such a right: LP applied

Manifestly, a very large number of women have had, now have, and can confidently be expected to develop an interest in or desire for an abortion; manifestly, at some point or points in their lives a great many women make it their objective or purpose to have an abortion. Thus if we approach the issue of abortion from the perspective given by a practice of rights thought of as supported by LP, it will follow immediately that being able to have an abortion when one is in fact desired is a prima facie good, the denial of which requires explicit and substantial justification. Because it is also known that there is likely to be opposition to having an abortion when desired, it is also at least initially plausible to think that there ought to be some species of right to have one.

The contrast between this perspective on the matter and what might be called the traditional approach to it is of course very great. The traditional approach (to abortion and to a great many other moral issues) is to assume that the individual's interests, desires, and so forth are suspect, are probably guilty in some way, and to search revelation, natural law or right, tradition, the needs of the moral or legal community, or some other body of transcendent truth for (the expected) evidence that satisfying, acting on, or even having the particular interests and desires in question is indeed blameworthy and is therefore to be prohibited, prevented, punished, exorcised. No one who has read the by now voluminous anti-abortion literature can fail to be impressed by this among its characteristics. It is increasingly common for anti-abortion writers to concede that back-alley abortions are unpleasant and regrettable, that unwanted children enter life under great disadvantages, perhaps that the burgeoning world population threatens all life with catastrophe. It is rare indeed to encounter the view that the interests and desires, objectives and purposes, that (after all) make up so much of the lives of human persons are themselves deserving of immense respect and support.

The practice of abortion 63

Given this circumstance, little or nothing of a practical sort could be accomplished simply by stating LP in abstract formulation and pointing in a general way to its obvious applications to the question of abortion. Even if we do not regard interests and desires as guilty, we are all too wont to denigrate them with adjectives such as *mere*; to think of them as fleeting, evanescent, and insignificant. Purposes and objectives that are "merely individual" are also thought to be eligible for this treatment. We have been taught to think that what matters in life is virtue and duty, the sacrifice of individual interests and objectives to high moral principles and transcendent truths, the subordination of the individual to the community, the nation, the church. Thus even so erudite and incisive a student of the abortion issue as Professor Noonan has argued that the pro-abortion movement has taken much of its strength from "a trend to reject all codes of morality" and "a desire to be free of a code of morality."[6]

But there is nothing "mere," "insignificant," "unprincipled," or a-, non-, or immoral about respect for the interests and desires, objectives and purposes of individual human persons. Nor is there anything abstract about the significance of LP in its application to the question of abortion. Admittedly some interests and purposes are more substantial, more lasting, more important than others. One of the advantages of approaching questions about rights from the perspective of LP is that the latter allows of a ranking of interests and desires and hence provides logical space for the judgment that some, but by no means all, of them deserve the special protections afforded by establishing rights to act on them. But it could hardly be suggested, especially by anti-abortionists, that a woman's interest in having an abortion is trivial or insignificant. Having elevated child-bearing and rearing to the status of acts of the greatest possible sanctity, having treated motherhood and its duties as sublime and life-pervasive, anti-abortionists can hardly turn about and dismiss a woman's interests and desires in respect to them as transient and insubstantial.

Accordingly, I will resist the temptation to elaborate on the significance of the more obvious of the interests (for example, those that concern pregnancy and childbirth themselves) which a right to abortion on demand would protect. But there is one aspect of this matter, one that connects directly with the theory of rights, which requires discussion.

The value, to its possessor, of a right is not restricted to the protections it affords at the moment or moments of its exercise (in the sense of the actual doing of the protected act—in this case the actual having of the abortion). Its value projects back and out from that moment to the whole skein of thoughts and actions that precede it in more or less connected ways, and it projects forward into the continuing life of the actor after that moment. I personally have had relatively few occasions explicitly to assert and exercise my right to freedom of speech against specific challenges and challengers. But the knowledge that I have that *right* is a recurrent influence on my activities. I think thoughts, make plans, attend to events in my society, consider modes of action, and so forth in ways that would be impossible or that would be done under very different circumstances if I were living in Chile, Uganda, or the Soviet Union. And my life

64 *Equality, authority, rights, and philosophy*

following any exercise of the right has, if anything, been yet more markedly different than it would have been in the absence of the right.

Consider in this perspective the position of women in societies that have not established a right to abortion on demand. Consider in particular their position in respect to sexual relationships (and the entire constellation of potentially joyful experiences that radiate around such relationships) during those stretches of their lives in which they do not want to undertake the bearing and rearing of a child. It is no exaggeration to say that these relationships, which can be so beautiful, so sublime, so life-enriching and enhancing, are commonly sources of anxiety, sometimes of fear, sometimes of something close to terror. And for good reason. Assume "the worst" occurs and the woman becomes pregnant. If she is married and chooses to carry the fetus to term and to raise the child, her plans for her own life will certainly be significantly affected and may have to be entirely given up. If she seeks *permission* to have an abortion, she faces official interrogations, hearings, the making of judgments—in short, gross intrusions by strangers into the most intimate aspects of her life. For much of human history her alternative has been the debilitating and very likely dangerous ministrations of the illegal abortionist. And in either case, especially if she has the abortion, she must face the guilt and the shame that societies insistently impose on women who have not taken "due care." If she is unmarried, the entire experience is in all likelihood very much the worse, and its adverse effects might well continue through the remainder of her life.

Under these circumstances, which have been relieved but by no means eliminated owing to improvements in and the easy availability of contraceptive devices (relieved, that is, for those who have not been taught to feel ashamed of using such devices), the absence of a legal right (liberty) to abortion on demand projects its destructive consequences backward and forward in time (from the moment at which the right would actually be exercised) and inflicts those consequences on much of the woman's life.

The contrast between such a circumstance and one in which a right to abortion has been established could hardly be sharper. In the latter case, women can enter into that whole array of life experiences that radiate out from sexual relations secure in the knowledge that control of the effects of those experiences on their lives is largely in their hands; secure also in the knowledge that they can exercise that control in dignity free of clumsy and unwelcome intrusions. I would not deny that it is possible to enter imaginatively and sympathetically into the differences between these two situations and nevertheless conclude against a legal right to abortion on demand. I do not see how it is possible for anyone who appreciates the enormous differences between them to deny that there is a powerful case for such a right.

Arguments against a legal right (liberty) to abortion

There are of course a number of additional arguments that are commonly advanced by proponents of abortion on demand. Many of these concern social

The practice of abortion 65

consequences—the ill consequences of prohibiting abortions and the good consequences of a right to it. Although cogent and indeed persuasive in many instances, the use of these arguments in support of an individual right would introduce complexities (having to do with the so-called utilitarianism of rights) which cannot be dealt with here.[7] Accordingly, and because I believe that the foregoing arguments constitute a strong case for a legal right (liberty) to abortion on demand, I leave the other arguments aside and turn to the case against such a right.

That there is such a case, and that it merits a serious response, has been implicitly conceded in the foregoing discussion. If opposition to a legal right to abortion on demand were without creditable foundations, if it were based entirely on prejudice, misinformation, manifestly faulty reasoning, and the like, mounting a detailed argument for such a right would by now have been shown to be an exercise in futility if not irrelevance. But this is manifestly not the case. There are substantial arguments against a legal right to abortion on demand and we will have to concede to them on some points.

Arguments grounded in characteristics of the fetus as such (as opposed to the potential that the fetus carries)

The fetus as animate

The least complicated of the arguments against abortion are based on principles such as the "sanctity of life" or "reverence for life" (as, for example, in the well-known formulations of St. John-Stevas and Albert Schweitzer). These principles require that the life of all animate, organic things be protected and even revered; that it never be intentionally or perhaps even knowingly destroyed if it is at all possible to avoid doing so. Given that from conception, certainly from implantation, the (embryo-cum-)fetus is undoubtedly animate, it follows that abortion, which is the knowing, in most if not all cases the intentional, destruction of the life of the fetus can be justified, if at all, only in cases in which it is the only alternative to the knowing, perhaps the intentional, destruction of some other living thing. Traditionally, this has been taken to mean that abortion is justified only if refusing it will cause the death of the mother, perhaps even constitute the intentional killing of the mother.[8] And because advances in medical science have all but eliminated the possibility that such dilemmas will in fact present themselves, abortion is virtually always wrong.

There is very little that can be said for this argument. As noble as the sanctity of life principle may at first sight appear, accepting and acting consistently on it would, of certainty, lead to horrendous and utterly indefensible results. I will give but one of the many examples that not only support but require this judgment. In preparing for most medical procedures, doctors and nurses use antiseptics that are known and intended to destroy the lives of countless animate things. It could not be said that doing so is indispensable to preserving other lives, particularly not the life of the patient. Countless patients survived medical procedures

66 *Equality, authority, rights, and philosophy*

very nicely before antiseptics and indeed germs were discovered. More to the point here, given the availability of antiseptics, antibiotics, and other such medications, we could now postpone their use until such time as definite evidence of infection presented itself. Since infection would very often not develop, such a practice would save the lives of untold numbers of living things at minimal if any risk to patients.

But such a procedure would be unthinkable. Let one human person die or even suffer from it and its outrageous character would be condemned by everyone who heard of it. We do not treat all animate things as of equal value. Avoiding the slightest risk to some creatures—say, sentient creatures—justifies the destruction of millions of animate but insentient ones. The most generous thing that could be said for the proposal to do otherwise is that it would reflect a truly wild and irrational form of sentimentality. To pretend that we do in fact or would ever take such a proposal seriously would be the sheerest hypocrisy.[9]

The fetus as sentient

The argument from the merely animate character of the fetus, then, is no argument at all. But the fetus as such is not merely animate; from a short time after implantation it begins to show clear signs of sentience or what is sometimes called simple (as opposed to reflexive or self-) consciousness. These signs multiply rapidly in the early stages of its development and are undeniable through much of its existence. Thus with the possible exception of its very earliest stages the fetus as such falls under the protections, whatever they are, of any principles that hold for sentient life, not just those that protect life itself.

There is at least one principle that applies to all sentient but no nonsentient life, and that is the principle that forbids cruelty.[10] Thus if there were grounds for saying that abortion as such is cruel it would be categorically impermissible. Equally, if a particular person's desire for an abortion proceeded exclusively from cruel motives or dispositions—say, to torture a fetus at an advanced stage of development after it had been removed from the womb but before it died, or simply because that person took pleasure in the thought of any suffering the fetus might undergo during abortion—that abortion would be wrong.

There are, however, no grounds for treating abortion as such as a cruel act. "Cruelty" requires that the act be done for the sake of producing pain or other suffering. There may be individuals who seek abortions out of such motives, but there is surely no evidence to support the generalization that all or any significant number of persons do so. Anyone who did so, moreover, would have to have the abortion performed in a medically improper manner since all accepted procedures employ techniques, such as the use of anesthetics, designed to eliminate pain on the part of the fetus and pain and suffering on the part of the mother. It may be true, however, that the possibility of pain increases as the fetus develops. If so, this would be one of a number of considerations in favor of having abortions performed at the earliest possible date in the pregnancy. It is also true, to reiterate, that we have identified a condition under which abortion cannot be justified.

The practice of abortion 67

A further albeit less demanding principle that holds for sentient creatures concerns what we might call insensitivity or indifference. In extreme forms insensitivity is difficult to distinguish from cruelty. But one can be insensitive to another creature without positively seeking to harm it or to cause it to suffer. This is a more plausible charge against those seeking abortions. They do not cruelly or maliciously seek to cause the fetus to suffer, but they are insensitive to the fact that it is impossible to achieve their objective without causing severely adverse effects for the fetus. They and those who defend them simply do not concern themselves with, do not care about, the consequences of their actions for the fetus.

This charge has a more plausible ring than that of cruelty. It takes a good part of its plausibility from the fact that a considerable number of persons view the fetus as nothing more than a bit of tissue or a blob of coagulated protoplasm and accordingly believe that no consideration whatever is owed to it. Thus we have stories, retailed by anti-abortionists, such as the tale of the couple who, despite wanting a child and fully intending to try to conceive again in a few months, sought an abortion so that a mistimed pregnancy would not interfere with a planned vacation. More generally, since abortion is the destruction of the fetus, the charge that those who seek or support the procedure are insensitive, even indifferent, to a sentient organism has an air of plausibility about it.

If more credible than the charge of cruelty, however, the allegation that abortion involves indifference or insensitivity is also wide of the mark. Those who deny that the fetus is sentient are mistaken. But if they are genuinely mistaken in their views in this regard, they cannot also be indifferent to the pain that the fetus undergoes. And for those who recognize its sentience, seeking or defending abortion may be a question not of insensitivity to the fetus but of placing higher value on the interests and desires, objectives and purposes, of the mother than on the survival of the fetus. To choose a greater good over a lesser one is not in itself to deny or to be indifferent to the lesser good. In other circumstances, not faced with such a choice, the very persons who favor abortion may well show the most exquisite sensitivity to the well-being of the fetus. Certainly it is common for women who support abortion on demand and indeed who have had abortions to take every possible care for the fetus during a desired or merely accepted pregnancy and to go out of their way in assisting others who are pregnant.

The point of these last remarks can be generalized. Criticisms that focus on alleged defects of character, motive, or disposition on the part of proponents of abortion beg the issue in question. If abortion is right or justified, it is not wrong or a defect of character to seek it or to defend it. No doubt individuals have sought and defended abortions out of bad motives and owing to serious defects of character. But one suspects that their numbers are at least matched by those who oppose abortion out of a belief that pregnant women ought to be made to carry and to rear the child as due punishment for carelessness, promiscuity, or even Eve's primeval sin against God. (A view that the fetus, if it had views, or the child that the fetus becomes, might find something less than flattering!) No

68 *Equality, authority, rights, and philosophy*

amount of railing against either sort of person will help us to decide the merits of the issues about abortion.

Cruelty and insensitivity to the fetus, then, are as wrong as cruelty and insensitivity to any sentient creature. But the question remains whether abortion is wrong *because* the fetus is a sentient creature. Here again, if the value to the mother of a right to abortion is even remotely as great as I have suggested, the answer is clearly in the negative.[11] Even if we put the matter in the crudest of quantitative terms, since the fetus is merely sentient, the instant of pain that it may undergo in abortion simply cannot begin to compare with the fear, the mental anguish, the frustration and derangement of life plans, that unwanted pregnancies impose on women. But *of course* it is *wrong* to put the matter this way; it is wrong to act as if human persons are as it were to be weighed on the same moral scales as merely sentient creatures.

The fetus as possessed of reflexive consciousness

Animate and *sentient*: those two terms exhaust the list of undoubted and undoubtedly morally relevant properties of the fetus as such.[12] Because the fetus has these properties it falls under the protection of moral principles of undoubted gravity and importance. But there is simply no case at all for thinking that those protections do or should extend to the refusal of a right to abortion on demand. Any conflict between those principles and the principles that celebrate and defend significant life values of human persons must be decided in favor of the latter.

It is sometimes suggested, however, that the fetus as such, at least at some stages of its development, displays some degree of complex or reflexive consciousness, not merely sentient or simple consciousness. It not only feels pain in a purely phenomenal sense that we can detect with (and indeed define in terms of readings on) scientific instruments, but it is aware of pain, may seek to avoid it, may fear it, may suffer anguish in respect to it, and so forth. If this is true, the case for thinking of the fetus as human in a moral as well as a purely genetic or biological sense would be stronger, and hence the argument that the mother should have a right to prefer her interests and desires to the survival of the fetus would be vastly more difficult to make.

The evidence proffered in support of this characterization of the fetus concerns its alleged ability to adapt to changes in its environment in ways at least analogous to the deliberate, intentional adaptations made by human persons and higher animals. Some of this evidence is purely biological or neurological. Heartbeat, brain waves, the chemical composition of blood and other bodily fluids and substances alter in response to various changes in the environment. But changes of this sort are common to all animate creatures and do not support the contention in question.[13] Other evidence has at least something of a behavioral dimension and can be interpreted to indicate primitive kinds of intentionality, purposiveness, and consciousness of self. For example, the position of the fetus in the womb is known to change in response not only to chemical changes

The practice of abortion   69

that as it were produce their own effects in it but to such influences as pressures on the womb resulting from changes in the mother's posture and related events—changes the response to which would not appear to be dictated by the changes themselves. If we can say that the *fetus changes* its position in the womb in something like a knowing, intentional, chosen response to such pressures, we would have at least a primitive kind of reflexive consciousness.

This evidence is difficult to interpret and evaluate. Part of the difficulty is due to lack of clarity in the concepts we use (and, as matters stand, must use) in interpreting it. The notion of reflexive or complex consciousness (and the idea of human personhood in the moral sense that is intimately connected with it) has a relatively straightforward and unproblematic application to the ordinary human person of, say, more than a couple years of age. In the absence of evidence of the influence of drugs, serious disease, blows on the head, and so forth, such persons present what can properly be called the paradigm of reflexive consciousness; the pattern or family of characteristics that they so abundantly and continuously display are what we *mean* by reflexive consciousness. But as we move away from the paradigm case, the clarity of the concept and the certainty with which we apply it slips away from us. As we consider persons who are very drowsy but not asleep, under the influence of hypnosis, drunk or otherwise drugged, temporarily amnesiac owing to an injury or severe emotional stress, suffering severe depression in the psychiatric sense, mentally defective owing to birth trauma, we are increasingly doubtful as to what to say. The same is true of movement down the ranks of the animal kingdom and, for some, of movement up the ranks of increasingly complex and adaptive machines. Because the fetus is, on any reading of the evidence, very far indeed from the paradigm case of reflexive consciousness, it is not surprising that there is controversy over how to characterize it.

There is also a special problem involved in judgments about the fetus in this regard. The problem arises from one of the elementary but also elemental facts concerning it, namely, that it is in the womb and hence can interact with those (namely, us) who must make the judgments[14] only in the most narrowly circumscribed ways and for the most part only through the medium of elaborate scientific instruments (instruments that play no role in our ordinary uses of the concept of reflexive consciousness). There is a family of concepts the applicability of which makes up our notion of reflexive consciousness. "Intention," "deliberation," "choice," "reasoning," "understanding," "judgment," "having an interest" (and of course a number of more specifically moral and jural concepts to which I return below) are among the more important of these. When we can apply these concepts to a person or other creature in a positive way, we have no difficulty about characterizing that person or creature as possessed of some degree of reflexive consciousness. If, as I believe, Wittgenstein and others are correct that these concepts are built up in the course of, that their uses and their meanings take their characteristic shapes from, the interactions in which they figure and which they partly constitute, then the fact that our interactions with the fetus are so severely limited goes far to explain the difficulties we experience in trying to apply these concepts to the fetus. As Roger Wertheimer has said:

70   *Equality, authority, rights, and philosophy*

> There isn't much we can do with a fetus; either we let it out or we do it in.... As things stand, the range of interactions is so minimal that we are not compelled to regard the fetus in any particular way.[15]

Because the interaction is minimal rather than nonexistent, it may be that something at least analogous to reflexive consciousness can cogently be attributed to the fetus. If so, the case against cruelty and indifference would certainly take on additional dimensions, as would the argument against utterly casual, thoughtless uses of any rights to abortion that might be established. Given that there is no evidence supporting such attributions prior to what has traditionally been called quickening, it may be that these considerations support a strong moral preference for abortions prior to that development and in any case as early as possible.

In addition to these speculations, however, there are a number of certainties concerning the alleged reflexive consciousness of the fetus as such. Prominent among these certainties are the following: *none* of those moral and jural attributes that we alluded to above has any application whatsoever to the fetus. A fetus cannot be generous or selfish, kind or malevolent, honest or dishonest, courageous or cowardly, just or unjust. Accordingly, a fetus cannot deserve praise or blame, cannot be found guilty or innocent.[16] Again, the fetus can be said to have needs and sensitivities and to undergo damage and pain. It is for this reason that notions such as good and bad treatment apply to it (just as they apply to all animate organisms). But not even the most expansive interpretations of the available evidence suggest that it is capable of anxiety, fear or anguish, repose, equanimity or happiness (except, of course, in the sense of "happy as a clam"). The fetus does not have hopes that can be dashed, expectations that can be disappointed, desires that can be frustrated, objectives that it can fail to attain.

These last remarks are of course no more than an elaboration on the contention that our interactions with the fetus are extremely limited. One further such elaboration may be forgiven. The fetus can be said to be a subject of our moral actions; it cannot be an agent in our moral interactions. Together with certain propositions about the logic of the concept of rights which were touched on above, it follows from these facts about it that the fetus should not be thought of as a bearer or possessor of rights. To have a right is to be in a position to choose to exercise that right or not, to waive it if one wishes, to hold others to their obligations respecting it, or to release them from those obligations. And to be a participant in the practice of rights is to be subject to the duties and obligations that correlate with the rights of others. The fetus is capable of none of these (if it is capable of any) actions. Accordingly, while the fetus is properly regarded as the subject of good and bad (including morally good and bad) treatment by human agents, it is not properly regarded as bearing, possessing, or exercising rights or of having its rights respected or violated.

It follows from the last of this set of certainties that one of the strongest possible arguments against a legal right to abortion on demand—namely, that such a right would conflict with the established and justified rights of the fetus—is

The practice of abortion   71

without foundation. It follows from the entire set of certainties, and from our entire discussion of reflexive consciousness, that the evidence on this subject adds very little to the arguments against abortion which are based on the undeniable fact that the fetus is animate and sentient. In particular, there is virtually no basis for the claim that the fetus as such is a human person in a moral as well as a biological sense or that it should be protected by those moral principles that apply distinctively to creatures who are human in the moral sense.

Arguments grounded in the potential carried by (immanent in) the fetus as such

Abortions do not destroy human persons. Abortions destroy fetuses. Of course we know that the fetus will, with due care on the part of human persons (and a little luck), almost certainly become a human person. This fact does not warrant us in saying that a fetus *is* a human person. The fact that a bowl of batter will, with due care (and a great deal of luck) become a gorgeous and delectable soufflé does not transmute the bowl of batter into a soufflé. A soufflé is one thing, a bowl of soufflé batter is another. A fetus is one thing, a human person is another. No amount of emphasis on the indeed wonderful genetic and other biological properties of the fetus can change this.

Still, we treat the bowl of soufflé batter differently from, say, a dustpan of dirt swept up from the kitchen floor. Since the bowl of batter is not notably admirable or useful as such, our doing so makes no sense apart from what the bowl of batter can become. If we admire and enjoy soufflés, we can hardly be altogether contemptuous of or indifferent to the batches of batter from which they rise so majestically. If we assign great value to human persons, we can hardly altogether withhold value from the fetuses from which human persons develop. Thus the question is not whether to assign value to the fetus but what sort of value to assign to it and how to assess that value when serving and respecting it conflicts with the value we accord to human persons and the quality of lives they are able to lead.

Before taking up the latter question—which is of course the crucial one under this heading and perhaps in the whole issue about abortion—there are two associated questions that require discussion. The questions concern the "slide" down one or another of the "slippery slopes" that are said to descend precipitously from the plateau of safe argumentative ground that both pro- and anti-abortionists seek to attain and hold.

Many contemporary anti-abortionists want to defend the fetus but to allow the use of contraceptives (and perhaps masturbation, so-called unnatural sexual acts, and so forth). Most pro-abortionists want to allow destruction of the fetus but to disallow infanticide (and the killing of other creatures who are human in the biological sense but who are said not to be human persons in the full moral sense of the term). Pro-abortionists regularly contend that anti-abortionists cannot rationally or nonarbitrarily stop the "slide" or "regress" to positions that they themselves reject. If it is the fetus's potential to become a human person that requires

72   *Equality, authority, rights, and philosophy*

a prohibition against abortion, and if that same potential is immanent in any spermatozoon or ovum, then should there not also be a prohibition against the use of contraceptives, against masturbation to climax, against "wasting" the fluids by ejaculating them into various "inappropriate" orifices? Indeed if human beings have the capacity to produce ova and spermatozoa, should they not be prohibited from any actions or practices that may damage, destroy, or fail to utilize that capacity? If poor dietary habits, the use of alcohol, tobacco, marijuana or other drugs, excessive work, too little sleep, and so forth produce sterility, impotence, or frigidity, should they not be banned? Should vows of chastity and the beliefs and teachings that promote them not be forbidden? With comparable gusto anti-abortionists contend that there is no rational barrier to the "slide" or "progress" of the pro-abortion position to defense of a right to destroy any and all creatures who are like the fetus in lacking those attributes that define a human person in the full moral sense. If it is true that the cortical development necessary to full reflexive consciousness is not complete until approximately the infant's first birthday, is infanticide not every bit as defensible as feticide? If the development of full personality is prevented or arrested due to disease, accident, or other untoward events, should not those who are burdened by the life of the unfortunate victim of such events have a right to take that life?

It is not surprising that both sides have had difficulty in dealing with these questions and meeting these objections. The anti-abortionist can hardly resist the move from arguments grounded exclusively in the characteristics of the fetus as such to arguments relying on what it will become. But from the moment that move has been made the argument has to contend with the fact that the fetus represents (among other things) one moment or stage in a continuous biological process that can be, in the wider sense of the word, aborted at any moment or stage. If it is the culmination of that process that matters, one interruption in it can be made to appear as indefensible as any other. The pro-abortionist is faced with a comparable difficulty. As we have seen, concepts such as "human person," "moral personality," "reflexive consciousness," "capacity for distinctively human interaction" apply over a range or continuum of cases that is by no means precisely delineated. They are, in Wittgenstein's fashionable phrase, family resemblance concepts for the proper use of which it is impossible to state necessary and sufficient conditions. Moreover, many if not all of the characteristics over which their applications range are themselves fluid and developmental, not static or fixed. The moral personality of a two-year-old child is a vastly different thing than that of an adult.

Recognizing that, and why, both positions face such closely analogous difficulties ought to persuade us to a certain humility in discussing these matters. The game of trading charges in this regard is an amusement in which it is easy enough to score points; but the high scores that result aren't likely to signal progress in resolving issues about abortion.

For what it is worth, I am inclined to allow that there is a valid and morally significant distinction between conception (or perhaps implantation) and everything that precedes it. The union of a spermatozoon and an ovum (or that union

The practice of abortion   73

plus segmentation and implantation) produces a new entity with characteristics not possessed by its causal antecedents in the biological process, characteristics deserving of at least the kinds of moral consideration discussed above. Abortion *is* a more serious matter than the use of contraceptives. But the distinction between a fetus and an infant is at least as clear and at least as morally significant. This is true from the outset (that is, from parturition), and the clarity and moral significance of the distinction are heightened and enhanced very rapidly from the instant of birth forward. From that instant the infant displays a repertoire of behaviors (crying, gurgling, sucking, eye and other facial and bodily movements) which are either impossible in the womb or impossible for us to perceive and interact with when occurring in the womb. Items in that repertoire, as well as the remarkable responses they commonly evoke in the human persons about the infant, multiply in number and increase in complexity in ways that are not only extraordinary (except that they are entirely ordinary!) but that could not occur if the creature remained a fetus. Given these facts, and given that our moral conceptions and relationships concern the experiences we in fact have and the interactions in which we in fact engage (if only vicariously), it would be astonishing if the fetus–infant distinction ceased to be accorded substantial moral significance. The infant is not a human person in the full sense; there are significant distinctions between the infant and the child, the child and the adolescent, and so forth. (One of these is that, in my view, the infant and the youngish child should not be thought of as bearers of rights.) But this does not alter the fact that there is a clear and morally significant distinction between the fetus and the infant.

But should that distinction be accorded the degree of significance necessary to justify a legal right to abortion on demand? If there were no substantial, no weighty considerations in favor of such a right, the answer to this question would be no. If sexual relations, pregnancy, childbirth, and child rearing were biologically, economically, socially, emotionally, and above all morally trivial, inconsequential, and easily accommodated, the fact that the fetus is biologically human and is very likely to become a human person if not aborted would be enough to justify narrow limitations on abortion. But of course the conditional just mentioned is wildly counter-factual. Sexual relations, childbearing and rearing, especially for women, are manifestly among the weightiest, the most consequential and demanding, of life's experiences. Because this is so, it is difficult to think of any very large number of actions that are prima facie more eligible for the protection of a legal right (liberty) than the act of having an abortion.

Against the argument for such a right stands the potential for human interaction, human personhood and personality, that is immanent in the fetus. A particular instantiation of that potential is destroyed every time an abortion is performed. This is no insignificant consideration. But there is a material difference between potentiality and actuality. The millions of women whose day-to-day lives are so heavily affected by the availability (or not) of a legal right to abortion are not to be thought of in the subjunctive or the future tense. Their

74 *Equality, authority, rights, and philosophy*

interests and desires, their objectives and purposes, and the joy and delight, the pain and the anguish that they experience in pursuing their objectives are real and material, vivid and intense. It is in no small part because the human person that the fetus becomes will have such experiences that we ought to value its potential. It is dubious in the extreme to claim that we place immense, even absolute value on what the fetus will become at the same time that we go on sacrificing vital aspects of the well-being of those who now are what the fetus may someday be. If sensitivities even comparable to those sometimes lavished on the potential carried by the fetus are allowed in respect to the actuality presented by women, the case for a right to abortion on demand would be very strong. But such "evenhandedness" would be altogether misplaced. Beyond those characteristics of the fetus as such that were discussed above, the fetus is a bundle of human potential. But the woman who may want (now or sometime) but cannot have an abortion is a thinking, judging, feeling, hoping, believing human person who suffers in a here and now that may last much of her life.[17]

To deny a legal right (liberty) to abortion is knowingly to condemn very large numbers of actual human persons to pain and anguish and severely to restrict the freedom and quality of life of many more. We must accord this preeminently moral feature of the situation the serious consideration it obviously deserves. If we do so, the uncertain protection[18] that prohibiting abortions provides the fetus will not stand against the argument for a right to abortion on demand.[19]

The major (secular) arguments against a legal right (liberty) to abortion on demand have now been considered. Before concluding this part of the discussion, however, two related but in some respects distinct objections must be considered.

First, there is the objection that according a right to abortion will have psychological or cultural (that is, causal) consequences going beyond the effects of abortion itself. Specifically, it will produce a generalized weakening in respect for and the resolve to protect life and it will lead to the acceptance of infanticide, euthanasia, and other forms of killing. To my knowledge this objection, as commonly encountered as it now is, has not been formulated with the precision necessary to a determination of whether the empirical evidence that its cogency presupposes is in fact available. Nor has that evidence been produced.

For present purposes the more important consideration is that establishing the truth of the empirical propositions on which the objection depends would not itself constitute a conclusive argument against a legal right to abortion on demand. If a right to abortion is justified, and if the alleged causal consequences of according that right are objectionable, it would be open to us to accord the right and to take independent steps to prevent the objectionable consequences from ensuing. The most important of such steps would be to show that, and why, infanticide, euthanasia, or whatever kind of killing we wish to oppose is distinct from abortion such that the latter is justified and the former is not and to try to get others to accept that judgment. Doing this much would presumably help to block the objectionable consequences. It would also put us in a position to

The practice of abortion   75

defend whatever legal prohibitions against other forms of killing prove to be necessary to our objective.[20]

The second objection (or group of connected objections) relates to concessions that I have made to anti-abortion arguments. I have agreed that the fetus has moral value and standing and found that certain ways of treating it are morally wrong. If so, the objection runs, will not a legal right (liberty) to abortion on demand encourage, indeed license, wrongful treatment of the fetus?

There are actually several objections lurking here. The first is essentially the same as the objection just rejected. And the answer to it is the same. If certain ways of treating the fetus are known to be wrong, indeed if the argument for abortion itself includes a demonstration that they are wrong, then a right to abortion could be shown to "encourage" the wrongful treatments only by establishing contingent causal connections that have not in fact been established and that in any case would not be decisive against a right to abortion. Nor could such a right be said to "license" the wrongful treatments in the sense of explicitly and positively providing a warrant for them.

It might be argued, however, and this is the second of this second set of objections, that a legal liberty does license wrongful treatments of the fetus in the sense that it withdraws legal protection from it and leaves the question of how it will be treated to the discretion of private persons. But the assumption on which this objection rests is false. To accord a legal right to abortion on demand no more withdraws all legal protection from the fetus than does according a right to kill animals for human consumption withdraw such protections for animals as, for example, are provided by laws against cruelty to them. If cruelty or insensitivity were features of abortion itself, this argument would be cogent. Because they are not, the argument fails.

The third and last of this set of objections is that the right itself will be abused and that abuses will be difficult or impossible to prevent. People will seek and will obtain abortions for reasons as bad as or worse than those of the avid vacation seekers mentioned earlier. I don't suppose anyone knows, or knows how to find out or predict, exactly how often this sort of thing has occurred or will occur. Most rights are sometimes abused in the sense that people put them to uses distant from and even antithetical to the interests and objectives in terms of which the rights are usually justified. Think of the abuses of the right to private property—for example, the ways in which wealthy property owners hold the disadvantaged to the strict letter of their obligations in respect to those rights. Think of the abuses that have been made of rights such as freedom of speech, press, and association by individuals seeking to destroy such rights altogether. Where the argument for the value of these rights has continued to command widespread allegiance, the recurrence of such abuses has not been viewed as a sufficient reason for disestablishing the rights themselves.

There are, however, conceptual issues of some importance here, one of which points ahead to questions about moral rights in the sense of liberties and both legal and moral rights in the strict sense. The first point takes us back to the logic distinctive of a right. Rights are conclusive against some range of known or

76 *Equality, authority, rights, and philosophy*

anticipated objections. In the case of a legal right (liberty), the right is conclusive against all legal objections to the action protected by the right. Now, one could attempt to define the legal right to having an abortion in such a way as to exclude from the actions protected by it abortions sought for indefensible reasons. In the same way, one could define the rights of contract so as to exclude from them, say, the right of a wealthy person or a bank to foreclose on a mortgage held against a poor person unable to meet the mortgage payments. This would be to preserve the stringency or conclusiveness of the warrant the right provides but to restrict the range of objections against which it is in fact conclusive.

But there is another kind of move available, one that is preferable in this kind of case. It is well established that it can be morally wrong to do something that one has a legal right to do. No legal action can be taken or brought against the person who exercises the right in a morally wrongful manner, but that person is nevertheless subject to certain kinds of criticism and disapproval. For reasons that I will take up in the next section, this seems to me to be the best way of handling the kind of abuse of the legal right (liberty) to abortion on demand that I am now discussing.

The case for a legal right (liberty) to abortion on demand deserves acceptance. The considerations in favor of this right are firmly grounded in deep and vital human interests and purposes, interests and purposes that themselves arise out of some of the most continuing and morally salient dimensions of the lives of human persons. The arguments against the right are sufficient to establish that the fetus should be accorded moral value and standing of a kind that any moral person will respect and seek to protect. They are not sufficient to disjustify the right. The fetus is an animate and barely more than sentient creature with the potential to become a human person. It would be wrong to prefer preservation of instances of it to the service of profound and pervasive concerns of actual human persons.

Can a moral right (liberty) to abortion on demand be justified?

Some arguments for a legal right (liberty) to abortion on demand rely heavily on distinctive characteristics of legal prohibitions or requirements such as that they are enforced by the coercive power of the state. Given the widespread and cogently argued disagreement over abortion, for both normative and prudential reasons the state ought to withdraw and let the issue be resolved by the moral rather than the legal community.[21]

Although not without their merits, I have not relied on such arguments here. Rather, I have contended that the moral case for abortion on demand is very strong and that it deserves the positive support that is accorded by giving it the standing of a right. (If this argument were widely rejected, I might fall back to the "weaker" position that abortion ought to be "decriminalized." But that would be a tactical retreat.) For this reason, my argument for a legal right (liberty) is also an argument for a moral right (liberty) to that action. There ought to be such a moral right.

The practice of abortion   77

Accordingly, the only distinct issue to be taken up under the present heading concerns the implications, for the B's, of A having a moral right (liberty) as well as a legal right (liberty) to abortion on demand. In the latter case the implication is that B cannot properly act to make abortion legally wrong, and cannot attempt to punish A for having an abortion or punish any other person for giving A an abortion that A desires. In the former case, B cannot properly contend that it is morally wrong for A to have an abortion and cannot bring moral criticism to bear on A for doing so. Thus far the implications are entirely parallel. But there is at least one important difference between the two cases. In the law, any given abortion either is or is not legally wrong. That is the only judgment that the law as such can make. But morality and moral judgment commonly allow of differentiations that are more subtle and refined than are ordinarily possible in the law. The B's might accept the position that there is a right to abortion and accept the implication that they should therefore ordinarily refrain from criticizing A's for seeking or having one. Consistent with this position, however, they might hold out the possibility of making and expressing a number of kinds of judgments about conditions ancillary to or associated with the seeking and having of abortions. To our vacationists, for example, they might say: "We recognize and respect your right to abortion on demand and we will interfere in this case only to the extent of saying that we think your reasons for wanting this abortion are vile and repugnant." Persons who said this kind of thing about any very wide array of reasons for having an abortion would probably demonstrate by doing so that they did not in fact accept that right. It is nevertheless a valuable feature of moral as opposed to legal rights that genuine acceptance of and respect for them is compatible with recognizing and forcefully recording one's objections to their abuse. Thus a moral right (liberty) to abortion on demand is valuable both for the protections it accords the A's and for the flexibility of response that it makes available to B's who respect A's right.

Can a legal or moral right in the strict sense to abortion on demand be justified?

As noted earlier, it is a feature of the concept of a right in the strict sense that such rights impose some definite and affirmative obligation or obligations on some identifiable B's. The concept itself, however, tells us no more than this. Specifically, it tells us nothing about the incidence or the content of those obligations in respect to any particular right.[22] Thus there could be a legal or a moral right in the strict sense that imposed obligations on doctors or other qualified medical personnel, on hospitals and clinics, on the state, on insurance companies, and the like. And the obligations could be to perform or to see to or to pay for the performance of abortions; to do so unqualifiedly on demand, only in the first trimester or under other conditions; to provide postabortion care and counseling; and so forth through a considerable list of possibilities.

Because I cannot begin to deal with this array of possibilities, I restrict myself, by way of concluding this chapter, primarily to comments on the possible obligations of medical or paramedical personnel qualified to perform

78 *Equality, authority, rights, and philosophy*

abortions. Given that some persons in this category hold strongly felt moral objections against abortion, can we say that the right to abortion on demand includes the right to demand that persons competent to perform an abortion actually do so? Specifically, does a woman have a right to demand an abortion from a medically competent (and otherwise available) individual who personally believes that abortion is morally wrong? Is the argument for a right to abortion on demand strong enough to justify the imposition of such an obligation on persons who do not find that argument convincing? (Note that the question also arises in somewhat less dramatic ways in respect to persons other than those who actually perform the operation. It arises in regard to nurses and many others who must assist more or less directly with the procedure. And in jurisdictions in which the government has undertaken to provide or to assist with the costs of abortion it arises in some degree in respect to all citizens or subjects.)

The answer to these questions is a qualified yes. It is yes because (1) the argument for abortion on demand is very strong and (2) because, as things stand, a woman cannot safely (or even surely) abort herself. Owing to (1), we can say that the views of those who contend that abortion is morally indefensible are not well grounded. Having considered the arguments for this position and found them wanting, we cannot turn about and say that they nevertheless provide adequate support for the position they defend. Owing to (2) we can say that the right to abortion on demand could be, as a practical matter, a nullity if abortions could not in fact be obtained from those competent to perform them. Thus if it were the case that the demand for abortions were too great to be met by those both competent and willing to perform them, there would be adequate justification for establishing either a legal or a moral right (or both) in the strict sense that imposed (on those medically competent to do so) an obligation to provide abortions. (There is also adequate justification for using public funds to pay for abortions for persons—in jurisdictions with free enterprise medical practice—who cannot afford them.)

The yes is qualified for the same kinds of reasons that have convinced a number of societies to qualify the obligations imposed on pacifists and other conscientious objectors to do military service in what are believed to be justified wars. It is not that their arguments are judged to be convincing. If that were the case, others would have to give up their position in favor of the position of the pacifists. But where the position of the pacifist or other objecting position is believed by others to be cogent and sincerely held, and where it is believed that the justified objectives can be achieved while conceding something to the views of the objectors, an effort is made to find ways of making such concessions. Conditions of this kind have not always been satisfied in respect to abortion. But because they do seem to be satisfied at the present time, it would be morally insensitive (it would be a violation of LP) not to accommodate to the views of those who object to abortion insofar as we can. Thus we should establish both a legal and a moral right in the strict sense to abortion on demand. And so far as we can do so without nullifying the right, we should excuse from the correlative obligations those persons for whom abortion remains morally unacceptable.

Conclusion

The concept of a right is one of the most widely used, and most commonly abused, items in our moral and political lexicon. We hear claims to an extraordinary variety of rights and we find rights attributed to an astonishing diversity of creatures and things. Although this proliferation represents a kind of tribute to the not inconsiderable success of a comparatively recent legal and moral innovation of genuine value, there is reason to view the proliferation with skepticism. We may be experiencing a kind of inflationary spiral that will end by unnecessarily diminishing the real and distinctive goods that can be obtained with this part of our conceptual currency.

This concern, however, does not properly extend to the campaign for a right to abortion on demand. In adopting the language of rights, pro-abortionists have made precisely the correct conceptual choice. As I have tried to show, "a right" provides the conceptualization, and hence the moral and jural attribute, exactly appropriate to the case that the pro-abortionist wants to make. For this reason, because that case is very strong, and because its strength derives in no small part from the support it receives from the principle (LP) which provides the optimum basis for defending individual rights, a right to abortion on demand is exactly what women ought to have.

Notes

1 See Wesley N. Hohfeld, *Fundamental Legal Conceptions*, ed. W. W. Cook (New Haven: Yale University Press, 1919).
2 See Richard E. Flathman, *The Practice of Rights* (New York: Cambridge University Press, 1976). A number of the questions taken up in this chapter are discussed in greater detail in this work.
3 Rights in the sense of powers and immunities have less relevance to issues about abortion, and I will simply give an example of each to make the distinctions somewhat clearer than they are in the above schema. A standard example of a right in the sense of a power is the legal capacity to make a will. It would be impossible to make a will apart from the constitutive rules of will making. But A's power to make a will imposes no obligations on B. What it does is make B liable to become a beneficiary of A's will should A choose to exercise her power to write one. When A actually makes a will that includes B, rights in the strict sense are likely to result. A standard example of an immunity is represented by the Fifth Amendment provision prohibiting compulsory self-incrimination in certain classes of cases. Ordinarily the prosecutor, judge congressional investigating committee, and the like have authority to require an accused person or witness to testify, and the latter are under a liability to be questioned and have an obligation to respond when questioned. But A's immunity qualifies that authority and its correlative liabilities and resultant obligations and puts the prosecutor, judge, congressional investigating committee under a disability to ask certain classes of questions.
4 There is of course controversy concerning how this distinction should be drawn and what inferences can be made from and concerning it. I will be elaborating and defending my use of the distinction below. But that there is and must be some such distinction could hardly be controverted. For a vigorous defense of the distinction, see Michael Tooley, "Abortion and Infanticide," in *The Rights and Wrongs of Abortion*, ed. Marshall Cohen, Thomas Nagel, and Thomas Scanlon (Princeton: Princeton University Press, 1974).

80　*Equality, authority, rights, and philosophy*

5　I will take the occasion provided by this turn in the discussion to remark on a point concerning abortion itself. It is commonly suggested that the pro-abortion position implies or otherwise invites insensitivity and worse toward life forms that, as with the fetus, lack characteristics of full human personhood or personality. I deal with aspects of this argument below. But it is worth emphasizing the point made in the text above, namely, that our duties to human persons who lack a part of the usual complement of characteristics are commonly and rightly thought to be much stronger, much more demanding, than those owed to persons with no disabilities. The judgment that a member of some class departs in some way from the usual characteristics of the class to which she or it belongs cannot itself settle the question of how she or it ought to be treated.

I permit myself one further aside of a somewhat polemical nature. I am inclined to think that the attitude of anti-abortionists toward women commonly presents an extreme case of the kind of recklessness toward normal human persons mentioned above. It is admitted that women are deeply affected by pregnancy, childbirth, and child rearing, and so forth. But it is assumed that "they can take care of themselves" in these regards, that is, that they do not require the help provided by such things as rights to abortion. This attitude might be acceptable, might even be a kind of compliment, if they were in fact allowed to take care of themselves, that is, to handle sexual relations, pregnancy, and the like in their own way(s).

6　John T. Noonan, Jr., ed., *The Morality of Abortion* (Cambridge, MA: Harvard University Press, 1970), p. xv.

7　The most compelling among the additional arguments, and those that introduce the fewest complexities, concern the ways in which respect for the interests and desires, objectives and purposes, of women carries over to respect for the interests of other persons involved in or affected by the abortion decision.

8　The distinction between knowing and intentional destruction of the fetus is at the basis of what is commonly called the doctrine of the double effect. I do not find the distinction or the doctrine helpful in respect to questions about abortion, but I cannot deal with the matter here. For a sensitive and helpful discussion, see esp. Philippa Foot, "The Problem of Abortion and the Doctrine of Double Effect," *Oxford Review* 5 (1967): 5ff.

9　On this point, see Werner J. Pluhar, "Abortion and Simple Consciousness," *Journal of Philosophy* 71 (1974): 165.

> As sentience ... grows dimmer and dimmer as we descend toward ever simpler organisms, the *prima facie* wrongness of destroying an organism inevitably decreases in proportion, ultimately to a degree of negligibility where it becomes in practice more misleading to affirm than to deny that there remains a residual *prima facie* wrongness at all, since it is standardly overridden by just about any countervailing consideration, moral or other.

> It does not follow that no consideration whatever is owed to life as such. The wanton, pointless destruction of any living thing, aside from being terribly stupid from a self-interested point of view, is indefensible. As Pluhar suggests, the point is rather that terms such as *wanton* are not and should not be employed if the killing finds justification from the resultant improvements in the well-being of higher creatures.

10　It is, I think, conceptually impossible to be cruel to a creature or thing—a microbe, a plant, and so on—incapable of any kind of pain or undergoing any kind of suffering or anguish.

11　I leave aside the fact that humans routinely destroy and cause pain to sentient creatures for reasons vastly weaker than those that support a right to abortion on demand. Many of these practices are clearly indefensible. It should nevertheless be said that if one were to start a campaign against mistreatment of sentient creatures, on any view

The practice of abortion 81

of the matter abortion would have to take a much lower priority than those many practices that are virtually without justification.

12 Of course the fetus as such has a veritable host of other properties. Among those that figure with disturbing prominence in the anti-abortion literature are its undeniable aesthetic properties. The fetus is commonly said to be very beautiful: delicate in features, extraordinarily intricate in its complexities, and so forth. Insofar as I can judge from photographs I have seen, I concur with these judgments. The judgments are also true of, for example, snowflakes and rock crystals. And these are reasons, albeit certainly not moral reasons, for preserving snowflakes and rock crystals under some circumstances. They are not reasons for countenancing adverse effects on human beings. Nor, incidentally, are they reasons that pro-abortionists should adopt for protecting the fetus. If it turned out that some or most fetuses were ugly, would we therefore be justified in destroying them?

13 Of course some of this "biological" evidence, particularly evidence concerning the central nervous system, distinguishes human fetuses from other creatures and establishes that they have the neurological potential for (the neurologically necessary conditions of) reflexive consciousness. But this evidence bears on the question of the potential immanent in the fetus, not the actuality that the fetus as such presents. I take up the question of potentiality in the following section.

14 It is hardly irrelevant to this matter that the fetus does not itself have the concept of reflexive consciousness—or any other concept—and for this among other reasons cannot tell us that it deserves this characterization. On this point, see Tooley, "Abortion and Infanticide," in *Rights and Wrongs of Abortion*, ed. Cohen *et al.*

15 Roger Wertheimer, "Understanding the Abortion Argument," in *Rights and Wrongs of Abortion*, ed. Cohen *et al.*, p. 44. A really uncompromising interpretation of Wittgenstein's discussion of logical privacy might support the conclusion that the very idea of applying the above concepts to the fetus is and must be incoherent. The conditions necessary for such an attempt to so much as get a foothold, the argument would run, are simply not satisfied. I will not try to develop such an argument here, but the possibility, which is suggested by Wertheimer's remarks as well as my own, is worth exploring.

16 The constant references to the innocence of the fetus, to abortion as the taking of innocent life, are of course misplaced. Aside, perhaps, from contexts involving religious doctrines concerning original sin, the concept of innocence has no more application to the fetus than the concept of guilt. (And of course in the Christian religious doctrine, if the fetus is a human being it is guilty, not innocent.)

17 For an extreme case of this sort of "impartiality," see Baruch A. Brody, "Abortion and the Sanctity of Human Life," *American Philosophical Quarterly* 10 (April 1973): 133ff. Brody argues that a fetus may be aborted to save the life of the mother only if the following conditions are satisfied: (1) in the absence of an abortion both the mother and the fetus will die "relatively soon"; (2) the decision to abort the fetus (rather than let the mother die and save the fetus) is made by a fair—that is, presumably a random—procedure. In short, in Brody's view there is no morally relevant difference between the mother and the fetus. For the full range of Brody's views on this subject, see his book *Abortion and the Sanctity of Human Life* (Cambridge, MA: MIT Press, 1975).

18 Although I have chosen not to emphasize the kind of consideration alluded to in the text, it is worth noting that at least some of the adverse effects of prohibiting abortion fall with virtual certainty on women, while the benefits, to the fetus, of the prohibition are uncertain at best.

Having allowed questions of a probabilistic sort into the discussion to this extent, it should also be mentioned that questions about abortion would be substantially complicated if in fact so few women wanted to bear children that a right to abortion actually threatened the continued existence of the human race. Because this is not the

82 *Equality, authority, rights, and philosophy*

case, I will take up these complexities only to the extent of saying that it is less than obvious that denial of the right would be the morally appropriate response to such a development. It is not self-evident that the fact that women have the biological capacity to conceive and bear children justifies treating them and their lives as resources implicitly available for this or any other project.

19 The important reflections of Judith Jarvis Thomson and Mary Anne Warren should be mentioned at this point. Thomson calls our attention to how seldom any of us are legally or morally *required* to make sacrifices even remotely comparable to those involved in unwanted pregnancy, child rearing, and the fear thereof. See her "A Defense of Abortion," in *Rights and Wrongs of Abortion*, ed. Cohen *et al.* Warren presents an analogy that helps to focus thought on the sacrifices we would be willing to make or impose on behalf of potential such as the fetus carries. She asks us to imagine (I have entered some minor modifications in her analogy) that our bodies could be split up into parts with each part (like so many plant cuttings) capable of becoming or generating a human person. If so, we would be presented with a choice between keeping our bodies whole and thereby wasting the immense human potential they carry or splitting them up so as to let that potential be realized. Perhaps some truly heroic persons would be willing to sacrifice their lives so as to utilize their capacity in this regard to the full; perhaps some number of others would be willing to give up an arm, a leg, some flesh from an inconspicuous part of their body, and so forth. Would there be any justification of requiring anyone to do any of these things; for punishing them or holding them morally blameworthy if they refused? See Mary Anne Warren, "The Moral and Legal Status of Abortion," *Monist* 52 (1973): 42ff. For a related analogy, see Tooley, "Abortion and Infanticide," in *Rights and Wrongs of Abortion*, ed. Cohen *et al.*

20 Owing to the reliance my argument for abortion makes on reflexive consciousness and moral interaction, a word must be said about kinds of killing, in addition to abortion, that would appear to be justified by that argument. I refer in particular to cases in which a human person ceases to display reflexive consciousness and ceases to be an agent in (as opposed to a subject of) moral interactions. If the loss is known (that is, known with the greatest certainty medical science allows) to be permanent, the case for a right to take the life of the erstwhile person seems to me to be at least as strong as the case for a right to abortion. It is, in fact, clearly stronger in one obvious respect; namely, that the organism in question does not possess the potential carried by the fetus. Such cases, however, are seriously complicated (as against the case of abortion) by two factors, the first of sometimes wrenching practical difficulty but of no great theoretical significance, the second of both practical and theoretical significance. The first is that it is often difficult to determine who should have the right to terminate the life of the organism. In the case of the fetus the mother's interests are sufficiently clear and paramount to make this decision unproblematic in most cases. But when tragedy befalls mature persons the matter is often anything but clear. The second complication arises from the fact that, unlike the fetus, such organisms have histories as persons in the full moral sense. These are largely histories of interactions with others who continue to be persons, interactions that will of course have produced attitudes, beliefs, emotional ties, and so forth that do not simply cease at the moment the interactions cease.

This second consideration is not a reason against a right to terminate the life of an organism that was once a person. It is a reason to expect that exercising such a right will be an agonizing, wrenching experience for those who must decide whether to do so and to expect that the latter will in fact often make great sacrifices rather than take the life. (Just as the fact that mothers, at least those not taught to look on the fetus as some kind of punishment inflicted upon them, can easily imagine a personal history for the fetus explains that they so often make the extraordinary sacrifices that the bearing and rearing of children entail.)

The practice of abortion 83

For present purposes, however, the importance of the second consideration is that it provides the necessary distinction between the fetus and persons who have temporarily lost reflexive consciousness and the capacity for moral agency and interaction. Unlike the fetus, they do not merely have the potential to develop these characteristics, they have a history of such characteristics. And because they have such a history, they have a relationship to other moral agents that no fetus as such can ever have. For an opposing position, see Eike-Henner Kluge, *The Practice of Death* (New Haven: Yale University Press, 1975), ch. 1.

21 See, for example, Wertheimer, "Understanding the Abortion Argument," in *Rights and Wrongs of Abortion*, ed. Cohen *et al.*, the final paragraphs.

22 In fact, the obligations are sometimes specified in the rules that establish the right; sometimes they must be inferred from the characteristics of the right itself and what would be destructive of or perhaps necessary to its successful exercise.

Part II

Situating and disciplining freedom

6 Kinds of freedom (1987)

A baby emerges from the womb. Nothing apart from itself is moving it, but it moves nevertheless. It is self-activated, possessing what Aristotle called *energeia*.

Some of the baby's movements go unimpeded. It extends its legs, twists and turns. Other movements encounter obstacles.

Does a case like this give us the conditions necessary to our notions of freedom and unfreedom; the conditions sufficient to those notions? Of course we use the words "free," "freely," and "freedom" where there is neither self-activation nor a genuine possibility of obstacles to movement. Free-falling objects and branches swaying freely in the breeze are not self-activated; the notion of an omnipotent God excludes the possibility of effective obstacles; accounts of ghosts and creatures of science-fiction often achieve their distinctive flavor by denying or severely qualifying this possibility; a cloud-free sky, a complexion free of blemishes, does not depend literally or straightforwardly on either condition.

Just because of these characteristics, the latter uses of "free" and its cognates and counterparts are sharply and strikingly different from uses concerning ourselves and higher-order animals. Such uses render uninteresting if not pointless the contrasts we draw between freedom and unfreedom in our lives.

The two conditions with which I began do seem to be necessary elements in our concept of our own freedom and unfreedom. Are they jointly sufficient to that concept? A prominent account of freedom, which forms the conceptual foundation of a moral and political theory of recurrent appeal, answers this question in the affirmative.

Thomas Hobbes portrayed not just human beings but all higher animals as self-activated in a very strong sense. Impulses that originate within these creatures are the necessary and (given their physical makeup and certain very general features of their environment) sufficient conditions of their movements. He contended that these creatures should be said to be free just insofar as their movements are unimpeded by forces or obstacles external to themselves, unfree just insofar as those movements are effectively impeded or prevented. Information about the two conditions is all that is needed, indeed is all that can properly be employed, in discourse about their freedom and unfreedom.

88 Situating and disciplining freedom

Hobbes's account has served as a starting point for much subsequent discussion in moral and political philosophy. Friendly critics, who think the account is correct in its essentials but in need of amendment, have observed that the notion of acting involves such attributes as intentionality and purposiveness, and they have incorporated distinctions between mere movement and action on the one hand and mere obstacles versus impediments knowingly and intentionally placed or left on the other. These amendments do complicate, as against Hobbes's often highly mechanistic account, the concept of agents or actors to whom human freedom can be attributed. For example newborn infants, although not likely to be confused with a waving tree-branch, are not regarded as experiencing the same kind of freedom and unfreedom as mature persons. The intention of these friendly critics is nevertheless to stay close to Hobbes's account.

Less friendly critics have urged far-reaching alterations and additions. On their view we cannot say that a person is free unless we have criteria for deciding which impulses, which intentions and purposes, ought to be or are worthy of being pursued. Freedom is achieved only if the persons in question distinguish good and bad, right and wrong, worthy and unworthy conduct. In addition, the persons to whom freedom is attributed must employ such distinctions in choosing more or less extended or encompassing plans of action. Finally, on some theories of freedom the chosen courses and plans of action must actually be good, right, or worthy and the criteria by which this is decided must themselves be correct or at least justified criteria. The conditions of saying that a person is free have been greatly complicated by comparison with Hobbes's rudimentary account.

Perhaps we can deal with the differences among these accounts by using the simple device I have already introduced, the notion that there are "kinds" of freedom. If we set aside tree branches and cloud-free skies, the following list identifies, in terms of their characteristic conditions and elements, the different "kinds" of freedom that can be extracted from the discussion to this point. Self-activated movement plus the possibility of obstacles to that movement give us freedom$_1$ and unfreedom$_1$ or "freedom of movement." Intentional or purposive action plus the possibility of impediments deliberately placed or left by other intentional and/or purposive agents are the elements of freedom$_2$ and unfreedom$_2$, or "freedom of action."[1] Intentional and/or purposive action taken in the more or less rational pursuit of an intelligently (and at least in that sense independently) conceived plan or project that is consonant with norms or principles that the agent believes to be justified, plus the possibility of impediments deliberately placed or left by other intentional or purposive agents, are the conditions of freedom$_3$ and unfreedom$_3$, or "autonomy." These same conditions plus the proviso that the action is taken to satisfy, and in fact satisfies, norms or principles that are authoritative in the agent's community, give us freedom$_4$ and unfreedom$_4$, or "communal freedom." These same conditions again plus the requirement that the authoritative norms and principles be certifiably worthy of endorsement give us freedom$_5$ and unfreedom$_5$, or "fully virtuous freedom." (For convenience of reference a somewhat modified version of this list is given in the

Kinds of freedom 89

Appendix to this chapter.) We would expect controversy over how these kinds of freedom should be evaluated, but the several kinds are importantly distinct and each of them can be seen to have an established place in our thought and action. The point is not to give one among them priority but simply to keep them distinct so that thought and action about them can proceed in a clearheaded manner.

Such conceptual pluralism or latitudinarianism has been powerfully resisted by the major writers on the topic of freedom. Consider the most familiar philosophical controversy concerning freedom, that between advocates of negative and positive conceptions. Roughly, proponents of theories of negative freedom recognize $freedom_1$ and $freedom_2$, sometimes $freedom_3$. They strongly deny that $freedoms_{4-5}$, which are the favored and the characteristic notions of theorists of positive freedom, are kinds of freedom at all. The requirement that the agent's action satisfy some criterion or norm (other than being the agent's action), and that the norm itself be worthy, it is argued, confuses freedom and unfreedom with such quite different things as virtue and vice. A conception that imposes these further requirements disallows perfectly familiar and intelligible attributions of freedom. More serious, it encourages a host of restrictions on freedom in the name of freedom itself, thereby creating both conceptual conundrums and moral and political enormities. Critics of negative theories of freedom, in their turn, contend that $freedoms_{1-2}$, perhaps even $freedom_3$, allow of saying that a person is free or has acted in freedom despite being in the grip of, despite being "enslaved" by, impulses, passions, and desires that are harmful to the agent or to arrangements that the agent does or should value. Because freedom and slavery are incompatible, a theory that produces or allows such a result cannot be accepted.[2]

A somewhat less dogmatic response to my list of five kinds of freedom and unfreedom allows that there are such distinctions but argues that no one of the distinguished kinds can stand alone. The several kinds of freedom are a part of a larger, encompassing, and normatively more attractive concept, one of full or perhaps genuine freedom. For example Franz Neumann (1957), contributing to a tradition that is foreshadowed by Aristotle and is powerfully expressed in Machiavelli, Rousseau, and Hannah Arendt, argued that the "negative" or "juridical" elements in freedom (stressed by theorists of my $freedoms_{1-2}$) and the "cognitive" elements (stressed by theorists of my $freedoms_{4-5}$) must be supplemented by a "volitional" component that is most satisfactorily expressed by certain theories of political democracy. In its fullest or most complete form, our conception of freedom unites several complementary elements or moments and takes on a specifically political character. Partial notions such as $freedom_1$ and $freedom_2$ are intelligible to us. But they are intelligible because (only if?) we have the full or complete conception and are able to grasp the partial notions as elements thereof.

If any of these contentions are correct, we may be obliged to reject the claim of MacCallum (1967) and Feinberg (1980, esp. the first essay) that there is a serviceable distinction between conceptual and normative questions about

90 *Situating and disciplining freedom*

freedom. There is no single concept of freedom that we can hold constant as we debate normative questions such as the rank that should be assigned to freedom among other perhaps competing desiderata. Freedom is an "essentially contested" concept that cannot be elucidated or construed apart from a larger pattern of argumentation concerning the moral and political issues in which freedom is implicated. To achieve agreement concerning what freedom is and is not would be to achieve consensus concerning a wide array of moral and political issues.

It is certainly false to say that there is nothing settled, that there are no agreed points, concerning the concept of freedom. "Freedom" is a concept in nontechnical English, one governed by rules that we know as competent speakers of our language and that inform and constrain our uses of the concept. We are not in the position of having nothing more than a term or signifier (an "articulate sound" as John Locke would say) and needing to construct a concept from the ground up. Were we in the latter circumstance, the disputes I have been mentioning would not be disputes at all but mere sets of stipulations with no intelligible relations to one another.[3]

MacCallum's now familiar triadic analysis (1967), moreover, seems to me to provide a perspicuous identification of important parts of what we share as competent speakers. Theories of human freedom that have no place for agents, for obstacles, or for objectives pursued are vulnerable to powerful objections. Their proponents must show either that they in fact encompass those elements or that there is good reason to alter our shared concept of freedom.

But MacCallum's analysis, valuable as it is, gives us no more than a framework in which to think about freedom. Major conceptual questions that it insistently leaves open, questions about the range over which the "term variables" (agents, obstacles, objectives) can move, are at the center of cogently conducted but heated disputes among competing theories of freedom. However we resolve such questions as whether a person's action or course of action must satisfy a normative criterion, or a worthy normative criterion, in order to be free, it is clear that the putative ends or purposes must be intelligible as such, that is, as possible ends or purposes. As Benn and Weinstein put the matter, "it is apposite to discuss" whether an action is free

> only if ... [the end it pursues] is a possible object of reasonable choice; cutting off one's ears is not the sort of thing anyone, in a standard range of conditions, would reasonably do, i.e., "no one in his senses would think of doing such a thing" (even though some people have, in fact, done it). It is not a question of logical absurdity; rather, to see the point of saying that one is (or is not) free to do X, we must be able to see that there is some point in doing it.
>
> (1971, 194–211, 310)

As the example makes clear, what counts as a reasonable choice, what is regarded as intelligible, varies from society to society and may be a matter of dispute within a society or culture. The conceptual point, however, is well-taken.

The position in respect to freedom, then, appears to be of a kind familiar to students of a number of the concepts salient in political and moral practice. As with justice, rights, authority, and obligation (among others) we share enough about freedom to allow mutually intelligible use of the notion and enough to dispute cogently concerning it. But it has proven difficult to arrive at a systematic analysis that is generally or even widely acceptable. Quite well-defined accounts, each of which finds support in and from what we share, have been in competition for more than two centuries.

Can we improve upon this position? It should not be taken for granted that we can. Despite close attention from powerful and well-instructed minds, on central questions the theory of freedom has been at something of a stalemate for a considerable period. The competing positions are supported by argumentation that has the marks of pertinence and plausibility. Perhaps the best that we can hope for (no small thing) is clarification and improved comprehension of alternative understandings.

The springs of philosophical hope, however, have been replenished (at least in my own case) by comparatively recent work concerning language and meaning, action, agency and personal identity, and philosophical and empirical psychology. Done largely by investigators not directly concerned with the topic of freedom, studies in these areas seem to promise fresh perspectives on issues about freedom. As is frequently the case, they do so in part by calling attention to unexamined assumptions common to the competing positions.

Many writers in the negative-freedom tradition, to take a salient example, tend to think (or at least are said by their critics to tend to think) of self-activation in terms of passions, desires, interests, and the like, conceiving of these as mental or even physical (neurophysiological) states or events occurring within and moving the agent's body. The agent is held to be free if the resulting movements are not effectively impeded from outside. Proponents of the theory of positive freedom agree that self-activated movement is sometimes directly prompted by such inner forces, but they are unwilling to regard such movements as free. On their view, freedom obtains only to the extent that inner forces are controlled by reason (or some analogue thereto such as judgment exercised by the agent's higher or better self) expressing itself in deliberately chosen and defended criteria, norms, rules, and laws. If there prove to be agents incapable of controlling the causal effects of their own passions and desires, other agents, frequently conceived of as possessing status or authority in a political society or community, make freedom possible by supplying the wanted discipline. In this way the norms of conduct said to be conceptually necessary to freedom come to be understood as external to agents, a circumstance that proponents of negative theories of freedom regard as the very paradigm of unfreedom.

We can begin to evaluate this dispute by asking questions such as the following: Is there such a thing as an objective, a purpose, an interest, or even a passion or desire, that can be *acted* upon (not to say achieved, attained, or satisfied), entirely without reference to criteria or norms or rules that have interpersonal standing? Contrariwise, is there such a thing as a norm or rule (in any sense

92 Situating and disciplining freedom

beyond an observer-detected regularity) that has not been accepted, subscribed to, or in some manner internalized by those whose conduct it actually governs? On the first question there is indeed reason to think of emotions such as fear and fright, joy and delight, longing and pining, as sheer happenings, as unchosen, undeliberated occurrences. We can study the conditions under which they occur in ourselves and others and, given the knowledge that such study affords, we can arrange our affairs so as to increase or decrease the probability that we will experience them. There is no further sense in which we do, or could, choose to have them or not. Moreover, for all practical purposes "having them" consists in the occurrence of (what Wittgenstein termed) certain "natural" or "primitive" expressions in certain "characteristic circumstances." These expressions and circumstances can be misdescribed in the sense that we can unwittingly make verbal mistakes in identifying them and we can deliberately misdescribe them in order to mislead others. But there is no other sense in which we can be mistaken or make mistakes concerning them.[4]

But even if having emotions is passive in these ways, is it plausible to regard evaluating the emotions we have, and acting on those evaluations, in the same manner? I experience fright, but do I not decide or judge whether the events that frightened me were dangerous or threatening and do I not (or at least can I not) choose to act one way rather than another in response to those events and my evaluation of them? Or more exactly, is it not the case that I *act* in response to those events and my emotions only if I choose one action as opposed to others? Of course such evaluations and choices are mine, are made by me. But they are neither passive nor personal in the same strong sense as emotions and passions (cf. Aristotle 1953, ch. 2, sect. 5). To begin with, they are the evaluations and choices that they are, each of them is *this* as opposed to some or any other evaluation or choice, by virtue of satisfying the criteria that govern *our* use of the concepts in which they are expressed and by which they are identified. These criteria do make reference to, do require the presence of, certain types or classes of circumstances, characteristics, or conditions. But the tie between the criteria and the conditions is not as close as with the concepts that identify passions and emotions. To substantiate my statement or claim that I had a frightening experience (as opposed to my having experienced fright), I have to show that something occurred which in fact put me or some other person or creature in some kind of danger. The "natural expressions" and "characteristic circumstances" mentioned above are the necessary and ordinarily the sufficient conditions of experiencing fright. By contrast, my claim to have had a "frightening experience" must be warranted by pointing to events that are or could plausibly be regarded as dangerous or threatening. Others can dispute the adequacy of the evidence that I adduce. Nor will just any evidence whatsoever, any consideration I choose to advance, count as justification for my saying that I "fled from," "stood up to," or "acted courageously in the face of" my fright. Many different things are relevant to supporting such claims and there is commonly room for cogently conducted dispute concerning the evidence adduced.

In this connection we may note further arguments, forcefully presented in social psychology, in theories of acculturation, socialization, and learning, and in the sociology of knowledge and belief, according to which the evaluations that persons in fact form and the actions they in fact take must be at least partially understood and explained in terms of beliefs and values, norms and expectations, shared among the members of communities, societies, and polities, cultures and civilizations. Philosophical psychologists in their turn have argued that this not only is but must be the case, and theorists of agency and personal identity have drawn on such argumentation in contending that the creatures who populate prevailing theories of freedom (roughly, those who are said by negative theories to be free but who must be called unfree by the criteria of positive formulations) could not be agents and could have no identities.

These arguments remain controversial in important respects, and in any case their bearing upon this or that theory of freedom needs to be worked out in detail. I will be giving them closer attention in later chapters. Even in the crude forms I have used, however, it is undeniable that the arguments sharply challenge understandings embedded in prevailing theories of freedom. If action involves evaluations and decisions that are public in the ways indicated, proponents of the theory of negative freedom (at least as described by their critics) would have to conclude that freedom (for human beings) is not only unknown but an impossibility. All action would be informed and hence in some measure constrained by considerations external to the agent. But the same reasoning implies that what theorists of positive freedom regard as a leading class of cases of unfreedom, namely, agents controlled by their passions, is and must be an empty class. If action is never an unmediated result of impulse, emotion, or passion, then there can be no case of action that is "enslaved" or unfree in this sense. Further, insofar as human action is norm- or rule-governed, to that extent it satisfies what is at least a necessary (and perhaps—when fully explicated—the sufficient) condition of freedom for the positive theorist.

It is possible, in short, that the dominant alternative theories of freedom are committed to an understanding of agency and action that renders freedom impossible for the first and inescapable for the second; unfreedom necessary for the former and impossible for the latter.

A similar suggestion emerges if we focus on the notion of a norm or rule as it has figured in leading versions of the negative and positive theories. Hobbes is famous for the argument that subjects or citizens are at liberty just insofar as their Sovereign has not promulgated laws or commands requiring or forbidding modes of conduct. Freedom consists of the absence of rules; their presence is a sufficient condition of unfreedom. Although modified in various ways by later proponents of negative conceptions of freedom, this view has been prominent in the negative-freedom tradition throughout its history. Proponents of the theory of positive freedom take a sharply contrasting position. On their view, free conduct conforms to norms; therefore norms requiring and forbidding conduct, so far from preventing freedom, are necessary to it. Here again there is reason to think that the competing theories in fact share a single misunderstanding, namely, an exaggerated view of the effects—whether for or against freedom—of rules. Writers otherwise as diverse as Oliver Wendell Holmes, Jr., the later

94 *Situating and disciplining freedom*

Wittgenstein, and Michael Oakeshott have urged that rules, that is, general and prospective guides to conduct, can do neither as much to agency and action as theorists of negative liberty suggest nor as much for it as proponents of the theory of positive freedom contend. Even rules that form a "strict calculus" (Wittgenstein) take the agent by the elbow, not by the throat. Theorists of negative freedom underestimate the extent to which human conduct must be rule-governed in order to be intelligible; proponents of theories of positive freedom underestimate the extent to which the most precisely formulated norm or rule, the most tightly integrated system of norms and rules, leaves scope for variations in conduct.

These and related possibilities are examined in the chapters that follow. To borrow James Madison's language in *The Federalist* 10, I propose to extend the sphere in which argumentation about freedom has been conducted; to extend argumentation to include considerations from the literatures mentioned above. In doing so I may bring about no more than an increase in the number of philosophical "factions." But this result may also "dissipate the force" of those factions and it is at least possible that it will contribute to "the equalization and assimilation of opinions and passions" that have been in contention in respect to freedom.

I will not, however, take my cues from the ardent and probably negative-liberty theorist Madison. Rather, I will initially look to the suggestive notion of "situated freedom" bequeathed to us by Hegel, implicit in most versions of the positive theory of freedom, and elaborated explicitly and self-consciously in later recognizably Hegelian thought. This strategy partly reflects what seems to me to be the current philosophical ascendancy of positive theories: it examines well-developed versions of that theory and attempts to determine whether their ascendancy is deserved. In this perspective my conclusion will be that the best versions of that theory contain vitiating defects. As I have begun to suggest, however, I will also argue that the notion that freedom is "situated" is separable from the characteristically "positive" aspects of the theory and contributes importantly to remedying difficulties commonly and in some measure correctly attributed to "negative" theories.

Appendix

Kinds of freedom distinguishable in the philosophical literature

* Freedom$_1$ and Unfreedom$_1$ or Freedom and Unfreedom of Movement
  Self-activated movement plus the possibility of impediments to the movement in question.
* Freedom$_2$ and Unfreedom$_2$ or Freedom and Unfreedom of Action
  Action attempted by an agent plus the possibility of impediments to that action placed or left by another agent or other agents acting with the intention of placing or leaving those impediments.
* Freedom$_3$ and Unfreedom$_3$ or Autonomy and Heteronomy

Action attempted by an agent in the pursuit of a self-critically chosen plan or project that the agent has reason to believe is consonant with defensible norms or principles, plus the possibility of impediments to that action placed or left by another agent or other agents acting with the intention of placing or leaving those impediments.

- Freedom$_4$ and Unfreedom$_4$ or Communal Freedom and Unfreedom
  Action attempted by an agent in pursuit of a plan or project chosen to satisfy, and in fact satisfying, norms or principles that are authoritative in the agent's community, plus the possibility of impediments to that action placed or left by another agent or other agents acting with the intention of placing or leaving those impediments.
- Freedom$_5$ and Unfreedom$_5$ or Fully Virtuous Freedom and Unfreedom
  Action attempted by an agent in the pursuit of a plan or project self-critically chosen to satisfy, and in fact satisfying, certifiably worthy norms or principles, plus the possibility of impediments to that action placed or left by another agent or other agents acting with the intention of placing or leaving those impediments.

Notes

1 It may prove necessary to recognize a variant of freedom$_2$ (and the other freedoms and unfreedoms to follow) in which the obstacles are not deliberately placed or left. According to most versions of Marxism, for example, the most important obstacles to freedom are not intentionally placed or left, if we take those expressions to mean placed or left by individuals or groups of individuals acting with the conscious intention of creating or maintaining the obstacles. On this and numerous related theories we can describe the most important obstacles as intentionally created only if we are prepared to talk about unconscious intentions or to attribute intentionality to impersonal agencies such as history, classes and class structures, forces and relations of production, and the like.

As John Gray has pointed out to me (personal communication), we might view social arrangements as impediments to liberty if they are alterable or remediable by human agency. If A is prevented from doing X by the class structure of A's society, and if that structure could in principle be altered by human decision and action, we can say that A is made unfree to X without imputing intentional or purposive interference to any assignable agent or agencies and without attributing unconscious intentions to a social class. By contrast, if A were prevented from doing X by an unalterable natural condition or circumstance, we would say that A was unable to X not that A was unfree to X.

The value of this suggestion can be seen by noting that conceptions of what is alterable and what is given and must be accepted themselves undergo change and that such changes are reflected in talk about freedom. When it came to be thought that full employment was an achievable social goal, the unemployed could cogently complain of their unfreedom without identifying the particular culprits who were keeping them out of work. As the possibility of full employment has again been called into question, we see renewed need to single out responsible parties.

It remains the case, however, that claims of unfreedom are typically accusatory; they charge some party or parties with responsibility for deliberate interference, not merely with causal influence. In part for this reason, we should endorse David Miller's further suggestion that claims and attributions of unfreedom require that some agent or agency

96 *Situating and disciplining freedom*

is morally (as opposed to merely causally) responsible for the obstacle or impediment to A's action. I disagree, however, with Miller's argument that for this purpose "morally responsible" should be limited to cases in which *B* has a moral *obligation* not to place or leave the obstacle or impediment that prevents or restricts *A*'s action. Unless we inflate "obligation" unduly, this restriction excludes cases in which *A* and others will properly say that *B* (perhaps along with others) is morally responsible for *A*'s unfreedom (see Miller 1983). I am indebted to conversations with Miller on this and related questions.

2 My scare-quotes around "enslaved" are in effect my first comment on this controversy. Talk of being enslaved is question-begging because to say that someone is enslaved has come to be equivalent to saying that she is unfree. Thus to say that passions and desires render a person unfree by enslaving her is to put the *explanandum* into the *explanans*.

   I should add a further comment concerning the above remarks. The distinction I have thus far drawn between negative and positive theories is nonstandard. The more usual distinction, familiar from the exchanges between Isaiah Berlin and Gerald MacCallum, turns on whether the agent must be free *to* achieve some objective or purpose, *to* serve some interest or satisfy some desire, as opposed to merely free *from* restraints and limitations. My larger purpose in drawing the distinction as I have done is to make conceptual connections between human freedom and human action and human unfreedom and attempted but prevented human action. Because all human action is intentional and purposive, human freedom must be freedom *to* as well as freedom *from.* In this respect I agree with MacCallum (1967). But this move does not itself establish the superiority of theories of positive freedom. The more controversial thesis of such theories is that the agent's purpose must be chosen to satisfy and must in fact satisfy some normative criterion, and, in some versions of the theory, that the criterion itself must be worthy. The mere fact that an agent has adopted and is engaged in the unhindered pursuit of an objective or purpose is not sufficient to warrant saying that she is free. It is this, or these, further requirement(s) and the attendant notion of a higher or better self that chooses worthy actions, it seems to me, that has aroused the concern of theorists of negative freedom such as Isaiah Berlin (1969).

3 Of course it doesn't *follow* that the features that are settled in our uses of the concept of freedom in contemporary English will also be found in the parallel or analogous concepts established in other times and places. It is not impossible that other societies and other cultures have or have had concepts of freedom that are radically different than ours. Determining the similarities and differences among historical instances of this (or any other) concept requires empirical study. But we know enough about the history of the concept of freedom to say that there has been and is a good deal of continuity and positive comparability among its uses. Our confidence in this knowledge is expressed in our ready willingness to say that other societies and cultures do or do not, did or did not, have the concept of freedom. On these and numerous other points I am indebted to conversations with Quentin Skinner.

4 The above remarks rely on Wittgenstein as he has been interpreted by David Sachs (1976).

References

Aristotle. 1953. *Nichomachean Ethics*. Baltimore: Penguin Books.

Benn, Stanley, and Weinstein, William. 1971. "Being Free to Act and Being a Free Man." *Mind* 80: 194–211.

Berlin, Isaiah. 1969. *Four Essays on Liberty*. London: Oxford University Press.

Feinberg, Joel. 1980. *Rights, Justice, and the Bounds of Liberty*. Princeton: Princeton University Press.

Kinds of freedom 97

MacCallum, Gerald. 1967. "Negative and Positive Freedom." *The Philosophical Review* 76: 312–34.

Miller, David. 1983. "Constraints on Freedom." *Ethics* 94: 66–86.

Neumann, Franz. 1957. *The Democratic and the Authoritarian State.* Glencoe, IL: The Free Press.

Sachs, David. 1976. "Wittgenstein on Emotion." *Acta Philosophica Fennica*, vol. 28, nos. 1–3. Amsterdam: North-Holland Publishing Company.

7 Is the positive theory of freedom a theory of freedom? (1987)

...

I

...

II

The notion that positive freedom is importantly distinct from negative freedom takes its plausibility from a fact that looms large in the views I have been considering, namely, that we can be unconstrained by "external" forces and yet be unable to carry out certain patterns of actions or achieve certain goals and purposes. But this plausibility disappears, Feinberg contends, when we recognize that constraints can be both internal and external and both "positive" and "negative" in character. Hobbes and others in the negative-freedom tradition focus on external, positive constraints such as "barred windows, locked doors, and pointed bayonets," and theorists of positive freedom urge attention to internal positive constraints such as brute desires and obsessions and compulsions. We must also recognize external negative constraints such as the lack of money, power, or other necessities for successful action, and internal, negative limitations such as the lack of ability, character, will, knowledge, and so forth. In Feinberg's words, freedom from negative constraints is the "absence of an absence, and therefore the presence of some condition that permits a given kind of doing. The presence of such a condition when external to a person is usually called an opportunity, and, when internal, an ability" (1980: 6).

When these several kinds of constraint are acknowledged, "there is no further need to speak of two distinct kinds of freedom.... A constraint is something—anything—that prevents one from doing something.... Thus, there can be no special 'positive' freedom *to* which is not also freedom from" (1980: 6–7). Feinberg follows Isaiah Berlin to the extent of allowing the possibility that a person might attain freedom from some hated constraint without having "formed a project on which the agent plans to act" and hence not yet involving consciousness of freedom to act in a particular manner. But he regards such cases as atypical (1980:

The theory of freedom   99

5). Thus the main concerns of positive theorists can be accommodated within a single concept of freedom. Achieving the qualities of self and character that these theorists prize can be understood not only as overcoming internal positive constraints such as compulsions but also as freeing oneself from the constraints imposed by the lack of such character, by the absence of certain abilities.

As I proceed I will argue that Feinberg unduly extends the notion of constraint and thereby distorts our thinking about freedom. But if we follow him in understanding "constraints" to encompass such notions as limitations and incapacities, and if we think of the latter in contrast with abilities, capacities, and opportunities, he provides a more parsimonious conceptualization than the negative–positive dichotomy.[1] If we combine this conceptualization with my objections to the distinction between situated and unsituated freedom, the task of theorizing about freedom assumes a different shape and character than that to which we have been accustomed. Most notably, the task ceases to be choosing between allegedly dichotomous, mutually incompatible theories. There are a considerable number and variety of characteristics and circumstances that contribute to or detract from freedom. What matters from a practical standpoint is the ways in which these combine and interact in particular action settings. What matters from a theoretical perspective is to identify, to order, and to assess the recurring kinds of characteristics and circumstances that create and constrain opportunities for action.

I adopt this conceptualization and use it to widen my discussion of positive theory arguments that certain kinds of "internal" forces "enslave" the persons who experience them. There are certainly forces that limit the possibilities of human action and there is much that occurs in human affairs that appears to support views such as Taylor's and Feinberg's. But positive theorists have misdescribed the phenomena that concern them and have exaggerated their significance for the theory of freedom. Developing this argument will help to reduce my list of five kinds of freedom and unfreedom and allow me to coordinate the remaining items on that list with the MacCallum–Feinberg thesis that there is a single concept of freedom.

III

If we leave aside limits imposed by what are widely accepted at any given time as the largely unalterable natural conditions of all human life, it would by now be difficult to deny that there are illnesses and disorders, commonly characterized as mental, that severely narrow (as against what have come to be our expectations) the range of actions possible for those who suffer those illnesses and which grossly distort their in some respects action-like performances. In some cases these limitations and distortions are so striking that others come to think of such human beings not as agents but as subjects, and to regard their performances not as actions but as movements or behaviors. These arresting and deeply unsettling phenomena provide a starting point for wider consideration of the thesis that factors "internal" to human beings render them unfree.

100 *Situating and disciplining freedom*

It will be instructive to notice at the outset the view taken of even the most extreme forms of mental illness by radical critics of the notion such as Michel Foucault, R. D. Laing, and Thomas Szasz.[2] Although differing from one another in important respects, these writers share the view that talk of mental illness is an expression of ideological thinking. They believe that such thinking, despite employing allegedly scientific—and hence morally and politically neutral— concepts such as "illness," "normal," and "well-adjusted," puts these concepts to repressive moral and political purposes.

Whatever else we may think of these critiques, they have two connected implications or consequences that are pertinent to present concerns; they situate the performances, both of those said to be mentally ill and of those who respond to them as such, in a social and political setting and they give a definite foothold to the concepts of freedom and unfreedom as those concepts have been used by proponents of the negative theory of freedom. Very palpable external restraints are placed on those characterized as mentally ill, and those who place the con- straints justify doing so with the claim that the "patients" violate established community norms and expectations and are dangerous to others as well as to themselves. On the assumption that the "patients" are in fact agents engaged in action, the imposition of these restraints easily warrants the conclusion that the patients have been made unfree.

This critique is indeed radical—radical in the fashionable sense of going to the roots. Its most radical aspect, however, is not its challenge to notions such as illness, normality, and good adjustment. The content of these has shifted about a good deal historically; it is less than surprising to be told that their uses in any culture or society reflect its dominant beliefs and values. Much deeper-going is the claim that persons judged to be, say, in a catatonic state, are nevertheless actors or agents engaged in action in the sense in which I have been using that term. This claim proposes a transformation of our concepts of agency and action and much of what depends upon them.

I do not say this to endorse any one of the diverse accounts of the protean phenomena that nowadays get called mental illness. Although skeptical about much of what is said concerning, and unsettled by much of what is done in the name of, this variegated conceptualization, I am not competent to pass on the intricate questions that make up the controversies concerning it. But it is, as I said, "by now difficult" to say that someone judged to be in a catatonic state is acting as opposed to moving, or perhaps behaving. It is difficult to say this because the concept "catatonic" (or less technically and more generally, "psy- chotic" or "insane") defines an outer limit of the widely received, I think it is fair to say the established, understanding of "action." We conceive of the movements of catatonics as the effects of some kind of force or forces (the exact "kind," of course, is a matter of wide and intense disagreement) that they are unable to control. Thus we do not hold them morally or legally responsible for the con- sequences of movements that occur when they are in that state, we sometimes feel justified in removing them from society, and we believe that they need the assistance of others—who often employ powerful countervailing forces such as

The theory of freedom   101

drugs, electrical currents, surgical knives—if they are to regain or to achieve the capacity for action.

I cannot assess the observations and interpretations out of which this understanding has been built. Certainly I cannot assess the large bodies of theory that attempt to render the observations and interpretations intelligible and that inform the numerous and often mutually incompatible practices that have developed concerning the mentally ill. My timorous venturing just across the borders of this (to me) dark territory is in the hope of achieving much more modest purposes. I seek to provide an anchor or to establish a benchmark for a discussion of internal sources of unfreedom, one that will hold for or not be deeply contested by readers less radical than Foucault, Laing, and Szasz. If we agree to some sense in which a human being who is in a catatonic, schizophrenic, or hysteric condition is unfree because of "internal" forces, we can use that agreement to discipline examination of other alleged but more disputed instances of internally caused unfreedom. More specifically and polemically, I have presented the foregoing remarks as preparation for suggesting that positive theory arguments about unfreedom involve either a conceptual mistake that is the other side of the coin of the mistake made by Foucault, Laing, and Szasz or a proposal for a conceptual transformation that would be at least as far-reaching, in a quite different direction, as the implicit proposals of these theorists. To anticipate, Foucault, Laing, and Szasz attribute agency, and hence the capacity for moral and political freedom (and responsibility), to persons regarded by most of us as incapable of it. Positive theorists deny agency and hence freedom to persons regarded by most of us as not only capable of but in fact exercising freedom in the very instances in question.

As a preliminary to presenting this argument, I reiterate a conceptual point already made. If widely received opinion about psychosis is correct, and if positive theorists are also correct to extend the same or a strongly analogous analysis to a further range of cases, the appropriate inference would not be that those for whom the opinion or the analysis holds are unfree; it would rather be that questions about freedom and unfreedom arise about them only if we are thinking of freedom$_1$ and unfreedom$_1$. Such persons do not satisfy conditions requisite to predication of freedoms$_{2-5}$ and unfreedoms$_{2-5}$. Putting the matter this way, it seems to me, sharpens the edge of the following question: Is this the appropriate way to think about those who would like to be cooperative, and forgiving but are persistently selfish, obstinate, and vindictive? Is it the way to regard those who agonize about their overeating, their smoking, their poor work habits, but who, perhaps despite every assistance and encouragement from family, friends, and fellow-workers, do not succeed in breaking these habits or reversing these tendencies?

In the hope of addressing these questions in an orderly manner, I posit a continuum moving from individuals entirely lacking in control over forces internal to them to those with control so complete as to be able to eliminate such forces. Anchoring one end of this continuum are the psychotics I have been discussing. Setting aside views such as Foucault's and Laing's, it is part of a widely influential understanding of such persons that they are so incapable of "responsibility

102 *Situating and disciplining freedom*

for self" that they can be said to be unfree only in the sense of unfreedom$_1$. There is *energeia* or self-activation and of course there can be impediments and obstacles to the movements produced. But questions about freedoms$_{2-5}$ and unfreedoms$_{2-5}$ arise about such persons only in the sense that others might attempt to cure their illnesses and thereby render them capable of moral and political freedom and unfreedom.

The other end of the continuum I am positing is occupied by creatures familiar enough in imagination and even belief but hard to come by empirically. Some conceptions of gods and goddesses, perhaps of angels, saints, and holy persons in certain religious traditions, are expressions of this ideal. In the more worldly (but far from mundane) realm of secular (or apparently secular) thought, this notion has been expressed in the ideal of a human life of fully self-critical, entirely presuppositionless, judgments and actions, an ideal that has been the aspiration of hubristic philosophers from Plato to Jürgen Habermas.

This continuum might be thought of as moving from entire unfreedom to perfect freedom. But this would be a mistake on several counts. In respect to the psychotic it would confuse unfreedom$_1$—and hence a lack of capacity for freedoms$_{2-5}$ and unfreedoms$_{2-5}$—with unfreedoms$_{2-5}$. In respect to gods and godlike philosophers it would either confuse omniscience with omnipotence or make the Stoic's mistake encountered earlier, namely, *equating* freedom and control of self. Most generally, and most importantly for the theory of human freedom and unfreedom, it would be to ignore such facts as that freedom in one respect often conflicts with freedom in another and that the value we place on freedom varies depending on the importance we assign to the actions we are free to take and the objectives we are free to pursue. Someone not far removed from the psychotic on the continuum might be free in ways very important to her or might have relatively few goals and objectives and hence might rarely experience the necessity of choosing among actions all of which she is free to do. On the other hand, because not even the most god-like of philosophers can be in two places at one time, entire control over their internal forces would not make their freedom "perfect" or "full." It makes good sense to talk of more and less freedom, but the notion of complete, or full, or perfect freedom is a misunderstanding.

A person's location on the continuum, then, may be relevant to assessing her freedom but it cannot itself settle that assessment. With this proviso in mind, let us consider a few of the large number of "stages" that might be singled out between the psychotic—call this position (a)—and the god-like philosopher. Leaving aside undoubted cases of organic disorders (such as epilepsy) and addictions that are agreed to be at least in part neurophysiological or biochemical, a next stage (b) might be occupied by persons suffering obsessions, phobias, and compulsions. Here again the ordinary uses of these terms attribute to the compulsive such characteristics as being "in the grip of" or "overcome by" some inner force. The kleptomaniac "cannot help herself"; when surrounded by the cornucopia of goods displayed in a supermarket or a department store her best efforts are not enough to prevent her from slipping items into her purse or under her coat. The acrophobic simply cannot maintain composure at the top of the

The theory of freedom 103

Eiffel Tower. If she is so foolish as to ascend, she will all but certainly panic and do harm to herself unless restrained.

In certain respects, then, notions like "phobia" and "obsession" overlap with "psychosis" and "insane." The reflection, deliberation, intention formation and revision, the choosing, deciding, explaining and justifying, the adapting to changed circumstances and accommodation to other persons, the following of rules, routines, and recipes, the making and correcting of mistakes—none of these components of "ordinary" or "standard" action and acting are present in those aspects of the phobic's or the compulsive's life in which the phobia or the compulsion holds sway. (Of course the compulsive or phobic, just as with the psychotic, may be the very paradigm of the ordinary or standard agent or actor in some or much of her conduct.) For these reasons, the responsibility of compulsives and phobics, and the appropriateness of blaming and praising, punishing and rewarding them for the specifically compulsive and phobic behaviors, is minimal if not nonexistent. Because these abnormalities are often quite specific and coexist with ordinary capacity for action in other respects, we expect those who suffer them to take such precautions as they can against their occurrence and their effects. But when they do occur our role is to help and to sympathize, not to blame or punish.

Here again, then, we can make good sense of the notion of inner forces taking control of, even (if we remember that it is metaphorical) enslaving, human beings. Nor is there reason to doubt that persons who suffer compulsions and obsessions would like to be freed of or from them. But this too is unfreedom$_1$, at most the aspiration to freedoms$_{2-5}$. In respect to her obsessions and phobias, the genuine compulsive or phobic is incapable of action and hence of freedoms$_{2-5}$ and unfreedoms$_{2-5}$. To relate to her on any other assumption, for example to accuse her of inadequate responsibility for self or to read her lectures about her failings of character, would be either stupid or cruel.

The movement of my continuum toward its appointed termination with the god-like philosopher could proceed in a wide variety of ways or through a considerable diversity of "stages." One perhaps not implausible sequence would be the following: (c) habits in the at least mildly pejorative sense in which we say that smoking and pot-taking are habits; (d) a wide variety of so-called akratic behaviors, cases in which a person fails to act in the manner or in pursuit of the end or goal that she herself identifies as right or best by criteria that she herself endorses; (e) habits in the benign or even favorable usage of theorists such as Edmund Burke and Michael Oakeshott; (f) the purely preferential and instrumental but perhaps exquisitely calculated choices of some utilitarianisms and of classical and neoclassical economic theories; (g) character traits or settled but principled dispositions à la Aristotle and such contemporary writers as Bernard Williams and Charles Taylor; (h) the casuistries, firmly practical, elegant in formulation, and deeply grounded in an elaborate system of reflections, of the scholastic moralist; (i) the thoughts and actions of the philosopher who would be divine if only she hadn't suffered the indignity of being created mortal.

I comment briefly on some of these (most particularly habits and the moderately technical notion of *akrasia*) just below. But I will assume that the idea

104 *Situating and disciplining freedom*

informing the progression from stage to stage is at least as available and as intuitively clear to readers of this book as are the notions of psychosis and obsessions, compulsions and phobias. For present purposes what is needed is not a detailed explication of these familiar notions but rather consideration of the bearing, if any, of the similarities and differences among them on theories of freedom and unfreedom.

It appears to me to be the Hegelian and the neo-Hegelian view that unfreedom, or no better than a thin, insignificant freedom, prevails until we reach (e) or even (f) on this continuum and that rich, fully significant freedom is a possibility only for those who have arrived at least at stage (g), perhaps at (h) in this sequence. (Note that in principle a person could be at various stages in respect to the several dimensions or aspects of life. At least this could be true up to [h] or [i].) If I am correct about this, two now familiar ways of interpreting this view emerge from my previous discussions. One of these is that the view equates freedom with various other values or ideals such as virtue, good character, authenticity, and the like. Those at stages (c) through (e) or (f) fall short of their own or their community's ideals in various ways and to various degrees. As we move from (f) or (g) toward (i), the degree and quality of freedom increase along with the extent to which the individual achieves (so far as she is not prevented from doing so by others) whatever ideals are in question. The second interpretation is the one I have been considering and that led me to posit the continuum. Movement along the continuum is not calibrated in terms of more or less virtue, higher or lower levels of achievement of valued objectives or states. Rather, it is from little or seriously inadequate control over inner forces to entire control over them. On this second interpretation, persons at stages (c) through (f) are treated as remarkably similar to psychotics in respect to their psychoses and obsessives in respect to their obsessions. Those who eat too much, work inefficiently, live fragmented, disorganized lives, have poor relationships with others, above all persons who are cowardly, selfish, unjust, illiberal, and the like are said to be in the grip of or overcome by some sort of internal but alien force. It is in this sense, it is for this reason, that they are unfree or enjoy no more than an impoverished freedom.

At least in respect to Charles Taylor, both of these interpretations are partly correct. Freedom is a kind of virtue and virtue is knowledge of self-in-community that makes possible rational control of action. Unfreedom is a kind of vice or evil when vice is an absence or failure of knowledge of self-in-community and of self-command which leaves the individual at the mercy of the irrational and nonrational forces that lurk in the subhuman recesses of the self. In a manner at least reminiscent of earlier versions of the theory of positive freedom, neo-Hegelian arguments combine these two doctrines.

If we exclude ordinary desires and compositional evaluations, and if we set aside psychosis and compulsions for the reasons discussed, the plausibility of the second doctrine is left to depend on those occurrences in human affairs that we would place at stages (c), (d), and possibly (e) on my continuum. In both (c) and (d) and perhaps in (e), certain of the elements that are prominent in our ordinary notion of action are thought to be very little in evidence or perhaps missing altogether. In the case of habits in the at least mildly pejorative sense expressed by talk of having the habit of smoking, the elements alleged to be missing are critical self-consciousness, deliberation, rationality, and even decision and choice. There are those who invariably reach for a cigarette as they swing their legs out of bed in the morning, on the appearance of a cup of coffee, in the course of starting their cars, answering their telephones, beginning lectures to their classes, and so forth. Their smoking in these and other circumstances is as if by rote or by the numbers. They pause for not so much as an instant. There seems to be no evidence of their asking themselves whether they want to smoke, should smoke, have already smoked enough that day, would do better to save their remaining cigarettes for later, or anything of the sort. In the more inclusive case of (d), which on some interpretations would in fact encompass (c), there may be reflection, an abundance of self-examination and criticism, ambivalence, dissonance, hesitation, vacillation, agonizing, and so forth. The akratic, in short, may give an appearance very different from the person "locked into" a habitual mode of behavior. Here the missing or inadequately represented element is more like Harry Frankfurt's "will" to act on the conclusions of one's deliberations, to implement one's "choices" in the sense of the results of one's deliberations. For all of her agonizing and self-castigation about past failures, despite her elaborate preparations, strategies, and scheming, the akratic cannot resist the cigarette, the rich dessert, the nasty comment about a colleague, the putting herself first. If the habitual smoker is "in a rut," of which she may no longer be aware and from which she does not try to escape, the akratic is aware of her deficiencies and failings but fails to correct or overcome them. In both cases, perhaps for different reasons or by different psychological mechanisms, it appears that the persons are controlled by some force or forces that are alien or at least inauthentic. Hence they are unfree. It also appears that they could be made free, or that their freedom could be enhanced, if other agents or agencies would remove them, even if forcibly, from their rut or would prevent them from acting in ways that they themselves may regret and even despise.

We do frequently talk in ways that seem to warrant such conclusions about habitual and akratic conduct. I will comment on these forms of speech in a moment. But we should first note some additional characteristics of each of these modes, characteristics that support quite different conclusions about them. Habitual conduct is properly contrasted with decisions reached and choices made as the more or less direct or immediate conclusion of reflection and deliberation. It is "matter of course" in the sense that the conduct occurs without critical reflection about its propriety or desirability when the agent finds herself (or thinks she finds herself) in the kind of circumstance or situation in which it has previously served. The person does not, in Hannah Arendt's phrase, "stop and think" (1977: 2:78; see also 88–89). There is no turning inward, no consideration of alternatives, no seeking of further information or advice. Nevertheless, even the most settled, the least reflective of habitual behaviors are only "robot-like," not the movements of robots. Even the monotonous, the dreary regularity with which

106 *Situating and disciplining freedom*

Able, a member of my car pool, lights up as she settles into the back seat each morning is broken if she hasn't seen to having cigarettes and matches in her purse. Nor is Able literally a "smoking machine"; her deadly instrument moves irregularly from hand-to-hand and hand-to-mouth, she puffs rapidly and then slowly, exhales first in my direction and then in that of another sufferer, she flicks her ashes sometimes on the floor, sometimes out the window, occasionally in the ashtray. These depressing sequences, moreover, are learned and practiced. Able knows how and how not to smoke. She conceives of herself as smoking in a sophisticated manner. There are many ways in which she would "not be caught dead" smoking. The angle at which she holds her head and her arm, the manner in which she holds the cigarette in her yellowing fingers, the ways in which she uses her inhaling and exhaling to punctuate her speech and to express her mood, all of this is ritual. If it is a ritual by now performed largely or even entirely without deliberation, if it is thoughtless in numerous senses of that word, it is nevertheless replete with intentionality and with purposiveness and it manifests choice and decision throughout. Although repeated many times each day by Able, and many times each day by millions of other human beings, each of these repetitions is a chosen, an enacted, performance, one that differs from every other.

Owing to these characteristics, each of these habitual performances is subject to evaluation. Each of them can be carried out elegantly or inelegantly, smoothly or awkwardly, efficiently or wastefully. More important for present purposes, as with any and all habits, the habit itself (taken to be the ensemble of actions that constitutes having the habit of smoking) is subject to evaluation as a good or a bad habit. Perhaps my morning companion no longer asks herself this question. Perhaps she hasn't asked herself this question for years. But at some point in her life history, at some level of self-consciousness, Able asked and answered it. Her habit developed because she repeatedly answered some formulation of the question in the affirmative. Having become satisfied with her answer, she has since had no more occasion to continue to ask it than a dispositionally courageous person has to ask herself whether she should be a coward. But any one of a wide array of events or occurrences might prompt her to ask it again. And if Able doesn't ask it, or asks it but comes to what others think is the wrong conclusion concerning it, she is subject to criticism. If those who know her are convinced that the habit has become so "deeply ingrained" that it is genuinely difficult for her to reconsider it or to consider it in an open-minded, balanced, manner, they may be sympathetic, patient, and gentle with her. They may decide that the habit has come to occupy so central a place in her life that it is better not to bring the matter up at all. But the same assessment, if combined with the view that smoking is a very bad habit indeed, that it is deeply harmful to herself or to others, may convince others that they are justified in employing measures so severe that they deprive Able of freedoms she had previously been enjoying (the same freedoms that will continue to be enjoyed by persons whose habits are judged to be good).

According to Amalie Rorty and other recent students of akrasia, akratic behavior is itself habitual (Rorty 1975: 193–212; Elster 1978). It differs from

The theory of freedom   107

habits such as I have just discussed in that it typically occurs when there is a conflict among two or more of a person's habits. On this account of the phenomenon, the Able of my car pool is a likely candidate for akrasia. Her habit of smoking coexists with a variety of others such as attending to her health and her good physical appearance, seeking the approval of others and avoiding actions distressing or annoying to them, being frugal about her money, and so forth. She took up smoking before it came to be thought harmful to health, when it was considered fashionable by all but the unfashionably ascetical or puritanical and even a mark of liberation on the part of a woman, and before her government had come to appreciate its potential as a source of revenue. As changes occur in these regards, Able's habit of smoking will increasingly conflict with other of her dispositions and inclinations and she may decide that it would be better if she "kicked" it. Not smoking may become what Rorty calls her "preferred judgment," continued smoking an "*akratic* alternative" to that preferred judgment. If she nevertheless continues to smoke she will in that respect become an *akrates*. Despite her sincere belief that she should not smoke, her concerted efforts to act on that belief, and her regret and perhaps even self-disgust at her failure to do so, her smoking continues unabated.

Traditional analyses of akrasia support the view that the akrates is unfree. For Socrates, a person who takes an action or follows a course of action that is wrong or less attractive than available alternatives is either ignorant of what she is doing (doesn't realize the consequences of her action or doesn't appreciate that it falls under a principle she rejects) or under some kind of compulsion. Plato simplified this view by treating all wrongdoing as a result of ignorance of the good. As Rorty points out, however, these analyses, and even Aristotle's more plausible view that akrasia is explained by mistakes of fact or of practical reasoning, "explain" the phenomenon by denying its existence. Their explanations do not explain akrasia, they explain it away. My smoker Able is by now well-informed about smoking. She knows the grim statistics about lung cancer, heart disease, and emphysema; she is intensely aware of the disapproval of others; she keeps accurate account of the money she spends on cigarettes and adverts frequently to the other pleasures she must therefore forego. In other regards, moreover, she maintains a close and effective discipline over her conduct. Although fond of rich desserts, she ends her meals with black coffee in order to remain trim and to save money; although intensely disliking her boss, she never permits herself so much as the mildest criticism of her. In most respects she is a paradigm of the "responsible self."

Of course there is weakness here, weakness that may deserve understanding and sympathy on the part of friends and acquaintances that would never occur to them in respect to other aspects of Able's conduct. Moreover, Able may talk about her smoking in ways which, if taken literally, suggest more than mere weakness. For example, she may say that she "can't help" smoking, or that it is "impossible" for her to stop doing so. These and many related locutions, which are characteristic of persons experiencing akrasia, might seem to support the view that the akrates is unfree.

108 *Situating and disciplining freedom*

The most serious difficulty with this analysis can be seen by noting that the akrates herself, despite using language that suggests unfreedom, continues to describe her smoking as mistaken or regrettable at least in the sense of not being the most desirable or best or right thing for her to do. Rorty argues that this does not mean that akrasia always involves conduct of a deeply or seriously mistaken kind; conduct that is immoral or seriously harmful to the agent or to others. On her analysis, the concept applies even if the akrates has no more than a mild preference for some alternative pattern of conduct.[3] But as the traditional term "weakness of will" suggests, akrasia involves some sense of shortcoming or deficiency, some at least mildly negative or critical self-assessment. Weakness and shortcoming, however, are not unfreedom. If the akrates were unfree, such self-criticism would be out of place. I cannot at once be unfree and *make* a mistake. If I am unfree in a particular respect I cannot *act* in that respect and hence I am not subject to criticism, by myself or by others, in that respect. (Of course I might be subject to criticism for past actions that led to my present unfree condition.) It is a condition of the applicability of "mistake," "criticism," and a whole host of evaluational concepts that I am an agent engaged in action.

Statements that appear to claim unfreedom should be understood, rather, as expressions of a two- or perhaps a three-fold regret, but a regret that is at least partially qualified. (i) Able regrets her continued smoking; there is an obvious alternative, one that she genuinely and sincerely prefers. (ii) She regrets the fact that she allows herself to be influenced by considerations—the anticipated pleasure of the cigarettes, the comradely support of other smokers—over which she could exercise control if she made a sufficient effort. (iii) She regrets earlier decisions and actions that established her habit of smoking and that make her susceptible to the continuing influence of considerations such as in (ii). But the regret is qualified or partial, not entire. From early in the history of her habit Able genuinely enjoyed smoking and she continues to do so. The cigarettes do taste good to her, do give her other pleasurable sensations; she enjoys the ritual, likes to discuss the differences among brands with other smokers, finds satisfaction in the thought that, unlike earlier generations of women, members of her generation are at liberty to smoke if they see fit. If she gave up smoking her sense of achievement would be qualified by regret over the loss of these pleasures. The considerations that influence the partially regretted action are not alien or external or inauthentic to her. They influence her, they have weight with or for her, because of beliefs, inclinations, and preferences that are among her characteristics as a person. She may succeed in changing herself in these respects, but until she does so her smoking remains an action that she takes.[4]

I suggested that positive theorists exaggerate the significance, for the moral and political theory of freedom, of the idea that desires, interests, inclinations, and so forth "enslave" the agent. There is no denying that something like this notion is frequently encountered outside of the pages of philosophical works. My argument that positive theorists exaggerate the significance of the notion is in two stages. I concede, *arguendo*, that "enslavement" occurs in cases of psychoses and obsessions and compulsions. But I contend that these are cases of

The theory of freedom   109

freedom$_1$, and hence are relevant to moral and political theory only insofar as it is possible to cure psychosis and addiction and hence make those who have suffered them eligible for predication of freedoms$_{2-5}$ and unfreedoms$_{2-5}$. To put this thesis somewhat differently, in the cases in which the language of brute and alien forces, and hence absence of agency, is appropriate, talk of "enslavement" is metaphorical and the "enslaving" forces should not be assimilated to the desires and interests that operate at stages (c) through (e) or (f) on the continuum I have posited. Second, I contend that talk of "enslavement" in respect to stages (c), and (d) is inappropriate; these stages—and more obviously (e) and (f)—should be understood in ways that leave agency largely if not entirely intact. Taylor is correct in his sometimes implicit thesis that notions such as making a mistake remain available in the cases that concern him, and hence he is also correct that freedoms$_{2-5}$ and unfreedoms$_{2-5}$ can be predicated of the actors in such cases. But he is mistaken in his view that evidence of the kinds he considers is sufficient to justify saying that those agents are unfree if we are thinking of unfreedoms$_{2-5}$.

In the light of these reflections, it appears that the versions of the positive theory of freedom I have examined combine, in an inappropriate manner, the two views that I suggested as ways of interpreting it. These theorists *are* working with an ideal of virtue or authenticity or integrity or good personal adjustment. They value and hope for persons whose actions are deliberately chosen to satisfy norms and principles that those persons correctly believe to be morally and otherwise worthy. And they are disposed to say that actions which do not meet these criteria are unfree. But they are unwilling to adopt in an unvarnished form the position that equates freedom and virtue or freedom and authenticity, unfreedom and vice or unfreedom and inauthenticity. Hence they seek plausibility for their uses of "freedom" and (especially) "unfreedom" by treating actions that are not morally or otherwise worthy as compelled by inner forces. I suggest that this move, although seeming to find support from certain ordinary modes of speech, misinterprets the locutions that appear to support it and leads to incoherence in the theory of freedom.

If we recur now to Feinberg's schema, it is evident that the foregoing remarks are primarily concerned with constraints of the internal, positive variety. Not only obsessions and compulsions but unevaluated desires, passions, habits, and so forth are treated by positive theorists as forces preventing the agent from acting as she should and as compelling untoward or inadmissible "actions." So understood, their discussions give an apparent plausibility to the argument that such persons are unfree.

The same passages to which I have been responding support the interpretation that the positive theory equates freedom with ideals of virtue and character. To see this, we need do no more than shift our focus to Feinberg's category of constraints that are internal but negative. In this perspective, those persons whom positive theorists regard as unfree (in ways that negative theories of freedom cannot accommodate) lack the qualities of character that are necessary conditions of proper action. Just as a person who is suffering from the negative external constraint of lack of money cannot buy a new car, so persons who lack

110 *Situating and disciplining freedom*

the qualities that positive theorists celebrate cannot act in a proper manner. By implicitly adopting Feinberg's notion of negative, internal constraints, they connect freedom with virtue without explicitly using an unvarnished version of the position that assimilates freedom and virtue.

My objection to the positive theory, then, is at three levels. In respect to psychotics, genuine compulsives, and the like, I allow that there is no action or agency and hence a kind of unfreedom. But this is unfreedom only if we are thinking of unfreedom$_1$. Questions about freedoms$_{2-5}$ do not arise about psychotics and compulsives. The second and third levels of my objection concern habitual actions and actions taken to satisfy evaluated passions, desires, and interests, objectives and purposes, evaluations that positive theorists disapprove and that the agent herself may regret in the qualified senses discussed above. I contend that such actions are the agent's own. The evaluations and choices that prompt them are authentic to the actor as she is and as she understands herself and should not be regarded, in Feinberg's language, as positive, internal constraints that compel movements or behaviors on the agent's "part." In the absence of external, positive impediments or constraints, these actions, however objectionable, are freely done, are done in freedom.

The third level of my objection can be put by stressing the respect in which the second objection is in effect conceded by positive theorists. When actions are called base as opposed to noble, cowardly as opposed to courageous, mean as opposed to generous, spiteful or vindictive as opposed to understanding, forgiving, or magnanimous, the actor is *criticized* and *blamed*. Such criticism abandons the view that the person in question was compelled by internal or any other forces. To save the notion that the actor is nevertheless unfree, a conceptual move is made that can be described in any one of three interrelated ways: in a vocabulary that equates freedom and virtue; by using "freedom" to refer to my kinds of freedom$_{4-5}$; as a readiness to treat the absence of virtue or good character as a negative, internal constraint that allows the agent to act but prevents her from acting in a noble, courageous, generous, understanding, forgiving, or magnanimous fashion.

Having separated this move from the positions criticized at my first two levels, how should we assess it? It will help to note again the difference between freedom$_4$ and freedom$_5$. Freedom$_4$ requires that the plan of action followed by the actor satisfy the criteria that purportedly inform the actions in question. This formulation does not specify *who* is to make the judgment whether the actions taken in fact satisfy those criteria. Most important, it does not specify whether (for purposes of assessing the freedom or unfreedom of the act and the actor) that judgment is to be made by the actor herself or by other parties. By contrast, freedom$_5$ clearly posits some species of interpersonally defensible judgment concerning the worthiness of the agent's objectives and hence excludes the possibility that the agent's own judgment, as such, could be conclusive.

In respect to freedom$_4$, the move that I am discussing takes plausibility from the fact that the agent who acts habitually says or shows that she partially regrets her action because it does not fully satisfy the criteria that she accepts and aims

The theory of freedom   111

to satisfy. Able aims to have cordial, harmonious relations with Baker and she partially regrets it when her actions produce tension and ill-feeling. Thus she criticizes herself for not having fully satisfied her own objectives. The language of freedom and unfreedom appears to obtain a foothold in this setting. Able does not want to disavow responsibility for the outcome, does not want to "cop out" or "pass the buck" to someone else. Yet something stands between her and her objectives. Because of this feature, it is not inconceivable that she would say of herself that she would be more free if that something were removed or brought under control.

I have argued, however, that if such talk is taken literally—whether by the agent herself or by other parties—it is incoherent. A person cannot at once, that is in respect to one and the same act or failure to act, claim that she was unfree and that she has *made* a mistake. Persons who talk themselves into such an incoherence in respect to their own conduct are either confused or, more likely, suffering from a more or less serious case of that mode of self-deception that existentialists call *mauvaise foi* (or perhaps it is deception of others and should be called, less esoterically, bad faith). Persons who interpret such talk on the part of others in this literal-minded way either misunderstand it (perhaps because they accept a certain theory of freedom) or are taken in by it.

The position of positive theorists is yet less plausible if we assign to other parties the judgment whether Able's actions serve Able's own objectives or meet her own criteria. Let us focus on cases in which Able is, on balance, satisfied with her actions but Charlotte and Dorothy, although raising no questions about Able's objectives, conclude that her actions in fact disserve those objectives and betray inadequate responsibility for self. For example, Able aspires to good relationships with her academic colleagues but frequently publishes sharply critical analyses of their scholarly work. Some at least of Able's colleagues resent this practice and are cool to her because of it. Charlotte and Dorothy attribute Able's conduct to jealousy and personal insecurity and urge Able to seek counseling so as to better understand and control her inclinations. They argue that following this course would enhance Able's freedom.

Able admits to a degree of jealousy of some of her colleagues and to insecurity about her own professional standing and achievements. She even allows that she would be happier if she were rid of these feelings. But she contends that the actions in question conform to the norms of academic life as she understands and accepts them and that she takes the actions for this reason. The resentment and cool relationships are the fault of her colleagues' failure to understand collegiality at its best.

Pressed by Charlotte and Dorothy, Able may be induced to claim that she is "free" to alter her practice out of deference to the feelings of colleagues. She may also contend that her colleagues are equally "free" to adopt her understanding of collegiality and thus to appreciate rather than to resent her practice. I suggest, however, that even such talk on Able's part would be an inappropriate concession to an unfortunate misconception held by Charlotte and Dorothy. The issue is not whether Able or her friends are free; that issue is already settled,

112 *Situating and disciplining freedom*

indeed tacitly acknowledged to have been settled. Rather, the issue is whether she or they are justified in their respective views concerning the norms that do and/or that should inform and govern academic life. The freedom of Able and her friends is a supposition of the disagreement between them concerning this normative issue. In attempting to transform the normative issue into a question about Able's freedom, Charlotte and Dorothy patronize—that is, insult—Able. If Able is a patient (or perhaps a charitable) as well as a clear-headed sort, she will explain this distinction to Charlotte and Dorothy. If they persist in their views despite her explanation, she will be presented with a choice between sympathizing with their incapacity and resenting their obnoxious conduct.

We can now set aside as irrelevant the differences between $freedom_4$ and $freedom_5$. Questions about the worthiness of Able's projects and objectives presuppose Able's freedom to choose and to pursue them. If she were unfree in these respects, the projects and objectives would not be *hers* and criticism of her would be misdirected. Given that she has chosen and pursued her projects and objectives, any number of issues can be raised about the merits of her choices and actions. To treat these as issues about freedom is to confuse the question whether Able is free with the quite different matter of the merits of Able's use of whatever freedom she has.

In sum, the concepts of freedom and unfreedom encompass my kinds of $freedom_{1-3}$. Persons or other creatures characterized by no more than $freedom_1$ are as yet neither free nor unfree by the criteria of $freedoms_{2-3}$, that is, by the criteria of the only kinds of freedom that can be thought of as moral and political in character. My supposed $freedoms_{4-5}$ and $unfreedoms_{4-5}$ are not kinds of freedom and unfreedom at all. They are made to appear as such (and positive theories are made to appear to be theories of freedom) by equating (confusing) freedom with abilities and virtues or unfreedom with the absence thereof (that is, with internal, negative constraints). All instances of $freedoms_{2-5}$ and $unfreedoms_{2-3}$ are situated as opposed to "brute," and most if not all such instances are situated in further respects that remain to be explored.

I conclude by explaining my earlier assertion that positive theories of freedom make the wrong kind of connection between freedom and virtue. Questions about virtue and vice, good and evil, right and wrong, are of course importantly related to freedom and unfreedom. To begin with, in our culture freedom is itself widely regarded as a good and various particular freedoms are regarded as especially valuable and important. If we simply accept the fact for now, for this reason the question whether an action is right or wrong, good or evil, virtuous or unvirtuous, often cannot be decided apart from, independently of, whether it is or will be done in freedom or in the exercise of a particular freedom. If Mr. Harding in Trollope's *Barchester Towers* had thought Eleanor's (supposed) willingness to marry Mr. Slope had been coerced or even manipulated, his readiness to accommodate himself to that arrangement would have diminished or disappeared. Although he despised the match itself, his belief that his daughter was acting in freedom was important in convincing him that he ought to accept it. If a despicable racist harangue is regarded as an exercise of freedom of speech, our

The theory of freedom   113

estimate of the importance of that freedom convinces many that the act should not only be allowed but protected. In short, the freedom or unfreedom of actions is itself sometimes a consideration in our moral and other evaluations of those actions. In addition, actions and proposed or attempted actions typically raise further moral or normative questions, questions about which our thinking may be influenced but is seldom settled by the fact that they are or would be done in freedom. Let us assume that Mr. Harding was right to respect his daughter's freedom and that we are right to protect the racist's speech. Let us further assume that Eleanor and the racist have a right to act as they see fit in these regards. It may nevertheless be that Eleanor would have been wrong to marry Slope and that the racist would be wrong to give her speech. The moral good that is freedom, even the good that is a freedom protected by an established right, coexists and often conflicts with other moral goods. If we tried to assess these actions without attending to the fact that freedom is involved (as Dr. Grantly was disposed to do and as opponents of racism sometimes do) our identification of the issues before us would be incomplete and prejudicial. But we might recognize and attach great significance to these features of the actions and yet conclude that other considerations, other values in question in the circumstances, should properly take precedence. For example, we might desist from any active attempt to prevent the actions and yet think less well of the agents for persisting in them.

As against theorists of Pure Negative Freedom, theorists of positive freedom are therefore correct in thinking that the theory of freedom is an integral part of the more general theory of morality. Questions about freedom are typically moral questions. But these theorists make the wrong kind of connection between freedom and other moral concepts. By making the question whether an action is done in freedom equivalent to the question whether it is virtuous, by equating freedom and virtue, they lose the independence of the concept and the value of freedom and they distort and simplify moral issues. On their construction, the moral good of freedom and of particular freedoms cannot conflict with the moral goods with which freedom is equated. If the racist is morally wrong to hold and to express her views, she is *therefore* unfree in doing so. As we have seen, on the "enslaved by desires" dimension of the positive theory, it follows that the racist cannot be criticized or blamed for the particulars of (what appears to be her thought and action but in reality is) her behaviors. At most we can criticize her for the train of failures of responsibility for self that have left her in the grip of such vile impulses. Setting this consequence aside, we now see that it is impossible for us to conceptualize the issue posed by her proposed speech as involving a conflict between (genuine) freedom and other moral values. Quite apart from anything we may or may not do, the racist is already unfree (or enjoying no better than an impoverished freedom); hence there can be no such conflict (or the conflict will be easily resolved against the impoverished freedom). Difficult and vitally important moral and political questions disappear.

Of course this or that theorist of positive freedom might well reach correct substantive conclusions about any number of moral issues. The theory of

114 *Situating and disciplining freedom*

positive freedom might be regarded as a theory of freedom in the powerfully moralized sense of a theory that tells us who *ought to be* free to do what. But equating "freedom" with "morally virtuous (or otherwise right or proper) action" conceals an important part of what is at issue in the judgments that the theory urges on us. We are conceptually blinded to the fact that the judgments propose limitations on freedom itself. Not knowing what is at issue, we are in no position to assess the merits of proposed resolutions of it. In the name of wedding freedom to reason and morality, the positive theory diminishes our ability to deal intelligently with moral issues involving freedom.

Notes

1 If we put Feinberg's suggestion in schematic form, we get something like the following:

Table 7.1 Freedom

	I *Constraints*		II *Opportunities*	
	C	D	E	F
	Negative	*Positive*	*Negative*	*Positive*
A Internal	lack of: knowledge skill will rationality etc.	psychoses neuroses compulsions cravings habits etc.	presence of items under IAC	presence of items under IAD
B External	lack of: money tools authority etc.	physical and other external impediments to action	presence of items under IBC	presence of items under IBD

Proponents of the negative theory such as Hobbes restrict "unfreedom" to persons and other creatures who are self-activated and whose circumstances put them in IBD; they restrict "freedom" to such persons and other creatures whose circumstances put them in IIBF. Later proponents of this type of theory, such as J. S. Mill and Isaiah Berlin (we might call them "welfare negative libertarians") also give attention to the constraints of IBC and to the opportunities opened up by IIBE. Proponents of the positive theory make IIAF as well as self-activation a condition of freedom and treat IAC as the chief source of unfreedom. They are also prepared to say that the constraints of IBD actually contribute to freedom if they help the agent overcome the limitations of IAC and IAD.

2 See Foucault 1973a, 1973b, 1973c, 1979a, 1979b, 1981; Laing 1969, 1972; Laing and Esterson 1970; Szasz 1968, 1970, 1974.

3 Perhaps even this is too strong. As Paul Brest has suggested to me, there might be an akratic good Samaritan, someone who cannot stop herself from doing good for others

The theory of freedom   115

at excessive cost to herself. A more moderate, confined, benevolence might be her preferred alternative. As I note in the continuation of the discussion above, however, this conceptualization would be untraditional.

4 Both purely habitual and akratic actions should be kept distinct from actions that are regarded as objectionable in kind but on balance justified or defensible in particular cases. To stay with the same example, it is easy to imagine an Able whose smoking is neither habitual nor akratic. She is well-informed about the consequences of smoking, has reflected carefully about this information, and deliberates about when to smoke and when not to. She knows that smoking has harmful effects on those who do it and on those exposed to the smoke of others. For these reasons she counsels others against smoking and she herself smokes only when alone. But she doesn't regret her smoking. She not only enjoys it but is convinced that stopping would have worse effects than continuing. On balance or all things considered, smoking is her preferred alternative. If there is regret at all, it will be over the fact that she has other characteristics—a tendency to nervousness, to gain weight, or whatever—that make smoking the least undesirable course of action for her. Many human choices and decisions, especially in moral life, have these characteristics.

References

Arendt, Hannah. 1977. *The Life of the Mind*. New York: Harcourt, Brace, and Jovanovich.

Elster, Jon. 1978. *Logic and Society*. New York: John Wiley.

Feinberg, Joel. 1980. *Rights, Justice, and the Bounds of Liberty*. Princeton: Princeton University Press.

Foucault, Michel. 1973a. *Birth of the Clinic*. New York: Pantheon.

Foucault, Michel. 1973b. *Madness and Civilization*. New York: Random House.

Foucault, Michel. 1973c. *The Order of Things*. New York: Random House.

Foucault, Michel. 1979a. *Discipline and Punish*. New York: Random House.

Foucault, Michel. 1979b. *Power, Truth, Strategy*. Atlantic Highlands: Humanities Press.

Foucault, Michel. 1981. *Power-Knowledge*. New York: Pantheon.

Laing, R. D. 1969. *The Divided Self*. New York: Pantheon.

Laing, R. D. 1972. *Self and Others*. New York: Penguin.

Laing, R. D., and Esterson, A. 1970. *Sanity, Madness, and the Family*. New York: Penguin.

Rorty, Amalie. 1975. "Akrasia and Conflict." *Inquiry* 23:193–212.

Szasz, Thomas. 1968. *Law, Liberty, and Psychiatry*. New York: Macmillan.

Szasz, Thomas. 1970. *Ideology and Insanity*. New York: Doubleday Anchor.

Szasz, Thomas. 1974. *The Myth of Mental Illness*. New York: Harper & Row.

8 Situating freedom (1987)

I

My chief purpose here is to elaborate, defend, and detail the implications of the thesis that freedom and unfreedom are situated.
...
For Rousseau the freedom of the state of nature might not be practicable or viable but it is of certainty conceptually and rationally non-moral. For this reason it is unworthy. If (contrary to fact) we had the option of returning to that condition, we should reject it in order to achieve the kind of freedom befitting our potential as human beings. By contrast, for Hobbes the freedom of the state of nature is worthy in conception—indeed is the only kind of freedom there is—but empirically or practically illusory. Hobbes was disposed neither to dismiss nor to demean self-engendered and unimpeded movement of the kind that Rousseau regarded as amounting to no better than an animalistic freedom. In Hobbes's view the difficulty is rather that self-moving and legally and morally unconstrained human agents so often collide and conflict that their freedom, though "morally" entire, is destructive of peace, of security, and hence of itself. Hobbes urges human beings to submit to the restrictions of organized social and (more especially) political life not so as to achieve more elevated or noble impulses and dispositions and hence a morally higher freedom but to reconcile freedom with peace and security and hence with itself. We exchange our unqualified but mutually destructive natural freedom for the bounded but vastly more secure and reliable "liberties of subjects."

Hobbes's argument for the rather thin situatedness he advocated is empirical and instrumental, not conceptual, mundane, and prudential, not moralizing. For all of its strident insistence, it is even made with a certain tinge of regret over the unfortunate fact that human beings and their world are such that the state of nature and its freedom are untenable. Situatedness is no more to be posited, stipulated, or assumed than it is to be celebrated as a good in its own right. It is to be understood and coolly accepted as a necessary means to ends and purposes given prior to it. It is by no means a condition necessary to our concept of freedom. On the contrary, our recognition that situatedness is necessary to the practical realization of freedom shows (to Hobbes's satisfaction) that the latter concept is logically prior to and independent of the former. We know what freedom is and why we want it and we situate ourselves in political society in order (among other things) to get it. Thus Hobbes would regard the position taken here as logically and conceptually mistaken and as confusing an end pursued with a means of pursuing it. Because in his judgment the means are indispensable to the end, and because Hobbes in fact confronted arguments that we should be forced to be righteous or good, not forced to be free, we do not find him objecting to the moral, political, or other normative implications of these mistakes. But materials out of which to form such an objection are available in his argument and it is tempting to permit ourselves the anachronism of imagining his fervent response to Rousseau and Kant and especially to Hegel and later Hegelian proponents of the positive theory of freedom. Because I have endorsed important aspects of his thinking about freedom, it is imperative that I show that he and other proponents of the negative theory are mistaken concerning the conceptual points just discussed (and that this mistake can be remedied without giving up the essentials of the negative theory).

We can begin by returning to the distinction between freedom$_1$ and unfreedom$_1$ and my claim that Rousseau would regard (if he employed the terminology) the freedom possible in his state of nature as freedom$_1$. This distinction (the distinction, not merely the terminology) has no clear or secure place in Hobbes's official conceptualization. He refuses to differentiate between the freedom of action and the freedom of movement.[1]

Hobbes's theory nevertheless provides compelling evidence for the importance of this distinction. Why *should* human beings accept the authority of political society? How can Hobbes himself conceive of and develop arguments for this imperative? What is he assuming about his fellow human beings when he addresses imperatives and arguments (these or any other) to them? The entire exercise takes its sense from an implicit distinction between purposeful, deliberately chosen actions that are defensible by some standard and mere movements which cannot be avoided and which "arise not for deliberation." In slightly different terms, the whole idea that the "liberties of subjects" are *preferable* to the freedom of the state of nature presupposes agents who make and act upon these distinctions. It presupposes the distinction between freedom$_1$ and freedom$_2$, and agents who make that distinction and apply it to themselves and to others.

The next step in my response to Hobbes was taken by Rousseau when he objected that Hobbes illicitly attributed social characteristics to creatures who he (Hobbes) claimed were in an entirely pre- or non-social situation or circumstance. Having conceptions of any sort becomes possible only after a series of accidents has brought numbers of human beings, who in their natural state scarcely recognize one another as of a distinct kind, into more or less steady and patterned contact with one another.[2] The advent of social relationships leads (in a manner that Rousseau regards as unabatedly mysterious) to the development of language and hence of the ability to make, to remember, and to communicate various distinctions.

On this view, situatedness in the sense of an at least minimal sociality is a necessary condition of the formation of anything that could be regarded as a

118 *Situating and disciplining freedom*

conception. It *seems* also to be an implication of the view that situatedness in this sense is a sufficient condition of those conceptions I found implicit in Hobbes's theory of freedom. In yet more forceful terms, it appears to be a necessary truth that situatedness and the conceptualizations it yields includes the distinctions between action and movement and between freedom$_1$ and freedom$_2$.

Rousseau's discussions of these points might be called mock-empirical or mock-historical in character. Cast in the "state of nature" idiom, they present themselves as an account of two states of affairs and of the transition from the one to the other. In fact, of course, Rousseau knew that he had no empirical evidence about the state of nature or the "earliest" states of sociality. He says we should "begin ... by laying facts aside" and enter instead into "conditional and hypothetical reasonings, rather calculated to explain the nature of things, than to ascertain their actual origin" (1950: 198).[3] In later jargons, his discussions might be called a priori, conceptual rather than empirical, an exercise in descriptive metaphysics, or the like. If we set aside the distracting talk about the state of nature, and particularly if we also follow Rousseau's lead in making the focus of our attention the fact that human beings are language-using creatures, we can put Rousseau's suggestive and—in my view—essentially correct understanding of situatedness and its significance on better foundations and into a less confused form.

...

II

...

Proponents of the main competing conceptions of freedom have tended to favor sharply different modes or species of sociality. We have already encountered the strong association between "deeper," more communitarian conceptions of society and the positive theory of freedom. Proponents of the negative theory, by contrast, have promoted individualistic, *Gesellschaft-type* understandings and arrangements. If Rousseau, Bradley, and Charles Taylor are clear examples of the former tendency, Hobbes is once again the leading example of the latter. Although favoring political absolutism in the sense of a government with unlimited authority to act as the Sovereign judges necessary, Hobbes was a thoroughgoing individualist who opposed limitations on conduct save those necessary to maintain peace and security. The picture is more complicated in respect to later theorists of negative liberty such as Bentham and Constant, Mill and Berlin, but it would undoubtedly be a distortion to portray any of these writers as enthusiasts for mechanical solidarity or anything approaching a *Gemeinschaft*.

As a matter of empirically grounded social theory, and particularly theory that issues in moral and political recommendations and prescriptions, I am inclined to think that there is good reason for the latter sympathies and tendencies of thought. Certain cultural, social, and political forms, especially those that are regarded as deeply situating human conduct, while not themselves excluding individual freedom, are inhospitable or unconducive to a number of freedoms that should be highly valued. But there is nothing direct, certainly nothing necessary, about these connections. There is nothing contradictory or incoherent about combining a negative theory of freedom with a preference for deeply situating, strongly communitarian arrangements. This would be true even if the association between communitarian-type societies and limitations on individual freedom were much closer and more direct than it is. Commitment to the negative theory of freedom entails nothing about the value of freedom by comparison with other values. A proponent of that theory might allow that communitarian arrangements systematically subordinate freedom to equality or fraternity or social justice and yet favor such arrangements. Such a person need only insist that arrangements which serve these other values do not *therefore* also serve freedom. (Bentham is a clear case of a theorist who insists on a negative conception of freedom but who ranks other goods—especially security of person and property—much more highly than freedom. Indeed Bentham is a clear case of a theorist who employs a negative concept of freedom as part of an antifreedom argument.) Again a theorist of negative freedom who valued freedom highly might favor communitarian arrangements on the ground that they diminish obstacles to action and hence maximize, at least by comparison with actually available alternatives, freedom itself. Finally, a proponent of the positive conception of freedom might argue for an individualistic, even an anomic society, on the ground that the genuinely worthy beliefs, values, and patterns of conduct necessary to true freedom develop only, or best develop, where authoritative cultural norms and social and political institutions are at a minimum.

To sum up this last stretch of discussion, the claim that situatedness is a postulate necessary to theorizing about freedom implies nothing as to how moral and political questions about freedom can or should be answered. This conclusion is reinforced by the more detailed and sophisticated account of situatedness to which I now turn.

III

"'I set the brake up by connecting up rod and lever.'—Yes, given the whole rest of the mechanism, and separated from its support it is not even a lever; it may be anything, or nothing" (Wittgenstein 1953: I, 6; hereafter cited as *PI*). This passage can be taken as a synecdoche for much of Wittgenstein's argument in the *Investigations*. Apart from the "mechanism" that consists of such Wittgensteinian elements as language-games, agreements in judgment, established conventions and rules and techniques for interpreting and applying them, shared or widely accepted propositions, characteristic patterns of thought and action, and the like—apart, that is, from life in something like a society—our experience of ourselves, of one another, and of the world we inhabit could be "anything or nothing." Life situated in such a "mechanism" is a condition of life that has meaning for those who live it.

The significance of Wittgenstein's contentions for our purposes can be appreciated by considering some of the views against which they—as distinct from

120   *Situating and disciplining freedom*

Rousseau's analogous views—were a reaction. Throughout the *Investigations* Wittgenstein is arguing against theories which claim that meaning and meaningfulness are dependent on social situation only in unessential or even superficial respects. Most of these theories tacitly concede that there is some sense in which, in Wittgenstein's words, "meaning is in language." Their task, accordingly, appears to be the same as Wittgenstein's, namely, to explain how this can be, how seemingly arbitrary sounds and signs—that vary widely from time to time and place to place—can bear meaning. But this appearance is deceptive. If we construe "language" broadly, the proposition that meaning is *in* language can serve as a kind of abbreviation of Wittgenstein's theory. In the theories he mainly attacks, by contrast, language is no more than a vehicle or medium by or through which meaning may be recorded and communicated. Meaning is not *in* language in the strong sense that without language there would be no meaning. Meaning is *in* something antecedent to or independent of language. We grasp, apprehend, or otherwise acquire meanings apart from language and then we contrive signs and sounds that we make to stand for those meanings. At least logically and in all likelihood temporally, there is first meaning and only later language. Language is derivative of, secondary and even epiphenomenal to, meaning. Thus the fact that natural languages in the sense of Greek or English or Chinese are social phenomena, in that they are shared among those who speak them, does not show that meaning or meaningfulness is essentially social in character.

In the discussion immediately surrounding the brake-rod-lever passage Wittgenstein is attacking versions of such theories according to which meaning resides in extralinguistic entities that are initially (again in a logical and in the first instances a temporal sense) perceived and identified apart from language. The word "lever" *means* a particular object (or class of objects) of experience. If I use the word "lever" meaningfully I am aware of that object and I employ the word to refer to or to stand for it. Of course the particular combination of sounds or signs that make up "lever" acquires meaning only when I or someone else uses it to stand for the object. But the choice of "lever" is perfectly arbitrary; any mark or sound would do as well. More important, meaning or meaningfulness is not dependent on language. The meaning or meaningfulness resides in, is constituted by, the object itself. We might even say that the "I," the experiencing subject or agent, is unessential. True, if neither I nor anyone else had experienced the object there would be no one for whom it was meaningful and no one who would have occasion to adopt a word to stand for it. But the object, which *is* the meaning, would or could just as well nevertheless exist. It is obviously a condition of meaningful experience that there be human beings who have such experiences; it is a condition of meaningful human language that there be human beings who have experiences and who mark them by language. But given these conditions, the meaning of the experiences and the language used to mark it is constituted by the objects experienced and marked. The locus, the substance or essence, of meaning is not in language and it is certainly not in the community of human beings who share language. Rather, it is in the extralinguistic world.

Situating freedom   121

Human beings (and presumably various nonhuman creatures as well) have the good fortune of inhabiting a world replete with distinct, distinguishable, and hence meaningful entities. They also have the good fortune of being able to discern and distinguish those entities. They do not create meaning by contriving language, they invest such language as they choose to contrive with meanings that they appropriate, ready-made as it were, from the non-or extra-linguistic world. If God or nature had been mechanically inclined, there might have been brakes, rods, and levers. If so, human beings (and perhaps other creatures) would be capable of experiencing them as such, that is, as distinct, recognizable objects or entities. If a human being (or another creature capable of making and remembering what Locke called "articulate sounds") did so, and if for some reason she decided to mark that experience with the sounds or signs "brake," "rod," and "lever," those markers would acquire the meaning they now in fact have.

On some versions of this object-word or name-thing theory of language it is alleged that there is no special difficulty about interpersonal communication. Language took its beginnings from single-handed linguistic creations. Individual persons assigned names of their own contrivance to objects that they personally experienced. And each of us can create new words in this same manner. But once I have created a word I can teach it to others. I simply call their attention to the object and indicate that I use a particular word to stand for it. They understand what my word means and hence are in a position—if they so choose—to use the word in the same way that I do. This process of "ostensive teaching" (As Wittgenstein calls it [*PI*, I, 6]) can be repeated for an indefinitely large number of words, among an indefinitely large number of persons, and over any number of generations. Through it, words that began as personal and idiosyncratic become public and common. With the passage of generations a great many of the objects that make up the world that human beings inhabit are named and later generations learn and accept much of the vocabulary invented by their predecessors. This vocabulary becomes sufficiently extensive and customary to constitute not merely language (as opposed to a collection of meaningless sounds and marks) but *a* language in the sense of French or German and *the* language of entire peoples.

Of course Wittgenstein agrees that languages are public. Nor does he deny that many of the particulars of French, German, etc., their orthographies, vocabularies, distinctive verb structures, and so forth, developed and achieved customary status through historical processes that could have eventuated differently and that may, in their continuation, yield large-scale changes in many of the characteristics of these languages. Indeed his account, not being founded on the notion that words name objects the characteristics of which are known apart from language, is much more open to variability and change in language than are the accounts against which he is arguing. What he denies is that language *could* be individual or personal in the sense I have been discussing and could have become public by a historical and hence contingent process. Language is necessarily, essentially, public.

The basic elements of Wittgenstein's argument for the necessarily public character of language are present in his objections to the object-word theory that

122 *Situating and disciplining freedom*

I have been discussing. But we can better appreciate his argument if we follow him in considering a variation on the object-word account that directly and explicitly challenges the view that some language, however it began, has become genuinely public. The variant in question (of which there are a number of versions) follows the object-word or thing-name account in holding that the meaning of a word is given by some extralinguistic entity for which the word stands or to which it refers. Its challenge to the shared, public character of language resides in its denial that one person can know the referents of another person's words. On some versions of the theory this difficulty presents itself in respect to "things" such as emotions and sensations that occur within the agent who experiences them and hence are not directly accessible to others. For example, I use the word "headache" to refer to pain that I am suffering. You cannot feel *my* headache. Hence you cannot know to what my word "headache" refers. In fact you too may have headaches and you too may use the word "headache" to refer to them. (God might know that this is the case.) But you cannot *know* that my word "headache" refers to the same kind of pain as does your word (and the reverse). We may suppose that we have this knowledge and we may act successfully on this supposition. But because the phenomenon to which my word refers is inaccessible to you (and the reverse), and because the meaning of words *is* their referent, you cannot know the meaning of my word (and I cannot know the meaning of your word). Language, or at least those parts of language that refer to states or events internal to the person who uses it (whose language it is), is necessarily private.

It is easy to see how the theory that these aspects of language are private can be extended to all of language. A premise sufficient to effect such an extension is that words which seem to refer to objects that are mutually accessible (stones, trees, etc.) in fact refer to images, percepts, sense data, or some other phenomena that are internal in the same way as sensations and emotions. If my word "tree" refers to an image or a sense datum in my mind, you can once again do no more than make suppositions about its meaning. On this view language ends as well as begins in experience that is not only personal but private. The idea that we do, or that we might some day come to, share a language (and all that depends upon it) is simply an illusion.

These theories of language and meaning have an obvious and an obviously important bearing on our present concerns. They support an understanding of action as meaningful (as a something rather than an anything or a nothing) despite not being situated in any sense beyond being located in a field of experience that is intelligible to the agent whose action is in question. If the word-object theory in the first form discussed is correct, an actor could identify herself and could discriminate among her various actions on the basis of nothing more than self-observation. If she entered into interactions with other persons she might observe herself taking actions that she could not take if she were isolated from others. And if those others had come to share her language through the process of mutual ostensive teaching, these actions and interactions might have the added dimension that is mutual meaningfulness. In these ways social dimensions would become a part of her understanding of herself and her actions. But these social dimensions would not be a necessary part of her self-understanding as an actor taking actions; they would be a necessary part of the meaning of only those of her actions that in fact involved her in interactions with other persons, and meaningfulness would be mutual only insofar as language had in fact come to be shared between or among them. If "necessarily private" versions of the word-object theory are correct, social dimensions in the sense of mutually meaningful action could enter into self-understandings either not at all or only in respect to those parts of language that refer to "external" phenomena.

Thus if these accounts of language and its meaning were correct they would support deeply atomistic understandings of action. They would support Hobbes's understanding of action in the state of nature (not surprising since Hobbes offers us an early version of the object-word theory of language). They would also support Humean and emotivist theories of that subclass of actions taken (according to these theories) as a direct, an unmediated, result of brute passions and desires. If the actor experiences a distinct and recognizable passion or desire, and if that passion or desire produces a distinct and recognizable action on the part of the actor, the conditions of meaningfulness have been satisfied. In identifying (naming) the desire and the action, the actor may employ language that (on the not-necessarily-private version of the object-name theory) she shares with others—even that she has learned from others; but for the purpose of accounting for the meaningfulness of her experiences this feature is nonessential. Thus whether it is impossible for others cogently to object to the action (as emotivists hold), or whether such objections are possible (as Taylor and MacIntyre contend), there is no difficulty about saying that such occurrences fall not only into the category "action" but into more differentiated categories that identify actions of particular kinds. Meaningful action that is radically unsituated, whether rare or commonplace, whether welcome, deplorable, or indifferent, is a conceptual possibility. Quite clearly, then, the adequacy of these theories is a matter of some moment.

Wittgenstein attacks these theories of language and meaning from a number of directions, his several lines of argument converging to show that they and everything that depends upon and follows from them is untenable. In the discussion leading to the brake-rod-lever passage he writes as if a major assumption of the object-word account is justified. The assumption is that an individual can create language that is meaningful to herself by inventing words and using them to stand for objects she has experienced. His initial attack is on the further and (apparently) more problematic proposition that she can make such language meaningful to others by ostensive teaching. He assumes that B (who is to learn the meaning of one or more of A's words) does not yet know any of A's language and hence that A cannot use words in teaching. A turns instead to a procedure very much like that which she herself followed in inventing the word for herself. Her attention had focused on a distinct object and she had invented a name to stand for it. To teach B the word, she uses gestures such as pointing to call B's attention to the object while pronouncing the word. The idea is to get B

124   *Situating and disciplining freedom*

to make the same association between object and word that B herself makes, thereby learning the meaning of the word.

It is worth emphasizing immediately that nonverbal actions are thus assigned a vital role in the theory. The theory is not an object-word theory but an object-action-word theory. There is an important respect in which Wittgenstein has no objection to this modification of what appeared to be the theory. He himself puts acting "at the bottom" of language (Wittgenstein 1969: 204; hereafter cited as *OC*). On the assumptions of the theory he is criticizing, however, appeal to actions such as pointing and demonstrating is illicit and shows the theory to be untenable. The theory itself provides no reason for thinking that the meaning of such nonverbal communicative devices will be any clearer than the meaning of the words they are supposed to teach. If A points or otherwise calls B's attention to an object that she (A) has singled out and to which she has given the name "stone," B might take her gestures to single out not the "entire" object that A has in mind but some feature of it such as its color, shape, location, hardness, and so forth. Or B might think that A is pointing past or through the stone to something beyond or beneath it. B might even take what A intends as pointing to be some altogether different signal, for example a warning or a supplication. Just as with words themselves, in the absence of an understood "mechanism" in which they have an established place and use, ostensive communications "can be variously interpreted in every case." For the object-word theory, our successful use of these modes of communication (which of course Wittgenstein himself does not for a moment deny) is as much in need of explanation as our successful use of words.

There are numerous additional difficulties with object-word theories taken as an account of anything like the languages that we in fact employ. They are implausible in the extreme concerning so-called logical words such as "and," "or," "if," and "then," concerning negatives, privatives, and demonstratives; in their most philosophically influential versions they depend on a notion of "simple" or "atomic" entities that cannot be cogently explained, much less defended. But let us leave these points aside and consider instead Wittgenstein's argument that the objection to ostensive teaching applies just as decisively against the assumption that A herself can create language for her private use by picking out objects and assigning names to them. In considering this argument we confront the deepest and most uncompromising sense in which, according to Wittgenstein, all meaning is situated.

As noted, in passages discussed thus far Wittgenstein allows, *arguendo*, the assumption that A herself knows the referent, and hence the meaning of the words she invents for her own use. But how does she know this? We are tempted to say "Of course she knows. She herself identified the object and assigned the word to it." The very fact that the process of assigning the word is purely arbitrary seems to exclude the possibility that anything could go wrong with it, that any sort of mistake could be made in carrying it out.

As Anthony Kenny points out, Wittgenstein has frequently been interpreted as allowing the (initial) assignment or definition but raising the question whether

A will later remember the definition correctly (Kenny 1973). On this view, A can successfully create language for herself but there is reason to doubt that she can successfully use it into the future. Having nothing to test her memory against, the objection goes, there is no way for her to be sure that her later uses of her words will stand for the same objects as those to which she initially assigned them. Thus for all she knows (can know), her entire "language" alters continuously as she uses it.

Kenny seems to me to be correct, however, in arguing that the difficulty Wittgenstein sees with the "necessarily private" version of the object-action-word account of meaning is deeper, or earlier, than this. Wittgenstein says:

> I speak, and write the sign down, and at the same time I concentrate my attention on the sensation—and so, as it were point to it inwardly.—But what is this ceremony for? For that is all it seems to be! A definition surely serves to establish the meaning of a sign.... But "I impress it on myself" can only mean: this process brings it about that I remember the connexion *right* in the future. [Emphasis in the original. Note that "right" is emphasized, not "remember."] But in the present case I have no criterion of correctness. One would like to say: whatever is going to seem right to me is right. And that only means that here we can't talk about "right."
>
> (*PI*, I, 258)[4]

The deeper problem, then, is not with memory. It is that there is no criterion of "correct" or "right" and hence nothing to remember correctly or incorrectly. Or as Kenny formulates the point, the measure or criterion of correctness and that which it measures or tests are one and the same (1973: 191–195). This is why whatever seems correct is correct; it is also why claiming that the word has been used correctly is like claiming that one copy of the morning newspaper has substantiated reports in another copy of the same paper (*PI*, I, 265), why I cannot show that I know how tall I am by putting my hand on the top of my head (*PI*, I, 279), and why my left hand can't give money to my right hand. "[J]ustification consists in appealing to something independent" (*PI*, I, 265), and the account in question does itself out of that possibility.

These arguments show that many views and much controversy concerning human freedom are untenable and confused because concerned with an impossibility. Hobbes imagined human beings who inhabit a meaningful world and live lives meaningful to themselves despite being so radically unsituated, so atomized and privatized, that one person's thoughts and actions have no meaning to or for any other person. Hume and Ayer, Taylor and MacIntyre, think they have identified human beings at least a part of whose experience—that part which involves sensations, emotions, and desires and hence much if not all of morals and politics—is unsituated in this radical sense. Hobbes seems to have found this notion attractive and to have wanted to maintain at least a measure of privacy of this radical sort. Rousseau was apparently ambivalent about it and the freedom he took it to involve but he concluded that it could be eliminated and that it would be better for humankind if such privatism were overcome and a deeply situated and more "positive" freedom achieved. Hume and Ayer thought such privatism inescapable and busied themselves with dispelling the illusion that there is an alternative to it. Taylor and MacIntyre, while thinking such a privatism all too real and all too prevalent, regard it as a lamentable consequence of specific and alterable historical and cultural developments that must be reversed if significant human freedom is to be regained. In short, controversy swirls about the alterability and the desirability of "something" that Wittgenstein shows to be an impossibility. If human thought and action—and hence human freedom and unfreedom—are meaningful (if they are *thought, action, freedom, unfreedom* as opposed to anything or nothing) they are not and cannot be private or unsituated in the deep sense these writers have in mind. If there is a something in human experience that corresponds to what these writers are trying to discuss—think they are discussing—when they inveigh for or against atomism, privatism, subjectivism, and unsituatedness, that something is outside of the realm of the meaningful and there can be no discussion concerning it.

IV

Does Wittgenstein advance positive or constructive generalizations parallel to those that make up the refuted object-word theory? Can the claim that meaning and language are situated in "mechanisms" and "practices" be elaborated in more specific, less metaphorical terms? If so, does the appropriate elaboration show that human actions are so impeded or constrained by the factors that actuate them that we should say they are unfree?

The answer to the first of these questions is primarily negative. Wittgenstein has no comparably systematic or comprehensive theory of language and meaning to put in place of the object-word account that he refutes. Unlike the proponents of that and analogous general theories, he thinks that the project of identifying the essential characteristics of language and meaning and providing an explanation for them is misbegotten. On the one hand, the languages we know display a "prodigious diversity" (*PI*, II, xi, 224) of characteristics and the idea of reducing these to an essence is a misunderstanding. On the other hand, we have no need, no use, for general "explanations" of language and meaning. The meaning of our language is in its use and our use is not only "in order as it is," "but open to view." Philosophical attempts to generalize and explain distort and confuse rather than clarify or illuminate. What is needed is not generalizations and explanations but descriptions of the specifics of our practice (*PI*, I, 109), descriptions that remind us of what we already know and thereby dispel the mists of misunderstanding rising from the misconceptions of philosophers. We can show that language does *not* have certain characteristics that have been attributed to it and offered as explanations for its meaning. As a part of showing this, certain positive generalizations emerge—such as that meaning is in language, that it is in "mechanisms" and "practices," that it is in the uses to which language is put. But these generalizations are crude and uninformative; they are of value primarily as antidotes to the equally crude but mistaken generalizations advanced by other philosophers.

Accordingly, Wittgenstein characterizes the results of his investigations as making up no more than an "album" consisting of "sketches" of our actual practices. But these brilliantly executed sketches can be read as elaborating somewhat on the extremely general propositions about mechanisms and practices and hence as giving an answer of sorts to my second question. To combine and follow out two of Wittgenstein's own figures, someone who peruses an album of family photographs is likely to come away with certain general impressions concerning that family. To peruse Wittgenstein's sketches of the family that is language and meaning is to learn that those whose activities make up the mechanisms and practices in which language and meaning are situated characteristically agree in many judgments, know about, accept, and generally follow a variety of rules, customs, and conventions, have been exposed to and have more or less assimilated certain kinds of training, and have mastered certain techniques of following rules and commands, of acting on advice and suggestion. This perusal, moreover, reminds us that there are certain very general facts of nature, facts to which attention is seldom given by participants in such practices, which must be more or less as they are if the mechanisms and practices are to remain more or less what they have become. We are also reminded that these circumstances do not always obtain; that human beings sometimes find one another and one another's activities alien, opaque, and incomprehensible.

I return to these notions—agreements, rules, training, and so forth—below. But we can see at once that none of them are at all technical. They recur in Wittgenstein's sketches because they are prominent in the activities and arrangements he is sketching. If they were not familiar, ordinary, and even homely notions they would not serve as "reminders" of what we already know and would not help to dispel the confusions created by philosophers. Arriving at and acting upon agreements, adopting and following rules, giving and receiving training and instruction, these are among our most familiar experiences. By invoking them in the course of his philosophical discussions, Wittgenstein gives a certain substantiality, a certain definiteness, to more abstract notions such as "mechanisms," "practices," and "language-games" and to the yet more general idea that meaning and meaningfulness are "situated" in character. At bottom, the situatedness of human affairs consists in such facts as that there are agreements and conventions, rules and directives, that people who share these thereby "know how to go on" in and with various activities, and so forth. As we might put it, when elaborated in these familiar terms the idea that meaning and meaningfulness are situated itself becomes a something, not an anything or a nothing.

What of the third question raised above? What bearing does this elaboration have on questions about human freedom and unfreedom? Of course it has the bearing already anticipated in my earlier discussions. Questions about freedom and unfreedom arise—as all questions do—only within the realm of the meaningful. We now see that this means that such questions arise only where human beings agree on certain judgments, only where some conventions and rules have

128   *Situating and disciplining freedom*

gotten established and are generally respected, and so forth. And it might be thought that this shows that Wittgenstein's views, if correct, do much more than identify the conditions that must be satisfied if questions about freedom are to arise and be discussed in a meaningful fashion. It might be thought that his views settle major questions about freedom. Notions like facts of nature, technique and training, custom and rule—even the notion of agreement in the Wittgensteinian sense of something about which a consensus exists despite not having been self-consciously and self-critically reached or adopted—these notions can easily be made to suggest limitation and constraint, restriction and obstacle. If the situatedness necessary to meaningfulness entails these elements, it might yet appear that human beings acquire the meaningfulness of their lives at the cost of their freedom.

The questions that present themselves in this regard concern such notions as obstacles and impediments, constraints, interferences, and restrictions. Are we to say that the features or conditions that Wittgenstein associates with meaningfulness are obstacles or interferences that render us unfree? At this stage my discussion will focus on the feature, namely, rules and rule-following, in respect to which an affirmative answer has at least initial plausibility. But I preface this discussion with some preliminary observations.

First, it is not to be thought that Wittgenstein himself has *any* questions about freedom—let alone the question whether the conditions of meaningfulness exclude or limit freedom—in mind. We can bring considerations from Wittgenstein's philosophy to bear on questions about freedom, but we cannot explicate "Wittgenstein's theory of freedom." Second, from a Wittgensteinian perspective the question I propose to address has more than a faint air of absurdity about it. Most generally, if there are meaningful questions about freedom and unfreedom, they quite obviously must arise under or within the conditions of meaningfulness. If the conditions of meaningfulness themselves categorically excluded freedom, there would seem to be no use for the concept "freedom" in meaningful discourse. This consideration suggests that my question will have sense, if at all, only if it is asked in much narrower terms, much more concretely. Did these rules, in this set of circumstances, interfere with or constrain these attempted actions to an extent that justifies us in saying that some person was made unfree? It is a delusion to think that there is a general analysis of the concepts "rule," "restraint," "freedom," and "unfreedom" which would allow us to conclude that rules as such exclude or impede, create or facilitate freedom or unfreedom.

But what is absurd in practice may seem plausible to the theorist. As we have seen, political theory is no stranger to the idea that society itself excludes or severely limits freedom. This notion is at work in various ways in state-of-nature and social-contract theories and something like it is not far beneath the surface in romantic individualisms and other theories that treat freedom as—in Charles Taylor's phrase—radical self-dependence. More pejoratively, the idea, though rejected, is taken seriously indeed in attacks on freedom as "license" or as "doing as one lists." Finally, what might be regarded as its opposite is frequently encountered in slogans such as "liberty is life under the rule of law."

Situating freedom 129

We should also note that Wittgenstein himself gives many pages to refuting understandings of rules and rule-following according to which a sufficiently detailed and integrated set of rules would "determine everything in advance," would settle every question that could possibly arise in the activity governed by those rules. Wittgenstein's concern in these passages is not to defend the possibility of freedom. Philosophers have tried to find in strictly drawn rules the source, indeed the necessity and hence the guarantee, of a kind of certitude of meaning and of truth without which meaningfulness and knowledge seem to them to be in jeopardy. Wittgenstein thinks that as a practical matter we are sometimes certain about meaning (and about truth, validity, and many other things), sometimes much less than certain. He agrees that rules and rule-following are prominent in meaningful speech and action and he allows that some (but not all) of the areas of greatest practical certainty—such as doing logic and arithmetic and playing certain games—are characterized by quite closely drawn rules. But neither these nor any of our other activities or practices achieve or permit the kind of metaphysical or guaranteed certainty imagined by philosophers. This ideal of a certainty that derives from rules that form a "strict calculus" is not a result of investigations in logic, mathematics, or any other subject matter, it is a requirement imposed in advance on such investigations. Wittgenstein rejects it not because achieving it would threaten freedom but for the same reason that he rejects the object-word account of language, namely, that it prevents us from seeing our practice as it actually is.

The details of Wittgenstein's discussions of rules and rule-following are nevertheless pertinent to the questions now before us. Some rules do require and forbid, direct and deflect. If we do not understand that rules can be substantial impediments and inducements to action we have not grasped the notion of a rule. Moreover, "rules," "rule-governed conduct," "rule-following," and the like bulk very large in Wittgenstein's writings. There are a number of passages in which he makes rules necessary to meaning and hence to meaningful thought and action. Of "not," its negative force and such facts as that a double negative yields an affirmative, he observes that

> There cannot be a question whether these or other rules are the correct ones for the use of "not." (I mean, whether they accord with its meaning.) For without these rules the word has as yet no meaning; and if we change the rules, it now has another meaning (or none), and in that case we may just as well change the word too.
>   (*PI*, I, remark appended to paras. 548–551; cf. *PI*, I, 558, and *OC*, 62)

At least in respect to the concepts under discussion in these passages, rules emerge as essential features of the "mechanisms" in which there can be a something as opposed to an anything or a nothing. Much more generally, Wittgenstein contends that all language "is founded on convention."[5] If we interpret "convention" to include prescriptive or normative rules, as opposed to regularities discerned by observers, this remark greatly extends the significance of the passages already cited.

130 *Situating and disciplining freedom*

We must also consider remarks that are yet more encompassing because they employ the concepts "normal" and "abnormal" as well as "rule" and "convention." "It is only in normal cases that the use of a word is clearly prescribed; we know, are in no doubt, what to say in this or that case. The more abnormal the case, the more doubtful it becomes what we are to say" (*PI*, I, 142). "Clearly prescribed," "we know," "are in no doubt," go together with numerous passages in which Wittgenstein writes as if prescriptive rules virtually settle what is thought, said, or otherwise done. For example, of someone who has learned how to pronounce the Cyrillic alphabet "we shall very likely say that he *derives* the sound of the word from the written pattern by the rule that we have given him" (*PI*, I, 162). Similarly, persons teaching algebra are likely to say to their pupils: "But surely you can see...," which "is just the characteristic expression of someone who is under the compulsion of a rule" (*PI*, I, 240, 238). Again: "Disputes do not break out (among mathematicians, say) over the question whether a rule has been obeyed or not." And: having mastered the colour concepts "it is a matter of course for me to call this colour 'blue'" (*PI*, I, 240, 238). But these certitudes, these matter-of-course derivations and applications, these compulsions, are hostage to "normalities" which, while no doubt defined or delineated by prescriptive rules and perhaps partly created and maintained by allegiance to such rules, could be otherwise. Prescriptive rules and rule-following are interwoven with and vitally dependent upon "mere" regularities. Where rules in the latter sense do not exist, prescriptive rules and rule-following lose their certainty and finally their sense. "And if things were quite different from what they actually are...; if rule became exception and exception rule; or if both became phenomena of roughly equal frequency—this would make our normal language-games lose their point" (*PI*, I, 142; II, xi, 226).

If we translate these discussions into the language of freedom and unfreedom we might well infer that our freedom is the price we pay for the meaningfulness of our lives. We are under the compulsion of rules and those rules are, in turn, hostage to a nature that we did not choose and that we can alter little if at all. But are these the appropriate inferences? To pursue this question let us consider more closely the "things" that must be more or less as they are. Wittgenstein's immediate example is homely in the extreme: "if it frequently happened" that for no obvious reason lumps of cheese grew or shrank, "the procedure of putting ... [them] on a balance and fixing the price by the turn of the scale would lose its point" (*PI*, I, 142; II, xi, 226). In this same connection he observes that "What we have to mention in order to explain the significance ... of a concept, are often extremely general facts of nature: such facts as are hardly ever mentioned because of their great generality" (*PI*, I, remark appended near paras. 142–143; cf. *OC*, 135, 338, 617). A certain constancy in the natural world is a background condition of rules and rule-governed activities and practices. But it would be wrong to think that these conditions themselves determine the content of the prescriptive rules—that they supply what moralists have called a Natural Law or a Natural Right that governs human affairs at least in the sense that in time a price will be exacted if the Law or Right is not heeded. Rather, they partly constitute

Situating freedom 131

the circumstances under which normative rules and rule-following—whatever their content—are *a possibility* for human beings.

This understanding is affirmed and deepened if we note that some of the general facts of nature that are in particular need of "mention" are facts about human beings themselves. All of Wittgenstein's examples of such "human" facts are mundane, but we may begin with an instance that is distinctive in being remarked with some frequency. For most human beings, use of color terms such as "blue," "red," and so forth is "matter of course." "There is," in other words, "in general complete agreement in the judgment of colours." But this agreement obtains only among "those who have been diagnosed normal." "There is such a thing as colour-blindness and there are ways of establishing it." These facts characterize "the concept of a judgment of colour" (*PI*, II, ix, 227). If these facts about human vision were otherwise, rules and rule-following—and hence the system of color concepts that we in fact have—would be impossible.

The case of colors stands out for remark because color blindness is fairly common and well understood. But capacities and characteristics akin to the ability to distinguish between colors are presupposed by all human activities and practices and hence by all rules and rule-following. Wittgenstein mentions various specifics in this regard. It is "natural" for human beings to know the position of their limbs even when they can't see them (*PI*, II, viii, 185–186), to see three-dimensionally (*PI*, II, xi, 198), to differentiate among the "aspects" of a drawing of figure (*PI*, II, xi, 213–214), to groan, grimace, or cry out when in pain (*PI*, I, 244), and to be sure how many toes they have despite wearing shoes (*PI*, I, 505; *OC*, 430). More generally, human beings characteristically respond in certain ways to teaching, training, and related experiences. Pupils grasp and accept what they are told or shown by their teachers. There is of course a sense in which it is *logically* necessary that for the most part they do so. I cannot doubt *this* without presupposing much else (*OC*, 115, 160). But Wittgenstein's point here is as much anthropological as it is a rejoinder to skepticism (or to the more grandiose delusions of those in quest of fully "critical," fully presuppositionless theories). Children who persistently doubted their teachers would be incapable of learning (*OC*, 283). Nor is the general point here limited to the young. "My *life* consists in my being content to accept many things" (*OC*, 344). There is an entire system of beliefs, indeed a "whole system of verification," that "a human being acquires by means of observation and instruction," one that provides a "picture of the world" that is the "background against which I distinguish between true and false" (*OC*, 279, 40). The "countless general empirical propositions" that make up this system, for example, that if someone's arm is cut off it will not grow again, if someone's head is cut off he is dead and will never live again, that cats do not grow on trees, that motor cars do not grow out of the earth (*OC*, 274; 282, 279), while not logically interdependent, "hang together" in our belief and thought. "We feel that if someone could believe the contrary he could believe *everything* that we say is untrue, could question everything that we hold to be sure" (*OC*, 279). "To have doubts about [these things] would seem to me madness"; if someone "were to pronounce the opposite of these propositions ...

132 *Situating and disciplining freedom*

we should not just not share his opinion: we should regard him as demented" (*OC*, 281, 155). "In order to make a mistake, a man must already judge in conformity with mankind" (*OC*, 156).

Elizabeth Anscombe has brought these Wittgensteinian thoughts directly to bear on prescriptive rules that enjoin and forbid. She writes:

> These "musts" and "can'ts" are the most basic expression of such-and-such's being a rule; just as they are the most basic expression in learning the rules of a game, and as they are too in being taught rights and manners.... These "musts" and "can'ts" are understood by those of normal intelligence as they are trained in the practices of reason.
>
> (1978: 323)

Prescriptive rules operate within the confines of the "natural" possibilities of human beings and their world. That is, it is characteristic for such rules to say that one must or must not act in a manner in which, as a matter of the Wittgensteinian facts I have been discussing, one plainly can act or can avoid acting. Thus such rules can be thought to narrow those natural confines, to place further limits upon us. Are they therefore impositions that are sources or causes of unfreedom? Let us follow Anscombe's discussion somewhat further. In some cases adults who are teaching prescriptive rules to children

> will physically stop the child from doing what they say he "can't" do. But gradually the child learns. With one set of circumstances this business is part of the build-up of the concept of a rule; with another, of a piece of etiquette; with another of a promise; in another, of an act of sacrilege or impiety; with another of a right.
>
> (1978, 321)

The child may sometimes resist or resent the particulars of such teaching—perhaps rightly so. And it is worth remembering that on some views *all* such teaching runs counter to the child's "nature" in the sense not only of her original physical and psychological makeup but of tendencies and psychological dynamics that can be channeled and directed, perhaps repressed or sublimated, but never eliminated. On these views, the process of "being trained in the practices of reason" is one of losing natural freedom and may be regarded as a process of being denatured. Note, however, that Anscombe writes of the buildup of the *concept* of a rule, of a promise, of an impiety. A child who lacks those concepts, whatever her psycho-physical characteristics, can neither obey nor disobey rules, can be neither polite nor impolite, pious nor sacrilegious. Accordingly, the child who lacks these concepts could be neither free nor unfree to conform to or rebel against rules, to respect the rights of others or to violate those rights. True, the concept of a rule loses application if exception becomes as frequent as rule. In *this* sense, the child who learns these concepts thereby learns to obey or conform. But learning this general lesson is not to learn to obey

Situating freedom 133

this rule under *these* circumstances, to keep *this* promise made to *that* person. Rather, it is to learn to be a participant in the practices of rules and promising, practices that include disobedience and promise-breaking. Moreover, learning these general lessons is "natural" in the sense of Wittgenstein's "general facts of nature." In Anscombe's words:

> It is part of human intelligence to be able to learn the responses to [musts and can'ts. If this weren't true, must and can'ts] ... wouldn't exist as linguistic instruments, and these things: rules, etiquette, rights, infringements, promises, pieties and impieties [and much, much more] would not exist either.
>
> (1978: 321)

None of this is to deny that "linguistic instruments" and the rule-governed practices of which they are a part can be repressive or otherwise objectionable. Talk of "what the reasonable man accepts," of learning "the practices of human reason," and the like must not be construed as an endorsement of passivity, Panglossianism, or even the kind of conservatism that tends to find merit in the particulars of established social and political arrangements and to counsel acceptance and accommodation. Wittgenstein and Anscombe are discussing conditions that are equally necessary to conservatism and radicalism, conformism and antinomianism, fatalism and activism. Decisions to accept or reject an arrangement or practice, a norm or rule, an order or a piece of advice, presuppose the setting that they describe. It remains to be seen whether reflections of theirs have a more immediate bearing on such decisions. But before pursuing that question I pause to underline an implication contained in the foregoing discussion.

V

The passages I have been considering deepen the senses in which rules and rule-governed conduct are "situated." Human and nonhuman nature provide the setting in which our conduct occurs, a setting that establishes conditions necessary to our conduct as we know it. If these general facts of nature were significantly different than we know and accept them to be, our concepts—and hence our activities and practices—would be impossible and/or quite different (*PI*, II, xii, 230). Taken at all literally, the notion of persons who are self-subsistent and whose conduct is sui generis is absurd because it denies or inadequately appreciates this fact. There are biologically human persons whose behavior departs strikingly from these regularities; noticing this may lend credibility to extreme versions of voluntarism, atomism, and "unsituatedness." The general facts of nature that Wittgenstein invokes are just that, that is, *general* facts; they are not necessary or even universal truths. But insofar as the behavior of a person or group is at variance with these general facts, to that extent the rest of us find it difficult to "find our feet with them" (*PI*, II, xi, 223; and see I, 206–207).

134 *Situating and disciplining freedom*

Conduct that is mutually meaningful—and hence *possibly* freedom-evaluable—is conduct within these general facts as they are accepted by the "reasonable" participants in a form of life. These facts, and the limits they "impose" on our conduct, are for the most part beyond our powers to change. For example, no amount of training, no regimen, will enable any of us to jump, unaided, twenty-five feet straight up from the surface of the earth, to develop gills instead of or in addition to lungs, and so forth. But it is misleading to say either that these facts are imposed on us or to say that we choose to conduct ourselves within the limits they set. These facts and the broad patterns of our conduct within them are integral to, not alien from or chosen as part of, our lives. Few if any of us decide to stand upright, to walk by moving first one foot and then the other, or to see figures three-dimensionally (albeit physically normal children who are in rebellion against their parents or teachers may adopt bizarre postures and gaits, may refuse to see the dimensions of figures presented in a geometry lesson, and so on). These and innumerable other modes of acting are "natural" in the sense that from very early on they "come easily" to us and we become habituated to and comfortable with them. Departures and deviations from them may indeed occur and may meet with surprise, disapproval, and punishment. It is nevertheless rare for them to be viewed as chosen or freely done, as required or compelled. In respect to much of the "common behavior of mankind" most of us simply are "at home" in and with our world and ourselves. Our nature and our conventions are interwoven; descriptive regularity and prescriptive rule are largely continuous one with the other. In these deep respects our lives are—ineluctably—situated.

VI

The passages I have been examining might be viewed as an essential background to those of Wittgenstein's discussions that bear more directly on questions of freedom and unfreedom, background to his treatment of rules that are more explicitly adopted or promulgated and to rule-following that is more self-consciously obedient or disobedient. But there is no sharp distinction, no clear demarcation, between "background" and "foreground," between the conditions necessary to rule-following that is freedom-evaluable and such rule-following itself. The anthropology discussed thus far does not settle whether self-conscious rule-following and rule-breaking is done in freedom or unfreedom; it does place constraints upon any discussion of that question.

Most definitely and undeniably, from a Wittgensteinian point of view any thesis to the effect that rules and rule-following *as such* contribute to or detract from human freedom will be not so much true or false as absurd. Secondly, the elements and characteristics that make up the general anthropology enter into, are a part of, all human action. We should not think of them as merely a stage on which, or even a stage-setting in which, action occurs; rather, they should be regarded as characteristics of the participants in the human drama, characteristics that influence all of the events and actions that occur in all of the plays that are performed. These general characteristics are compatible with a prodigious diversity of practices and activities, of decisions and choices, interactions and outcomes. But for philosophical purposes (whether those purposes are understood as achieving a general understanding of the diverse array, or, more modestly, as dissolving puzzles and conundrums that develop concerning this or that activity or practice) we must attend to the general characteristics.

Third and more specifically, in Wittgenstein's account rules and rule-following do not divide cleanly between, on the one hand, tacit, unstated and unself-consciously followed background agreements and norms and, on the other hand, explicit, codified, and deliberately obeyed or disobeyed rules or laws. Rather, all rules and rule-following present a complex combination or amalgam of these and other characteristics. Development of this third point should further clarify understanding of the relationship between situatedness and freedom.

Rules do not apply themselves. Whether as deeply settled, as matter of course, but as infrequently stated as the rules governing color concepts, or whether as clearly articulated but sharply controversial as the law that all eighteen-year-old males must register with the Selective Service system, rules must be applied by persons who are participants in or practitioners of the activity or practice of which the rules are part. To make such applications, to "know how to go on" with the activity, participants must know more than the formulation of the rules themselves and must have acquired qualities and abilities over and above the "background" characteristics discussed thus far. In some places Wittgenstein calls these further characteristics the "mastery of a technique" (*PI*, I, 199, 150). In another place he speaks of some of them as "knowing one's way about" in the activity in question (*PI*, II, xi, 203). "What tells us that someone is seeing the drawing three dimensionally is a certain kind of 'knowing one's way about'. Certain gestures, for instance, which indicate the three-dimensional relations: fine shades of behaviour" (*PI*, II, xi, 203).[6] These "techniques," this "knowing one's way about," are typically specific to an activity or perhaps to a family of related activities; experience with and training in that activity are virtually always necessary in order to acquire the techniques. Some learn more quickly and surely than others, and it is often difficult, or rather pointless, to set a minimum standard that must be satisfied in order to say that someone is "able to go on" (*PI*, I, 61). But in the circumstances in which questions of performance present themselves in practical form, this seeming indeterminacy does not prevent us from deciding who can go on and who cannot, who can go on fluently, easily, and sure-handedly, who is prone to mistake, to uncertainty, and to getting stuck.

There is nothing mysterious or even notably obscure in these notions. Consider activities involving, among other things, moderately complex or intricate physical skills and tasks. The rules for making omelettes and soufflés are readily available in any number of recipe books and cooking guides. If I wish, I can commit these rules to memory so that I can recite them flawlessly and in that sense teach them to others. Yet my omelettes and soufflés seldom come out well. Although I follow the rules closely, I am clumsy with the implements, my timing is poor, I do not adapt effectively to minor variations in ingredients and

136   *Situating and disciplining freedom*

equipment. There is a technique that I have not mastered. Consider Wittgenstein's account of teaching concepts:

> How do I explain the meaning of "regular," "uniform," "same" to anyone? I shall explain these words to someone who, say, only speaks French by means of the corresponding French words. But if a person has not yet got the *concepts*, I shall teach him to use the words by means of *examples* and by practice.—And when I do this I do not communicate less to him than I know myself.
>
> In the course of this teaching I shall show him the same colours, the same lengths, the same shapes, I shall make him find them and produce them, and so on. I shall, for instance, get him to continue an ornamental pattern uniformly when told to do so.—And also to continue progressions...
>
> I do it, he does it after me; and I influence him by expressions of agreement, rejection, expectation, encouragement. I let him go his way, or hold him back; and so on.
>
> Imagine witnessing such teaching. None of the words would be explained by means of itself; there would be no logical circle.
>
> (*PI*, I, 208)

When the student can continue a variety of patterns, do various progressions, and the like, he "has got" the concepts, and the role of the teacher is at an end. When I can successfully make a variety of omelettes and soufflés, with various pans, in my own kitchen as well as in the one at the cooking school, I have mastered these culinary techniques.

Can I now, that is, with nothing more, follow the rules of soufflé-making? Is the kind of tuition Wittgenstein describes sufficient to allow his pupil to follow the rules governing "regular," "same," and "uniform"? Given the way the examples have been presented (and continuing to assume the more general conditions discussed earlier), the answer is almost certainly "yes." But that is because the presentations assume that the learners understand and accept what Wittgenstein calls the purposes of the activities and the ways in which the rules and techniques contribute to achieving them. Wittgenstein says: "The game, one would like to say, has not only rules but also a point" (*PI*, I, 564). If we do not see the reason for a rule, the way it connects to the "point" of the game, we are puzzled as to what to do with or in response to it,

> as one wouldn't see the point ... of a rule by which each piece had to be turned round three times before one moved it. If we found this rule in a board-game we should be surprised and should speculate about the purpose of the rule. [He imagines someone speculating, "Was this prescription meant to prevent one from moving without due consideration?"]
>
> (*PI*, I, 567)

Wittgenstein is not advancing a fixed or a systematic teleology (any more than he is advancing a structuralism or a generalized *Rechtsstaatphilosophie*). If someone were to say "The purpose of language is to express thoughts," a proper rejoinder would be, "So presumably the purpose of every sentence is to express a thought. Then what thought is expressed, for example, by the sentence 'It's raining'?" (*PI*, I, 501). Purposiveness is a usual, an ordinary characteristic of human activities; it is sometimes helpful to remind ourselves of this fact. But there is no general purpose that is served by all of our activities, and there is no single, unvarying purpose or objective that is pursued in all instances of any kind, type, or class of activities. The purposes served by our rules and our rule-following are as diverse as our activities themselves. Any number of generalizations can be made. Capitalists seek to earn profits, coaches to win games, politicians to gain reelection. Someone who didn't understand these settled, ordinary purposes would have great difficulty in understanding the actions of capitalists, coaches, and politicians. For the same reason, capitalists or coaches who did not pursue these objectives would be eccentric and others would be at least initially puzzled and perhaps soon enough upset, offended, or even outraged by their actions. There are shared, established, ordinary purposes of activities and their rules and, pleonastically, the purposes of most participants coincide with them. But "subliming" or "hypostasizing" purpose is foolish; as foolish—and for the same reasons—as subliming "rule," "technique," or "fact of nature." Idiosyncratic, eccentric, and deviant purposes are not only possible but abound.[7] Indeed, "do I always talk with a very definite purpose?—And is what I say [or do] meaningless because I don't?" (*PI*, II, ix, 188).

The words "rules" and "rule-following," it emerges, refer to a large and diverse family of phenomena each member of which is itself a complex of elements or features. There are boundaries or limits to the family. For example, obeying a rule and acting on an inspiration

> are surely not the same. In the case of inspiration I *await* direction. I shall not be able to teach anyone else my "technique" of following the line. Unless, indeed, I teach him some way of hearkening, some kind of receptivity. But then, of course, I cannot require him to follow the line in the same way as I do.
>
> (*PI*, I, 232)

For the same reasons, obeying a rule is not something that only one person could do, that a person could do only once, or that one could do "privately." "['O]beying a rule' is a practice," a "custom," a "use," an "institution" (*PI*, I, 197–202). Sometimes, in some classes of cases, such practices become "matter of course"; practitioners can engage in them as if "by the numbers." In other cases there is much deciding and choosing, interpreting and adjusting, and hence there is likely to be disagreement and conflict. But in no case is this due to any magical properties of rules or any special illumination in the minds or distinctive foresight on the part of the rule-followers. Rather, it is because the several elements characteristic of rules and rule-following—the elements I have been discussing—have or have not coalesced with firmness and in harmony.

138 *Situating and disciplining freedom*

Where is the connection effected between "Let's play a game of chess" and all the rules of the game? Well, in the list of the rules of the game, in the teaching of it, in the day-to-day practice of playing.

(*PI*, I, 197)

Rules are not something apart from practice that can be invoked to explain the latter; they are part of practice, vary with variation in practices, and must be understood in or rather with them. (And doing so well takes practice.)

VII

Let us now return to our starting point in the last section of this chapter. It emerges that such questions as "What is *the* relationship between rules and freedom?" and "Do rules and rule-following as such contribute to or detract from freedom?" betray misunderstandings at one or more levels. To summarize: First, rules and rule-following do not constitute a single, homogeneous phenomenon; hence they cannot stand in an invariant relationship to freedom (or to anything else). Second, in respect to many rules and much rule-following questions of freedom simply do not arise in a significant manner. Rules and rule-following are among the conditions that must be satisfied *in order that* questions of freedom can arise. Third, there are cases of rules and of rule-following that are freedom-evaluable in certain respects. But such evaluations turn not on features common to all rules and rule-following (there are no such features) but on features of the particular rules themselves and of the circumstances and activities in which they present themselves to be followed or not. All rule-following requires choices as to "how to go on," as to what the rule requires or allows, as to what will count as obeying or disobeying the rule. These choices may be made and implemented under circumstances that will warrant us in saying that they were made in freedom or in unfreedom. But because the rules and rule-following themselves, that is, the rules and rule-following understood as a complex of elements such as I have been discussing, do not themselves dictate or determine the decisions and choices, it cannot be said that the rules and rule-following eliminate or guarantee freedom. Of course such rules and such rule-following are "somethings," not "anythings" or "nothings." Accordingly, the choices of persons whose acting takes place in a practice or setting which involves rules will be circumscribed in various ways and to varying degrees. Thus a number of possibilities present themselves. Insofar as these circumscriptions are objectionable to those to whom the rules apply, we have elements relevant to (although rarely if ever conclusive concerning) a judgment on their part that the rules detract from their freedom. Insofar as the circumscriptions prevent or deter others from actions that would interfere with my conduct, or require of others conduct that enlarges my possibilities of action, we have elements relevant to a judgment on my part that the rules enhance my freedom. There are numerous other such possibilities. But at this juncture the further point to underline (that is, further to the point that rules do not apply themselves) is that rules and rule-following are integral to human thought and action. We can object to the content of this, that, or the next rule; but to object categorically to rules and rule-following is incoherent because the objections cannot be framed or stated without presupposing and following various rules. Equally, to object generally is to put oneself at war with a distinctive feature of human life and hence with oneself as a participant in human life.

The fourth point, although less explicit in Wittgenstein's discussions, is an inference warranted by those discussions (as well as a proposition one would be hard put to deny from any perspective). The fact that there are rules and a general practice or pattern of rule-following does not and cannot itself settle the question whether this or that agent will follow particular rules, will endeavor to act in a manner consonant with the rules that apply to her. We must remind ourselves once again that if exception and rule, if obedience and disobedience, became phenomena of roughly equal frequency, rules and rule-following would be at an end. But equally, the concepts "rule-following," "conformity," and "obedience" require such further concepts as "disobedience," "deviance," "rule-breaking," and even "indifference to rules." The possibility of nonconformity is conceptually necessary to the practice of rules and rule-following in every sense of "rule" other than mere observer-discerned regularity. Indeed, the fact that there is a rule requiring a mode of action is itself always eligible to be regarded as a reason for refusing to perform an action in that mode.

To these four points we can add a fifth which is also recognizably Wittgensteinian in character as well as familiar from our most basic experiences with rules and rule-following. Rules do not stand in isolation one from another. We encounter them in systems, in sets, in constellations or combinations. And it is not infrequently the case that the rules that make up a system or a set conflict with the rules that make up another or others. For these reasons, the most steadfast, even the most unthinking, of rule-followers, will from time to time find herself with no practical alternative to conduct that violates one or more rules. Consideration of such occurrences might tempt us to say not that obedience to rules is unfreedom but rather that we are, at least sometimes, unfree to obey rules. This temptation should of course be resisted; in its generic formulation the view it advances confuses impossibility, even logical impossibility, with unfreedom. But we know that rule-makers sometimes seek to prevent or diminish freedom by entrapping the law-abiding among their subjects in a web of conflicting rules. And we also know that moderately skillful rule-followers can enlarge their freedom of action by taking advantage of unintended and perhaps inelimin-able conflicts within or among systems or sets of rules. In conjunction with the other considerations that have emerged from this examination of Wittgenstein, these commonplaces caution against generalizations concerning the relationship between rules and human freedom; they therefore also warn against the view that the situatedness of human activity tells for or against its (our) freedom.

140 *Situating and disciplining freedom*

Notes

1 His distinction between the freedoms of the state of nature and the "liberties of subjects" is not a distinction of kind in my sense. The criteria governing "freedom" are the same and the differences concern the source of the obstacles or impediments to movement and the reliability of the freedom of movement that remains despite them (see 1955: ch. 21).

2 Apparently following Locke, Rousseau thinks that human beings in the state of nature have "ideas" (perceptions) and experience a small number of feelings. These nameless percepts combine, in some manner that Rousseau prudently neglects to discuss, with instincts to produce the movements of human beings in their natural state. He also thinks that by nature human beings have, apparently in latent form, "free-will" and "the faculty of self-improvement." Whereas all other animals can only "submit" to their natural instincts and impulses, the human being "knows himself at liberty to acquiesce or to resist" and dimly senses the possibility of making himself into something different and better than he now is. Following Descartes, Rousseau regards these capacities as constituting the "metaphysical and moral" as opposed to the "merely physical" and "mechanical" side of mankind (see 1950: 209–210). The discussion of these points is confusing and probably confused. In particular, it is not clear whether these capacities actually operate in the state of nature or whether they are only latent in that state and are triggered into actuality by the onset of sociality and the language that comes with it.

3 The continuation of the passage quoted above shows that Rousseau was motivated in part by a desire not to offend religious sensibilities by seeming to deny that the Old Testament gives the correct history of the "actual origin" of human societies.

4 Wittgenstein is of course talking about the, in many respects, special case of sensations. But as I am interpreting his argument, the point he is making holds for all referents.

5 "And this language like any other is founded on convention" (*PI*, I, 355).

6 On what seem to be exceptionally quick learners, see his discussion of "calculating prodigies," persons "who get the right answers but cannot say how. Are we to say they do not calculate? (A family of cases)" (*PI*, I, 236). On minimum standards of competency, see especially the lengthy discussion of reading (*PI*, I, 156–171).

7 Their *possibility*, in fact, is conceptually necessary because it is by contrast with them or the idea of them that "ordinary" and "regular," "correct" and "incorrect," are delineated.

References

Anscombe, G. E. M. 1978. "Rules, Rights, and Promises." *Midwest Studies in Philosophy* 3: 123ff.

Hobbes, Thomas. 1955. *Leviathan*. Oxford: Basil Blackwell.

Kenny, Anthony. 1973. *Wittgenstein*. London: Alan Lane.

Rousseau, Jean-Jacques. 1950. *The Social Contract and Discourses*. New York: E. P. Dutton.

Wittgenstein, Ludwig. 1953. *Philosophical Investigations*. New York: Macmillan.

Wittgenstein, Ludwig. 1969. *On Certainty*. Oxford: Basil Blackwell.

9 Control, resistance, and freedom (2003)

As suggested, Nietzsche's remarks about Epictetus present in compressed form many of his thoughts concerning control and discipline. And the appropriations from Epictetus by Montaigne and Foucault underline some of the ways in which, for the two latter as well as for Nietzsche, control and discipline are essential to power and hence to freedom.[1] Their thoughts in these regards, to indulge an anachronism, have a strong Nietzschian accent.

One of the numerous ways in which Nietzsche follows Epictetus and Montaigne (and anticipates Foucault) in connecting control and discipline with freedom is articulated in the following remarks from early in Book Four of *The Will to Power*. "The faith in the pleasure of moderation—that pleasure of the rider on a fiery steed!—has been lacking hitherto.—The mediocrity of weaker natures has been confused with the moderation of the strong!" (Nietzsche 1967: sect. 870, p. 466). In this regard, he goes on to say in the next section, there is "a confusion [that] is quite natural, although its influence has been fatal: that which men of power and will are able to demand of themselves also provides a measure of that which they may permit themselves" (sect. 871, p. 466). Instancing some "great" men, he says that Handel, Leibniz, Goethe, and Bismarck existed "blithely among antitheses, full of that supple strength that guards against convictions and doctrines by employing one against the other and reserving freedom for itself" (sect. 884, pp. 471–472).

Employing a phrase that became popular among twentieth-century thinkers influenced by him, Nietzsche asserts that every doing is a forgoing. But he turns this sometimes disheartening and even enervating idea to the advantage of his conception of free-spiritedness. "What we do should determine what we forego; *by* doing we forego—that is how I like it, that is my *placitum* [principle]" (Nietzsche 1974: Four, 304, p. 244, first italics mine). Self-control is of great importance, but "those moralists" who make of it our first and foremost duty afflict those who submit to their demands with "a peculiar disease." Whenever a person who has embraced such teaching experiences a desire, a push or a pull, "it will always seem to him as if his self-control were endangered. No longer may he entrust himself to any instinct or free wingbeat" (Nietzsche 1974: Four, 305, p. 244). To the extent that I adopt the doctrine or dogma of self-control, I must also resist it and "lose … [myself] occasionally" (Nietzsche 1974: Four,

142 *Situating and disciplining freedom*

305, pp. 244–245). That magnanimity toward enemies discussed above must extend to that part of the self that is the enemy of the self's choosing what to do and what to forgo; that is the enemy of one's free-spiritedness and hence one's most valuable freedoms of action. But the magnanimity must be proud and strong, not submissive—even to the teaching that commends it. This recommendation applies to doctrines and dogmas concerning what is true as well as what is good and virtuous. Referring to a slogan that is often used against him, Nietzsche asserts of "Nothing is true; everything is permitted," that "Here we have real freedom, for the notion of truth itself has been disposed of" (Nietzsche 1956: Third Essay, XXIV: p. 287).

What, then, are free-spiritedness and the freedom of action that is among its chief expressions or manifestations? As we would expect from the opinions and arguments we have been considering, Nietzsche presents numerous examples and characterizations of both, but nowhere to my knowledge does he offer a definition of these terms or concepts. To define them would be futile because we experience them and their absence in a great and constantly changing variety of situations and circumstances. It would also be dangerous because definitions are always restrictive and narrowing; they blind those who accept them to the fluid multiplicity of free-spiritedness and freedom of action in our lived and imagined experience. In part for this, or these, reasons, it is difficult to locate Nietzsche's thinking on the grids or in the schemas that for many centuries have organized thinking about and disputations concerning these concepts.

To take instances of typologies that have been with us for several centuries, it would be not only difficult but misleadingly reductive to classify him, exclusively as it were, as a theorist of "negative" as opposed to "positive" freedom or as solely concerned with the "conditions" as distinct from the "ends" of freedom or the reasons for valuing it. Elements in the formulations of the several proponents of these sorting devices are all prominent in his thinking.

It is clear from the considerations rehearsed here, for example, that numerous among Nietzsche's discussions are directed against restrictions on and obstacles placed in the path of individual thinking and acting, placed by hegemonic social, cultural, and occasionally political norms and values, and by institutional and other controlling mechanisms and forces. Free-spiritedness and freedom of action are importantly "negative" in character; they consist importantly in escaping from or breaking the hold of such impositions and constraints. The clearest case is of course the imperium imposed and sustained by Christianity and its agents and operatives. Nietzsche thought that the preponderance of Christians were no less than enslaved by Christianity; reduced to a herd that was not merely informed and guided but indoctrinated, controlled, and directed, and their potential for freedom deeply diminished by Christianity and its shepherds. The thought that the Christian God was dead did not mean that, literally, everything is permitted, but it did mean that the hold of a myriad of unjustifiable constraints had been broken by those who had convinced themselves of this "death" and might someday be removed from all or most of those now under the Christian yoke. In this respect, to use a word that

Control, resistance, and freedom   143

most proponents of "positive" freedom abhor, the death of the Christian God was a liberation.

Although less vituperative concerning them than are many of his remarks about Christianity, Nietzsche had similar reactions to rationalism, customary morality, and to political doctrines such as nationalism, socialism, and what might be called democratism. We have seen that he placed substantial value on the first two and especially the second, but taken to excess they too could stifle thinking and reduce action to the dogmatic, the rote, and the formulaic. The thinking and often the acting of free spirits are importantly (but not exclusively) characterized by spontaneity, inventiveness, and unpredictability. When doctrines such as those just mentioned harden into dogmas, free spirits must resist their demands and assert their own individuality and independence. Their thinking and acting, as with Zarathustra's, thereby become distinctive, unorthodox, even idiosyncratic. Doing so of course arouses the ire of many. Accordingly, free spirits must summon their strength and stand against the attempts of the scientistic and stupidly virtuous to control and direct their thinking and acting.

Although only rarely addressing topics conventionally regarded as political, in *Human All Too Human* and a few other places, Nietzsche had some choice words for the doctrines mentioned above. "Socialism is the fanciful younger brother of the almost expired despotism whose heir it wants to be." Because it "expressly aspires to the annihilation of the individual," "it requires a more complete subservience of the citizen to the absolute state than ever existed before" and seeks to improve the individual into "a useful *organ of the community*." It is therefore "in the profoundest sense reactionary" (Nietzsche 1966: sect. 473, p. 173). Nationalism and its pet entity the nation itself are sources of the same and some additional evils. The nation "is in its essence a forcibly imposed state of siege and self-defence inflicted on the many by the few and requires cunning, force, and falsehood to maintain a front of respectability" (Nietzsche 1966: sect. 475, p. 174). When heated up by nationalisms it has many of the same repugnant characteristics and effects as socialism. Thus one "should not be afraid to proclaim oneself simply a *good European* and actively to work for the amalgamation of nations" (sect. 475, p. 175). And those many who want to make Nietzsche into an anti-Semite and a proto-Hitlerian would do well to consider the following:

> the entire problem of the *Jews* exists only within national states, inasmuch as it is here that their energy and higher intelligence, their capital in will and spirit accumulated from generation to generation in a long school of suffering, must come to preponderate to a degree calculated [albeit not by the Jews] to arouse envy and hatred, so that in almost every nation—and the more so the more nationalist a posture the nation is again developing—there is gaining more ground the literary indecency of leading the Jews to the sacrificial slaughter as scapegoats for every possible public or private misfortune.
>
> (sect. 475, p. 175)

144 *Situating and disciplining freedom*

Thus in the name of individuality and individual freedom of action, the free spirit will resist the nation, nationalism, and anti-Semitism. (Incidentally, Nietzsche's self-identification as a good European and a proponent of "the strongest possible European mixed race" is one of the few instances in which he embraces an ideal that he is willing to share with as many others as possible. More on this below.)

Nietzsche's thoughts about democracy are more complex and nuanced than those concerning the doctrines just discussed, and there are remarks that are, if somewhat grudgingly, supportive of it. (See, for example, Nietzsche 1966: sect. 438, p. 161.) But he shared the fear of many mid- to late-nineteenth- (and not a few twentieth-) century thinkers that democracy, often in alliance with religious forces, promotes a state every bit as absolute and destructive of individuality as nationalism and socialism. What I have called democratism, now widely know as popular, direct, deliberative, or participatory democracy, forwards a conception of government "as nothing but the instrument of the popular will, not as an Above in relation to a Below" with those Below prepared to resist its overweening tendencies, "but merely as a function of the sole sovereign power, the people" and looked to by the people to solve their every problem and to satisfy their every desire. Where this attitude and these expectations have become widely adopted, "the unknowledgeable will think they see [in the state] the hand of God and [will] patiently submit to instructions from above." Democratic government may then ensure, at least temporarily, "internal civil peace and continuity of development," but at the cost of a "unity of popular sentiment" assured by "the fact that everyone holds the same opinions and has the same objectives" (sect. 472, pp. 170–171). Although for the most part urging that free spirits maintain a "pathos of distance" vis-à-vis the state and the politics engendered by its authority and power, Nietzsche seems to recommend that they engage themselves to resist and promote resistance to the democratic as well as to the nationalistic and socialistic state. Here again, resistance is necessary to sustaining and enhancing freedom of thought and action.

Thus resistance, and the discipline required to achieve the power necessary to make it effective, are conditions of free-spiritedness and freedom of action. They are not the same as and should not be confused with the latter two because other conditions are often also necessary to make attempts at resistance successful and because there are forms of discipline that are inimical to freedom in both senses. It is, I think, fair to say that for Nietzsche discipline and resistance are necessary conditions of free-spiritedness in any culture or society that Nietzsche can imagine. And for those who succeed in maintaining a goodly amount of "solitude," of sustaining a "pathos of distance" vis-à-vis not only politics and government but society and culture more generally, they may be both necessary and sufficient conditions of becoming and remaining an "overperson." They are also strongly contributive to the freedom of action. But they are neither sufficient for nor necessary to the latter. They are not sufficient for reasons already stated, and they are not necessary to all freedoms of action because governments, societies, and cultures may be indifferent or even favorably disposed to many of the latter.

Control, resistance, and freedom   145

There is, however, plausibility to the thought that freedoms of action of the latter type will not be held in high esteem by those who have them.

Thus far, and with the qualifications concerning the conditions of freedom just entered, there are good reasons for thinking of Nietzsche as importantly a theorist of "negative" freedom, a theorist who thinks that unfreedom consists in a person being under restrictions and controls imposed by others, finds herself confronted with substantial obstacles to the thinking she desires to do and the acting in which she has an inclination or a will to engage. Unfreedom is undesirable because it is due to the presence of effective constraints—"brake-shoes" as Zarathustra calls them (Nietzsche 1957: Second Part, p. 108)—freedom is valuable because the individual is able to resist and overcome those constraints and hence is able to think and act as she is disposed to do. To recur to a formulation that I proposed in an earlier writing, on the considerations thus far examined, Nietzsche can be said to advance a notion of freedom and unfreedom the elements of which, schematically, are: "Action attempted by an agent plus the possibility of impediments to that action placed or left by another or other agents acting with the intention of placing or leaving those impediments" (Flathman 1987: p. 322). Freedom in this, I think familiar, sense consists in the agent successfully overcoming the impediments, unfreedom consists in the agent's being prevented from the desired action by the impediments. Of course Nietzsche places more emphasis than I did on the discipline and resulting strength that allows the agent to resist the impediments placed by others, but otherwise this formula captures much of what he says in pursuing the thought that "the tug towards freedom ... [is] the strongest drive of our spirit."

As anticipated, however, further qualifications need to be made to this reading—and hence this appropriation—of Nietzsche's thinking. The kind of qualification necessary is presaged when Nietzsche speaks of "Virtue [*virtù*?] as pleasure in resistance, will to power. Honor as recognition of the similar and equal-in-power" (Nietzsche 1967: Book Two, sect. 255, p. 148). Resistance to custom, convention, and authority is necessary to open up spaces for freedom and hence to give outlets for the will to power, outlets that are socially and culturally significant. But even if it does not have this other-regarding effect, resistance and the will to power that it discloses are sources both of visceral pleasure and the pleasure of being honored by those who deserve to be honored.

Enlarging on this point, the forms of discipline that enable resistance to others also contribute importantly to the possibility of saying, *con brio* as Nietzsche encourages us to put it, "yes to life." Looking back on his lifetime of thinking, in *Ecce Homo*, he says that he had "become the first to comprehend the wonderful phenomenon of the dionysian," which he here characterizes as the readiness to make a

> *supreme affirmation* born out of fullness, of superfluity, an affirmation without reservation even of suffering, even of guilt, even of all that is strange and questionable in existence.... This ultimate, joyfullest, boundlessly exuberant Yes to Life is not only the highest insight, it is also the

146   *Situating and disciplining freedom*

profoundest, the insight most strictly confirmed and maintained by truth and knowledge.

(Nietzsche 1979: pp. 79–80)

Of course this affirmation, which is enunciated in a great variety of locutions and rhetorics throughout the writings primarily consulted here, would not be possible without disciplined resistance to the array of "degenerated" instincts "which turn ... against life with subterranean revengefulness" (Nietzsche 1979: pp. 79–80). If we take the readiness to make the dionysian affirmation as the distinctive, the differentiating characteristic of the free spirit and the overperson, we can reaffirm the above reading that discipline and resistance, and hence freedom from degenerate outlooks, are necessary conditions of free-spiritedness. And if the free spirit must enact, must act upon, this affirmation, we can also say that a significant measure of freedom of action is also among the necessary conditions of free-spiritedness. But now freedom from and freedom to, rather than being for their own sake, are of inestimable value because they enable the affirmation, the Yes to Life. Removed from this Weltanschauung or Weltgeist, freedom to engage in action and perhaps freedom from constraints and controls might be trivial and perhaps diminishing.

At first and perhaps at second sight this construal is supported by some of the more pungent remarks of Zarathustra.

You call yourself free? I want to hear your sovereign thought, not that you have escaped from a yoke. Are you one of those who are *entitled* to escape from a yoke? There are some who cast off their ultimate value when they cast off their servitude. Free *from* something? What does Zarathustra care? But let your clear eyes show me you are free *for* something.

(Nietzsche 1957: First Part: p. 69)

To return to my earlier formulations, in the passages now under consideration Nietzsche can be read as advancing a notion of freedom as autonomy and unfreedom as heteronomy, when these notions are explicated as follows:

Action attempted by an agent in the pursuit of a self-critically chosen plan or project that the agent ... believe[s] is consonant with defensible norms or principles [or ideals], plus the possibility of impediments to that action placed or left by another agent or other agents acting with the intention of placing or leaving those impediments.

(Flathman 1987)

It would appear that an agent is entitled to be free of the yoke or yokes placed or left by others, to be free in a sense that a free spirit such as Zarathustra *would* care about, only if she has a "sovereign thought" that is and deserves to be genuinely her own. If she lacks such a thought, or perhaps thoughts, her unfreedom, her being heteronomized, may be beneficial to her.[2]

Control, resistance, and freedom 147

There is a temptation to go yet further and read Nietzsche as promoting a conception of freedom close to what I have called Fully Virtuous freedom (except that of Nietzsche we have to say "fully virtu-ous"). In this formulation, the above words "believes is consonant with defensible norms or principles" are followed by "chosen to satisfy, and in fact satisfying, certifiably worthy norms or principles [or ideals]." This reading is responsive to what is sometimes called Nietzsche's perfectionism. It is not enough that the individual's sovereign thought(s) be unquestionably her own; rather, that thought or those thoughts must be affirmed "without reservation" and this must be *because* it or they are "confirmed and maintained by truth and knowledge." Echoing widely circulated slogans such as "Ye shall know the truth and the truth shall make your free" (the motto of my university is *Veritas Vos Liberabit*), thus construed Nietzsche is a proponent of one of the most soaring versions of the "positive" theory of freedom, a version that not only distinguishes between higher and lower, better and worse selves— distinctions that Nietzsche unquestionably makes and that move him toward a conception of freedom as autonomy—but that specify that a self can be regarded as high or good only if its sovereign thoughts accord with truth.

This further interpretation, however, is clearly mistaken. There is no denying or wishing away the fact that in the passage quoted from *Ecce Homo*, Nietzsche makes a direct connection between the merits of a supreme affirmation and the fact that it is confirmed and maintained by truth and knowledge. But whose truth and whose knowledge? For reasons that have been rehearsed in detail above, it cannot be truth and knowledge as conventionally accepted in this or that society and culture. But we have also seen that Nietzsche identifies himself as a perspectivalist, as holding that truth and knowledge are always and necessarily determined from the perspective of some person or persons and that the idea of a higher theory, a metatheory, that can and should arbitrate among perspectives and determine what is TRUE and what counts as KNOWLEDGE is not only a fantasy but a dangerous delusion. (On this topic, in addition to works already discussed, see especially his "On Truth and Lies in a Non-Moral Sense" and the other early papers collected in Daniel Breazeale, editor and translator, *Philosophy and Truth*.)

Nietzsche is a "perfectionist" in the sense that he has formed and aspires to the realization of an idea, or rather an ideal, of a self or of selves that soars above the traditional, the conventional, and the orthodox. Moreover, he heaps derision and scorn not only on idealisms in the philosophical sense but on numerous of what we might call the ideals of life with which he was familiar. But while he gives various names to the ideal(s) that he admires—the free spirit, the overperson, and several others—he repeatedly insists that there is no single version of this generic ideal that should be preferred to all others. Just as he shared William James's admiration for polytheism and its diverse, fluctuating, and often conflicting conceptions of the divine or superhuman, so he thought that there are, and believed passionately that there ought to be, an irreducible multiplicity of ideals of life. As he put the latter conviction—with unequaled verve and exuberance:

148 *Situating and disciplining freedom*

> Whatever kind of bizarre ideal one may follow ... one should not demand that it be *the* ideal; for one therewith takes from it its privileged character. One should have it in order to distinguish oneself, not in order to level oneself.... "This is what I am; this is what *I* want:—*you* can go to hell."
>
> (Nietzsche 1967: Book Two, sect. 349, pp. 190–191)

Concluding thoughts

As with Montaigne, Nietzsche gives us no single, unified answer to our questions concerning how we should think about, and act concerning, the relationships between freedom on the one hand and discipline and resistance on the other. For both of them, and especially for Nietzsche, freedom is a multivalent concept and idea and it and various nearly cognate terms and related ideas such as liberty, liberation, and *laissez-aller* are used in a great variety of contexts and in respect to diverse circumstances. Moreover, ideas of freedom often appear without the word or words being used, their presence in Nietzsche's thinking being indicated by his use of the various notions that he regards as opposed to or in contrast with freedom. In these respects, his linguistic and rhetorical practices—leaving aside terms distinctive to him such as "free-spiritedness" and "overperson"—are for the most part familiar to us from our own discourses. If we find his thinking convincing we can readily appropriate it to our own and if we find it engaging but unacceptable, we can readily dispute it.

The opening sentences of the previous paragraph notwithstanding, there are several respects in which major tendencies in Nietzsche's thinking about the ideas and issues of concern here, if not systematic or even notably orderly, is not only accessible but quite clear. For present purposes, perhaps the three most important of his themes are those that I proceed to discuss.

First, there is no categorical or across-the-board opposition between freedom and discipline. Discipline is often necessary to both freedom of action and free-spiritedness and it often contributes to those desiderata even when it is not necessary to them. Nietzsche obviously prefers self-discipline to disciplines imposed by others, and for the free spirit this preference for it is categorical, in that the free spirit, even if she finds the particulars of disciplinary regimens in and takes them from social or cultural norms, must subject them to critical examination. If she accepts them she must in this way internalize them and in this sense make them her own. For the free spirit, disciplines not internalized in this way are antithetical to her freedom.

The free spirit will almost certainly recognize that numerous of the members of her society or culture are not given to or are incapable of critical assessment of social and cultural norms, and she will acknowledge that her own freedom may be enhanced by their uncritical submission to them. She may also feel some gratitude toward the "virtuous intellects" both for the reason just stated and because their compliance with the law of agreement and customary morality, and their attempts to impose them on her, will multiply the occasions on which she experiences the need to exercise a further discipline on herself, the discipline

Control, resistance, and freedom   149

necessary to resisting their demands and realizing the pleasures that such resistance, perhaps only such resistance, can afford.

The second and third themes are partly stated by or implied in the first, but go beyond them. Resistance, at least in the sense of standing against the demand that conventional disciplinary regimens be accepted uncritically, and often in the further sense that they often must be actively resisted, is essential to free-spiritedness and in many instances to freedom of action. Moreover, it is clear from Nietzsche's brief discussions of the state and politics that the possibility of a politically organized society that we might call livable or tolerable depends on the readiness of some considerable number of citizens—including citizens who may not qualify as free spirits in the strongest sense—to resist the government and its commands. In this respect, Nietzsche deserves to be numbered among those who give at least—but not more than—two cheers for democracy, and he sometimes appears to be friendly toward anarchism if it is the only alternative to despotism.

Third, Nietzsche recognizes that discipline and the strength necessary to resistance are almost certainly necessary to any considerable measure of freedom of action and contribute importantly to the vigorous and fruitful pursuit of his ideal of free-spiritedness. He does not, however, equate the third with either of the first two. It is possible to have numerous freedoms of action and not formulate an ideal for oneself, and if one has imagined and wished for an ideal, freedom of action does not guarantee that it will be effectively pursued. A further and quite vital point is that there are ideals—for example the Christian ideals as Nietzsche understands them—that manifest not disciplined free-spiritedness but despotic impulses on the part of their champions and uncritical submissiveness on the part of those who follow their promoters. (The passage that begins "Whatever bizarre ideal you may follow" notwithstanding, the pluralism of Nietzsche's idealism is not without its limits.) Free-spiritedness is almost certainly a condition of formulating and pursuing any ideal about which Nietzsche would say "This is what *You* are, this is what *You* want. *I* can't have it and you can tell me to go to hell," but it is not a sufficient condition of doing so. Formulating and pursuing an ideal that passes this test requires imagination and creativity, that is qualities of mind and more especially of spirit that cannot be analyzed—as free-spiritedness importantly is—in terms of what the free spirit is not and what she is against. We are on safe ground in saying that any ideal that Nietzsche would judge worthy would feature a strong commitment to overcoming those parts of the self that are against its idealized self, to self-making, and hence to some version of individuality. Exactly how individuality does or should manifest itself, however, cannot be predicted and certainly cannot be prescribed.

If this brief summary captures the main themes in, and theses advanced by, Nietzsche's thinking about freedom, discipline, and resistance, how should we assess them? It should be evident from the foregoing pages, from their tonalities and from the delight (which no doubt some will think excessive) that I evidently take in quoting from Nietzsche's work on these and related topics, that my own assessment is largely favorable. That this is the case, at least in regard to the

150 *Situating and disciplining freedom*

relationship between freedom and discipline, came initially as something of a surprise to me. When I began these reflections, I was suspicious of the view that the various familiar forms of discipline are necessary for freedom, contributive to it, or even compatible with it. (This suspicion did not extend to the idea that resistance is often not only contributive but frequently necessary to freedom. Given that discipline is almost always necessary to effective resistance, I was closer to accepting something like Nietzsche's view than I then realized.) Somewhat suspicious of my own suspicion, and knowing from previous readings that Foucault, Montaigne, Nietzsche, and Hampshire are enthusiasts for freedom but also for various types of discipline, the thought occurred to me that engagements with their formulations would be a fruitful way to test both of these suspicions.

Even as I complete this project, my present judgments must remain provisional, open to challenge and reconsideration. With one major exception with which I conclude, however, I now agree with much of what Nietzsche thought about these matters. Beginning with the third of the themes or theses summarized just above, I strongly agree—indeed in this respect have long since agreed—with Nietzsche's thoughts, both negative and positive, concerning ideals and the place that they should and should not have in our affairs.

An ideal is an idea or more or less integrated array of ideas to the realization of which an individual or some number of individuals aspire. It is regarded by those who embrace it as providing a standard of excellence or accomplishment, an excellence exceeding that which has as yet been achieved in their lives and in most cases in the lives of those with whom their lives are regularly involved or engaged. The ideal gives inspiration and a degree of direction to those who are committed to its realization and it provides a basis on which to critique arrangements and patterns of conduct that fall short of its demands.

As sources of inspiration, direction, and critique, ideals are valuable, and sometimes—as in the case of Nietzsche's ideal of free-spiritedness—of supreme value to those who espouse them. In providing grounds on which to critique conventional understandings and orientations, they provide those who hold them with reasons for distancing themselves from them, with the courage and strength necessary to resist the demands with which they are presented and to overcome the obstacles with which others confront them. For Nietzsche and for numerous other promoters of ideals, a person without an ideal, without a "sovereign thought," may be (perhaps by chance) free from many restrictions and hence may be free to do many things. But lacking a sovereign thought to inspire and captain their thinking and acting, their thoughts are likely to be commonplace and their actions lacking in self-control and self-chosen orientation.

As Nietzsche would emphatically say ("we exceptions to the rule" are the glory of but also one of the chief dangers to humane life), ideals can be and often are not only dangerous to but destructive of a "decent regard for the opinions of [hu]mankind" and hence the possibility of a minimal decency in human relations. The Christian ideals have enslaved much of Europe and more recently prominent ideals such as socialism and nationalism threaten a despotism unknown for several centuries. Even worthy ideals can engender dogmatism and

Control, resistance, and freedom   151

fanaticism. Lacking any commitment to moderation, politeness, and poise, any appreciation for the pleasures that come from respecting "forms," their proponents run a brutal roughshod over those who do not accept—and not infrequently a few of those who do—their ideal.

Since he was intensely aware of these dangers, one of the most appealing aspects of Nietzsche's conception of his ideal is his insistence on guarding it against its being put, by himself or others, to these nefarious purposes. If you can't have my ideal, the last thing I would want to do would be to level myself by imposing it on you. But this resounding and perhaps unprecedented declaration is surrounded by admonitions, to himself as well as to others, to discipline oneself to maintain *virtu's* of form such as those mentioned again in the previous paragraph. The ideal is of supreme value, but it can be realized only if those who cherish and promote it discipline themselves to enact these formal or adverbial virtues.

One final point regarding ideals as Nietzsche understands them. He is right, both conceptually and (if this is a distinction) normatively, to refuse to *identify* forming and pursuing his ideal with freedom. Freedom in the two main senses discussed here is a high-order value for Nietzsche, but—as with the *virtu's* just mentioned—it is to be kept distinct from his ideal. It is a condition of being in a position to enact one's ideal and it can contribute valuably to the ability to formulate an ideal that one wishes to embrace. By refusing, however, to identify acceptance and pursuit of an ideal—his or anyone else's—with freedom, he protects others from the enormities perpetrated in the name of forcing others to accept and live by an ideal they do not accept, the enormity of "forcing them to be free."

These appreciations of what I called the third of Nietzsche's themes also capture much of what I think merits endorsement in the two that precede it in my summary discussion. Nietzsche is correct that there is no categorical opposition between freedom and discipline. As Montaigne and Foucault also understood, in the entire absence of the various forms of discipline that they both strongly favor, thinking and acting deteriorate into "letting go," very likely into a form of self- and mutually destructive madness. (In this respect their thinking has many affinities with the thinking of Hobbes.) For Montaigne these forms of discipline are especially important for those who seek to make themselves—for example, to make oneself, as Montaigne essayed to do, in large part by writing oneself. For Nietzsche they are especially important for those who aspire to the closely related ideal of self-overcoming and free-spiritedness. But for reasons already discussed, it is also important, including to the free spirit, that they be exercised by those who aspire to other ideals or to none. In the absence of discipline there may be various freedoms of movement, but there is little if any freedom of action. (I return to this distinction below.)

Nietzsche is also correct to argue that self-discipline is to be preferred to disciplines imposed by others. This is, again, particularly the case with the free spirit but it is also true of anyone who aspires to achieve and maintain some degree of individuality. To repeat, it is unavoidable that some forms of discipline

152   *Situating and disciplining freedom*

will be found in and adopted from norms already widely shared. But the free spirit, and anyone else who recognizes the sometime need for resistance to such norms, must be capable of critiquing and standing against them. Disciplines never subjected to such critique are antithetical to the freedoms of the free spirit and endanger the freedoms of anyone and everyone.

As regards anyone and everyone, I write "endanger" rather than "antithetical to" for two reasons, the second and more important of which leads to the disagreement with Nietzsche that I anticipated above. The first is that the demand for a continuous and universally critical stance toward established conventions and norms is almost certainly unrealistic. Although claims that all freedoms are deeply situated and all selves deeply embedded are (dispiriting) exaggerations, they are exaggerations, not generally mistaken propositions. As Nietzsche himself repeatedly and in my judgement rightly insists, a recognizably civil society depends on a "law of agreement" and a customary morality that are not continuously or widely questioned. In railing against those exceptional, those "impatient" ones, who seek to "disrupt" these arrangements and conventions, and in saying that his hell would be a life of constant improvisation, he brings this understanding to bear on himself. And in acknowledging, gratefully we may say, the numerous respects in which he is benefited by the presence of a large number of readily trainable persons, he not only recognizes but endorses a conception of society and culture that includes these characteristics.

What, then, is there to disagree with? We might begin by saying that to the extent that Nietzsche generalizes his demand for a continuous critical stance toward the received and the conventional, he blurs a part of his own distinction between the free spirit and those who do not accept this ideal of life. For present purposes, a better way to put the objection may be that he risks violating his own strictures against imposing (a part of) his ideal on others. And if or insofar as he does so in the name of freedom, he moves his conception and valorization thereof in the direction of a notion of autonomy versus heteronomy rather than a conception of freedom of action.

In order to conclude discussion of this point it will be helpful to develop somewhat further the tripartite distinction among differing senses or uses of "freedom" and "unfreedom" already mentioned.[3] In the first, that is freedom of *movement*, freedom consists in the movement of a body or its parts not effectively impeded or obstructed by other persons or physical things. Unfreedom, accordingly, consists in attempts at or impulses to movement that are prevented by other persons or other bodies. Distinctive to this conception of freedom is that it requires, indeed allows, no reference to *why* the person or other body wants, desires, is disposed to, has the objective or purpose, to move in a particular direction. The clearest examples of freedom and unfreedom in this sense are reactions to stimuli or other causes such as the blink of an eye in response to a bright light and the jerk of a leg struck on the patellar tendon. If unimpeded, the movements are free, if effectively prevented by some other body or force, they are unfree. The theory called behaviorism (and not a few kindred theories) treats all or a very large number of the movements—the behaviors—of human beings as

Control, resistance, and freedom 153

instances of movements and aims to explain as many of them as possible on this model or understanding (the (in)famous Stimulus-Response theory). It treats "mentalist" explanations as delusions, impossibilities, or both.

By contrast, the theory of freedom and unfreedom of *action requires* reference to the "mentalist" components of actions. On the now widely accepted (generic) analysis of actions as distinct from movements, an action involves four main elements, namely a belief, a desire to act on that belief, the formation of an intention to do so, and the adoption of a purpose, goal, or end that the agent expects or hopes to be achieved by doing so. As with freedom of movement, unfreedom consists in the agent's attempt at action being effectively prevented. In most of its versions, however, unfreedom of action is brought about by the actions of other agents and hence requires attention to the beliefs, desires, intentions, and purposes of the agents who prevented the first party from successfully taking the action she attempted.

As already indicated in part, freedom in the sense of autonomy, and unfreedom in the sense of being heteronomized by other agents or agencies, adds further requirements to saying that an agent acted in freedom. These further requirements vary among the numerous theorizations of autonomy and heteronomy, but all of those known to me specify that the acting agent must be aware of (conscious of, as Nietzsche might say) her beliefs, desires, and so forth, and must subject them to some degree of critical assessment. If she has no self-critical awareness of the "why" of her attempted conduct she cannot be said to be autonomous and hence, on this conception of freedom, cannot be said to be free. And as her self-critical awareness diminishes, her autonomy and hence her freedom diminish with it.

By contrast with freedom as unimpeded movement, both freedom as unprevented action and freedom as autonomous conduct deserve to be regarded as ideals. But the latter is by far the more demanding of the two and for this reason allows of a fewer number of instances in which an agent can properly be said to have acted in freedom. Perhaps for this reason, champions of freedom as autonomy, including Nietzsche and perhaps Montaigne and Foucault, regard it as the higher of the two ideals. It is not difficult to understand the attractions of this view. Notions such as "the unexamined life is not worth living" and imperatives such as "know thyself," "overcome thyself," and "make thyself" all weigh in its favor. Anyone who places a high value on her own individuality will be attracted to it. Certainly such a person will be attracted to it as an ideal *of her own and for herself*.

There are nevertheless reasons to hesitate before the ideal of autonomy. One such reason is the following: Even if I regard the ideal as exclusively mine, make no attempt to convince others of its merits or hold them to it, in some of its versions it involves such a radical distancing from others as to amount to a disregard for them and possibly a readiness to appropriate them to my objectives. My quest for autonomy becomes so unqualifiedly self-regarding that I either isolate myself from others or treat them as means to my ends.

It might be thought that this objection applies to Nietzsche. His repeatedly expressed craving for solitude could be taken to indicate an indifference

154 *Situating and disciplining freedom*

regarding others, and his enthusiasm for the opportunities and other advantages made available to him owing to the "trainability" of most Europeans might suggest a crassly instrumental attitude toward them. I think, however, that this reading, while admittedly finding some support in his texts, is mistaken. He does seek to distance himself from others, but what he seeks is not isolation but a "pathos of distance." A person indifferent to others would experience no pathos in her relations and especially her non-relations with or to them. And the passages that suggest that he is prepared to "use" others for his own purposes must be read along with, and against, his many injunctions to politeness, fastidiousness, magnanimity, and like *virtu's* of form. These and many other of his injunctions apply not only to the stance he should take toward other exceptional persons but to all human beings. (This is one of several indications that there is a strong egalitarian component in his thinking.)

A second reason for hesitation before this ideal is the one already sketched above. If or to the extent that I hold others to the ideal of autonomy, that ideal becomes a weapon, at least a rhetorical and perhaps a more material weapon against them. If another person claims to have taken an action freely or in freedom, and if I am convinced that her action did not satisfy criteria of autonomy such as having subjected her beliefs, desires, and so on to appropriately critical scrutiny, I can deny that she acted in freedom. And if I further think that it is a mark against her that she fell short of autonomy, I may convince myself that I am justified in interfering in her thinking and acting so as to remedy this defect. I may show disrespect for her and I may convince myself that it is my duty to interfere in more material and potentially more efficacious ways.

Here again there are elements in Nietzsche's thinking that warrant bringing this objection against him. There is no shortage of remarks in which he evinces what has to be called disdain for the stupidly virtuous and those herd-like many whose lives consist in sheep-like submission to some shepherd. Here also, however, this criticism must be qualified. The *virtu's* on which he repeatedly and avidly insists may permit of expressing disdain in a philosophical treatise, but commitment to them, to standing pledge for one's word, to scrupulously avoiding actions that disrupt the workings of the law of agreement, are incompatible with the kinds of direct interference under discussion.

Consider in this regard a remark of his concerning politics, one that is relevant to the above discussion of democracy or democratism and that will lead us to a third objection to the conception of freedom as requiring autonomy:

> [I]f the purpose of all politics really is to make life endurable for as many as possible, then these as-many-as-possible are entitled to determine what they understand by an endurable life; if they trust to their intellect also to discover the right means of attaining this goal, what good is there in doubting it? They *want* for once to forge for themselves their own fortunes and misfortunes; and if this feeling of self-determination, pride in the five or six ideas their head contains and brings forth ... there is little to be objected to, always presupposing that this narrow-mindedness does not go so far as to

Control, resistance, and freedom 155

demand that *everything* should become politics in this sense, that *everyone* should live and work according to such a standard.

(Nietzsche 1966: sect. 438, p. 161)

Disdain, yes. But with regard to a chief source of interference with the beliefs and actions of the many, Nietzsche explicitly counsels against it, requiring only that their beliefs and chosen forms of action not be made mandatory for him.

Briefly stated, a third objection to the ideal of autonomy and the conception of freedom that its proponents frequently advance is that it underestimates or otherwise mischaracterizes action and acting, tending to assimilate them to movements or behaviors. Otherwise stated, ideas of autonomy and of freedom as (conceptually) requiring autonomy exaggerate the differences between autonomy and action. No one among the four generic components of action are merely unconsidered responses to stimuli. Beliefs, desires, intentions, and purposes are always chosen from among alternatives and, typically, are chosen among and often against alternatives that compete with or are either conceptually or materially (or both) incompatible with those chosen. Moreover, framing an intention and adopting a purpose rarely if ever will tell the agent which among alternative courses of action will best enact the intention and achieve the purpose. Of course awareness of alternatives, critical reflectiveness as to why one among them is here and now chosen over the others, and the self-discipline to act as one thinks best, vary from action to action and agent to agent. Deeply ingrained beliefs, strongly felt desires, conventional and habitual intentions and purposes may reduce awareness and reflectiveness to minimal proportions. But if there is no awareness and no reflectiveness we are in the presence of a movement not an action.

Some may think that this is no more than, is "merely," a conceptual point. But if there is such a thing as a "merely" conceptual point, the one before us is not an example. Insofar as we recognize persons as agents attempting to engage in action we attribute—accord—to them qualities that are different, if at all, only in degree from those exalted and privileged by theories of autonomy and of freedom as requiring autonomy. Such differences as there are between the actions of agents and the actions of those who are autonomous are far from sufficient to justify the view that only the successful attempts at action of the latter deserve to be thought of as done in freedom. They are obviously insufficient to justify preventing the actions of agents on the ground that doing so is necessary to make them free.

Is Nietzsche guilty of underestimating action and exaggerating the differences between it and autonomy? The answer is at once a No and a Yes. When, in passages such as the one just quoted, he speaks of "intellect," self-determined wants, ideas of the endurable and the unendurable, and the like, he attributes characteristics of agency and action to the many. In respect to these dimensions of his thinking and others rehearsed in considering the previous two objections, the answer is No. When he indulges himself in expressions of contempt for the abjectly submissive herd, of those who "let themselves go" and descend into

156 *Situating and disciplining freedom*

madness, the answer is Yes. There no doubt are human beings about whom these characterizations are apt. But if thinkers from Aristotle to Hampshire are correct that action is the staple ingredient in, an elemental feature of, human life, generalizations of the latter sort are as misleading as they are dangerous to human freedom.

For now I can say that my brief attempt at an assessment of Nietzsche's thinking has led to a balance strongly in favor of his views concerning freedom, discipline, and resistance. Where his formulations prompt objections, I very often find that in other passages he responds effectively to them or gives me reasons to qualify my concerns. As with Foucault and Montaigne, my engagement with his thinking has strengthened my commitment to views I earlier held and has also convinced me that reservations I previously had to positions akin to his are either unwarranted or less damaging than I earlier thought. It is of course my hope that others who follow my explorations of his extraordinarily rich and supple reflections will arrive at a similar conclusion.

Notes

1 It might be thought that the latter three are less attentive than is Nietzsche to the respects in which control and discipline emanate from and are, in part, imposed on the individual by society and culture. But this would be a mistake in all three cases. A substantial part of Epictetus's thinking is concerned with slavery and his attempts to cope with it. Montaigne's awareness of and even his readiness to go along, at least outwardly, with custom and convention are if anything more pervasive and emphatic than Nietzsche's. And Foucault repeatedly underscores the respects in which the regimens recommended by Epictetus are rarely invented by individuals but come to them via their participation in cultural conventions and practices.
2 Bill Connolly has suggested to me that the concept of "autonomy" does not adequately capture or express those of Nietzsche's thoughts presently under discussion. Although I think it works well as regards the ideas and forces that Nietzsche opposes, I agree that it does not convey the sense of exuberance and abundance that Nietzsche associates with the free spirit.
3 The following remarks draw on Flathman, 1987.

References

Flathman, Richard E. 1987. *The Philosophy and Politics of Freedom* (Chicago: University of Chicago Press).
Nietzsche, Friedrich. 1956. *The Genealogy of Morals*. Trans. Francis Golffing (Garden City, NY: Doubleday).
Nietzsche, Friedrich. 1957. *Thus Spake Zarathustra*. Trans. Marianne Cowan (Chicago: Gateway Editions).
Nietzsche, Friedrich. 1966. *Human, All Too Human*. Trans. R. J. Hollingdale (Cambridge: Cambridge University Press).
Nietzsche, Friedrich. 1967. *Will to Power*. Trans. Walter Kaufmann and R. J. Hollingdale (New York: Vintage Books).
Nietzsche, Friedrich. 1974. *The Gay Science*. Trans. Walter Kaufmann (New York: Vintage Books).
Nietzsche, Friedrich. 1979. *Ecce Homo*. Trans. R. J. Hollingdale (London: Penguin Books).

Part III

Opacity, liberalism, and individuality

10 Individuality, plurality, and liberalism (1992)

At what we might call the arithmetic core of their meanings, *individual* (particular, single) and *plural* (two or more) are conceptually interwoven. *Plural* and hence a plurality requires countable and hence individualizable entities, and *individual* makes a distinction only if there are two or more such entities. In this elementary—but also elemental—sense, descriptive and evaluative theories of individuality and plurality are mutually dependent and complementary, not opposed or contrary one to the other.

Perhaps influenced by these considerations, various social and political doctrines, especially versions of liberalism, aver that in fact individuality and plurality are complementary and often synergetic phenomena. The diversity of perspectives, beliefs, purposes, and styles that individuality involves are possible bases or starting points for a plurality of groups and associations, perhaps even cultures and traditions;[1] for its part, a plurality of the latter may stimulate, support, or otherwise enable individuality.[2] On this understanding, which I call complementarism, theories or practices that promote either individuality or plurality at the expense of the other would appear to diminish or even jeopardize both.

At the level of generality at which I have thus far stated complementarist views, the support they offer to values prominent in liberalism should make them attractive to anyone of a liberal persuasion. They are certainly to be preferred to monistic, organicist, and strongly communitarian doctrines that deny the reality or disdain the worth of everything—particularly of individuals and their individuality—less than "the whole." Their merits relative to more insistent forms of individualism is a more complicated matter that will occupy us as we proceed. Perhaps, however, there are forms of individualism, liberal or otherwise, as foolish as its holistic antagonists allege, so foolish as to mimic holism by denying the reality of anything but individuals or the possibility that groups and societies, traditions and cultures, can contribute to individuality. If so, it is easy to think of reasons for setting them aside in favor of an understanding along the lines sketched above.

...

160 *Opacity, liberalism, and individuality*

I

...

II

...

Both cooperation and conflict, both mutually gratifying complementarity and the most one-sided domination, presuppose substantial self- and mutual understanding on the part of those who are party to the relationship. This being the case, the very prevalence of cooperation and conflict in human affairs may explain the tendency of otherwise sharply divergent views to take the presence of such understandings for granted. Would attention to this shared but seldom-examined assumption help us to assess the disagreements we are considering?

In the literatures directly pertinent to our topic, such attention is most frequent in thinkers pessimistic about the likelihood of fruitful cooperation and complementarity, inclined to view relationships in their societies as systematically diminishing all or most of the individuals and groups involved in or affected by them. From Jean-Jacques Rousseau to Alexis de Tocqueville and Karl Marx, from Max Weber, Sigmund Freud, and Nietzsche to Erving Goffman and Michel Foucault, we have heard that our institutions and our practices are structured in ways that none among us knowingly or intentionally brought about and few if any of us understand; that our thinking and acting within the confines of these settings and arrangements is suffused and largely controlled by assumptions of which we are at best dimly aware. Some of our most treasured convictions—for example, that our political, economic, and social arrangements were made by us or are subject to remaking by our own decisions and choices, that our beliefs are held and our actions taken for good reasons, that we are sometimes constant, sometimes wavering in our judgments, sometimes agree, sometimes disagree with one another but that we understand ourselves and one another—are for the most part illusory. And not far below the surface of our societies, just beneath the superficial or even epiphenomenal diversities that some of us celebrate and others of us lament, there is a dreary uniformity that is all the more deadening because it is unrealized by us.

From this latter perspective the pervasiveness of complementarism—in liberalism and elsewhere—has to be regarded as a symptom of one of the worst diseases that afflict our thinking. And the least treatable form of that disease is complacency and the dismissive attitude toward theorizing commonly associated with it. If or to the extent that our condition is as these radical critics portray it, complacency is the last thing to which we are entitled, and theorizing concerning the deepest of our assumptions about individuality and plurality is among our most urgent needs.[3]

III

The least disputable of the limitations on our self- and mutual understandings concern our capacities to sustain awareness of anything approaching the full

Individuality, plurality, and liberalism   161

range of the assumptions and beliefs that inform our judgments and intentions and hence the actions we take. However we may have arrived at the various items making up our array of beliefs, in altering that array and in drawing on it to form and act on intentions, we necessarily leave unexamined many of the beliefs of which it consists. Let us consider anew and attempt to follow out the leads given by a salient example of this view.

"When we first begin to *believe* anything, what we believe is not a single pro-position, it is a whole system of propositions. (Light dawns gradually over the whole.)" "It is not single axioms that strike me as obvious, it is a system in which consequences and premises give one another *mutual* support." "All testing, all confirmation and disconfirmation of a hypothesis takes place already within a system. And this system is not a more or less arbitrary and doubtful point of departure for all our arguments … [it is] the element in which arguments have their life" (Wittgenstein 1969, hereafter *On Certainty*, 141, 142, 105).

If we are tempted to read these passages as constituting a manifesto of philosophical holism, perhaps of some species of social or political organicism or corporativism, we must realize that they are part of a larger view according to which the systemic character of our believing and thinking, the very quality that gives them life and strength, also diminishes our capacity to assess and adjust, reconsider and revamp, indeed to summon to our own and to one another's awareness, many of the elements of which the system has at any time come to consist. "It may be … that *all enquiry on our part* is set so as to exempt certain propositions from doubt, if they are ever formulated." Many of our beliefs "lie apart from the route travelled by inquiry." "Much seems to be fixed, and it is removed from the traffic. It is so to speak shunted unto an unused siding. Now it gives our way of looking at things, and our researches, their form. Perhaps it was once disputed. But perhaps, for unthinkable ages, it has belonged to the *scaffolding* of our thoughts" (88, 211–212). "If the true is what is grounded, then the ground is not *true*, nor yet false." "The difficulty is to realize the groundlessness of our believing" (205, 166).

By comparison with a number of the other formulations that (from at least Immanuel Kant forward) are responsible for the wide influence of views of this kind, in the altered perspective in which we are now viewing it, Wittgenstein's version might be called moderate in character. On his account, the "unthought" may, here and now, be psychologically or even ontologically inaccessible to us, but it is not logically or epistemologically before or beyond our thinking. Although all certainty and all doubt, all reflection and judgment, presuppose that some beliefs "stand fast" (115, 160, 163, 156) as we form and act on, assess and revise others, it is not impossible that new circumstances will prompt us to question those that had previously gone unconsidered—even if for "unthinkable ages."[4]

Nor is Wittgenstein's argument a skepticism in the dogmatic form of a denial of our capacity to arrive at warranted beliefs, beliefs that pass the tests or satisfy the criteria appropriate to deciding whether to hold them. The passages I have

162   *Opacity, liberalism, and individuality*

been quoting, rather, are part of an argument that certitude concerning our beliefs, while never warranted ("grounded") in the supposititious, superstrong sense of being incorrigible or invulnerable to the very possibility of cogent questioning or dispute, is sometimes adequately warranted, sometimes not. Indeed they are part of an argument that has been styled complacent or conservative because of its affirmation that we often do know how to go on, that the combination of our native capacities and the languages, practices, and institutions that have developed among us enables (of course it does not guarantee) mutual intelligibility, successful attempts at action, and so on. Nor is there any reason to doubt that this going on can and does include forming, revising, and acting on conceptions of oneself and of others, noticing and responding to similarities and differences, entering into agreements and disagreements, and generally engaging in the kinds of thinking and acting of which human relationships commonly consist. In these respects, and despite the qualifications we have already encountered and will consider in more detail, Wittgenstein's investigations not only support the possibility of complementarism but identify ways in which individualities and pluralities stimulate and support one another. We might go further and say that his reflections promote the stance toward the possibility of complementarism that I entertained above.

The charge of complacency is badly misdirected if it accuses Wittgenstein of anything like the generally approving and optimistic attitudes toward extant political, social, and moral practice that I attributed to the American pluralists. Nothing in Wittgenstein's work suggests that individuals or groups are or will be gratified by the conceptions they form of themselves and others, by the character of the relationships that develop among them, by the outcomes of their actions and attempts at action. The characteristics that Wittgenstein identifies as sometimes enabling self-understanding and mutual intelligibility are consistent with relentless tyranny and intractable conflict, with extensive, intensive, and fruitful cooperation, with substantial dispersion and mutual indifference.[5]

It is true that much of Wittgenstein's later work is directed against philosophical doctrines that (wittingly or otherwise) have induced disillusionment and even despair in some quarters by insisting on criteria of "meaning" and "truth," "knowledge" and "understanding," "validity" and "justification," that cannot be satisfied. In dissolving these misconceived requirements, he clearly intends to provide reassurance against the most unqualified and unnerving forms of skepticism, solipsism, and nihilism, and he may bolster confidence in the ordinary procedures, the homely everyday standards, that those requirements are intended to discredit and to replace. No one closely acquainted with Wittgenstein's zigzag, maddeningly complex writings, with his often immediate problematizing of the very notions on which he himself has just relied, could believe that it was any part of his intention to engender generalized complacency in his readers. Nevertheless, a main reason for the kind of theorizing that Wittgenstein called *philosophical* (or at least what Wittgenstein himself identified as a main impetus to his own "philosophical investigations") is such facts as the following: "We do not *command* a clear view of our use of our words." The "aspects of things that are most important for us are hidden because of their simplicity and familiarity. (One is unable to notice something—because it is always before one's eyes.) We fail to be struck by what, once seen, is most striking and powerful" (Wittgenstein 1953, hereafter *Philosophical Investigations*, I, 122, 129). We become "entangled in our own rules" and fall into the kinds of contradictions that lead us to say such things as "I didn't mean it like that." "The civil status of a contradiction, or its status in civil life: there is the philosophical problem" (I, 125). Accordingly, a stated objective of his philosophizing is to "assemble reminders" of what we are ignoring or have overlooked or forgotten and thereby to provide a kind of "therapy" that can "unt[y the] knots in our thinking."[6] Whatever Wittgenstein's estimation of the probability of success in these activities, his evident belief that they are possible qualifies his views concerning the limitations on our thinking and acting. This and related qualifications that will be considered below constitute a major dimension of his thinking, a dimension that, again (and by contrast with the other investigators of the "unthought" that I gestured toward above?), affirms the *possibility* of complementarity and complementarism.

Close attention to the actual uses of our words and the standards of intelligibility and understanding actually employed in our practices and activities, then, can dissolve puzzles and paradoxes, enhance confidence, and diminish tendencies to angst. But it may also heighten awareness of ways in which our languages and practices (along with and in part due to the ways in which they are serviceable for us) are incomplete and indeterminate, opalescent, opaque and occluded, are of the ambiguous, the dissonant, and the incomprehensible in our experiences of ourselves and others. In short, Wittgenstein's analyses of the conditions necessary to the self- and mutual intelligibility that are (I am thus far assuming) presupposed by individuality and plurality can also be read as identifying circumstances under which those conditions are not and perhaps cannot be more than partially satisfied.

We have already seen that for Wittgenstein many of our most firmly fixed beliefs (whether held individually or, more frequently, shared more or less widely) are obscured from our view by the further beliefs for which they provide the "ungrounded grounds." Insofar as these most firmly fixed elements of thought include our beliefs about the similarities and differences between ourselves and others, we comprehend the relationships and interactions that those beliefs inform primarily to the extent that we have a grasp of the overall system or web or gestalt of beliefs of which they form a part. It is difficult and in various circumstances impossible for us to break into, as it were, the system so as to attend to its various parts. To this extent, the results of Wittgenstein's investigations can be said to circumscribe the possibilities for complementarity and complementarism.

(Do his reflections therefore promote a more skeptical stance toward the possibilities for individuality, plurality, or both? If liberalism presupposes these possibilities, do his reflections cast doubt on its tenability? Or is it possible that the very circumscriptions and qualifications that he identifies

164 *Opacity, liberalism, and individuality*

advantage individuality and plurality? Do they give us reason to qualify the assumptions with which I began and the connected view that both individualities and pluralities flourish best when there is complementarity among and between them? Are they consonant with and supportive of those differentiating and perhaps mutually isolating agent-relative and voluntarist elements that some liberal thinkers have taken from theology and philosophy and that I forward below? No on the first two counts, Yes on the others.)

"Our language forms an enormous system. And *only* within *this* system has a particular bit the value we give it" (*On Certainty*, 410, emphasis added).

> "I set the brake up by connecting up rod and lever."—Yes, given the whole of the rest of the mechanism. *Only* in conjunction with that is it a brake-lever, and separated from its support it is not even a lever; it may be anything, or nothing.
>
> (*Philosophical Investigations*, I, 6, emphasis added)

Accepting, that is, thinking and acting within, these systems or mechanisms, games, gestalts, or webs is not a defect or failure. "And that something stands fast for me is not grounded in my stupidity or credulity," not "hastiness or superficiality," not something done "out of thoughtlessness" (*On Certainty*, 235, 358, 657). "But it isn't that the situation is like this: We just *can't* investigate everything, and for that reason we are forced to rest content with assumption. If I want the door to turn, the hinges must stay put" (343).[7]

Assuming for the moment that the perimeters of such entities or units are clearly delineated (an assumption that will have to be qualified below), these pronouncements carry implications and consequences of some moment for the concerns of this essay. Consider:

> If someone wanted to arouse doubts in me and spoke like this: here your memory is deceiving you, there you've been taken in, there again you have not been thorough enough in satisfying yourself, etc., and if I did not allow myself to be shaken but kept to my certainty—then my doing so cannot be wrong, even if only because this is just what defines a game.

Faced with such challenges, indeed, "I find it quite correct for someone to say 'Rubbish!' and so brush aside the attempt to confuse him with doubts at bedrock." Equally, however, "I hold it to be incorrect if he seeks to defend himself (using, e.g., the words 'I know')" (497, 498).

Suppose that "we" who are "guided … by the propositions of physics" meet a people who

> instead of a physicist … consult an oracle. (And for that we consider them primitive.) Is it wrong for them to consult an oracle and be guided by it?—If we call this "wrong" aren't we using our language-game as a base from which to *combat* theirs?

Individuality, plurality, and liberalism 165

Or yet closer to home:

> But what men consider reasonable or unreasonable alters. At certain periods
> men find reasonable what at other periods they found unreasonable. And
> vice versa.
>   But is there no objective character here?
>   *Very* intelligent and well-educated people believe in the story of creation
> in the Bible, while others hold it as proven false, and the grounds of the
> latter are well known to the former.
>
> (336)[8]

Of course most senses of "combat" presuppose some degree of mutual understanding, some overlap or consilience among the language-games of the combat-
ants. Thus if combat is possible, couldn't we also give our adversaries reasons
for our views? Indeed, "wouldn't I give him *reasons?* Certainly; but how far do
they go? At the end of reasons comes *persuasion.* (Think what happens when
missionaries convert natives.)"[9] And as we may well be reminded by the
example of missionaries, "where two principles really do meet which cannot be
reconciled with one another" by reason, persuasion, or even combat, "then each
man declares the other a fool and a heretic" (609, 612, 611)—and acts on that
declaration.
    Language-games, forms of life, and the various less encompassing "systems"
in which thought and action occur enable mutual understanding and various
modes of cooperation and conflict among those party to them. In the setting of
the shared beliefs, rules, and conventions that constitute such a system, we sometimes even "say of some people that they are transparent to us." The very features of language-games that enable such relationships and interactions,
however, also diminish or disable these possibilities between or across the
boundaries of the games.

> It is, however, important as regards this observation [of transparency] that
> one human being can be a complete enigma to another. We learn this when
> we come into a strange country with entirely strange traditions; and, what is
> more, even given a mastery of the country's language. We do not *under-
> stand* the people. (And not because of not knowing what they are saying to
> themselves.) We cannot find our feet with them.
>
> (*Philosophical Investigations*, II, xi, p. 223)

Nor are the experiences of opacity, occlusion, and even stark incomprehensibility restricted to encounters with distant or otherwise unfamiliar traditions and
forms of life.

> I believe that every human being has two human parents; but Catholics
> believe that Jesus only had a human mother.... Catholics believe as well
> that in certain circumstances a wafer completely changes its nature, and at

166 *Opacity, liberalism, and individuality*

the same time that all evidence proves the contrary. And so if [G. E.] Moore said "I know that this is wine and not blood" Catholics would contradict him.

(*On Certainty*, 239)[10]

Do the "Wittgenstein" and the "Moore" of this passage understand the "Catholics" that figure in it? The former two, we can presume, have frequently encountered and very likely have had explained to them not only these particular beliefs but the larger set of tenets of which the doctrines of immaculate conception and transubstantiation are parts (we can presume this because the beliefs are, and for a long time have been, prominent in the traditions and culture in which "Wittgenstein" and "Moore" had their upbringing and lived their lives). That set of beliefs, we can also presume, includes numerous items that "Wittgenstein" and "Moore," whether or not they regard them as religious beliefs, fully accept (for example, the set of beliefs enunciated in Moore 1959). By these far-from-negligible criteria the answer to my question is yes. As Wittgenstein says in a related context:

In one sense, I understand all he says—the English words "God", "separate" etc. I understand. I could say: "I don't believe in this", and this would be true, meaning I haven't got these thoughts or anything that hangs together with them.[11]

Yet these particular beliefs of the "Catholics" seem to contradict beliefs about which "Wittgenstein" and "Moore" are entirely certain; indeed, they seem to contradict beliefs that are among the "grounds" of much else that "Wittgenstein" and "Moore" believe (240). On this view, even if "Wittgenstein" and "Moore" understand what we might call the propositional content of the beliefs of the "Catholics," they could understand how the "Catholics" *could* accept those beliefs only if they gave up much of what they themselves now believe, only if they were "converted" to the system of beliefs that the "Catholics" accept and think within.

There are numerous cases in which I not only do stand firm against the beliefs of others—including others in the community or communities of which I am part and with which I identify—but am justified in doing so in that everything in my system of beliefs supports—no, *requires* my doing so.[12] Am I then also justified in claiming that I understand the views I am rejecting? The sentence that completes the paragraph just quoted reads: "But not that I could contradict the thing"; and Wittgenstein then considers the objection " 'Well, if you can't contradict him, that means you don't understand him. If you did understand him, then you might.' " To which he responds: "That again is Greek to me. My normal technique of language leaves me. I don't know whether to say they understand one another or not" (Wittgenstein 1967a, hereafter *Lectures and Conversations*, p. 55).

Let us pause to consider whether we have reached points on which there is convergence between these parts of Wittgenstein's thinking and views concerning individuality and plurality that have for some time been widely accepted in

Individuality, plurality, and liberalism   167

numerous modern Western societies and that are regarded by many as essential to any form of liberalism. Religious beliefs and believing, it is widely held, are categorially different from beliefs and believing of other kinds. As it is sometimes put, religion is at least partly a matter of faith or deep conviction, not of knowledge or even of belief in the ordinary sense of a view I hold because of evidence or argumentation and that is more or less readily susceptible to revision or rejection. This is one of a number of reasons why attempts to promote or to impose uniformity of religious belief and practice fail to achieve their objectives as they engender intractable conflict and inflict grievous harms. And for many it is for the same reasons that there must be toleration of a wide diversity of religious beliefs and practices. In this regard, plurality and perhaps individuality are, in a deeper-than-usual sense of the expression, *faute de mieux*.

It is a further point—further both to the commitment to toleration that I cautiously attributed to modern Western societies and to the passages I have quoted from Wittgenstein—to claim that proponents of differing religious beliefs often do not understand one another. Beginning with the former, it is widely thought that tolerance presupposes understanding sufficient for disapproval as distinct from bare recognition of difference or incompatibility.[13] Just as, on this view, we cannot "tolerate" that which we think good or right, neither can we be tolerant (or intolerant) of that about which we are unable to form a judgment or make an assessment. Is this insistently judgmental, even censorious, character of our thinking about toleration partly responsible for the grudging, regretful, even sour quality often characteristic of relations marked by tolerance? If so, what would be the practical consequences of a more radical view (whether or not it is Wittgenstein's) according to which often or even for the most part we have no more than partial understandings of religious confessions other than our own? Would such a view engender or permit a stance more supportive of religious diversity than mere tolerance of it? A more generous and in that sense a more liberal doctrine of religious freedom?[14] Or would recognition of the limitations on our understandings engender anxieties so unnerving as to make mutual tolerance—hardly to be despised—impossible for us?

It is clear that Wittgenstein regarded religious beliefs and believing (or beliefs and believing that are genuinely religious, as we should perhaps say) as marked by certain characteristic features. For example, in religious matters "you don't get … the form of controversy where one person is *sure* of the thing, and the other says: 'Well, possibly'." "There hasn't been opposed to those who believe in Resurrection those who say 'Well, possibly'." "This is partly why one would be reluctant to say: 'These people rigorously hold the opinion (or view) that there is a Last Judgement.' 'Opinion' sounds queer." "It is for this reason that different words are used: 'dogma', 'faith'." "We don't talk about hypothesis, or about high probability. Nor about knowing." "In a religious discourse we use such expressions as: 'I believe that so and so will happen,' and use them differently to the way in which we use them in science" (*Lectures and Conversations*, pp. 56–57). Sometimes a person gives

168 *Opacity, liberalism, and individuality*

> up a practice when he has seen that something on which it depended is an error, but ... this is not how it is in connection with the religious practices of a people and what we have here is *not* an error.[15]

These passages affirm an assumption tacitly at work in the discussion thus far, namely, that we sometimes understand or misunderstand religious thinking and acting in the sense that we identify or misidentify them *as religious*. Moreover, in understanding that religious discourse is usually characterized by a certain configuration of characteristics and the absence of a number of others that are typical of science, mathematics, and so on, we do more than classify or categorize. Identifying thoughts and actions as religious is integral to engaging with and otherwise relating to them. Our identifications carry with them expectations and criteria of judgment that inform and guide us as we "go on" with our religious (and our antireligious) activities.

Let us combine this claim with remarks considered earlier in which Wittgenstein says that we often understand many of the individual words and propositions that occur in religions that we do not accept, and perhaps understand yet more of the discourse of religions that we accept wholly or in part. Bringing these elements together has the effect of replacing the (philosopher's?) dichotomy "understand/don't understand" with a diverse and unstable array of possibilities that includes understanding in some respects but not others, various combinations of understanding and misunderstanding, not knowing whether we understand, and mixtures of certainty and uncertainty as to whether the notions "understanding" and "misunderstanding" have any application in the circumstances in which we find ourselves. My apparently univocal question, Do "Moore" and "Wittgenstein" understand the "Catholics"? masks many different questions, some of which make little or no sense; when unpacked, my "question" has many different answers or none. (Hence the "answers" have a diversity of implications for judgment and action vis-à-vis religion.)

Wittgenstein effects this and like substitutions throughout the entire domain of believing and doubting, judging and assessing, agreeing and disagreeing. Contrary to the assumption that I have been making, Wittgenstein's "unit of analysis" concepts—system, culture, form of life, language-game, and practice—do not differentiate sharply distinct domains of thought and action. Perhaps because "God" and the other concepts characteristic of religious discourse "are among the earliest learnt" (*Lectures and Conversations*, p. 59), Wittgenstein is confident that we are, or at any rate often are, able to recognize and relate to religious beliefs and practices. Nevertheless, "different connections would make [a set of statements] into religious beliefs, and there can easily be imagined transitions where we wouldn't know for our life whether to call them religious beliefs or scientific beliefs" (p. 58). (Creation science?) But this situation, so far from being unique to or even distinctive of religion, is characteristic of all our language-games.[16] Like the concept of game from which it might be viewed as a projection, "language-game" itself (and hence religion, logic, politics and all other language-games) is a family-resemblance term, one that gathers a number

Individuality, plurality, and liberalism   169

of phenomena with recognizable and for some purposes salient similarities but no single common element or set of elements that is the necessary and sufficient condition for its correct use. The absence of such a commonality, and of the univocality and certitude that some philosophers who hanker for commonality believe it would make possible, is not a defect, does not disable our ordinary, routine, unhesitating uses of the concept.[17] But it does mean that sometimes we will "not know for our life" whether to call something a language-game, a game, a religious or scientific belief, *and so on* (*Philosophical Investigations*, I, 65ff.).

In various combinations and intensities, such mixtures of luminosity, transparency, and fluency with opacity, hesitation, and doubt obtain through the entire inventory of the concepts we have, have had, and might come to have, through all of the thinking and acting that we do in and with these concepts. Not only is it "a matter of course for me to call this colour 'blue'" but "there is in general complete agreement in the judgments of colours made by those who have been diagnosed normal [e.g., not color blind]" (I, 238; II, xi, p. 227). But equally, any number of considerations can be assembled to "show the indeterminateness in the concept of colour or again in that of sameness of colour."[18] "Just try—in a real case—to doubt someone else's fear or pain" (*Philosophical Investigations*, I, 303; cf. I, 391). But equally:

> I am sure, *sure*, that he is not pretending; but some third person is not. Can I always convince him? And if not is there some mistake in his reasoning or observations? "You're all at sea!"—we say this when someone doubts what we recognize as clearly genuine—but we cannot prove anything.
>
> (II, xi, p. 227)

> It is certainly possible to be convinced by evidence that someone is in such-and-such state of mind, that, for instance, he is not pretending. But "evidence" here includes "imponderable" evidence...
>
> Imponderable evidence includes subtleties of glance, of gesture, of tone.
>
> I may recognize a genuine loving look, distinguish it from a pretended one (and here there can, of course, be a "ponderable" confirmation of my judgment). But I may be quite incapable of describing the difference. And this not because the languages I know have no words for it. For why not introduce new words?—If I were a very talented painter I might conceivably represent the genuine and the simulated glance in pictures.
>
> (II, xi, p. 228)

And so on

There is no doubt that Wittgenstein had an abiding interest in religion and its place in our forms of life. Along with reflecting about its distinctive characteristics, however, in the passages considered above he is using religious examples to call attention to characteristics that obtain in respect to *all* knowing and believing, *all* thinking and acting, characteristics that sometimes enable and enrich,

170 *Opacity, liberalism, and individuality*

sometimes circumscribe and prevent, mutual understanding and the kinds of interaction that it makes possible. On his readings of the forms of life, language-games, and practices with which his investigations were concerned, what I (but not Wittgenstein) have called the conditions of complementarity are sometimes satisfied, sometimes not; most often they are satisfied in some respects, not satisfied in others. If we want to find out where, when, and to what extent they are satisfied, his advice, succinct in the giving, arduous in the following, is "don't think, but look!" (I, 66).

IV

Let us recall in somewhat enlarged terms some of the issues and disagreements that prompted us to examine Wittgenstein's investigations. Here are some of the more striking claims advanced by those who profess to have "looked" at individuality, plurality, and related matters in modern Western societies. (1) Whether forced or otherwise, the members of these societies are compressed or are congealing into a mass of unthinking look-alikes among whom individuality and plurality are no more than marginal possibilities. There are many shared beliefs and values, numerous and insistently enforced conventions, norms, and expectations, but these work against, not for, plurality and especially individuality. (Tocqueville, Thoreau, William James, Nietzsche, Weber, Ortega y Gasset, Arendt, Goffman, Oakeshott.) (2) These societies have dispersed or are steadily fractionating into an atomized and anomic array of individuals and insular groups among whom mutual understanding is for the most part impossible. Individualism and other forms of idiosyncrasy and parochialism are rampant, but they breed frustration and despair, suspicion and antagonism, not fulfillment, mutual appreciation, or cooperation. (Emile Durkheim, Dumont, Leo Strauss, contemporary communitarians such as Charles Taylor, Robert Nisbet, Ivan Illych, Alasdair MacIntyre.) (3) Some of these societies present a gratifying mix of commonality, individuality, and plurality, which is, or with relatively modest modifications could become, the basis for a fruitful combination of cooperation and competition. (American pluralists, Marx in his more optimistic moments, much liberalism from John Stuart Mill, if not from John Locke, to Rawls and Richard Rorty.)

These sustained, self-consciously developed accounts are reflections of beliefs that present themselves, in various combinations, in the views of those who "look" in the sense (perhaps closer to the one Wittgenstein had in mind) of "keeping their eyes open" as they go about the activities of every day. (1) As members of these societies we are constrained and oppressed by an intrusive state and its bureaucracy, by the tyranny of the majority, of the rich or the poor, of the multinational corporations or the military-industrial complex, the media, the dominant gender or race, or of some other more covert or for other reasons less readily identifiable hegemon (2) Crime, substance abuse, and many other forms of deviance and degradation are rampant; laxity and self-indulgence are manifest in the refusal of parents to parent, of teachers to teach, of workers to

Individuality, plurality, and liberalism 171

work and managements to manage, of governments to govern with an eye to anything more than the present moment or the preservation of their power. (3) These societies are basically satisfactory; certainly they are to be preferred to all the historical and contemporaneous alternatives.

Wittgenstein neither arbitrates among these sweeping generalizations-cum-evaluations nor attempts to settle the numerous more delimited points of disagreement and dispute out of which grand controversies of these kinds arise. His investigations direct our attention to the features of our experience that produce and sustain these divergent accounts and assessments of it, but the suppositions behind his advice to look, not think, strongly suggest that resolving the disagreements falls less to philosophers or theorists than to all of us as participants in social and political life.

Should it be among our objectives to resolve them? Or are there respects in which individuality, plurality, or both are protected or otherwise advantaged by these diversities and conflicts? Does (would) concern for individuality and plurality press us, as liberals or otherwise, to be "critical" as "far down" and as "far out" as is possible for us, down or out far enough to find or create greater common ground?

From Socrates's animadversions concerning the unexamined life through Hegel's celebration of Reason to Jürgen Habermas's promotion of undistorted communication, much in our tradition returns affirmative answers to these questions. Self- and mutual understanding—what Charles Taylor thinks of as clairvoyance concerning our beliefs and values and their harmony or disharmony with both our deepest or truest selves and with the norms, mores, and aspirations of our society and our culture is or should be our ideal.[19] We should regard opacity and occlusion in the same ways that we look on ignorance and irrationality, that is, as defects to be remedied where possible, deficiencies that should be regretted where they cannot be eliminated.

Although hardly characteristic of Wittgenstein himself, these aspirations are not generally, certainly not categorically, disqualified or discredited by his investigations. However, along with his assiduous efforts to clarify this, that, and the next of our confusions, he denies that the unthought in our thinking prevents us from "going on," suggests that the groundlessness of our believing, the indeterminacy in our rules, the often enigmatic character of others and indeed of our selves are sometimes essential to our doing so.

Should we go further than he did and say that limitations on our self- and our mutual understandings provide protections for and otherwise enhance individuality and plurality? As to the first point, there is indeed reason to think that the hinges that are most likely to stay put so that I or we can act (and therefore possibly enact and reenact myself or ourselves) are those of which I am unaware or aware that I *must* let stand as they are if the door of action is going to turn.[20] On the second and yet more provocative point, if you (they) do not understand me (us), or do not know whether you understand me or not, your ability to enter into my affairs, certainly your capacity to do so skillfully and especially insidiously, is diminished. Argumentation, persuasion, command and other forms of authoritative direction,

172 *Opacity, liberalism, and individuality*

and even coercion presuppose some degree of mutual understanding; even successful manipulation requires understanding on the part of the manipulator, misunderstanding on the part of the manipulated. Of course territorial and other boundaries, property and other rights, law, morality, polities, and the conventions of polite conduct all afford protections—among other things they afford—against these influences and intrusions. But these arrangements and institutions, in addition to being variable in their efficacy and making substantial demands on the resources of those they are intended to protect, can be efficacious only to the extent that they themselves restrict and indeed intrude. By contrast, when we stand to one another's beliefs as Wittgenstein described his (?) relation to certain of the beliefs of Catholics, then we are at a loss regarding the particulars of those beliefs and hence regarding one another insofar as we hold and act on them. We identify the beliefs as such, and one another as holders of beliefs, on the basis of aspects of one another that we do understand, and we can act with and against one another in these respects. But because the beliefs in question do not mesh, join, or even meet, we can act neither with nor against one another in respect to them.

Let us briefly consider some yet headier and perhaps more disconcerting possibilities that have been explored and even promoted by thinkers far more explicit than Wittgenstein in their desire to protect and enhance plurality and especially individuality. In seeking an assured basis for that species of individuality that they called "tranquillity" (*ataraxia*), the Pyrrhonians among both ancient and early modern skeptics (Sextus Empiricus, Michel de Montaigne, Pierre Bayle, David Hume) found inadequate (or overly demanding of efforts and other resources to maintain) the cultivated indifference to others promoted by much Stoicism and (later) by reclusives and misanthropes such as Rousseau (in some among his many moods!) and Thoreau. The skeptics relied, rather, on the protections provided by the impossibility of knowing the truth or falsity of what they and others believed. Even if we can understand one another's beliefs in the senses that Wittgenstein says he can understand the beliefs of the Catholics, recognition of the impossibility of determining the truth or falsity of those beliefs eliminates the only (as it were) objective or even fully exchangeable justifications for acting on our own and against others' beliefs. Sextus, Montaigne, and Hume among others, and Hobbes in respect to religious beliefs, promoted these views in the hope of stilling or calming the destructive dogmatisms, enthusiasms, and fanaticisms generated by convictions of the truth of my or our views, the falsity of yours.[21] More important, they and later writers influenced by them let their skeptical dispositions—and their reasons for valorizing what they hoped would be the consequences of wide cultivation of like dispositions—extend from the content of our beliefs to our believing itself and thereby to that whole range of our understandings of one another that are concerned with our believing and our acting on our beliefs. Rejecting the view that we hold our beliefs because of something apart from us and in principle accessible to all of us, that is, because of properties of the subjects or objects of our beliefs (e.g., the properties that make the beliefs true), they explained the phenomenon of believing in terms of attributes of those who hold beliefs. They and their successors in this regard then

Individuality, plurality, and liberalism 173

summoned for this explanatory purpose attributes to which, on their view, persons other than those holding the beliefs have restricted access and sometimes no access, for example, the individual person's passions or desires, or her unconscious; the traditions, conventions, language, and so forth, of the community or group; the "standpoint" or "consciousness" of the class or caste.

In the first form discussed, acceptance of a skeptical outlook largely deprives others of the possibility of refuting my beliefs and hence of the *justifications* for actions vis-à-vis me that may be provided by evidence or argumentation showing that my beliefs are false. On the extension of skepticism just outlined, you are also unable or little able to understand why I hold my beliefs, how I came to hold them. It follows that the *possibility* of your acting skillfully and efficaciously to alter my beliefs is diminished, if not eliminated. Your actions or movements may, in fact, affect my beliefs and those of my actions informed by those beliefs, but they do so more by chance than by your design.

These limitations on the very possibility of mutual access and influence (as distinct, again, from limitations deliberately created and sustained by me or by us) were greatly extended by later writers, some of whom are successors to earlier skepticisms. One particularly far-reaching extension (which ended if it did not begin in a dogmatic albeit a domain-restricted skepticism) can be understood in (roughly) the following manner: If meaning in the sense in which we say that language and other signs are meaningful is a function of truth and falsity (depends on the truth-evaluableness/falsifiability of the propositions that purport to be meaningful), then skepticism about truth and falsity provides the much thicker insulation of mutual meaninglessness. Logical empiricism adopted this theory of meaning, and those members of this school of thought who were also robust emotivists (for example, A. J. Ayer and Moritz Schlick) combined it with the claim that the "propositions" distinctive of ethics, aesthetics, and religion are not truth-evaluable and hence are meaningless. On this alarming view we are, in the most literal sense, meaningless to one another throughout the entire axiological realm, have access to and can deliberately influence one another only to the limited extent that we understand the psychological states that our (pseudo)propositions "evince."[22]

Whether or not the emotivists regretted these enormous circumscriptions on mutual intelligibility (if regret is an evaluative term, they would have to have held that it would be meaningless for them to *say* they regretted them),[23] there are no signs of regret concerning the conclusions, which are analogous to those of the emotivists in their unqualifiedly voluntarist or agent-relative character, reached by say, William James, Søren Kierkegaard, or the Jean-Paul Sartre of *Being and Nothingness*. Nor is regret a pervasive feature of those postmodernist doctrines that have assaulted the enlightenment ideals mentioned earlier by insisting on an *inpensee* irremediably beneath or apart from our thinking, on the radically indeterminate, aporia- and caesura-ridden character of our "texts" and "text-analogues" and so forth, that is, on the various ways in which our claims to mutual intelligibility are delusive, if not vain, conceits.

Lurking and sometimes explicit in these several views are variants of the idea that I initially drew out of some of Wittgenstein's observations, namely, that

174 *Opacity, liberalism, and individuality*

opacity creates spaces protective of individuality and plurality, makes it difficult and sometimes impossible for those who are other to individuals or groups to know or understand them well enough to diminish their distinctiveness by acting with or against them. If individuality means that, in fact, there are individuals who in some or all of their thought and action (as well as in their physical makeup) are not assimilated or assimilable to, commensurate or commensurable with, one another, then on these doctrines individuality is an ineliminable feature of the human condition.

Reactions to the views I have sketched (perhaps including the tendency to ignore or deflect attention from these elements in Wittgenstein's thinking) leave no doubt that this is an idea that is deeply disturbing to many. Nor are these reactions surprising. Few would deny that in fact we often fail to understand one another; and the claim that in important respects we cannot but fail to do so is familiar enough among the philosophically inclined. But the further proposition that these limitations should be protected, welcomed, and even cultivated challenges the soaring aspirations I mentioned earlier—and much more. It would appear that to accept this proposition is to reject, in the name of the value of individuality and perhaps of certain forms of plurality, not only manifestly unrealizable ideals of entire, opacity-excluding mutual transparency but the very doctrine that I and numerous others have treated as a main support for individuality and plurality. For those who accept this proposition, most versions of complementarism are enemies, not friends, of individuality, quite possibly of plurality.

V

We are on, or rather over, the brink of absurdities that I have been trying to avoid from the first words of this chapter.

Pressed very hard, the view that there is not (or should not be) *any* mutual intelligibility makes (would make) individuality and plurality at once unavoidable and impossible, thereby falling into incoherence. If my or our distinctiveness, in all but the most crudely physical respects, owes nothing to, is unknowable by, and hence is impervious to others, then, humanly speaking, it is invulnerable, guaranteed. Individualities and pluralities are not achievements, they are divine or natural facts, unalterable by humankind.[24] All of the apparent cases of individuality- or group-destroying impositions, oppressions, and controls are and must be illusory.[25] But equally, individuality and plurality are impossible because neither term draws any distinction. Even if I could know, realize, or somehow experience my own characteristics, my inability to know or understand the characteristics of anyone else would prevent me from regarding my self as distinctive, from viewing myself as characterized by individuality. And assuming that we can know our characteristics as a culture, society, or group, our inability to understand the characteristics of any other such entity would prevent us from regarding ourselves as one among a plurality of entities.[26]

The (fraternal) twin of this absurdity is the view that there is (or should be) no opacity or mutual unintelligibility among us because in all but physical respects

Individuality, plurality, and liberalism   175

we are (should make ourselves, or otherwise become) one with one another, form an internally undifferentiated whole or wholes that is or are fully intelligible to us. Here individuality and plurality in the sense of diversities within the whole appear to be rendered impossible while their opposites, oneness or unity, are made necessary. Once again, however, the distinctions or contrasts on which the cogency of these claims depend have been conceptually obviated.

From a Wittgensteinian standpoint, the attempt to press as hard on notions like opacity as I have tried to imagine defeats itself because it presupposes the very thing that the attempt purports to question or to deny, that is, *some* mutual intelligibility.[27] This does not mean that mutual intelligibility, or any particular distribution of intelligibility and unintelligibility, is divinely or metaphysically guaranteed to us; it only means that some such intelligibility is presupposed by the activity of thinking about the extent to which we are and are not, should seek to be or to avoid becoming, intelligible to one another.[28]

Setting these absurdities aside helps us to see that the attitudes and reactions toward intelligibility and unintelligibility that are familiar among us are as variable as the distributions of the two. As Wittgenstein's discussions would suggest (are intended to reflect?), we sometimes sanctify and worship that which is beyond our understanding, sometimes contemn and attempt to obliterate it. In some settings familiarity, obviousness, and transparency breed indifference and contempt; in others they are sources of reassurance, of comfort, and of contentment. Some people and some groups are assiduous in their efforts to disclose themselves fully to and to engage regularly and deeply with numerous others; they dislike and distrust the unknown and the uncertain, the protective and the private, the reclusive and the exclusive.[29] Others seek to sustain and to cultivate the latter conditions and qualities, viewing disclosure as display and theatricality, regularity and predictability as monotony, exposure as vulnerability, engagement as mutual intrusion, cooperation as dependency and diminution. More commonly, perhaps, individuals and groups manifest one of these outlooks in some of the domains of their activities, quite different ones in others.

As the last observation (and indeed much of what I have considered in this essay) suggests, it is deeply implausible to think that one or another of these patterns or modes is categorically or even generally to be preferred to the other. Thinking and acting within the conditions necessary to both, preferring one to the other, are matters of practical (that is, of circumstantial) judgment. There has been, however, a tendency—including a tendency within complementarism and liberalism—to favor the first of the two patterns I sketched, a resistance and not infrequently an antagonism toward the second. In the (liberal?) spirit of counter-cyclical pedagogy, let us therefore take somewhat further our exploration of the advantages and disadvantages of the latter.

There is no denying the risks, including those to individuality and plurality, involved in embracing and promoting mutual indifference, misanthropy, and isolation. Having disabused us of the self-defeating versions of this program, Wittgenstein himself signals some of the dangers here when he observes that people who find themselves at a loss with one another—and who can't or don't

176 *Opacity, liberalism, and individuality*

want to ignore one another altogether or in the respects in which they find one another incomprehensible—often call one another fools and heretics. This brief but pregnant observation reminds us that various heavier-handed kinds of impositions remain possible, under some circumstances are made easier and hence more likely, by limitations on mutual understanding. Where we are as brute facts to one another, *ressentiment*, fear, anxiety, and even certain unthinking forms of disdain and megalomania sometimes prompt us to behave toward one another in the brutal ways all too characteristic of our conduct toward animals and our natural environment generally.

Typically, these impositions are more costly, inefficient, and hence self-limiting than forms of interaction and influence that benefit from some degree of mutual understanding. Any number of political thinkers (perhaps most elegantly David Hume) have emphasized, for example, that political rule based entirely on brute force is not so much as a possibility; rule relying heavily on force is certain to be ineffective and likely to be short-lived in that those exercising it will soon be forced to give way to others. Perhaps more relevant here, it is arguable that such impositions, whether political or otherwise, are less damaging to individuality and plurality than modes of influence and control that work, as it were, through the beliefs, values, and judgments of those influenced and controlled. To the extent that my individuality or the distinctiveness of our group, society, or culture consists of my or our desires and interests, of the beliefs and values I or we hold, of the dispositions and aptitudes I or we have cultivated, impositions of these kinds may leave individuality and plurality intact.

Of course, these qualities can be eroded and sometimes destroyed by the infliction of prolonged pain and suffering, by subjecting individuals and groups to compulsions and restraints that prevent them from acting on their beliefs and values, from putting their aptitudes to use.[30] Along with bearing in mind the resources needed to make and sustain such impositions on any very large number of people, we want to distinguish as well as we can between the effects of physical impositions and those of the terror, indoctrination, manipulation, and so forth that commonly accompany them, and we do not want to forget those who have sustained and even heightened their individuating characteristics despite imprisonment and other forms of confinement and constraint, torture and severe physical deprivations. Nevertheless, and whatever might be the most effective means of preventing and combating such evils, we certainly do not want to pretend them away or to be careless concerning them.

The individualities and pluralities that we have encountered in Wittgenstein are in the setting of various degrees and forms of commonality and mutual understanding. The beliefs and values, aptitudes and dispositions, that I and we acquire and develop are formed and altered as I or we encounter (directly and vicariously) the thoughts and actions of others. How I or we respond to those encounters is itself in varying degrees understandable by myself (ourselves) and others.

To the extent that we understand that we do not understand these responses, or even understand that we do not know whether our notions of understanding get any foothold concerning them, it is open to us to regard them as loci of

Individuality, plurality, and liberalism   177

individuality and plurality and to look on them with either favor or disfavor, with relish and delight, or with fear and loathing. (If we do not understand even this much, the matter, as Hobbes somewhere wryly says, "arises not for deliberation.") As with reactions to other phenomena that we call mysterious, which of these responses this or that person or group makes may itself be among the most mysterious of our experiences.

To the extent that we understand more than this, additional and more differentiated possibilities may present themselves. Understanding that you believe X but not why you believe it, I may distance myself from you generally or in respect to this among your beliefs. Or I might approach very close indeed, might be so attracted by your belief that I want to become as one with you in holding and acting on it, or so affrighted by it that I want to extirpate your belief and, if necessary, you. Which of these and the very large number of other attitudes I adopt and courses of action I take will be influenced by many considerations in addition to my assessment of your belief.

The figure transcribed by this chapter approximates a circle. Examination of the conditions of complementarity has confirmed and extended the understanding that individuality and plurality are conceptually interwoven. Nor has our examination discountenanced the complementarist expectation that, existentially, individualities and pluralities will often be mutually enhancing. I have nevertheless ended a little apart from where I began. I have done so because I found reason to think that both individuality and plurality can be advantaged by circumstances often judged to be incompatible with or uncongenial to them, disadvantaged by conditions that influential versions of complementarism affirm and promote.

For reasons mentioned at intervals through the chapter and reiterated in somewhat different terms just above, the considerations I have adduced and the conclusions I have reached resolve few, if any, of the moral and political issues encountered in the course of the reflection. The only doctrines that I have claimed to invalidate defeat themselves without my help, and my attempts to delineate possibilities and desirabilities have been in terms much too general, to settle questions of action or policy.

There may, however, be a modest upshot along the ideological—and to that extent the practical—dimension that I have tried to maintain. In foregrounding and valorizing not only difference, separation, and incompatibility but indeterminacy, opacity, and incomprehensibility, I have urged favorable consideration of features of human affairs that have no better than an insecure place in liberal thinking, that are accorded much greater prominence in doctrines and outlooks widely regarded to be illiberal. But if liberalism does value individuality and plurality, and if these features of human affairs protect and enhance them, then the porous and fluctuating ensemble of ideas that we call liberalism would be the better if it were more accommodating to, more welcoming of, them.[31]

178 *Opacity, liberalism, and individuality*

Notes

1 A newcomer to the neighborhood with an enthusiasm for tennis but no partners takes to hitting tennis balls against a wall of the local school. Seeing her do this, another resident in the same plight approaches to propose a game at the somewhat deteriorated municipal court. The game attracts the attention and interest of others, leading to an active tennis club, which also builds a swimming pool, a badminton court, and starts a child-care center.

What if my tennis enthusiast has just arrived not in a neighborhood in which tennis is widely known and accepted but in a culture unfamiliar with it? Familiar with it but regarding it as frivolous and self-indulgent? Acceptant of it for men but decidedly not for women? As different as initial and perhaps continuing reactions to her wall volleying would certainly be, perhaps...

2 Two newcomers to a community with an active tennis club are pressed to join. Newcomer Able overcomes her theretofore reclusive and otherwise reticent disposition and becomes an active player with an unusual style of play, as well as a distinctive participant in social life centering on the club. Reacting against what she experiences as unwelcome pressure, newcomer Baker refuses to join, and the encounter prompts her to begin writing introspective poetry that is opaque but beguiling to the cloistered writing group with which she occasionally meets.

It is unlikely that many of the inhabitants of the city of Kandahar will have opportunities to join tennis clubs, much less likely that women inhabitants of that city will do so. But then there was a time when there was no such thing as the game of tennis, later times when it was unknown or known but unplayed over most of the globe...

3 We might say that the radical critics I mentioned are united in rejecting G. W. F. Hegel's claim—the quintessential claim of the quintessential complementarist—that theorizing is now unnecessary because Reason has already triumphed within and among ourselves and our practices.

4 In order to write a check and subtract the amount on the ledger I must "hold constant" the system of banking, of numbers, of addition and subtraction, I must assume the durability of paper and of writing in ink, the postal system and everything that it depends on, and so forth through a very long list. But there are those who reflect about and otherwise attend to these components of actions such as mine, and even the familiar act of writing a check *might* prompt me to join their company.

5 Familiarity with the substantial and growing biographical materials available concerning Wittgenstein will hardly encourage the thought that he was approving of or optimistic concerning the state of political, social, or moral affairs in his own time. Aside, however, from brief remarks such as his characterization of his times as "in ... darkness" (*Philosophical Investigations*, Preface), Wittgenstein's philosophical works largely avoid these topics and issues.

6 Wittgenstein, 1967b, 452. For purposes of this discussion I deliberately de-emphasize Wittgenstein's view that much of his philosophical work was occasioned by the confusions generated by previous philosophers. I assess this aspect of his view in *Toward a Liberalism* (1989), esp. ch. 1.

7 "My *life* consists in my being content to accept many things" (*On Certainty*, 344). "What has to be accepted, the given, is—so one could say—forms of life" (*Philosophical Investigations*, II, xi, 226).

8 Very intelligent and well-educated people believe in liberalism, socialism, and communitarianism, in supply-side economics, conspiracy theories of the assassination of John F. Kennedy, the right to abortion on demand, the deterrent effect of the death penalty, the harmfulness of eating red meats, the efficacy of psychoanalysis, while others hold these beliefs to be proven false, and the grounds of the latter beliefs are well known to those who hold the former ones.

Individuality, plurality, and liberalism   179

9 Thinking the thought that Wittgenstein here recommends might be assisted by attention to works such as Tzvetan Todorov's *The Conquest of America* (1984).
10 As through much of *On Certainty*, Wittgenstein's reference to Moore is primarily to the latter's "In Defence of Common Sense," ch. 2, in G. E. Moore (1959).
11 *Lectures and Conversations*, p. 55.
12 Cf. *On Certainty*, 667. It is perhaps worth underlining that these of Wittgenstein's discussions are askew of much of the debate currently conducted in terms of dichotomies such as holism–atomism, communitarianism–individualism, embodied–disembodied or encumbered–unencumbered selves.
13 For critical discussion of this view, see Raz (1986), esp. ch. 15.
14 Cf. José Ortega y Gasset: "Liberalism … is the supreme form of generosity; it is the right by which the majority concedes to minorities and hence it is the noblest cry that has ever resounded in this planet." Regrettably, this "cry" is now largely stifled. "The mass … does not wish to share life with those who are not of it. It has a deadly hatred of all that is not itself" (1932, 83–84).
15 Ludwig Wittgenstein, *Remarks on Frazer's "The Golden Bough,"* quoted in Peter Winch (1987, 109).
16 Of the Wittgensteinian categories, "language-game" is perhaps the most appropriate for thinking about religion in modern Western societies. One might use the usually more encompassing "form of life" in thinking about, say, medieval European Christianity or Islam in contemporary Iran. But the observations that follow apply to all of the "unit of analysis" concepts that Wittgenstein employs.

17   The more narrowly we examine actual language, the sharper becomes the conflict between it and our requirement [i.e., the connected requirements of commonality, univocality, etc.]. (For the crystalline purity of logic was, of course, not a *result of investigation*: it was a requirement.) The conflict becomes intolerable; the requirement is now in danger of becoming empty.—We have got on to slippery ice where there is no friction and so in a certain sense the conditions are ideal, but also, just because of that, we are unable to walk. We want to walk: so we need *friction*. Back to the rough ground!

      (*Philosophical Investigations*, I, 107)

18 Wittgenstein 1978, hereafter *Remarks on Colour*, I, 17. This work assembles a large array of considerations that support the generalization I quote above.
19 Taylor (1976), esp. pp. 160ff and (1986), vol. 1, esp. essays 1, 2, and 4; vol. 2, esp. essays 5, 7, and 8.
20 The first of these formulations ("unaware") is close to Oakeshott's in *Rationalism in Politics* [1962] and to more general doctrines about the role of "prejudice" in thought and action from Edmund Burke to Hans Georg Gadamer. The second ("aware that I *must* let stand") has many affinities with Oakeshott's treatment (*On Human Conduct* (1975), Essay 1) of the distinction between the theorist whose task is constantly to interrogate the presuppositions of her understandings and who is thereby disabled from action and the practitioner who treats the identifications and understandings of which her thinking now consists as diagnoses and prescriptions, that is, as invitations to action rather than to further theorizing. The latter also resembles Hannah Arendt's concern that the injunction "stop and think" stills the impulse to action (see esp. *The Life of the Mind* (1978), vol. 1). On all of these doctrines, thinking in the sense of unremitting questioning of the beliefs and understandings that we have thus far acquired is a siren's song to which we often must—willfully—close our ears if the life of action is to continue. Is this why these thinkers are widely regarded as antiliberal and even illiberal? Can liberalism accommodate these views? Can it do so to a yet greater extent than I have suggested some versions of it have already done so?

180 *Opacity, liberalism, and individuality*

It is striking that contemporary proponents of self- and mutual clairvoyance and rationality in ethics such as Charles Taylor and Alasdair MacIntyre also promote community and solidarity, values previously forwarded by conservative thinkers such as Edmund Burke, Joseph de Maistre, and François Chateaubriand, who thought they could be sustained only where the ultimately mysterious character of the human condition was not only accepted but cherished.

21 Because they do not discredit my *belief* that my views are superior to yours (or, in Hobbes's case, the propriety of the sovereign establishing and requiring public acceptance of a single religion—and in some respects moral—view), as thus far described these arguments could be said to promote toleration of the type that involves disapproval of the beliefs or practices tolerated.

22 Ayer (1946), esp. chap. 6; Schlick (1962).

23 Cf. Wittgenstein, *Tractatus* (1922), and "A Lecture on Ethics" (1965).

24 Or, on the Kantian version, synthetic a priori truths, truths that reason must accept, cannot alter.

25 Thus, pressed not quite so hard in this direction, these considerations yield blindness to or complacency concerning some of the ugliest moments in human experience. Retreating to what Isaiah Berlin calls the Inner Citadel, I close my eyes to, or look with indifference on, the worst that others do not only to my family and friends but to me. See Berlin (1960), esp. pp. 135–141. I return to this point below.

26 In short, pressing very hard on the reality or desirability of mutual unintelligibility (or, as we see just below, their opposites) is one of the ways in which theorizing about individuality and plurality can make itself ridiculous. Although I attempt to give it a Wittgensteinian rendering, the paragraph above can be viewed as a gloss on Rousseau's discussions of the state of nature in his *Discourse on the Origin and the Foundations of Inequality among Men* and his *Essay on the Origin of Languages*.

27 Trying to question mutual intelligibility is itself a language-game that presupposes shared beliefs, rules, and so forth; the notion of "simple" or "atomic" entities (e.g., internally undifferentiated individuals or groups) on which the activity depends is meaningful only by comparison with some notion of a complex entity; the activity presupposes a logically "private" language; and so on through a considerable number of the main elements of Wittgenstein's thinking.

28 The creatures about whom Rousseau speculated and who figure in the more robust versions of the Babel story are not metaphysical impossibilities, but such speculation and story telling is possible only for those among whom there is mutual intelligibility. It is well to remember, however, that Rousseau also anticipated Wittgenstein's view that the very conditions and characteristics that allow us to engage in mutually intelligible speculation, story telling, and so forth, also limit our understandings of our own and one another's performances.

29 Among the remarkable features of the thinking of Hannah Arendt is that she promotes self-disclosure and mutual involvement, disdains the private, but treasures the uncertain, the unknown, and the mysterious.

30 Cf. Elaine Scarry (1985).

31 Antagonism toward (fear of?) indeterminacy and opacity is one of the reasons that group theories such as those of von Gierke and Dumont, and communitarian theories that insist on deeply situated and harmonized selves, have difficulty sustaining a place for individuality. Suspicion of these features of human affairs also does something to explain the implicit tension between individuality and plurality in forms of pluralism that officially reject corporativism and the notion of group personality but nevertheless treat individuals and their characteristics as functions of intragroup dynamics. Finally, a certain underestimation of ambiguity and mutual incomprehensibility may help to explain the almost heroic (certainly the powerfully willful) character that thinkers such as James and Nietzsche, Oakeshott and Arendt, must attribute to those who achieve and sustain individuality. For James and Nietzsche, individuals must

Individuality, plurality, and liberalism 181

continuously fight off the pervasive demand for conformity powerfully imposed by the "herd." Oakeshott and Arendt agree with this. But the former, like James and Nietzsche, diminishes the difficulty by treating the messages and intimations that I receive from others and from the traditions and conventions of my society as invariably ambiguous, as *requiring* interpretation. Each of us can, and all too many of us do, go very far in surrendering this interpretive task to others, but this fault or failing dramatizes what it cannot alter, namely, that it is I who has surrendered myself to others. By contrast, Arendt can be said to deepen the difficulty by locating the meanings of my "actions" entirely in the responses of others to them, in the stories that others tell about what I do. In this respect, and despite her unremitting antagonism toward him, Arendt adopts the least estimable aspect of Hobbes's thinking.

References

Arendt, Hannah. 1978. *The Life of the Mind*, 2 vols. New York: Harcourt Brace Jovanovich.

Ayer, A.J. 1946. *Language, Truth, and Logic*. New York: Dover.

Berlin, Isaiah. 1960. *Four Essays on Liberty*. London: Oxford University Press.

Flathman, Richard E. 1989. *Toward a Liberalism*. Ithaca: Cornell University Press.

Moore, G. E. 1959. *Philosophical Papers*. London: George Allen and Unwin.

Oakeshott, Michael. 1962. *Rationalism and Politics*. London: Methuen.

Oakeshott, Michael. 1975. *On Human Conduct*. London: Oxford University Press.

Ortega y Gasset, José. 1932. *The Revolt of the Masses*. New York: W.W. Norton.

Raz, Joseph. 1986. *The Morality of Freedom*. Oxford: Clarendon Press.

Scarry, Elaine. 1985. *The Body in Pain*. New York: Oxford University Press.

Schlick, Moritz. 1962. *Problems of Ethics*. New York: Dover.

Taylor, Charles. 1976. *Hegel and Modern Society*. London: Cambridge University Press, 1976.

Taylor, Charles. 1986. *Philosophical Papers*, 2 vols. London: Cambridge University Press.

Todorov, Tzvetan. 1984. *The Conquest of America*. New York: Colophon-Harper & Row.

Winch, Peter. 1987. *Trying to Make Sense*. Oxford: Basil Blackwell.

Wittgenstein, Ludwig. 1922. *Tractatus Logico-Philosophicus*. London: Routledge & Kegan Paul.

Wittgenstein, Ludwig. 1953. *Philosophical Investigations*. Trans. G. E. M. Anscombe. New York: Macmillan.

Wittgenstein, Ludwig. 1965. "A Lecture on Ethics." *Philosophical Review* 74: 3–12.

Wittgenstein, Ludwig. 1967a. *Lectures and Conversations on Aesthetics, Psychology, and Religious Belief*. Ed. Cyril Barrett. Berkeley: University of California Press.

Wittgenstein, Ludwig. 1967b. *Zettel*. Eds. G. E. M. Anscombe and G. H. von Wright. Trans. G. E. M. Anscombe. Oxford: Basil Blackwell.

Wittgenstein, Ludwig. 1969. *On Certainty*. Ed. G. E. M. Anscombe and G. H. von Wright. Trans. Denis Paul and G. E. M. Anscombe. Oxford: Basil Blackwell.

Wittgenstein, Ludwig. 1978. *Remarks on Colour*. Ed. G. E. M. Anscombe. Trans. Linda L. McAlister and Margarete Schättle. Berkeley: University of California Press.

11 Of liberty, authority and power (1993)

There is no mistaking Hobbes's admiration for distinctive individualities. Along with the exquisite intellectual constructs devised by geometers, self-enactment of the kind exemplified by Sidney Godolphin may well have been the form of human making that he treasured most deeply. Unlike numerous other thinkers of this sensibility, Hobbes was never tempted by the view that the bulk of humankind exists for the sake of the gallant, noble or merely uncommon few. He never entertained the idea that the no-more-than temperate, the imprudent or even the vain-glorious (all of whom engage in the making, mismaking and unmaking of their own lives and selves) can justifiably be subordinated to the rule or sacrificed to the needs or wants of those of superior character or accomplishment. The most noble or cultivated of humankind must acknowledge natural equality and must accommodate themselves to arrangements necessary if naturally equal human beings are to keep company with one another. Those capable of enacting a distinctive individuality are to do it within these constraints. (Those who reject this imperative thereby show themselves to be arrogant and vain-glorious rather than noble.)

Hobbes's egalitarianism is manifest in his argument for the right of nature and for a single set of laws of nature to which all human beings should in prudence/morality subscribe. He clearly and rightly thinks this argument consistent with his commitment to individuality. The right of nature and the voluntarist theory of obligation that is one of its corollaries are at once egalitarian and individualistic. Peace and self-preservation are conditions of a diversity of felicities, not ends in themselves. The further laws of nature consist primarily of formal or adverbial considerations that individuals consult and adapt as each of them pursues their felicity as they see it. A society whose members act steadily on Hobbes's prudence/morality would feature both commonalities or uniformities of kinds associated with egalitarianism and a diversity of ends and purposes, dispositions and temperaments. It was Hobbes's purpose to theorize the possibility of this combination and perhaps his aspiration to bring into being societies that actually achieve and maintain it.

On my reading, Hobbes intended his treatment of commonwealth, sovereign authority and power, and the other most specifically political aspects of his theory to further this project, to serve his dual but complementary egalitarian

Of liberty, authority and power   183

and individualistic objectives. This is by no means a usual reading and Hobbes puts difficulties in the way of sustaining it. In arguing for absolute and preferably monarchical government he appears to favor sharply defined hierarchy and strictly imposed uniformity and conformity. He proposes collective political makings by which everyone in a particular territory submits to a single person who thenceforth controls and directs their lives.

…

I

…

II

…

III

It is to achieve protections of freedom of action that the right of nature does not and cannot provide, to make our natural freedom effective as a means to our felicity, that we are to agree to the creation of a politically organized society and to submit to the authority of its Sovereign. Political society and its authority are not for their own sake or for the sake of some good or value superior to or independent of the freedom and felicity of its individual members; rather, they are precisely for the sake of the latter.[1] If it were impossible for political society to diminish the unfreedoms of the state of nature there would be no reason to institute it or submit to it. If this or that political society fails to protect its members against those disorders that threaten the conditions essential to freedom and felicity—life itself plus those things necessary to "living well"—then the obligation to submit to it ends with the only reason for such submission.[2]

How then are we to construct and sustain a political society that will serve these purposes as reliably as our nature and circumstances permit? How should and should not Sovereigns and their subjects go about pursuing these objectives?

Recall that Hobbes recognizes two basic processes of constructing commonwealth, by "institution" or mutual covenant and by "acquisition" or submission to life-threatening power. Of these two, the former is apparently most favorable to legitimacy and hence to stable and effective governance. Acting on the basis of the prudential reasoning I have been discussing, each of us makes the following covenant with all of the others (except the Sovereign) who will thereafter form the political association: **"I authorize and give up my right of governing myself, to this man, or this assembly of men, on this condition, that thou give up thy right to him, and authorize all his actions in like manner."** This procedure, Hobbes says, produces not mere "concord" but "a real unity of them all, in one and the same person" and "is the generation of that great LEVIATHAN … to which we owe … our peace and defence" (Hobbes 1962a, hereafter *Lev.*, Ch. 17, p. 132).

184 *Opacity, liberalism, and individuality*

Hobbes does not think that this procedure has ever been or ever would be followed, this formula enacted, in exactly these terms. He says it is "as if every man should say" these words to every other, indicating that he is identifying the requirements that commonwealths by institution should satisfy as best they can. If there are commonwealths that can be placed in this apparently favored category, they deserve that standing because their members testify, over time and through a variety of doings and forgoings, that they subscribe to their authority. To repeat, "state of nature" and "commonwealth" are analytic not historical or otherwise descriptive concepts and Hobbes never seriously entertained the idea of an abrupt and decisive movement from one of these "states of affairs" to the other. He is a contractarian thinker, but only in that he insists that there can be political authority and obligation exclusively where there is some meaningful sense in which subjects have voluntarily subscribed to them.

Hobbes nevertheless does much to encourage the conclusion that commonwealth by institution is neither a possible nor a prudentially desirable state of affairs for human beings as he describes them. Oddly given the views I have just attributed to him, he frequently writes as if such a commonwealth could only be constructed by the deliberate, self-conscious decision of some number of assignable persons who assemble specifically for this purpose. He gives us numerous and carefully articulated paragraphs concerning the decision procedures of such assemblies, meticulously elaborates the formula that the covenant must take and the speech-acts by which consent must be given, painstakingly distinguishes between the covenant among subjects and the authorization each subject gives to the Sovereign (see, e.g., *Lev.*, Ch. 18, pp. 134–136; Hobbes 1972, hereafter *DC*, Ch. VI, pp. 174–176). At the same time, he gives us an abundance of reasons for thinking that it would be grossly imprudent for any person to enter into such an assembly, to make such covenants and authorizations. Given his account of human nature and the human condition, we have little reason to expect the establishment of commonwealths by institution. If political societies that take their beginnings in this way are the only ones that are fully legitimate, we cannot be surprised by Hobbes's own concluding judgment that "there is scarce a commonwealth in the world, whose beginnings can in conscience be justified" or even by his sometimes nostalgia for the ancient time in which "the duties of men ... as subjects" were "delivered ... either curiously adorned with verse, or clouded with allegories, as a most beautiful and hallowed mystery of royal authority; lest by the disputations of private men it might be defiled" (*Lev.*, "A Review and a Conclusion," p. 506; *DC*, "The Author's Preface To The Reader," p. 95).

Hobbes never wavered in his view that human affairs are untenable without the discipline of political authority. Because he also anticipated Hegel's judgment that Socrates had destroyed forever the possibility of a "happy" or enchanted acceptance of such discipline, it would appear from these and related passages that he in effect gave up on the possibility of commonwealth by institution, looked instead to the less attractive but pragmatically more realistic commonwealth by acquisition. If human beings cannot successfully operate the complex, rationality- and trust-demanding procedures necessary to construct and

Of liberty, authority and power 185

sustain the former, they do and in prudence should submit when confronted with the life-threatening power that is the origin of the latter. As Rousseau and numerous other critics have complained, Hobbes is in fact a theorist of the ugly proposition that might makes right. His talk of science and reason, equality and liberty, covenant and consent, rights and duties, authority and obligation, is no better than camouflage for the despotism of the strong or the cunning over the weak or credulous.

As a historical matter Hobbes clearly thought that most if not all known political societies took their origins from force or fraud. Nor is there any doubting his conviction that these and other repugnant devices and methods are necessary to effective rule. Even if a commonwealth by institution somehow developed, its sovereign would be distinguished from its subjects primarily by the fact that he "hath the use of so much power and strength … that by terror thereof, he is enabled to form the wills of them all, to peace at home, and mutual aid against their enemies abroad" (*Lev.*, Ch. 17, p. 132).

Rousseau's critique, however, overlooks the fact that Hobbes's thinking provides even greater reasons for pessimism concerning the prospects of stable or lasting commonwealths by acquisition than for the likelihood of commonwealths by institution. It is believable that Hobbesian human beings will voluntarily and prudently submit, here and now, to the power another or others have temporarily acquired. His theory of natural equality, artfully elaborated in his several quite detailed and insightful accounts of sedition and rebellion, makes it very difficult to believe that power sufficient to compel continued obedience can be sustained for long and even more difficult to believe that very many human beings will or in prudence/morality should choose to remain faithful to the agreement by which they initially submitted. His movement from commonwealth by institution to commonwealth by acquisition compounds rather than abates the difficulties of his specifically political theory.

We might, then, adopt the familiar view that Hobbes is simply confused. He wants active, forceful government but fails to see that his own theory makes such government impossible. More plausibly, we might say that he is clear-headed but deeply pessimistic. He thinks human affairs would go better if there were such government but is convinced that the very characteristics of human beings that make it desirable also make it highly unlikely. Scorning as he does the delusive notion that a miraculous transformation of human nature can be effected by his own theorizing or by the happenstance emergence of something like a government, those parts of his thinking that show the desirability of wide-ranging and effective governance also and necessarily provide reasons for doubting that it can be established and sustained.

There is an additional possibility, one that acknowledges Hobbes's deep skepticism and considerable pessimism but also makes greater sense of the care that he lavished on commonwealth by institution and on the entire elaborate array of liberties and rights, obligations and duties, proprieties and improprieties of which his civil philosophy largely consists. On this third view, Hobbes did want to convince us that commonwealths can be valuable additions to God's creation,

186 *Opacity, liberalism, and individuality*

can make worthy contributions to individual freedom of action and felicity. He also wanted to persuade us that they are best able to make such contributions if they are quite simple in form or structure, if the authority-cum-right of action of those who rule is closely akin to the right of action that every human being has by nature. But he thought extensive, expansive, ambitious government neither feasible nor desirable, no more likely to achieve its objectives than ambitious and vainglorious individuals, as likely to do harm to itself and others as are the latter. Perhaps not significantly more optimistic concerning the probability of "temperate" government than of conduct of this sort on the part of private persons, his constant insistence on the difficulties of establishing and sustaining governmental authority and power is counsel not of despair but to a more substantially political version of the kind of prudence represented by his notion of temperateness. Some of this guidance, concerning appropriate objectives and how and how not to pursue them, is explicitly addressed to sovereigns and constitutes Hobbes's theory of temperate rule or statesmanship: He also has many words for those who, by whatever process, have become subject to a politically organized and governed association.

IV

The best known of Hobbes's words to sovereigns urge them to insist on and otherwise act to protect their absolute authority. Equally, the most widely discussed aspect of his advice to subjects concerns their obligation to obey their rulers and thereby make efficacious governance possible. But much of his advice to rulers urges temperateness in the use of their authority and many of his counsels to subjects are admonitions to confine and delimit their specifically political commitments and relationships. They are to understand political association as instrumental to their individual and hence non- or extra-political purposes and they are to act in ways that, because temperate, help to temper the conduct of their fellow subjects and their rulers. In the admittedly unlikely event that these several counsels were widely and steadily heeded, the distinctive and inherently dangerous mode of keeping company that is political association might ameliorate somewhat the difficulties of the human estate.

In order to be effective the Sovereign must be invested with all but absolute authority. As Hobbes understands absolutism, this means that there can be no law that the Sovereign cannot rightfully promulgate, no command that she cannot properly issue. There are laws and commands that it would be morally wrong for her to issue (for example those that would be cruel or vengeful), but the duty not to do so is owed to God not to her subjects and the latter have no political or legal right to enforce it. In strict jural terms we should eliminate the qualifier "all but" from the statement that the Sovereign must have absolute authority. Properly speaking, this qualifier speaks not to the Sovereign's authority but to the obligations of subjects that ordinarily correlate with it. There are commands that subjects are not obligated to obey, or rather that they have a natural right to disobey; but in Hobbes's view this natural right, while it may reduce the Sovereign's power, does not diminish her de jure authority.

Of liberty, authority and power   187

It is important to notice a distinction Hobbes makes between two senses of or moments in absolutism and the quite different arguments he gives for each of them.

When a number of people covenant with one another to create a political association they necessarily claim entire right or authority to do so. (Equally, when a number of people simultaneously or successively submit to the power of the same person, they each claim the right or authority to do so.) How they exercise that authority, for example whether they make that government absolute or qualify its authority in certain ways, is a question they must regard as within their authority to decide. They may decide to make the government absolute or to limit, divide, or otherwise qualify the authority of government in certain ways; in either case it is they who make the decision and who therefore claim the right or authority to do so. (Again, as a matter of right the same is true of those who negotiate an agreement with someone who is threatening their lives.) This is nothing other than the prepolitical right each of us has by nature. As Hobbes incisively puts it: "This device therefore of them that will make civil laws first, and then a civil body afterwards (as if policy made a body politic, and not a body politic made policy), is of no effect" (1962b, hereafter *Elements*, II, B, Ch. 1, p. 318).

In this its founding moment, political authority is necessarily absolute. The alternative to absolutism is not limited authority, it is anarchism. However it is exercised or implemented, absolute authority is the basis of all systems of rule. This is a truth of reason, an indisputable deduction from the meanings of the words "authority," "rule," and "government" (see esp. *DC*, Ch. VI and *Lev.*, Ch. 20). I wouldn't put it quite as Hobbes does, but his point is well taken and should not be pretended or wished away.

Hobbes makes the further argument that those who covenant to create authority ought to invest it with the entirety of their natural authority. This further argument is not and cannot be a deduction in Hobbes's or any other useful sense of that word. Rather, it is an experiential or prudential judgment, a prediction or wager as to how best to achieve the purposes for which the political society is instituted. Hobbes argues repeatedly and vigorously for this judgment, but he is evidently aware that his own account of absolutism in the first sense is reason for wariness concerning absolutism in the second and indeed concerning government of any sort. He insists that the commonwealth must have entire formal or jural authority but he also sustains the individual's natural right to disobey laws and commands that she thinks contrary to her purposes in submitting to political rule. When a subject reaches this conclusion, she and her Sovereign are in the state of nature in respect to the disagreement between them.

Thus Hobbes's first political counsel only appears to be absolutism in both senses, in fact privileges absolutism in a sense that is individuating because it depends on the willingness of each and every potential subject to enter into and sustain the covenant with some number of others.

Later I assess the effects of this qualification on the power of the Sovereign and hence on the prudence of her provoking, and of individual subjects engaging in, acts of disobedience. Consideration of other aspects of Hobbes's advice to sovereigns will prepare the way for this discussion.

188 *Opacity, liberalism, and individuality*

Hobbes argues that those human rulers invested with absolute authority should nevertheless exercise that authority only to the extent necessary (of which they must be the judges) to maintain the peace and defense essential to the felicity of their individual subjects. Perhaps more important, his skepticism leads him to the view that Sovereigns who pursue objectives significantly beyond peace and defense will almost certainly fail to achieve them and are very likely to lose their authority in the process.

Let us begin with the question of peace and war among commonwealths. Once political authority has been instituted, the first duty of the Sovereign is to protect her subjects against attacks from abroad. Owing to the incessant possibility of such assaults, the Sovereign must be constantly vigilant and always adequately prepared to fight effectively. But Hobbes is far from a supporter of bellicose or expansionist policies. Because no preparation can assure victory,

> such commonwealths, or such monarchs, as affect war for itself ... out of ambition, or of vain-glory, or that make account to revenge every little injury, or disgrace done by their neighbors, if they ruin not themselves, their fortune must be better than they have reason to expect.
>
> (*Elements*, II, B, Ch. 9, p. 384)

> The subjects of those Kings who affect the Glory, and imitate the Actions of Alexander the Great, have not always the most comfortable lives, nor do such Kings usually very long enjoy their Conquests. They March to and fro perpetually, as upon a Plank sustained only in the midst, and when one end rises, down goes the other.
>
> (Hobbes 1971, hereafter *Dialogue*, p. 60)

Temperate conduct and comfortable living not the teeter-totter existence of those who, hybristically and vain-gloriously, overestimate their knowledge and power. These same themes reverberate through Hobbes's treatment of domestic governance.

Hobbes thinks that we can have partial and for some purposes serviceable knowledge of one another's desires and thoughts. Setting aside doubts whether his theory actually warrants this possibility, it is plain that on that theory the Sovereign's knowledge of and capacity to govern her subjects (as with their knowledge of and ability to influence or control one another) can be no more than partial and can never be secure into the future. Like his brief but chastening advice concerning war and peace, his theory of jurally absolute but practically limited domestic government elaborates these skeptical views.

"[O]f the voluntary acts of every man, the object is some good to himself" (*Lev.*, Ch. 14, p. 105). For this reason alone, it is *possible* for the natural person whom I make my sovereign to pursue my ends if and only if her ends and mine happen to coincide. What is more, not actually being a god, my sovereign can know my ends, and hence can know whether our ends coincide, only to the limited extent that she as one human being can know and understand the

Of liberty, authority and power 189

passions, deliberations, stipulations and so forth of me, another such being. For all of her formal *authority* to act, the sovereign's *abilities* to do so are as severely limited as those of any other person.

Why then should we create sovereigns and submit to their rule?

Perhaps we should answer, as in consistency Hobbes himself must and does answer in part, that we should do so on the wager that the sovereign's ends and our own will coincide often enough that the advantages outweigh the disadvantages.

This is only part of Hobbes's answer. For the most part writing of the office of the Sovereign and its formal authority, only rarely discussing the personal qualities appropriate to holding that office, Hobbes recognizes that ruling is a distinctive activity, he distinguishes good and bad ruling, and he counsels sovereigns—primarily in the name of their own self-interest—to rule well rather than badly. Ruling well does not require the impossibility of pursuing the ends of someone other than the ruler or the near impossibility of acting only if the ends of the ruler and those of the ruler's subjects coincide. It requires, rather, that rulers be especially attentive to a distinction that reason urges on all human beings, namely between the ends of our actions and the conditions under which we are most likely to be successful in pursuing whatever ends we have. Necessarily pursuing their own ends, and *urged* to consider that due to their position their ends will more often than is usual coincide with the ends of those others who are their subjects, sovereigns have a special responsibility to attend to the conditions necessary to the successful pursuit of the kinds or classes of ends that experience and reason have shown to be most common among humankind. (As such, Hobbes argues that the sovereign's personal ends will very likely be encompassed within these classes.)

It is a signal advantage of this view that on it the inherently uncertain business of "searching hearts" is largely irrelevant to ruling. To repeat a passage quoted above, "let one man read another by his actions never so perfectly, it serves him only with his acquaintances, which are but few," while "[h]e that is to govern a whole nation, must read in himself, not this or that particular man; but mankind." To discharge their offices well (and hence to keep them), rulers must discern "the similitudes of **passions**, which are the same in all men, **desire, fear, hope, &c.**; not the similitude of the **objects** of the passions."

Relieved of, or rather largely excluded by incapacity from, the duty to know and advance the particular ends of their individual subjects, the Sovereign is nevertheless confronted with the arguably greater difficulty of "reading mankind" and pursuing what has traditionally been called the common good. Recognizing that from Plato forward the daunting character of these tasks had been taken as reason for pessimism concerning government and everything that has been thought (however absurdly) to depend on it, Hobbes continues the lines of thought I am tracing in ways that permit him to "recover some hope" that "the disorders of state" can be "taken away" (*Lev.*, Ch. 31, p. 270).

Concerned with the conditions of felicity not felicity itself (and not even *the conditions* of the integration of self or self and community, moral perfection,

190 *Opacity, liberalism, and individuality*

perfect freedom, and like repugnant fantasies), the deep and transcendental truths that Plato and his successors thought good rulers must know are in fact irrelevant to governance. The "only science necessary for sovereigns and their principal ministers" is the "science of natural justice" (*Lev.*, Ch. 31, p. 270). Hobbes convinced himself that he had so well "read mankind" that it would largely suffice for sovereigns to read Hobbes. Apparently eschewing the skepticism that I have attributed to him, he modestly claimed to have "put into order, and sufficiently or probably proved all the theorems of moral doctrine, that men may learn thereby, both how to govern, and how to obey." Almost all that is necessary for good government is that "this writing of mine may fall into the hands of a sovereign, who will ... by the exercise of entire sovereignty ... convert this truth of speculation, into the utility of practice" (*Lev.*, Ch. 31, p. 270). (Note that even this ill-considered remark recognizes the need for a "converting" that Hobbes has no reason to think so much as possible.)

Hobbes's "hope," however, the success of his project of employing absolute government to increase the prospects of human felicity, requires sovereigns and subjects to draw and act on several further inferences from the arguments thus far considered. The most general of these, from which Hobbes draws at least three subordinate inferences, is that sovereigns will limit themselves to governing primarily by law and that subjects (as such) will relate to one another and to their sovereigns first and foremost as obeyers of the civil law. (Hobbes is a theorist who urges rule primarily by law, but not a theorist of the "rule of law" when that phrase means that rule contrary to or by any means other than law is illegitimate.)

The "skill of making, and maintaining commonwealths consisteth in certain rules, as doth arithmetic and geometry; not, as tennis-play, on practice only" (*Lev.*, Ch. 20, p. 158).[3] The rules of arithmetic and geometry are "certain" in the sense of beyond dispute. Their certainty in this sense depends on another, namely the clarity or "perspicuity" of the definitions that mathematicians have stipulated and from which their further reasoning and their conclusions proceed. Analogously, by promulgating positive laws sovereigns define the terms in which thereafter their subjects (again as such as distinct from persons acting and interacting in ways not covered by law) make their "calculations." Perspicuous laws provide a settled basis on which the members of a commonwealth can maintain a modus vivendi despite the mutual antagonisms, misunderstandings, and unintelligibilities that result from their individuating characteristics.

The first of the inferences subordinate to the proposition that sovereigns should rule by law is that it "belongeth to ... the office of a legislator" to make the laws as perspicuous as possible (*Lev.*, Ch. 30, pp. 255–257). The second and third such inferences can be viewed as elaborations on differences between positive laws and their model, the stipulations of mathematicians. The former of these is simply a deduction from one such difference already noted, that the Sovereign's definitions are invested with authority and hence binding. Viewed in comparison with geometry, the point here is that law is not a system in the rigorous sense of a mathematics and hence sovereigns are advised but not obliged to

Of liberty, authority and power   191

maintain consistency between their new or altered laws and those they have pre-viously promulgated. Subjects should not be punished for obeying only one of two or more laws that make mutually incompatible demands upon them (as also they are excused from "obedience" if a "law" is so lacking in perspicuity that it is impossible for them to know what would count as obeying it), but conflicts among laws or between them and other desiderata do not invalidate or justify disobedience to any law. Hobbes refines this proposition in various ways, but in its fundamentals it is simply a corollary of his absolutism.

Together with his absolutism, the first subordinate inference might lead us to expect Hobbes to recommend extensive and encompassing legislation, to urge the sovereign to promulgate numerous laws governing many aspects of life in the commonwealth. If law eliminates or obviates the consequences of disagree-ment and mutual unintelligibility, why shouldn't the Sovereign use it freely and widely?

In fact, while reiterating that the Sovereign must have complete discretion concerning the number and scope of the laws promulgated, Hobbes proposes two criteria of "good laws," namely perspicuity and "needful," and interprets them in ways that imply (albeit Hobbes is not invariably faithful to the implication) the desirability of narrowly limited legislation.

"Unnecessary laws are not good laws; but traps for money: which where the right of sovereign power is acknowledged, are superfluous; and where it is not acknowledged, insufficient to defend the people" (*Lev.*, Ch. 30, p. 256). What does Hobbes mean by "needful" and its contrary "unnecessary"? Consistent with his view that freedom of action is necessary to felicity, his answer is that the

> use of laws ... is not to bind the people from all voluntary actions; but to direct and keep them in such a motion, as not to hurt themselves by their own impetuous desires, rashness or indiscretion; as hedges are set, not to stop travellers, but keep them in *their* way. And therefore a law that is not needful, having not the true end of a law, is not good.
>
> (*Lev.*, Ch. 30, p. 256, italics added)

Still, the presence of words such as *direct*, *hurt* and *impetuous desires* in this passage might be construed as recommending a highly active legislator, a pater-nalistic or even a moralistic governance. Hobbes does not rejoin directly to this interpretation but his rejection of an inference that might seem to be licensed by his absolutism is instructive concerning it. It might be thought, Hobbes con-siders, that "a law may be ... good, when it is for the benefit of the sovereign; though it be not necessary for the people; but it is not so. For the good of the sovereign and people, cannot be separated" (*Lev.*, Ch. 30, p. 256). Knowing as we do that the good of the Sovereign qua natural person is in all likelihood dif-ferent from the good of her subjects, and taken together with his revealing use of the metaphor of travelers and hedges, this caveat makes it sufficiently clear that by needful and unnecessary Hobbes means what we have by now been led to expect. Generically, those laws are needful that are essential to reduce the

192 *Opacity, liberalism, and individuality*

incidence of conditions adverse to the felicity of the individual members of the commonwealth. Equally, laws that have any other objective are "unnecessary" and should not be adopted.

We also know that for Hobbes the condition most generally destructive of felicity is death and that the condition most likely to result in premature death and otherwise most adverse to felicity is civil war and violent conflict generally. We can therefore infer that the most needful laws are those that prevent or (more soberly) diminish the frequency of the former and the severity of the latter, the least needful are those that restrict activities that do not or are unlikely to lead to war and violence. Prudence and reason in the conduct of private individuals are defined by reference to felicity, needfulness and unneedfulness in law (hence prudence or temperateness in the conduct of sovereigns) by reference to the conditions essential to the pursuit of felicity by those composing the commonwealth.

We do not yet have a complete account of good and bad law and rule. To complete our account, and to see its place in the highly estimable civil philosophy with which Hobbes has gifted us, we need to understand how and why the two criteria of good laws are complementary.

The perspicuity of a law "consisteth not so much in the words of the law itself, as in a declaration of the causes, and motives for which it was made. This is it, that shows us the meaning of the legislator" (*Lev.*, Ch. 30, p. 256). Good laws must have "preambles" that explain how they are to be understood. Assuming that the legislator has succeeded in making "the reason perspicuous, why the law was made," the law itself "is more easily understood by few, than many words." Why is this? Why would the clarity of the law not be enhanced by elaboration and explication within as well as without it? Hobbes's answer is consonant with if not required by his larger philosophy, but it at least appears to confound the argument he is here advancing:

> For all words, are subject to ambiguity; and therefore multiplication of words in the body of the law, is multiplication of ambiguity: besides it seems to imply, by too much diligence, that whosoever can evade the words, is without the compass of the law. And this is a cause of many unnecessary processes. For when I consider how short were the laws of ancient times; and how they grew by degrees still longer; methinks I see a contention between the penners, and pleaders of the law; ... and that the pleaders have got the victory.
>
> (*Lev.*, Ch. 30, p. 256)

These remarks are less than encouraging concerning the prospects of good law. Words being necessary to the formulation and promulgation of laws, all words being subject to ambiguity and the multiplication of words therefore compounding ambiguity, the legislator's prospects of achieving perspicuity in laws are less than bright. However well the legislator has "read mankind" and mastered the science of natural justice, however satisfied she may be (in her own

Of liberty, authority and power 193

mind as we might put it) with her reasons for thinking a law needful, she can have no assurance of making those reasons or the law itself clear to her subjects and hence no assurance of enhancing the prospects of felicity by promulgating it. A perfect law is an impossibility, a good law and hence a good system of laws extraordinarily hard to achieve.

V

These deep-going complications in Hobbes's theory of governance are rooted in the fundaments of his thinking. The problematic character of *making* good law dramatizes and compounds difficulties faced by all those who must keep company with others. Placed by God in a universe that is largely devoid of meaning and in close association with other creatures who are naturally intelligible to them only in the limited respects in which they were severally created alike, each of them must *make*, largely if not entirely for herself and primarily by the device of arbitrary stipulation, sense of the universe and of those others she encounters. To the extent that she and some number of others succeed in doing these things, they must then find means, again by artifice, to communicate with one another and to order their affairs in terms of the meanings they have respectively devised.

Nothing in Hobbes's analysis suggests that these things will be done easily or with steady success and Hobbes could not have been unaware that his argument for the farfetched device of Leviathan magnifies his own conception of the difficulties.

For reasons suggested earlier, we might stop here. We might read Hobbes's civil philosophy as ironic if not a *reductio*, as an argument or even a demonstration that government, if possible at all, is far more likely to compound than to ameliorate the ineliminable "inconveniences" of keeping company.

Insofar as "reading" means "appropriating to my or our own purposes," something close to this response will be hard to avoid—harder, I hope, after what follows in this text. But even this understanding of reading is incoherent apart from some notion (however resistant to generalizable articulation) of grasping the intentions of the author and thus the senses of the text under consideration. We are, I think, obliged to recognize that Hobbes's was the more complicated intention of conveying *both* the possibilities *and* the limitations of Leviathan, the at least possible gains as well as the probable losses of my submitting to the rule of another who by my own lights is far more likely to be worse than better than myself.

Hobbes was a proud and buoyant man inclined to regard the human predicament as a bracing challenge, not a circumstance sickly to lament. Reflecting as they do the difficulties of all human endeavor, to take the problems of governance as reasons for forgoing its possible advantages would be tantamount to forgoing the pursuit of felicity.[4] If barely possible for those of the species who have the least "worthiness,"[5] this was not a course Hobbes was prepared to accept for himself or recommend to others.

As with his treatment of the language of natural science, Hobbes's discussions of political and legal language and their limitations are meant to encourage

194 *Opacity, liberalism, and individuality*

sovereigns to make their laws as clear and readily followed as possible. Every law, nevertheless, increases the number of words that must be perspicuous to large numbers of persons few of whom can be personally known to the sovereign. In part for this reason, and because laws that are unneedful or inperspicuous advantage the enemies not the friends of the law, good sovereigns "sometimes forbear the exercise of their right; and prudently remit somewhat of the act, but nothing of their right" (*DC*, Ch. VI, p. 181).

VI

Sovereigns who respect the forgoing counsels of prudence, especially the last of those counsels, greatly advantage the liberty and hence the possibility of felicity on the part of their subjects. "The greatest liberty of subjects dependeth on the silence of the law" (*Lev.*, Ch. 21, pp. 165–166). "In cases where the sovereign has prescribed no rule, there the subject hath the liberty to do, or forbear, according to his own discretion," that is by exercise of her right of nature. Such cases are *necessarily* very numerous:

> all the motions and actions of subjects are never circumscribed by laws, nor can be, by reason of their variety; it is [therefore] necessary that there be *infinite* cases which are neither commanded nor prohibited, but every man may either do or not do them as he lists himself.
>
> (*DC*, Ch. XIII, p. 268, italics added)[6]

These as it were natural or ontological limits on governance do not provide a liberty wide enough for human beings as Hobbes understands them. Metaphor, hyperbole, periphrasis, and rhetorically convenient borrowings of the languages of his opponents are concatenated in underlining this point:

> As water inclosed on all hands with banks, stands still and corrupts; ... so subjects, if they might do nothing without the commands of the law, would grow dull and unwieldy; ... Wherefore ... it is against the charge of those who command and have the authority of making laws, that there should be more laws than necessarily serve for good of the magistrate and his subjects. For since men are wont commonly to debate what to do or not to do, by natural reason rather than any knowledge of the laws, where there are more laws than can easily be remembered, and whereby such things are forbidden as reason of itself prohibits not of necessity, they must through ignorance, without the least evil intention, fall within the compass of laws, as gins laid to entrap their harmless liberty; which supreme commanders are bound to preserve for their subjects by the laws of nature.[7]

The hortatory quality of this passage, while no doubt conveying the genuineness of the sentiments it expresses, also foregrounds the fact that it and Hobbes's other counsels to sovereigns are just that, advice that, as a matter of authority, of

Of liberty, authority and power 195

justice and of right, sovereigns are entirely at liberty to reject. Having authorized all of the Sovereign's actions, subjects may be "harmed" but cannot be "injured" by any of them, have no constitutional, legal, or other institutionalized right to or means of redress against any of them. Whether members of a commonwealth by institution or by acquisition, subjects can do little more than "hope" that their sovereigns conduct themselves in a temperate manner (see esp. *Lev.*, Ch. 20, pp. 150ff.).

Subjects have no such rights, can only hope for prudence in their Sovereign. But just as sovereigns are also natural persons with the usual complement of desires and aversions, strengths and weaknesses—and hence persons to whom counsels of prudence/morality can be addressed—so no human being is merely or exclusively a political subject the entirety of whose conduct is or should be governed by her political obligations. Keen to disqualify (almost) all purported agent-neutral and hence generalizable claims against the Sovereign (and hence to do what he can to eliminate or weaken group or collective as distinct from individual disobedience),[8] Hobbes insists that our "true liberties" consist not of those freedoms of action left to us by the grace or prudence of the Sovereign but rather of those "things, which though commanded by the sovereign, . . . [we] may nevertheless, without injustice, refuse to do" (*Lev.*, Ch. 21, p. 163).

These "true liberties" consist of those aspects of our right of nature that each of us must retain. They explicitly include "the liberty to disobey" commands "to kill, wound or maim himself; or not to resist those that assault him; or to abstain from the use of food, air, medicine, or any other thing, without which he cannot live" and to refuse "to accuse himself" of a crime without assurance of pardon (*Lev.*, Ch. 21, p. 163, p. 164). Consistently if nevertheless surprisingly given his general animus against group resistance, while in general I cannot "resist the sword of the commonwealth, in defence of another man, guilty or innocent,"

> in case a great many men together, have already resisted the sovereign power unjustly, or committed some capital crime, for which every one of them expecteth death, whether have they not the liberty then to join together, and assist and defend one another? Certainly they have: for they but defend their lives, which the guilty man may as well do, as the innocent.
>
> (*Lev.*, Ch. 21, p. 165)

Remembering that Hobbes is thinking not of mere life but of "living well," this catalog of true liberties can hardly be regarded as inconsequential. Much more important is the reasoning that leads to it, reasoning that will readily support additions to the liberties that Hobbes explicitly lists. As if to counterbalance his (too) ready imputation of tacit consent, Hobbes says that authorizations of the Sovereign's actions, and the obligations thereby undertaken,

> must either be drawn from the express words . . . or from the intention of him that submitteth himself to his power, which intention is to be understood by the end for which he so submitteth; . . . namely, the peace of the subjects within themselves and their defence against the common enemy.

196 *Opacity, liberalism, and individuality*

In what we have reason to regard as the most consequential class of cases, words that we may have spoken are to be set aside in favor of intentions and ends.

> [T]he obligation a man may sometimes have, upon the command of the sovereign to execute any dangerous, or dishonourable office, dependeth not on the words of our submission; but on the intention, which is to be understood by the end thereof. When therefore our refusal to obey, frustrates the end for which the sovereignty was ordained; then there is no liberty to refuse: otherwise there is.
>
> (*Lev.*, Ch. 21, pp. 164–165)

The Sovereign will by right make and act on her own judgments concerning these matters. In these as in all other respects, the Sovereign's right to do so is simply the right of nature that she has done nothing to relinquish or transfer. Those persons who are or have theretofore been her subjects will by natural right make their own judgments. If one or more of them decides, contrary to the Sovereign's judgment, that the end for which they submitted is served by refusal to obey, their obligation to obey is annulled and they join the Sovereign in the state of nature, return to that condition in which they as well as she have the right to do all they judge necessary to their preservation and well-being. From this moment, they have as much right to resist, attack, and if necessary to kill the Sovereign as the Sovereign has right to attack and if necessary to kill them.

Who will win the fights that are likely to ensue? Does Hobbes accord a natural right to disobedience confident that subjects will rarely if ever successfully exercise it; confident even that he will have convinced subjects that it is manifestly imprudent to attempt to exercise it? Before trying to answer these questions, we should underline the significance of the fact that they arise so prominently and urgently in Hobbes's thinking. Let us emphasize again that, because the rights in question in effect cancel one another, civil *philosophy* as such cannot answer the questions. Both the Sovereign and the subject confront prudential questions in both of the senses Hobbes uses. Neither of them can have certain knowledge of the answer to them and in answering them as best they can they must gather and assess the pertinent facts in the light of their personal desires and aversions. This feature of the situation underscores Hobbes's distinction between persons and subjects, perhaps also his related distinction between the artificial and the natural persona of the Sovereign. The obligations that define and govern the performance of the role of subject do not answer the question. When confronting it, those persons who are also subjects must think themselves out of that role and instead consult the considerations appropriate to their conduct as natural persons. If Hobbes's sovereigns are more deeply politicized creatures than their subjects, if artificial and natural or private and public considerations are harder to differentiate in their cases, not a little of Hobbes's advice to them appeals to their personal interests.

Further and more general aspects of these distinctions will emerge as we proceed. But let us address the question of who is likely to win if and when push comes to shove between sovereigns and subjects.

Of liberty, authority and power 197

It is a question of power; and Hobbes has made it clear that no individual person has or can hope to keep for long power sufficient to assure triumph in conflicts with others. If it follows that prudent subjects will avoid these confrontations wherever possible, the aspects of the situation thus far considered would seem to recommend the same inference to sovereigns. Taken together with Hobbes's other counsels to sovereigns, his doctrine of the true liberties of subjects suggests that prudent rulers will "sometimes forbear" the use of their authority rather than provoke uncertain trials of strength by commands that threaten the life or well-being of their subjects. If the Sovereign has as much, or more, at stake in the preservation of commonwealth as her subjects, she no more than they will put it unnecessarily at risk.

Perhaps these trials are not uncertain or are so little uncertain of outcome that sovereigns have no reason to avoid them. Granted that the Sovereign cannot have scientific knowledge that she will be the winner in all such confrontations, perhaps she is furnished with such an abundance, such an overwhelming superiority, of power that she has no practical reason for hesitation. Is not the whole objective in creating a commonwealth to provide its Sovereign with "the use of so much power and strength ... that by terror thereof, he is enabled to form the wills of them all, to peace at home, and mutual aid against their enemies abroad"?

Of what power and strength does the Sovereign have "the use"? Her own personal or natural capacities being insufficient, how does she augment them sufficiently to "terrorize" the throng of individuals, whose congenital unruliness can hardly have been diminished by the teaching that they have a right to resist her, who she is to govern?

As a metaphysical individualist and nominalist Hobbes insists that collectivities are and can be nothing but aggregations of their individual members gathered under a single name. A commonwealth is a "real unity," but only in the sense that a

> multitude of men, are made **one** person, when they are by one man, or one person, represented; so that it be done with the consent of every one of that multitude in particular. For it is the **unity** of the representer, not the **unity** of the represented, that maketh the person **one**. ... and **unity**, cannot otherwise be understood in multitude.
>
> (*Lev.*, Ch. 16, p. 127)[9]

If the artificial person who is the Sovereign is to have greater power than the natural person who she also is, it must consist "in the power and the strength, that every of the members have transferred to him from themselves by covenant."

On the same radically individualistic doctrine, "it is impossible for any man really to transfer his own strength to another, or for another to receive it." Therefore, "it is to be understood, that to transfer a man's power and strength, is no more but to lay by, or relinquish his own right of resisting him to whom he so transferreth it" (*Elements*, II, A, Ch. 6, p. 310).

Quite obviously, on this account the Sovereign, in particular that monarchical Sovereign that Hobbes strongly prefers, will be advised to "forbear" issuing

198 *Opacity, liberalism, and individuality*

commands that any but the feeblest of her subjects are likely to have reason to resist. If her other subjects do no more than "lay by" as she does combat with those who exercise their natural right to defend themselves against her, her chances of defeating any single opponent are no better than even. And if, perchance, her commands provoke the combined resistance of several subjects, her chances of victory are manifestly nil. If the "essence" of the power of "a body politic ... is the not-resistance of the members" (*Elements*, II, B, Ch. 1, p. 320), we are out of the equality of the state of nature, if at all, only to the extent that subjects do not find the Sovereign's commands threatening to their preservation or well-being.

If this is a difficulty in Hobbes's thinking, he was evidently aware of it and made various gestures toward diminishing it. The passage just quoted first says that the Sovereign "ought ... in all actions to be assisted by the members," albeit it immediately goes on to say "at least not resisted by them" and finishes with the words about essence quoted above. With one exception this pattern is repeated in the discussion of this topic in the several works. In *De Cive* he first says "not resist." He then construes this to mean "that is ... refuse him not the use of his wealth and strength against any others whatsoever" and "conveys to [the Sovereign] ... the right of his strength and faculties." But he ends the discussion by repeating the *Elements* formulation that "because no man can transfer his power in a natural manner" the authorization involves "nothing else than to have parted with his right of resisting" together with the commitment "not to assist him who is to be punished" by the Sovereign (Ch. V, pp. 170–171, 176).

The first statement that addresses this issue in *Leviathan* claims that commonwealths are the greatest of human powers because "compounded of the powers of most men, united by consent, in one person ... that hath the use of all their powers depending on his will" (Ch. 10, p. 72). The accounts of "laying down," "renouncing" and "transferring" a right, however, as well as the later discussion of the basis of the Sovereign's right to punish her subjects, revert to the language of "standing aside."

> To **lay down** a man's **right** to any thing, is to **divest** himself of the **liberty**, of hindering another of the benefit of his own right to the same. For he that renounceth, or passeth away his right, giveth not to any other man a right which he had not before; because there is nothing to which every man had not right by nature: but only standeth out of his way, that he may enjoy his own original right, without hindrance from him; not without hindrance from another. So that the effect which redoundeth to one man, by another man's defect of right, is but so much diminution of impediments to the use of his own right original.
>
> (*Elements*, Ch. 14, p. 104)

The Sovereign's right to punish "is not grounded on any concession, or gift of the subjects" but simply in her own right of nature now "strengthened" because "left to him alone" by the covenants and authorizations of her subjects (*Elements*, Ch. 28, p. 229).

Of liberty, authority and power 199

In this last passage Hobbes once again speaks of the obligation of subjects to "assist him that hath the sovereignty, in the punishing of another; but of himself not" (*Elements*, Ch. 28, p. 229). Despite the vacillations that I have just followed, the recurrence of this notion, together with the manifest weakness of the Sovereign's position on the "stand aside" view, may be sufficient reason to think that some version of this view represents his most considered position. Exactly which version? We have seen his doctrine that individual subjects have an obligation to undertake "dangerous and dishonorable offices" only if they themselves judge that their refusal to do so will directly jeopardize the purposes or ends for which they entered into the commonwealth. Given that the in any case powerful urge to the preservation of life and well-being has been enhanced by the natural right to protect them against all threats, we have to assume that most subjects will be disposed to resist the Sovereign's attempts to inflict any very severe punishments on them. Thus there is excellent reason for other subjects to expect that assisting the Sovereign in this activity will be a dangerous business that they will undertake only at their own discretion and in most cases with a good deal of hesitation. It looks as if the obligation to assist the Sovereign, despite being a feature of civil society, is *in foro interno*. It also looks as if, for all of her authority, the Sovereign's power is mainly on paper, that the Leviathan is indeed a paper tiger.

There is one substantial but by no means entire qualification to this conclusion. The character of the qualification, together with the fact that it is the only one, tells us a good deal concerning Hobbes's thinking about government and politics. In "A Review, and Conclusion" that Hobbes appended to later editions of *Leviathan*, he proposed a twentieth law of nature that reads as follows: **"that every man is bound by nature, as much as in him lieth, to protect *in war* the authority, by which he is himself protected in time of peace"** (italics added).[10] As we are led to expect by the phrases "by nature" and "as much as in him lieth," Hobbes allows important exceptions to this obligation.

> [A] man that is commanded as a soldier to fight against the enemy, though his sovereign have right enough to punish his refusal with death, may nevertheless in many cases refuse, without injustice; as when he substituteth a sufficient soldier in his place.
>
> (*Elements*, Ch. 21, p. 165)

This particular excusing condition, and the more general one provided by having "a timorous nature," are taken away from "he that enrolleth himself a soldier or taketh imprest money." More important:

> when the defence of the commonwealth, requireth at once the help of all that are able to bear arms, every one is obliged; because otherwise the institution of the commonwealth, which they have not the purpose, or courage to preserve, was in vain.
>
> (*Elements*, Ch. 21, p. 165)

200 *Opacity, liberalism, and individuality*

Viewed as a kind of culmination of Hobbes's overall theory of political obligation, more particularly viewed in the light of the internally dissonant discussion of which it is immediately a part, there is a strained, unconvincing quality to this the least qualified of his exhortations to support the Sovereign. The final sentence concedes that the Sovereign lacks the power to compel her subjects to fight on her behalf, makes it clear that the preservation of commonwealth depends upon the self-chosen and largely self-sustained allegiance of subjects. Because Hobbes himself has made such fidelity appear unlikely if not ill advised, his argument is about as likely to encourage Sovereigns to expect active assistance from their subjects as it is to inspire fear of Sovereign power in subjects.

Notes

1 This is true of all association with other people. "We do not ... seek society for its own sake, but that we may receive some honour or profit from it; these we desire primarily, that secondarily" (*DC*, Ch. I, p. 111).

2 In saying "the only reason for doing so" I am setting to the side Hobbes's argument that God commanded us to create and submit to political society. If we tried to harmonize the two arguments we might say that God issued this command out of benevolent concern for the earthly freedom and felicity of the human beings She had created. Presumably She would command disobedience to political societies that did not achieve this goal or at least conscientiously pursue this purpose. Officially, Hobbes himself cannot claim to know God's intentions in this or any other regard and ought not to speculate concerning them. God's commands are simply God's commands and it is not for us to wonder why. It is for this reason that Hobbes's "Christian" arguments are the most unqualifiedly deontic aspects of his thinking (and loom largest in those interpretations of his work that construe him as a strictly deontic moralist and political/jural theorist.)

   It is for the same reason that there is considerable tension between Hobbes's secular and his religious or theological argument for obedience to government. Hobbes's secular argument not only licenses a good deal of disobedience but encourages withdrawal from and the destruction of political societies under a considerable and by no means improbable array of circumstances. But his Christian argument relies almost entirely on the Pauline doctrine of strict obedience to all earthly authorities and makes justified disobedience nearly impossible. As a speculation, this may be because his Christian argument was addressed primarily to people who would disobey and disrupt political society for reasons other than to protect their earthly freedom and felicity.

3 In saying "not ... on practice only" Hobbes allows that skills learned by practice and not embodied or embodiable in rules do play a role in making and sustaining commonwealths. The most important of such skills are those that he discusses (for example in *Lev.*, Ch. 30) under the heading of public "instruction" as distinct from law. On the reading I am presenting these parts of Hobbes's argument have a problematic place in his civil philosophy.

4 In theological terms, if Hobbes did not permit himself the conceit of judging the human condition to be a manifestation of God's benevolence, neither was he prepared for the impiety of imputing to God the cruelty of having altogether withheld from humankind the wherewithal of activities that She had made unavoidable for them and of arrangements necessary to tolerable success in those activities.

5 In Chapter 10 of *Leviathan* Hobbes distinguishes the "worthiness" of a person from the "worth or value; and also from his merit, or desert." Whereas all of the latter

Of liberty, authority and power 201

depend in one way or another "on the need and judgment of another," "worthiness ... consisteth in a particular power, or ability for that, whereof he is said to be worthy: which particular ability is usually named FITNESS or aptitude" (p. 79). My suggestion is that he thinks some persons have more, some less, worthiness to pursue felicity under the less than propitious circumstances in which human beings find themselves.

6 Although Hobbes does not here mention his views about the limitations of language and what might be called the rule-skepticism that it implies, his emphasis on the variety of actions can be read as saying that actions are too diverse to be encompassed, "perspicuously" or perhaps at all, by the general and prospective rules through which sovereigns are urged to govern.

7 *DC*, Ch. XIII, pp. 268–269. Together with his admiration for the brevity of the ancient laws, the last sentences of this admirable paragraph dramatize the enormous gulf between Hobbes's thinking about law and governance and the assumptions and practices that have become commonplace in the centuries that divide him from us. The idea that a citizen or subject of a modern state could "easily remember" all of their laws, and that each and every of the plethora of legal prohibitions are dictated by reason, is simply comic. Or rather it is tragi-comic because, in the words of his next sentence, nothing is now so familiar as citizens entrapped by and losing their harmless liberties to the laws and regulations of the modern state.

8 Hobbes underlines this point by arguing that the Sovereign ought to accord individual subjects something approximating rights against her in various respects.

> If a subject have a controversy with his sovereign, of debt, or of right of possession of lands or goods, or concerning any service required at his hands, or concerning any penalty ... grounded on a precedent law; he hath the same liberty to sue for his rights, as if it were against a[nother] subject.
>
> (*Lev.*, Ch. 21, p. 166)

Because such matters are personal or even private to the individual in question, they are not likely to become a basis for group or collective action that threatens the Sovereign's authority or power.

9 Cf. his distinction between a "multitude" and a "people" in *DC*, Ch. XII, pp. 250–251.

Hobbes's use of an organic analogy to represent Leviathan, and the famous Frontispiece to *Leviathan* that appears literally to "embody" all of the subjects in the single body of the Sovereign, have misled his readers on this point. The "animal" that is Leviathan is "artificial" not natural, is a machine, engine, or "automaton" not an organism and Hobbes carefully distinguishes its several parts (*Lev.*, "Author's Introduction," p. 19). The "body" depicted in the Frontispiece, the drawing of which Hobbes closely supervised, meticulously maintains the separate identities of the numerous individual bodies (persons) of which it is composed. Hobbes's most extended treatment of identity, in *De Corpore* (1962c), Ch. 11, strongly underlines these points.

10 P. 504 ... We should interpret this law to hold for civil as well as international wars. Equally, the law would deserve the degree of special attention Hobbes gives it only if war is taken to mean actual fighting against an armed and organized force, not that "known disposition to" conflict that is pervasive in human affairs and not the Sovereign's attempts to prevent and punish the disobedience of individual subjects. It is clear from his numerous discussions of sedition that Hobbes thinks that the first two types of conflict are the chief threats to commonwealth and its purposes.

References

Hobbes, Thomas. 1962a. *Leviathan.* Edited by Michael Oakeshott, with an Introduction by Richard S. Peters. London: Collier Books.

202 *Opacity, liberalism, and individuality*

Hobbes, Thomas. 1962b. *Elements of Law*. In *Body, Man, and Citizen: Selections from Hobbes's Writings*. Edited by Richard S. Peters. London: Collier Books.

Hobbes, Thomas. 1962c. *De Corpore*. In *Body, Man, and Citizen: Selections from Hobbes's Writings*. Edited by Richard S. Peters. London: Collier Books.

Hobbes, Thomas. 1971. *A Dialogue between a Philosopher and a Student of the Common Laws of England*. Edited and with an Introduction by Joseph Cropsey. Chicago: University of Chicago Press.

Hobbes, Thomas. 1972. *De Cive or The Citizen*. In *Man and Citizen: Thomas Hobbes*. Edited by Bernard Gert. Atlantic Highlands: Humanities Press.

12 Strains in and around liberal theory

An overview from a strong voluntarist perspective (1998)

The recent theoretical literature in and around the ideology of liberalism is profuse, rapidly burgeoning, and sharply conflicted.[1] Contemporary discussions reenact a by now richly diverse history of moral and political reflection.[2] Complicating matters further, both recent writings and the tradition they continue are refractions of disputes in the wider and yet more controverted domains of general opinion and public policy. In the hope of making some overall sense of these multiplicitous phenomena, I begin with and then explore the deficiencies of a rough but I hope serviceable distinction between "agency"- and "virtue"-oriented liberal theories. This exploration will identify a few characteristics common to nearly all liberalisms, but its more salient outcome will be to underline that there is no liberalism as such, that the term refers to a diverse, changing, and often fractious array of doctrines that form a "family" only in the most extended of Wittgenstein's famous uses of that term (1953, paras. 65–81). I suggest, moreover, that we extend the family further by appropriating into it elements from modes of thinking usually and on the whole rightly regarded as a- or illiberal.

Agency liberalism

Liberal theories of this type foreground a number of interwoven elements. Of these the most important is the individual person as actor, initiator, producer, creator. Theorists of the agency liberal persuasion are more interested in action than in thought. They do not deny that reasoning and reflection can and should play a role in action, but they stress that most forms of action involve elements distinct from thinking. Their philosophical and empirical psychologies foreground less exclusively cognitive or ratiocinative elements or forces such as desire, intention, imagination and will. As classically formulated by Hobbes (1962), in the agency liberal view reason is a "scout" for the passions and desires; it neither can nor should aspire to be their master.

Echoed more or less audibly by later thinkers such as Benjamin Constant (1988), John Stuart Mill (1951), Raymond Aron (1957), Isaiah Berlin (1969), H. L. A. Hart (1962), Stuart Hampshire (1983, 1989), and Bernard Williams (1985), the theory of action and of reason prevalent in agency-oriented liberalisms manifests a distinctive

204 *Opacity, liberalism, and individuality*

combination of attitudes or judgments, a combination that many critics—from both within and without liberalism—think is internally conflicted or otherwise unacceptable. On the one hand, agency liberals are confident concerning the capacity of human beings not only for self-movement but for self-definition and for what Michael Oakeshott (1975) calls self-enactment. Given tolerably favorable circumstances, human beings are able to identify and act to obtain desired objects and objectives, form and execute intentions, adopt and pursue ends and goals. In the course of doing these things they develop and sustain personalities or characters that distinguish them one from another. On this construal, agency liberals idealize individual human beings as restless, pulsating sources and loci of singular ideas and ideals.

On the other hand, liberal thinkers of this orientation manifest a certain skepticism. Although not dogmatic or programmatic skeptics in any technical epistemological sense, they doubt the power of reason or mind to arrive at general truths, especially general truths concerning morals and politics.[3] At the same time, they fear the effects of attempts to subjugate thought and action to a rigorous rule of reason.

Agency-oriented liberals are, both descriptively and normatively, theorists of individuality and of other modes of plurality. It is at once a fact and a good that human beings form desires for a large and shifting variety of objects, adopt and pursue a wide and changing array of purposes, value and disvalue a fluctuating diversity of persons and things. Descriptively, these diversities and this flux, certainly forces tending to produce and sustain them, are observable in all human affairs. These sources of energy and divergence can be contained or stifled in varying degrees by social and moral, political, and legal forces and devices. But attempts to suppress or control them commonly provoke resistance that testifies to the persistence and power of diversifying impulses and desires in human thinking and acting.

Numerous facts about human beings and their affairs are indifferent from a moral or otherwise evaluative standpoint; numerous others are bad or evil. But for agency-oriented liberals, two connected considerations recommend the judgment that the human characteristics and proclivities I have been mentioning ought to be valued and encouraged, even celebrated.

Most important, it is either exclusively or primarily by acting on passions and desires, and by pursuing ends and purposes chosen to satisfy passions and desires, that human beings are able to obtain what they themselves regard as goods and to avoid what they judge to be harms or evils. In language frequent in agency liberal discussions, desire fulfillment or satisfaction is the only or the chief means of and to well-being. Hobbes adopts the first, stronger view. For him, good and evil consist exclusively in the satisfaction or frustration of actually and perhaps occurrently experienced passions and desires. "Felicity," the only overall end or good of human life that Hobbes recognizes, consists exclusively in more or less regular success in obtaining the objects of the passions and desires.[4]

Most agency-oriented liberals take the second and weaker view. They affirm or at least entertain a possibility that Hobbes rejects, namely of criteria of value

Strains in and around liberal theory 205

that are partially independent of desire. If, for example, someone desires to become a slave, and does so for its own sake rather than because of a circumstantial judgment that slavery will maximize her desire satisfaction or felicity, Mill and perhaps Constant appear to think that this desire and hence its satisfaction are bad in themselves or because they are virtually certain to diminish well-being. Likewise but more insistently, Judith Shklar (1984) and Richard Rorty (1989), whose thinking is at once importantly within but also against agency-oriented liberalism, argue that the impulse to be cruel to others, and hence acting on that impulse, is unqualifiedly bad or wrong. More generally, a variety of recent thinkers (e.g., Elster, 1979; Hare, 1981; Scanlon, 1982; Griffin, 1986; Raz, 1986; Sen, 1987), who for present purposes can be classified in the same way as Shklar and Rorty, argue that occurrent desires are sometimes "adaptive" or otherwise distorted such that their satisfaction results in ill- rather than well-being. And Shklar, Stuart Hampshire, and Jean-François Lyotard (1991; Lyotard and Thébaud, 1992) contend that there are certain minimal requirements of justice that must be respected and hence ought to be enforced regardless of the present distribution of desires. Even if they don't manage to say it with Hobbes's resounding aplomb, however, all of these thinkers agree with Hobbes's assertion that "as to have no desire, is to be dead: so to have weak passions, is dullness" (1962, ch. 6). A multiplicity of desires and desire satisfactions is the necessary albeit not the sufficient condition of human well-being.

It is also a fact that desires and purposes frequently conflict, and this further fact warrants the inference that legal and other restrictions must sometimes be placed on attempts to satisfy desires and achieve purposes. Equally, hopes and fears, beliefs and values sometimes converge or complement one another. Because these latter eventualities may enhance the prospects of present and continuing gratifications, efforts can and should be made to harmonize, or at least mutually to accommodate, the desires that occur both within and among individuals and groups. But this observation brings us to the second consideration supporting a favorable evaluation of the sources of subjectively based individuality and various other forms of plurality. Diversity, dissonance, and even conflict between and among desires enlivens and invigorates those whose desires they are. Whatever other effects doing so may have, experiencing dissonance, disagreement, and conflict animates what Mill calls the "meaning," for or to me, of my beliefs and values and thereby also animates my individuality. And the competitions that disagreements stimulate often energize capacities for effective action and hence for mutual as well as self-gratifications. There is no individual and certainly no collective *Summum Bonum*, but the prospects for individual and collected felicity are heightened rather than diminished by dissonance, divergence, and even strife.

The features discussed thus far are core commitments of agency liberalism. The other elements commonly found in theories of this type, some of which I now briefly discuss, should be understood as corollaries of or supplements to their conceptions of agency and action and their strongly favorable valorization not only of plurality but especially of that extreme form of plurality that is individuality.

206 *Opacity, liberalism, and individuality*

Just as agency liberals are not dogmatic skeptics, so they are neither anarchists nor radical antinomians (albeit their emphasis on individuality likens them to individualist anarchists and their disposition to a certain incredulity makes them receptive to the rule skepticism of antinomians). In the hope both of containing destructive forms of conflict and enabling mutually advantageous forms of cooperation, agency liberals promote rational or reasonable patterns of interaction and accept that principles, rules, and established practices sometimes contribute to these objectives. But all such constraining and directing devices are or ought to be adopted for the sake of the felicity of individuals. If or to the extent that principles and rules, duties and obligations disserve felicity, they should be altered, revoked, and if necessary disobeyed. Perhaps most important, there is a tendency among agency-oriented liberals to view principles and rules as primarily (to borrow yet another term from Michael Oakeshott, 1975) adverbial, as concerned less with ends and purposes, rights and duties, and more with the manner in which or the sensibility out of which each individual does whatever she chooses to do. If there is a primary political virtue it is civility, and there is a good deal of emphasis on moral virtues (or *virtùs*) such as magnanimity and fastidiousness, courage and free-spiritedness.

The notion of equality has a fundamental place in agency-oriented liberalism, but it is first and foremost equality in the sense articulated by Hobbes's notion of the Right of Nature. Every individual ought to be accorded standing as an end-defining and end-seeking agent. The very fact that I have chosen an end or purpose is reason for thinking that it is a prima facie good for me to achieve it. If others are disposed to prevent me from doing so, the burden of justification falls on them. If stated as a principle rather than a right, this becomes what I have elsewhere called—perhaps tendentiously—the Liberal Principle (Flathman, 1987, 1989).

Looking ahead a bit, it is true that something like this notion of equality is also prominent in the thinking of virtue-oriented liberals such as T. H. Green (1986), Leonard Hobhouse (1964), John Rawls (1971, 1993) and Ronald Dworkin (1977, 1978). In the views of these latter thinkers, every agent is entitled to that respect from others necessary to sustain her self-respect and hence her capacity to define and pursue a conception of her good. This notion of equality can even be associated with the "recognition" that Hegel (1977) says we all crave or ought to crave. But in the virtue liberal formulations I am now discussing, equality, respect and recognition are deeply conditional. I am entitled to standing and respect as an agent only if my desires, goals and purposes meet the criteria of justice, of reason, or of like standards. Recall what Rawls famously (or infamously) says of those "who find that being disposed to act justly is not a good for them": "their nature is their misfortune" and is no reason for the more favorably endowed to hesitate before punishing them for their failings (1971, p. 576).

Liberty or freedom of thought and action is also fundamental to agency-oriented liberalism. Liberty is understood as "negative" rather than "positive" in Berlin's sense (or "modern" rather than "ancient" in Constant's diction) and notions such as "forced to be free," "perfect service is perfect freedom" and "you shall know the truth and the truth shall make you free" are regarded as at once oxymoronic and repugnant. Liberty, however, is an instrumental not an a priori and certainly not an unqualified good. It is chief among what Rawls (in the most important of his agency liberal moments) calls the "primary" goods (1971), a good that one must enjoy in order to satisfy effectively whatever desires one may have and in order to pursue whatever ends and purposes one may adopt. Thus agency-oriented liberals allow the necessity of restrictions on liberty, but they are as congenitally wary of such restrictions as they are skeptical of foundationalist accounts of liberty or its value.

Hobbes and perhaps Montaigne are protoliberals of the agency type or orientation. In the early history of liberalism as a named idea and force the chief examples of agency orientation are found in Humboldt (1993), Constant, and parts of J. S. Mill (especially his emphasis on individuality and on meaning as distinct from truth). Among more recent thinkers, the most prominent representatives of this mode of liberal thinking are Aron and Berlin, Hart and Hampshire. George Kateb's promotion (1992) of a liberal individuality deeply indebted to Emerson and Whitman represents a distinctive and distinctively engaging variant of agency liberalism, as does the in some ways similar thinking of Will Kymlicka (1989). There are obvious objections to classifying thinkers such as Jean-François Lyotard as liberals of any sort, but elements of agency-oriented thinking are evident in the latter's work with Thébaud, *Just Gaming* (1992), and especially in *The Inhuman* (1991).

Virtue liberalism

In the second type of liberal view, virtue liberalism, life is or can be just and humane, is or can be appropriate to humankind, only if or to the extent that all public and much private thinking and acting are governed by beliefs that are arrived at under the discipline of intersubjective reason or "deliberative rationality." In a good, just, or humane—hence in this view liberal—society the interpersonal standing of the most operative or controlling beliefs will be underlined or augmented through procedures that inscribe those beliefs in principles and rules that have legal or otherwise authoritative standing. The most basic of these disciplining norms either are not instrumental at all (as in Kant, 1948) or have deontic standing sufficient to withstand (in reason if not in wayward fact) the pressures and temptations of fluctuating desires and interests.

For virtue liberals, ends that are shared or in common are superior to those that disaggregate or divide, and some ends (and hence some desires, intentions, and so on) are—as in Kant and Rawls—categorically inadmissible. There is a realm that is properly "private," but the scope of the private domain is to be determined by public reason and is properly susceptible to delineation and discipline by public procedures and processes. In the public domain, reason, deliberative rationality, and reasoned justification, and the principles and norms that are their favored yield, are to govern. Passion, desire and interest must submit to the discipline of reason and reason-based principles and rules. Moreover, for

208 *Opacity, liberalism, and individuality*

virtue liberals the distinction between public and private is deployed to circumscribe the authority of the state and law but not the authority of reason and morality.[5]

In virtue liberalism there is typically more emphasis (than in agency liberalism) on substantive or material equalities and on the conditions and arrangements that create and protect such equalities, an emphasis that is particularly pronounced in late-nineteenth-century "New Liberalism" (Freeden, 1978) and in the welfare state liberalisms that are importantly the heir of the former. There is also more enthusiasm for democracy, the latter understood less as a form of *cracy* or rule (which is how agency-oriented liberals, most of whom favor but do not enthuse over democracy, tend to regard it) than as a "way of life" (Dewey, 1927) or a preferred mode of collective action and governance. These tendencies are especially prominent among thinkers such as James Fishkin (1983) who identify themselves as liberal democrats.[6]

Among earlier writers usually classified as liberals, the thinking of Locke (1960) and Kant, Hegel as interpreted by Shlomo Avinieri (1972) and importantly by Charles Taylor (1979), Rousseau (who in my judgment is no liberal at all), and the utilitarian, empiricist-scientist and protosocialist parts of Mill all manifest the characteristics of virtue liberalism. The classic proponents of this version of liberalism are Kant, T. H. Green and Leonard Hobhouse. Among contemporary thinkers, John Rawls and Jürgen Habermas (1984) are the most influential representatives of this orientation. The large literatures affirmatively influenced by these two thinkers give their versions of virtue liberalism great prominence in recent discussions.[7]

For Rawls, justice is the first virtue of a politically organized society. The principles of justice, arrived at by a combination of rationality and reasonableness, have "absolute weight" vis-à-vis all other considerations. All questions concerning the "basic structure" and "constitutional essentials" of politically organized society are to be resolved by "public reason" (1993).

It is true that these virtue elements in Rawls's thinking (as with Habermas's) coexist with other features that are arguably more agency oriented in character or tendency. In Rawls's case, the chief example is that his first principle of justice accords to each citizen such rights to the "basic liberties" as are consistent with all other citizens having the same rights. This principle generates duties or requires virtues, but only in that it is both a duty and a virtue to respect the rights of others. Again, Rawls insists that there is a rationally irreducible plurality of conceptions of the good and appears to argue that, outside of the basic structure, choices among such conceptions should but need not be disciplined by justice or public reason. In company with his recent arguments that even justice should be "political not metaphysical" and ought to seek no more than an "overlapping consensus" on beliefs and values (1993), these features of Rawls's theorizing distance him from Green and Hobhouse and from more uncompromisingly virtue-oriented contemporaries such as William Galston (1991), Amy Gutmann (1980) and Steven Macedo (1990), all of whom share Habermas's view that, ideally, no domain of thought and action would be exempt from the requirements of deliberative rationality and morality.

Strains in and around liberal theory 209

But Rawls is unwavering in his insistence that justice must take precedence over all considerations that compete or conflict with it, and he clearly thinks that both fair and stable cooperation depends on strict adherence to the principles of justice that ought to govern the basic structure. More ominously, as his apprehensions about stability lead him (most emphatically in 1971, book 3) to "thicken" his theory of the good and otherwise to concern himself with the development of moral character, the agency-oriented elements in his thinking give way to moralistic and indeed to moraline formulations (tendencies prominent in the New Liberal British thinkers and also pronounced in Habermas's thinking).

On my reading, the types of thinking that I have delineated under the rubric "virtue oriented" dominate contemporary liberal theorizing, particularly in the United States. I cannot survey all of the literatures that lead me to this generalization, and it is yet more obvious that I cannot attend in adequate detail to the many differences among thinkers of this general tendency. Important theories such as those of Joseph Raz (1986), John Charvet (1981) and T. M. Scanlon (1982) share some of the characteristics I have mentioned, but also depart importantly from the pattern I have sketched. James Griffin (1986) and Amartya Sen (1987), in their own ways, can be read as seeking a harmonization of what each takes to be best in agency- and virtue-oriented liberalism. Recent attempts to move liberalism closer to classical republicanism (e.g., Ackerman, 1989) continue but also effect important changes in virtue-oriented liberalism. If Michael Walzer (1983) is regarded as a liberal, his work shows the affinities, already evident in T. H. Green, between virtue liberalism and communitarianism of the kind now associated with writers such as Michael Sandel (1982) and Charles Taylor (1989). As with *liberalism* itself, *virtue liberalism* is a family resemblance term, and the dispute between virtue liberals and communitarians is a family quarrel (see Honig, 1993).

Agency liberalisms, virtue liberalisms and strong voluntarism

Both agency and virtue liberalisms presuppose and endorse a weak form of voluntarism, a version of that doctrine that consists primarily in a distinction between chosen and intentional actions on the one hand and causally explainable movements or behaviors on the other. And some virtue theories—such as Kant's in the moments at which he emphasizes Will as a necessary activating agency in conduct—move, formally toward strong voluntarism. But these moves are compromised by other elements in virtue-oriented theories, elements that are resisted by agency liberals and rejected by strong voluntarists and willful liberals.

On the one hand, virtue liberal theorists tend to be impressed by the weaknesses of agents that are unaided and undisciplined by public reason, that is, by the constraints of reasoning that shows itself to be intersubjectively valid by being articulated in designated public forums following agreed procedures and canons of argumentation. The persons who predominate in virtue liberal theories (especially in those recent examples of such theories that promote the welfare

210   *Opacity, liberalism, and individuality*

state—Rawls, Habermas, Raz, Gutmann and Galston are good examples) need not only a lot of help but a good deal of discipline and control. At a minimum, these persons need the protections and other advantages provided by living in company with associates who are for the most part just and otherwise virtuous. And most persons also need more affirmative forms of assistance, material and otherwise.

In these respects contemporary virtue liberals have been influenced by Left and Right critiques of liberal societies and perhaps also by difficult-to-classify critics such as Michel Foucault (1980). Even if the abilities and arts of agency are valued—all theories that can usefully be called liberal value these abilities and arts to some extent—the confidence that Hobbes, Humboldt and Constant have in the capacity for such agency is at once diminished and feared. Without a good deal of public help, most human beings deteriorate into what Oakeshott (1975) calls the individual manqué and perhaps deteriorate further into that ressentiment-laden creature that he calls the anti-individual.

In the latter mood, so to speak, virtue liberals want weak voluntarism so as to be able to ascribe responsibility and to justify censure and punishment. This is of course the Nietzschean critique of weak voluntarism. Weak voluntarists impute freedom of will sufficient to warrant ascription of responsibility and hence blame. But their voluntarism is insufficient to allow them to celebrate self-enacted individuality and the deviance and disobedience that, as weak voluntarists-cum-virtue liberals see it, are too often the yield of such individuality.

Willful liberalism

If there is or could be such a thing as willful liberalism, it is or would be an accentuation and intensification of agency liberalism.

Willful liberals place yet greater emphasis (greater than, for example, agency liberals such as Mill and Berlin) on the irreducible diversity of divergent, incommensurable, and perhaps interpersonally or inter-subjectively inexplicable goods, ends, and especially ideals. Rather than Reason, its chief emblem is Will construed as largely or at least finally mysterious.

This cardinal feature of willful liberalism is obscured by the insistence of late-nineteenth-century strong voluntarists such as William James (1968) and Nietzsche (1955, 1956, 1967, 1974)—and, later, of Oakeshott and Berlin—on the prevalence of homogeneity and conformity, of the masses, the herd, the tyranny of the conventional and the majority. The individuality and plurality that these thinkers treasure are assured only in the sense that human beings harbor a potential for them. But this potential has been largely annulled or crippled by moraline doctrines such as Christianity, Kantianism, socialism and, yes, the virtue, welfare and democratic liberalisms that purport to value and to serve it. Thus this latent possibility must be freed, must be fought for (importantly by contesting the doctrines just mentioned). This leads thinkers such as William E. Connolly (1991) and Chantal Mouffe (1993) to insist on the agonal character of Nietzschean, pluralist and other strong voluntarist doctrines. But it also leads

Strains in and around liberal theory 211

them to a greater faith in democracy than I and most strong voluntarist liberals are able to sustain. As I suggested earlier, numerous agency liberals follow Max Weber in emphasizing the *cracy* part of the internally dissonant concept of democracy, and some of them follow Hobbes in fearing that its *demo* part enhances the dangers of the *cracy* that it legitimates.

In these respects willful liberalism has affinities with libertarianism and especially with various strains in romanticism. The notion of liberation from state and other forms of power is reminiscent of libertarianism and even of individualistic anarchism, and the notions of self-making, self-enactment and self-fashioning have manifest affinities with major tendencies in romanticism and expressivism.

These comparisons, however, are seriously misleading. As against libertarianism, especially in the recent American and British formulations that identify with so-called classical liberalism and promote laissez-faire or market economies, strong voluntarists from Montaigne and Hobbes to Nietzsche, James and Oakeshott are interested in the making of lives not in the making of livings. They find the economistic character of much libertarianism dreary and dispiriting.

The strong voluntarist attack on romanticism is less widely appreciated. In Nietzsche's phrase (1967), strong voluntarists view romanticism as a form or "letting go," as a lack or want of discipline.[8] The discipline strong voluntarists favor, moreover, must begin with quite rigorously impositional social and cultural training, with what Nietzsche calls "preparations" and what Oakeshott speaks of as schooling (1989, 1991) that engenders fluency in the various "languages" that have evolved into modes of experience or traditions of thought and sensibility. In this respect there are important continuities between the strong voluntarists and Wittgenstein's account of the ways in which "agreements in judgment" get established, agreements that allow of "knowing how to go on" in various practices and activities but also provide the settings in which and the materials out of which disagreements in opinion, often unresolvable, emerge (1953, paras. 241–242). The view, mistakenly attributed to strong voluntarists such as Nietzsche, that self-enactment is done in isolation or solitude, that one makes oneself and one's life out of materials entirely of one's own creation, is a serious misunderstanding. The Nietzschean free spirit attempts to achieve distance from society and especially politics, but it is a "pathos of distance" and the "pathos" part of this formula testifies to the fact that the free spirit remains deeply, albeit never complacently or even comfortably situated in a tradition, culture and society.

The strong voluntarist ideals of individuality and self-enactment require that over time initial social and cultural training and discipline be transformed into self-discipline, must give way to that "self-overcoming" that is a necessary condition of free-spiritedness. To the extent that such a transformation is achieved, homogeneity and commonality, dependency, conformism and ressentiment concerning remaining differences and inequalities are replaced by diversity and individuality disciplined by adverbial *virtùs* such as civility, magnanimity and fastidiousness.

212 *Opacity, liberalism, and individuality*

As with the work of all true artists, the arts of self-making require a never to be permanently stabilized combination of discipline and invention; discipline grounded in familiarity with the past and the present together with invention that departs from past and present configurations in unpredictable and often initially incomprehensible ways. In part because the specific forms of discipline necessary to self-making are importantly similar to those promoted by *virtù* theorists such as Machiavelli, we might call willful liberalism "*virtù* liberalism." For reasons that probably don't need to be stated, we do better to call it virtuosity liberalism—virtuosity in the making of lives.

Willful or virtuosity liberalism, and hence strong voluntarism, is essential to a recognizably liberal society at least in the sense that I have elsewhere called minimal (Flathman, 1992). There must be a substantial number of associates who for the most part "take care of themselves," who do not need to be "cared for" by others or by society. And there must be associates who, by cultivating virtuosities such as civility and especially magnanimity, care for others in the sense of not inflicting themselves harmfully or destructively on the latter.

Beyond this necessary minimum, willful or virtuosity liberalism is a form of idealism, a radically individualized version of what is now called—often misleadingly—perfectionism.[9] As such, it cannot be imposed, perhaps cannot even be socially or politically cultivated. Nietzsche declares himself an Argonaut of his idealism, not its evangelist and certainly not its drill instructor. Insofar as he "teaches" his idealism, he does so by example and more particularly by inspiriting writing not by direction or imposition. This understanding seems to me to be true to what is best in the liberal tradition.

Liberalism and public policy

Willful or virtuosity liberalism provides no recipes, decision procedures or logarithms for the making of public policy. It bears upon but is radically indeterminate concerning virtually all of the major issues that now animate public life in more or less liberal societies. But I must leave aside this huge question (and hence much of the literature currently being produced by *soi-disant* liberals and their ideological opponents). So as not to end this essay on a banal note, I nevertheless hazard the observation, prompted in part by my reading of the works of Lyotard, Hélène Cixous and Catherine Clément (1986), and Luce Irigaray (1985), that the ideas and ideals of willful or virtuosity liberalism have a particular pertinence to thinking currently being pressed by the oppositional forces most important to the liberal societies of our time—that is, the racial, feminist, and gay and lesbian liberation movements.

Notes

1 The bibliography of a recently published work on liberal political theory, restricted primarily to books, runs to well over one hundred items (Johnston, 1994). The bibliography of a survey of recent political theory, most of which is in or in the vicinity of liberal theory, runs to twenty-seven closely packed pages (Galston, n.d.).

Strains in and around liberal theory 213

2 Recent histories of liberalism include works by Arblaster (1991), Clarke (1978), Collini (1978), Freeden (1978, 1986) and Holmes (1984).

3 In the traditional distinction, they are Pyrrhonic rather than academic or dogmatic skeptics.

4   The words "good" and "evil" are ever used with relation to the [desires or passions of the] person that useth them: there being nothing simply and absolutely so; nor any common rule … to be taken from the nature of the objects themselves.

           (Hobbes, 1962, ch. 6)

Because Hobbes regards this as a conceptual as well as a psychological truth, for him it makes no sense to say that a desire or passion is good or evil in itself. But he thinks that having desires and passions is a necessary condition of there being goods and evils and hence gratifications and frustrations. Although it is less widely recognized in the Hobbes literature, he also holds that there are certain passions that must never be acted on, in particular the passion (often showing itself as "vainglory") that consists in denying that natural equality of all human beings that is the basis of the "Right of Nature."

5 So-called interest-group liberalism, a variant of the American version of political pluralism, and also arguments for "neutralism" such as that of (the early) Ackerman (1980) and especially of Charles Larmore (1987), are positions or tendencies of thought engagingly intermediate between my agency and virtue types. The idea that politics and government do—and *should* at least in the sense that there is no practicable alternative—respond to and service subjectively determined interests aligns these positions with agency-oriented liberalism. On the other hand, the notion that individuals can, frequently do, and in any case ought to subordinate their individual interests to the extent necessary to form groups with shared or common interests, and the further notion that there are procedural principles and rules that, because rational, are neutral to or among the competing group interests, move thinking of this kind toward virtue liberalism.

6 Without using the distinction between agency and virtue liberalism, Christopher Berry (1989, 1993) has effectively underlined differences among liberals concerning democracy.

7 The foregoing remarks underline the point that I regard the agency/virtue differentiation as more perspicuous than the familiar distinction between deontological and ideological liberal doctrines.

8 Nietzsche in particular thought that romanticism leads to rabid nationalisms in which the "letting go" takes collectivist forms that are immensely destructive. Berlin, among other agency liberals, is endlessly ambivalent on this question.

9 This designation is misleading because "perfectionism" is commonly construed (e.g., by Rawls, 1971, pp. 325ff.) as promoting *the* perfection to be sought by or appropriate to all human beings or all of the members of a society. Strong voluntarists and willful liberals insist that all human beings must create and pursue their own ideals, must perfect themselves by their own lights. Nietzsche's characteristically pungent remarks memorably capture the spirit of this latter, distinctive, form of idealism:

    Whatever kind of bizarre ideal one may follow … one should not demand that it be *the* ideal: for one therewith takes from its privileged character. One should have it in order to distinguish oneself, not in order to level oneself.

As regards his own "strange, tempting, dangerous" ideal of free-spiritedness, the ideal "of a spirit who plays naively—that is, not deliberately but from overflowing power and abundance—with all that was hitherto called holy, good, untouchable, divine," he declares that he "should not wish to persuade anybody" of its merits (1974, pp. 346–347). Indeed, he would not "readily concede *the right to it* to anyone. My ideal is *mine*. This is what *I* am; this is what *I* want:—*you* can go to hell!" (1967, pp. 191–192; emphases added).

214 *Opacity, liberalism, and individuality*

References

Ackerman, Bruce (1980). *Social Justice in the Liberal State*. New Haven: Yale University Press.

Ackerman, Bruce (1989). "Constitutional Politics/Constitutional Law." *Yale Law Journal* 99: 453–547.

Arblaster, Anthony (1991). *The Rise and Decline of Western Liberalism*. Oxford: Basil Blackwell.

Aron, Raymond (1957). *The Opium of the Intellectuals*. Garden City: Doubleday.

Avinieri, Shlomo (1972). *Hegel's Theory of the Modern State*. Cambridge: Cambridge University Press.

Berlin, Isaiah (1969). *Four Essays on Liberty*. London: Oxford University Press.

Berry, Christopher (1989). *The Idea of Democratic Community*. New York: St. Martin's.

Berry, Christopher (1993). "Shared Understanding and the Democratic Way of Life." In John Chapman and Ian Shapiro (eds.), *Democratic Community*. New York: New York University Press.

Charvet, John (1981). *A Critique of Freedom and Equality*. Cambridge: Cambridge University Press.

Cixous, Hélène, and Clément, Catherine (1986). *The Newly Born Woman*. Minneapolis: University of Minnesota Press.

Clarke, Peter (1978). *Liberals and Social Democrats*. Cambridge: Cambridge University Press.

Collini, Stefan (1978). *Liberalism and Sociology*. Cambridge: Cambridge University Press.

Connolly, William E. (1991). *Identity/Difference*. Ithaca, NY: Cornell University Press.

Constant, Benjamin (1988). *Political Writings*. Cambridge: Cambridge University Press.

Dewey, John (1927). *The Public and Its Problems*. New York: Henry Holt.

Dworkin, Ronald (1977). *Taking Rights Seriously*. Cambridge, MA: Harvard University Press.

Dworkin, Ronald (1978). "Liberalism." In Stuart Hampshire *et al.* (eds.), *Public and Private Morality*. Cambridge: Cambridge University Press.

Elster, Jon (1979). *Ulysses and the Sirens*. Cambridge: Cambridge University Press.

Fishkin, James (1983). *Justice, Equal Opportunity and the Family*. New Haven: Yale University Press.

Flathman, Richard E. (1987). *The Philosophy and Politics of Freedom*. Chicago: University of Chicago Press.

Flathman, Richard E. (1989). *Toward a Liberalism*. Ithaca, NY: Cornell University Press.

Flathman, Richard E. (1992). *Willful Liberalism*. Ithaca, NY: Cornell University Press.

Foucault, Michel (1980). *Power/Knowledge*. New York: Pantheon.

Freeden, Michael (1978). *The New Liberalism*. Oxford: Clarendon.

Freeden, Michael (1986). *Liberalism Divided: A Study in British Political Thought 1914–1939*. London: Oxford University Press.

Galston, William (n.d.). "Political Theory in the 1990's: Perplexity Amidst Diversity." Unpublished manuscript.

Galston, William (1991). *Liberal Purposes*. Cambridge: Cambridge University Press.

Green, T. H. (1986). *Lectures on the Principles of Political Obligation and Other Writings*. Cambridge: Cambridge University Press.

Griffin, James (1986). *Well-Being*. Oxford: Clarendon.

Gutmann, Amy (1980). *Liberal Equality*. Cambridge: Cambridge University Press.

Strains in and around liberal theory 215

Habermas, Jürgen (1984). *The Theory of Communicative Action* (2 vols.). Boston: Beacon.

Hampshire, Stuart (1983). *Morality and Conflict*. Cambridge, MA: Harvard University Press.

Hampshire, Stuart (1989). *Innocence and Experience*. Cambridge, MA: Harvard University Press.

Hare, R. M. (1981). *Moral Thinking*. Oxford: Clarendon.

Hart, H. L. A. (1962). *The Concept of Law*. Oxford: Clarendon.

Hegel, G. W. F. (1977). *Phenomenology of Spirit*. Oxford: Oxford University Press.

Hobbes, Thomas (1962). *Leviathan*, Michael Oakeshott, ed. London: Collier.

Hobhouse, Leonard (1964). *Liberalism*. New York: Galaxy.

Holmes, Stephen (1984). *Benjamin Constant and the Making of Modern Liberalism*. New Haven: Yale University Press.

Honig, B. (1993). *Political Theory and the Displacement of Politics*. Ithaca, NY: Cornell University Press.

Humboldt, Wilhelm von (1993). *The Limits of State Action*, J. W. Burrow, ed. Indianapolis: Liberty.

Irigaray, Luce (1985). *This Sex Which Is Not One*. Ithaca, NY: Cornell University Press.

James, William (1968). *The Writings of William James*. New York: Modern Library.

Johnston, David (1994). *The Idea of a Liberal Theory*. Princeton: Princeton University Press.

Kant, Immanuel (1948). *Groundwork of the Metaphysic of Morals*. London: Hutchinson.

Kateb, George (1992). *The Inner Ocean*. Ithaca, NY: Cornell University Press.

Kymlicka, Will (1989). *Liberalism, Community and Culture*. Oxford: Oxford University Press.

Larmore, Charles (1987). *Patterns of Moral Complexity*. Cambridge: Cambridge University Press.

Locke, John (1960). *Two Treatises of Government*. Cambridge: Cambridge University Press.

Lyotard, Jean-François (1991). *The Inhuman*. Stanford: Stanford University Press.

Lyotard, Jean-François, and Thébaud, Jean Loup (1992). *Just Gaming*. Minneapolis: University of Minnesota Press.

Macedo, Stephen (1990). *Liberal Virtues*. Oxford: Oxford University Press.

Mill, John Stuart (1951). *Utilitarianism, Liberty and Representative Government*. New York: E. P. Dutton.

Mouffe, Chantal (1993). *The Return of the Political*. New York: Verso.

Nietzsche, Friedrich (1955). *Beyond Good and Evil*. Chicago: Henry Regenry.

Nietzsche, Friedrich (1956). *The Genealogy of Morals*. Garden City: Doubleday.

Nietzsche, Friedrich (1967). *The Will to Power*. New York: Vintage Books.

Nietzsche, Friedrich (1974). *The Gay Science*. New York: Vintage Books.

Oakeshott, Michael (1975). *On Human Conduct*. Oxford: Oxford University Press.

Oakeshott, Michael (1989). *The Voice of Liberal Learning*. New Haven: Yale University Press.

Oakeshott, Michael (1991). *Rationalism in Politics*. Indianapolis: Liberty.

Rawls, John (1971). *A Theory of Justice*. Cambridge, MA: Harvard University Press.

Rawls, John (1993). *Political Liberalism*. New York: Columbia University Press.

Raz, Joseph (1986). *The Morality of Freedom*. Oxford: Clarendon.

Rorty, Richard (1989). *Contingency, Irony, and Solidarity*. Cambridge: Cambridge University Press.

216   *Opacity, liberalism, and individuality*

Sandel, Michael (1982). *Liberalism and the Limits of Justice*. Cambridge: Cambridge University Press.

Scanlon, T. M. (1982). "Contractualism and Utilitarianism." In Amartya Sen and Bernard Williams (eds.), *Utilitarianism and Beyond*. Cambridge: Cambridge University Press.

Sen, Amartya (1987). *On Ethics and Economics*. Oxford: Basil Blackwell.

Shklar, Judith N. (1984). *Ordinary Vices*. Cambridge, MA: Harvard University Press.

Taylor, Charles (1979). *Hegel and Modern Society*. Cambridge: Cambridge University Press.

Taylor, Charles (1989). *Sources of the Self*. Cambridge, MA: Harvard University Press.

Walzer, Michael (1983). *Spheres of Justice*. New York: Basic Books.

Williams, Bernard (1985). *Ethics and the Limits of Philosophy*. London: Fontana.

Wittgenstein, Ludwig (1953). *Philosophical Investigations*. New York: Macmillan.

13 Here and now, there and then, always and everywhere

Reflections concerning political theory and the study/writing of political thought (2006)

> … as it were between the games.
>
> Ludwig Wittgenstein

Both political theorizing and the study/writing of the history of political thought have many and varied exemplifications. Accordingly, it is difficult to generalize confidently concerning the relationship(s) between them. Briefly, political theorizing has commonly been, and ought to be, characterized by some combination of, on the one hand, critical assessments of prevalent political and related concepts, ideas, institutions and practices, and, on the other, attempts to imagine and articulate political ideals that serve both as criteria for critical assessment of extant ideas and arrangements and as proposals for a politics that is improved by normative standards. In its historical manifestations it is of course also an attempt to understand the concepts, issues and ideas to which it is addressed. This chapter then juxtaposes this conception with some leading views – which also may be regarded as idealizations – of the aims and methods appropriate to the study/writing of the history of political thought.

I

I take these to be importantly distinct activities or modes of thinking. Insofar as I advance a general view of the relationship(s) between them, it is that political theorizing provides historians of political thought with important parts (but not all) of their subject matter, while historians of political thought may provide, have sometimes provided, political theorists with an improved grasp of some of the concepts, ideas and ideals with, in and about which to think. They may also provide, have sometimes provided, an enlarged and in that respect an improved perspective on the questions they address and the answers they are inclined to give or to reject to those questions.

One way to expand somewhat on this view is to underline the idea that political theorists provide historians of political thought with part but not all of their subject matter. As regards the studies of the history of political thought that I was required to read as a graduate student,[1] we can pretty well do without the

218 *Opacity, liberalism, and individuality*

qualifier 'but not all'. These students (and many still writing) thought that there was a relatively short list of 'canonical' political theorists and the texts they produced; they devoted their efforts almost exclusively to identifying what they took to be the main concepts, ideas, ideals and arguments that formed the bodies of the texts that those canonical theorists wrote. There were (and are) minor differences among the lists with which they worked (and still work) but it would not be far wrong to say that those who made (and still make) it onto the list were understood to have a conception of political theorizing closely similar to the conception I have sketched above. Insofar as the texts in question contained elements that did or do not fit this conception they were (and in many quarters are) regarded as irrelevant to the study of the history of political theory.

A second way to expand on it is to emphasize the words 'critical assessment' and 'a politics improved by normative standards' in my earlier characterization of political theorizing. The students of the history of political thought to whom I just alluded (for convenience of reference I will call them 'students of the canon') understood the political theorists that they studied to be exposing mistaken views concerning political concepts, ideas and practices and to have the objective or purpose of replacing them with a correct, right or true account of them. They understood the canonical thinkers to be attempting to tell their readers what questions should be asked and how and what they ought to think about them and hence how and how not to act; that is, they were prescribing the form and character that policies ought to have. The students of the canon further thought that if, or to the extent that, the canonical theorists 'got it right', their theories tell *us* how and how not to think and act and how *our* policies ought to be conducted. Of course these canonical students disagreed with some of the political theorists that they studied, and they disagreed with one another as to the merits of the various views that they encountered in the course of their studies. But they agreed concerning the generic objectives that political theorists should pursue and that it was their task as students of political theory to make the results of that pursuit available to their own readerships. Insofar as they thought of themselves as political theorists as well as students of the history of political thought they pursued the same generic objectives as did their canonical predecessors. It is of course a controversial question how far they or those that they studied have achieved their practical objectives.

This understanding of how to study/write the history of political thought came under heavy attack in the latter part of the twentieth century (with, of course, some earlier anticipations) and the attack on it has continued with many refinements and with steadily increasing force in the ensuing years. Both the attack and the refinements have continued into the present century. In referring to the aforementioned large and growing group of writers as 'students' of the canonical history of political thought rather than as 'historians' of political thought I am 'acknowledging' (in something like Stanley Cavell's use of 'acknowledging')[2] what is arguably the broadest objection that these twentieth- (and of course twenty-first) century critics have entered to the studies of political thought that were dominant for much of the previous century, namely that in the proper sense of the term they were not *historical*.

Reflections concerning political theory   219

J. G. A. Pocock, looking back over historiographical thinking in roughly the last half of the twentieth century, has recently provided a characteristically elegant summary of this criticism. Referring to Quentin Skinner's early article 'Meaning and Understanding in the History of Ideas' (1969), 'which came to be the manifesto of an emerging method of interpreting the history of political thought', he credits Skinner with having

> demonstrated that much of the received history of that activity suffered from a radical confusion between systematic theory (or philosophy) and history. The greater and lesser texts of the past were interpreted as attempts to formulate bodies of theory whose content had been determined in advance by extrahistorical understandings of what 'political theory' and 'history' should be and were. This confusion led to errors including anachronism (the attribution to a past author of concepts that could not have been available to him) and prolepsis (treating him as anticipating the formation of arguments in whose subsequent formation the role of his text, if any, had yet to be historically demonstrated). After treating these fallacies with well-deserved ridicule, Skinner contended that the publication of a text and the utterance of its argument must be treated as an act performed in history, and specifically in the context of some ongoing discourse. It was necessary, Skinner said, to know what the author 'was doing'; what she or he had intended to do (had meant) and what she or he had succeeded in doing (had meant to others). The act and its effect had been performed in a historical context, supplied in the first place by the language of discourse in which the author had written and been read; though the speech act might innovate within and upon that language ... the language would set limits to what the author might say, might intend to say and be understood to say.[3]

In treating 'classical' or canonical texts' [*sic*] as themselves providing everything necessary to understand them, and as addressing 'perennial questions' or 'unit ideas', students of political thought produced not histories but what Skinner called 'mythologies'.[4]

In the passage quoted and some of the later pages of the same essay, Pocock is looking back at some of the key moments in the emergence of what has come to be called the 'Cambridge' or 'contextual' school of thought concerning the methods and objectives appropriate to studying and writing the history of political theory (and intellectual history generally). As he goes on to note, and as Skinner and other members of this contextualist school have emphasized, important changes, including disagreement among those who accept the basic tenets of the approach, have developed.[5] I comment on some of these later in the chapter but my purposes in the first parts of the chapter will be best served by using the distinctions I have thus far drawn, that is among an (idealized) conception of political theory, a prominent understanding of the history of political theory (the canonical conception) that brings a strongly analogous understanding of political theory to the study of its history, and the alternative approach to

220　*Opacity, liberalism, and individuality*

studying/writing the history of political theory (the contextualist approach) just sketched. As a means of doing so I make use of the main terms of my title, interpreting them in part through an overlapping but not equivalent set of distinctions proposed by the political philosopher Michael Oakeshott.

II

It is obvious, but nevertheless still worth mentioning, that all political theorizing, and all writing concerning the history of political thought, are in one or another here and now (as distinct from the everywhere and always). The thinkers that we regard as political theorists thought and wrote, think and write, in a time and place specific to them; writers concerning the history of political thought, whatever the then and there that is their focus, perform their studies and their writings in an identifiable – that is their own – times and places. All thinking and writing, however much its authors are concerned with a then and there of another specified time and place, are in the mode of the present, in the mode of the here and now. Insofar as they refer, explicitly or implicitly, to the past, that past is what Oakeshott calls the 'present past'.[6]

Oakeshott distinguishes, however, between the present 'practical past' and the present 'historical past'. If, or to the extent that, political theorists are interested in the past (as distinct from the everywhere and always), their interest is predominantly if not exclusively in the past as it bears upon the present interests and desires, objectives and purposes, of the theorist. The political theorist, *qua* political theorist, has no interest in, no use for, there's and then's that have no bearing on the here and now (though of course she or he may be influenced, knowingly or unknowingly, by there's and then's that in fact have a bearing on the here and now and it may be illuminating for historians of political thought to show that this is the case). In this respect, the interest of the political theorist in the past is, generically, the same as that of the moralist, the statesman, the businessman or the cook. For reasons already discussed, the same is true of canonical students of the history of political theory who understand it to be a search for correct answers to 'perennial questions', that is questions of present and future importance.

By contrast, contextualist historians of political thought – again as such and in what may be an idealized understanding – generally have no interest in the bearing of the concepts and ideas they study on the here and now. They seek to understand the emergence of concepts and ideas from the confluence of languages, intentions, thinkings, actings and other events that preceded and surrounded them; they seek to identify the meanings of the concepts and ideas in the then's and there's in which they, as evidenced by the texts and text analogues that come to the historian's attention, played a significant role. Mentions of the bearing of the ideas and events on the here and now of the historian (to say nothing of the everywhere and always) are – to update Stendhal – like the ringing of a cell-phone in the concert hall.

As with the distinctions drawn earlier, it is clear that those just sketched distinguish among ideal-types or, in terms that Oakeshott uses in discussing the

Reflections concerning political theory 221

'Modern European States', 'ideal characters'.[7] Just as Oakeshott does not claim that all or even any modern European states have or have had, exclusively, the defining characteristics of either a *societas* (a politically organized society with no common purpose) or a *universitas* (a society held together by a common purpose), he does not claim that all instances of thinking and writing concerning the past fit neatly into the categories 'practical past', 'historical past' or 'past past'. But he does claim that the elements or components of all such instances can be parsed, can be distinguished and differentiated, by using those categories. He also claims that doing so provides the criteria relevant to evaluating the merits of the thinking and writing that one is assessing.

In the next section of my chapter, I consider the value of his distinctions and of the related distinctions introduced earlier. In particular I consider whether employing these distinctions helps to identify congruencies and complementarities as well as differences among the understandings and approaches that the distinctions differentiate. Before doing so I should say a bit more about the third pair of terms in my title, that is the always and everywhere.

Taken in full seriousness, that is, as the view that there are questions pertinent not only to all known but to all possible (human?) experience, and that there are answers to those questions that not only are but must be true or valid of all human experience, this notion or view now seems to me to be little better than fantastic. If, as I think is the case, I was once attracted to it, just about everything that has transpired in the century in which I have lived most of my life, and not a little that has been recovered from earlier thinking and acting, has disabused me of it but not of the conviction that political theorizing as identified above is a possible and a valuable form of thought/action. But if we are to understand what many theorists and not a few political actors have thought they were doing, or understood themselves to be trying to do, we have to recognize that the notion of the everywhere and always, and the possibility – certainly the desirability – of giving that notion what Oakeshott and other Philosophical Idealists call 'fully coherent concreteness', has played and continues to play an important role in political and other modes of theorizing and (regrettably) in not a little political acting.

Leaving aside religious thinkers, it is more than merely arguable that Plato, Kant, Bradley and other Philosophical Idealists (Hegel is a difficult case) have understood their thinking about the here and now and the there and then to be also – and more importantly – thinking about the always and everywhere. Oakeshott himself saw no prospect of actually attaining to the fully coherent concrete whole, but he continued to think that the idea of such an attainment, even if only flickering in the back of the thinker's mind, was – at least for the philosopher as distinct from the theorist – a valuable, perhaps an indispensable heuristic. If Oakeshott wrote any history (which is doubtful) it was the history of historiography, that is, the history of the emergence of the 'postulates' of the activity of being an historian. His writings concerning the 'Modern European State' and related essays quite clearly do not, are not intended by him, to satisfy his own criteria of historical study. In his terminology, they are reflections on the

222 *Opacity, liberalism, and individuality*

practical past. Another thinker who comes to mind in this connection is Hannah Arendt. Numerous of her writings make references and allusions to past there's and then's and her perceptions concerning the rise of what she calls 'the social' may be of interest to historians, but we will be sorely disappointed if we look to her for instruction concerning, certainly of explanations for, the there's and then's that she instances. She too is a paradigm example of history viewed from the perspective of the practical past. The same might also be said of Leo Strauss.

It is at least arguable that Thomas Hobbes thought that important aspects of his thinking, those that he pleased himself to call scientific, had a character similar to Oakeshott's heuristic conception of the always and the everywhere. He of course admitted (no, insisted) that his science of the political (and the moral) took its beginnings from stipulations that could have been otherwise. But he thought that, once accepted, what he called ratiocination (the 'adding and subtracting' of the meanings of the stipulated terms) would lead to indisputable conclusions that would hold always and everywhere unless the stipulations were changed. With an important qualification, the same can be said concerning some of those political theorists that are called utopians. Of course these theorists, perhaps most notably Karl Marx but also Jürgen Habermas, would not have said that the utopian parts of their theories were true of any actual there or then or here and now, but they held that once put in to practice their theories would be true always and everywhere in the future. As Marx sometimes put it, history, that is significant change, would end. The history of political thinking could still be investigated and recounted, but it would have no bearing on the present or the future – would be purely antiquarian. There are places in which these theorists write as if they are studying the history of political (and other modes of) thought and action, but when they do so they understand themselves to be identifying a progression that could, or should, have only one culmination. By contrast, Philosophical Idealists such as Plato and Bradley thought that their theories identified and rendered reality as it has always been and can only be, all appearances to the contrary being just that, appearances.

III

The views and understandings considered thus far emphasize the differences between political theorizing and the study/writing of the history of political thought and among contrasting and competing approaches to the latter. But they also implicitly call attention to commonalities among these modes of inquiry and reflection. If there were no commonalities, comparison among them would be, if not impossible, of little fruition. Given that there are some significant commonalities, there is the possibility of complementarities as well as differentiations among and between them.

The obvious commonality among the canonical and contextual conceptions of the study/writing of the history of political thought is two-fold: in Oakeshott's terminology, they are both concerned (but for different reasons) with the present past, with the past as it is, here and now, perceived, understood and interpreted

Reflections concerning political theory 223

by those who study it. In an historical perspective, however, this is also true of political theorizing, even theorizing that aims to discern and articulate the everywhere and always. Reflections with this objective are of course carried out in a specific time and place and necessarily engage with, and reflect on, concepts and ideas that have come to the theorist from present and past formulations.

This commonality between political theorizing and studies concerning the history of political thought coexists with, and, I argue, creates the possibility not only of some meaningful comparisons but also of degrees of complementarity between these two forms or modes or intellectual activity. Those conventionally regarded as political theorists, say Hobbes or Mill, thought and wrote, in the there and then of their own time and place, a there and then that can be fruitfully identified by students of the history of political thinking. Important aspects of their thinking may be revealed by close examination of both the there and then in which their thinking took place and of the earlier then's and there's that figured, importantly (however knowingly or self-consciously) in their reflections and articulations. Many if not all of the concepts and ideas that political theorists critique and on which they seek to improve have lengthy and complex histories; as with the rest of us, political theorists, however extrahistorical (transcendental?) their objectives may be, become familiar with parts of their histories as they learn to think in and about them. In both their critical and constructive activities political theorists often attempt to effect changes in the stock of ideas and concepts that they inherit; but neither the changes nor the continuities in their formulations can be understood, by the theorists themselves or by their audiences, apart from their histories. Thus just as political theorists provide historians of political theory with important parts of their subject matter, so historians of political theory can be valuable co-political theorists by enlarging and deepening their command of the concepts and ideas in and about which they think. If political theorists aim to think constructively concerning the ideas and concepts that interest them, it is plausible to think that their theorizing will benefit from having a clear understanding of the meanings that those ideas and concepts have acquired and have become available to them. The work of John Rawls is instructive in this respect. It might be argued that the concepts and conceptions that he employs in *A Theory of Justice* (1971) can be understood without reference to the history of their uses in contractarian, utilitarian and related movements of thought and action that preceded his writing. Rawls locates his reflections in the contractarian tradition and contrasts them with utilitarianism, but he provides little of the details of either of what he recognizes as the historical antecedents of his thinking. As becomes clear from his later (including posthumous) publications, however, his thinking was importantly inflected by the histories of these ideas.[8]

Interregnum I

It is arguable that the possibility of complementarities of the kinds mentioned was significantly enhanced as the differences between political theorizing and

224   *Opacity, liberalism, and individuality*

among differing ways of studying/writing the history of political thought became more clearly delineated, a development that so far as I know (a 'so far as' that could *easily* be exaggerated) did not become clearly discernible until, at the earliest, the later years of the nineteenth century and perhaps not until the emergence of the Cambridge or contextualist school. Of course there have been histories from Herodotus and Thucydides forward and there were histories of philosophy (for example that of Diogenes Laertius), many of which recount and interpret the political ideas that their authors thought were influential in the events that were the subject matters of their histories. Many thinkers now conventionally regarded as political theorists gave those histories close attention – Machiavelli being only the most obvious example. So far as I have been able to determine, however, it was not – Vico may be a partial exception – until the late nineteenth and more likely the early parts of the twentieth century, that studies of the history of political (and philosophical) thought were distinguished from either political theorizing or general histories of policies, philosophy and related dimensions of human experience. In the early nineteenth century, William Whewell wrote a history of moral and political thought, Henry Sidgwick later did the same, while in the seventeenth, eighteenth and nineteenth centuries several histories of philosophy were written by German, French and other scholars. My impression is that these were in the 'canonical' mode. What seems clear is that in the last one hundredplus years there have developed improved distinctions between political theorizing and the study of the history of political thought, as well as among various alternative modes of studying the latter. However one assesses the merits of inquiries and reflections in the several modes, it seems clear that the emergence of these distinctions has made possible the identification of complementarities as well as differentiations among the several modes of inquiry and reflection that are now distinguished. This is a major contribution of the contextualist school.

Whatever exact dating we assign to the emergence and clarification of the distinction between canonical and contextualist approaches with which I have been working, they are now well in place. And this enables us to ask concerning the ways they advantage and disadvantage one another. To begin with the question of the ways in which 'canonical' historians of the history of political thought may benefit from the researches of contextual historians of the subject, it is undeniable that, say, Sabine's discussions of Aristotle, Machiavelli or Hegel would have benefitted from a more detailed understanding of the contexts in which these thinkers formulated their ideas. At the same time, however, Sabine had made a close study of the texts of these writers and has provided others interested in them with detailed accounts of features prominent in those texts.[9] Of course the contextually oriented historian of political thought could acquire the same textual familiarity without any help from Sabine, but the texts in question are complex and subject to various interpretations, and reading, say, Sabine's accounts of them might inform or usefully jostle the mind of the contextually oriented historians in ways that enhance their own readings. Pocock, Skinner and other contextualists recognize that the writings of canonical historians have sometimes yielded valuable results.

Reflections concerning political theory   225

This brings me to a quite general question concerning the notion of context. The relationship between text and context is a variable and disputable, not an unequivocal feature of recovering and achieving an improved understanding of a text or text analogue. Consider the case of Hobbes. Pocock has located an important part of his thinking in the context of theological disputations;[10] A. E. Taylor and Howard Warrender place him in the context of natural law theories leading to Kant;[11] Skinner positions *Leviathan* in the setting of neo-classical rhetorical writings;[12] Richard Tuck treats him as continuing and developing neo-Stoical and sceptical constructions;[13] Steven Shapin and Simon Schaffer interpret him as participating in controversies concerning the appropriate methodologies of natural and mathematical sciences:[14] these students of his thought locate him in ways that can be historically validated. By contrast, Gregory Kavka and Deborah Baumgold see him as an early contributor to rational choice theory;[15] numerous students locate him in the tradition of contractarian thinking; Oakeshott characterizes him as a theorist of 'Will and Artifice' and more generally as a leading contributor to 'epic' political theory;[16] and so forth. To take but one of numerous other possible examples, J. S. Mill has sometimes been characterized as continuing but entering important modifications in Benthamite utilitarianism, as a liberal in the tradition of Constant, as an elitist individualist who is best compared with Emerson and Nietzsche and as a forerunner of twentieth- and twenty-first-century feminist theory. I do not think that I am the only student of these works who, despite important disagreements with them, has learned from all of these studies. None of these interpreters need disagree with the others.

Different as they are, these contextualizations can be viewed as complementary rather than competing or mutually exclusive. Hobbes and Mill are complex thinkers whose work can fruitfully be viewed from a variety of perspectives. Because both of them aspired to 'get it right' concerning some of the issues they addressed, they are appropriately classified and assessed as political theorists. Approached in this way, the (or at least a) context relevant to understanding and assessing their work is the history of other attempts, whether prior to, contemporary with, or later than their own thinking. Hobbes's blistering attacks on 'the vain philosophy of Aristotle' and 'Aristotelians', and his protracted diatribe against Cardinal Bellarmine and other theologians, cannot be understood or evacuated without a knowledge of what they said and especially what he took them to be saying. It is of course absurd (because both an anachronism and a prolepsis) to treat him as anticipating the thinking of Hume or Kant, but there is nothing absurd about critically comparing his sceptical nominalism with Hume's or his importantly naturalistic ethics with Kant's *Groundwork for the Metaphysics of Morals*. No one would dispute the importance of Mill's responses to Bentham and his father, but important aspects of his thinking also require attention to his critiques of Kant and Rousseau, his favourable citations of George Grote's study of Plato, the continuities and discontinuities between his and earlier writings concerning political economy. Anachronistic or proleptic as it may be, I have found it fruitful to read his *A System of Logic* with and against Wittgenstein's *Tractatus* and *Philosophical Investigations*.

226   *Opacity, liberalism, and individuality*

At the same time, Hobbes and Mill were engaged with and vigorously responsive to intellectual and political events of the here's and now's of their own times. In this respect studies of the more immediate contexts of their thinking are not merely valuable, they are indispensable. Despite the many earlier canonical commentaries on Hobbes's thought it is only recently that we have learned more than the barest details concerning his life and his many practical involvements. Thanks to the work of Skinner, Tuck, Malcolm and others, we now know a great deal about his activities;[17] and what they have taught us is illuminating about his thought as well as his life. Just as Peter Laslett, James Tully, John Marshall and others have transformed the study of John Locke, so the historians just mentioned have given us insights into Hobbes' thinking that could not have been achieved in any other way.[18]

The study of important political theorists is a cooperative activity that can be done in many ways and in the pursuit of diverse objectives. That differing purposes and 'methodologies' often lead to disagreements is not only to be expected but welcomed. To borrow a figure from the Preface of Wittgenstein's *Investigations*, the same thinkers can be approached afresh from difference directions, producing a picture of the 'landscape' that is their lives and thoughts. To repeat what I said above, that we now have a clearer understanding of differing conceptions of the study of political thought allows us to see the advantages and disadvantages of leading approaches and to understand ways in which their results complement as well as conflict with one another.

IV

I now revisit the distinctions that have been introduced thus far and ask to what extent they clearly distinguish among political theorists on the one hand, and, on the other, canonical students and contextualist historians of political thought. Do we in fact find thinkers and writers who, if not throughout the writings, in identifiable dimensions or aspects of their work, present clear examples of the several approaches or understandings outlined in previous sections?

I opined earlier that there are clear examples of political theorizing as I have characterized that form of thought and action. It is not merely that this is an in principle possible way or mode of thinking/acting. Rather, it is whether Plato, parts of Aristotle, parts of Hobbes and of Kant, Rousseau, Hegel and Mill exemplify it. Of course these writers thought in particular times and places and were influenced, sometimes knowingly sometimes not, by the conceptual and ideational resources that they inherited. These are aspects of their thinking that could be but seldom are investigated by canonical students of political thought and are intensively studied by the trademark methods of contextual historians of that subject. The political theorists just listed often critique, explicitly or implicitly, thinkers contemporary with them and those that preceded them (Plato critiquing the pre-Socratics; Aristotle critiquing Plato; Hobbes, Aristotle; Hegel, Kant; and so forth). But their purpose in doing so was not to explain or understand the past, it was to arrive at right answers to the questions they addressed and to present

Reflections concerning political theory 227

arguments supporting those answers. In Oakeshott's terms, their concern with the past was with the practical not the historical past, but with the qualification that theory could and should govern practice, that theorizing was the most valuable kind of practicing. Oakeshott may be justified in saying that they sometimes abandoned the role of theorist and became what he scathingly calls theoreticians. He makes this charge most explicitly against Plato but he seems also to have Kant and Hegel in mind and he certainly brings the charge against all those that he designated rationalists.[19] There are admixtures of concern with the past in their texts, but their primary purpose was to arrive at demonstratively true answers to questions of continuing import. This is the most distinctive feature of their thinking. That there are major disagreements among them, and that generations of scholars who have studied them disagree with some or all of their conclusions is important; but so is the fact that those among them that came later in time found themselves obliged to engage the formulations of their predecessors, and that generations of students and historians of political thought have felt the same obligation.

Interregnum II

What do professors of political theory teach? There is of course no single answer to this question, but the preponderance of the graduate programmes known to me (that is, those that include political theory) teach a remarkably similar selection of texts. And every such undergraduate programme also teaches a selection of those same texts. Why? It is no doubt partly because the canonical approach to the study of past political theorizing remains dominant in most universities and colleges. But while I have learned much and will surely continue to learn more from studies of that kind, I ask graduate students to read various selections of the canonical texts because doing so sharpens their thinking (and of course for the more mundane, professional, reason that when they go on to teach political theory they will be expected to be familiar with them). And I present various of those texts to undergraduates (very few of whom will go on to graduate study and academic careers) because I have found no better way to get them interested in and able to think critically about political questions. As is increasingly common in the political theory programmes known to me (and it is a welcome development) I try to take account of and present the findings of contextual histories; and there are always some students who find these to be the most engaging features of the classes I teach. But these are, and I expect they will remain, a small minority. Most of the best of the students I have been privileged to teach are primarily interested in the positions and the arguments for them that they find in the political theorists they read.

My remarks in Interregnum II provide plenty of evidence (if any were needed) that there are lots of examples of studies of political theory in the canonical mode. The fact that leading contextual historians have been drawn to critique such studies, and that they have no shortage of examples of such studies to critique, makes it clear that the canonical approach is very much alive (if not necessarily in the best of health). Accordingly, I turn quickly to the contextual

228 *Opacity, liberalism, and individuality*

approach. As before, the question is less whether strict or pure versions of the contextual history of political thought are in principle possible (albeit versions of that question may again arise), but whether or to what extent there are extant examples of such histories.

Contextualist historians of political thought distinguish their approach and their objectives most persistently and most sharply from those of canonical students of that subject. They of course attend closely to the texts of the thinkers they study, but they hold that the intentions of the authors they study and the meanings of the texts they have bequeathed to us cannot be adequately understood without attending to the contexts in which they were written (enacted), in particular the issues and choices that were before their authors and the languages and styles of argument and presentation that were available to their authors. Because these contexts are constantly changing, the notion that there are timeless, perennial, questions that can be addressed, and 'unit ideas' concerning them that express, even if with some variations, answers to those questions (questions concerning the always and everywhere and timelessly correct answers to those questions) is mythological and leads not to history but to mythologies. Of course in distinguishing their approach from the (generic) approach of the canonical historians, contextualists at least appear to be denying the actuality (the possibility?) of political theorizing as characterized here. The view that there are no timeless, perennial questions at least appears to deny the possibility of a mode of theorizing that identifies and seeks to find correct answers to such questions. I suggest below that there are some respects in which this appearance, if in fact it was ever advanced, is misleading.

Reverting to Oakeshott's distinctions, there are important respects in which contextual historians concern themselves primarily (but not, I argue, exclusively) with the historical not the practical past. They of course recognize that they work in the present past; that their historical studies are done in a here and now and are chosen and carried out in part in response to questions that previous or contemporary students of the past (and probably of political theory) have raised and attempted to answer. (An obvious example is the one already discussed: that is, the attention and energy that contextualists have devoted to critiquing the canonical approach. To mention but one prominent but more historical than historiographical example, consider the many ways in which the renaissance studies of Hans Baron figure in more recent studies of the same period).[20] More generally, there is a personal, one might say a subjective, quality to their work as to everyone's. Why does this or that person study past political theories rather than, say, current welfare policies in Denmark or relations between the Sunnis and the Shi'as in Iraq? Given a disposition to historical study, why does not one study the conflict between the Bolsheviks and Mensheviks or the Boer War? Given a disposition to study past political thinking, why does one study early-modern political thought rather than the history of utilitarianism or of contractualism from Locke and Kant to Rawls? However they may have developed, these dispositional preferences cannot be eliminated or entirely suppressed. But they can be explained and disciplined. In the course of their studies, contextualist historians have frequently made cogent cases for the value of their inquiries and for

Reflections concerning political theory 229

their claims that those of different moral, political and other sensibilities and orientations can and should endorse their historical claims.

Notwithstanding their recognition of these features of their work, contextualist historians claim that their primary objective is not to resolve, or to contribute to the resolution of, present practical political questions, but to better understand the past thinkings/actings that they study. To the limited extent that I am familiar with the studies of this school, I am convinced that numerous of them make good on this claim, this self-characterization. In my judgement especially clear cases are John Pocock's *The Ancient Constitution and the Feudal Law* (1987) and Noel Malcolm's studies of Hobbes, but there are lengthy stretches in the works of, for example, Skinner, Tully and Tuck that do so. Present or later contextualist historians – to say nothing of Nietzschean perspectivalists and postmodernists or deconstructionists – may be able to show that the studies of Pocock, Malcolm, Skinner *et al.* are influenced by normative or other 'practical' commitments; but I see no reason to think that doing so will impugn or discredit their historical claims. The only considerations that would discredit or qualify those claims is historical evidence that goes against them.

These thoughts bring me to complexities in, and some divergencies among, the contextual historians. This school of thought has produced an exceptionally large and wide-ranging corpus of historical studies and I have neither the space nor the competence to explore these matters in a thorough-going way. Guided in part by the distinctions I have been using, I will briefly discuss a selection of the studies of Quentin Skinner and some of those of Richard Tuck.

Along with Pocock and John Dunn, Skinner has forcefully critiqued canonical studies of the history of political thought. But he has responded with equal vigour to the charge that his studies are purely antiquarian, that they provide nothing of interest or value to political theorists and/or political scientists who address issues of present importance.[21] He emphatically does not claim to be offering specific solutions to particular current political problems but he, quite rightly in my view, insists that his historical investigations can contribute in valuable ways to our thinking about those problems. In one of several presentations of this view, and with reference to recent discussions of liberty, he writes:

> it is remarkably difficult to avoid falling under the spell of our own intellectual heritage. As we analyse and reflect on our normative concepts, it is easy to become bewitched into believing that the ways of thinking about them bequeathed to us by the mainstream of our intellectual traditions must be *the* ways of thinking about them. It seems to me that an element of such bewitchment has entered even into Berlin's justly celebrated account [of liberty or freedom). Berlin takes himself to be pursuing the purely neutral task of showing what a philosophical analysis of our concepts requires us to say about the essence of liberty. But it is striking, to say the least, that his analysis follows exactly the same path as the classical liberal theorists had earlier followed in their efforts to discredit the neo-Roman theory of free states.[22]

230 *Opacity, liberalism, and individuality*

Thus Skinner and other contextualist historians do two things at once: first, they inform the theorist of the historicity of his/her thinking; second, but relatedly, they inform the theorist of a historical continuity in which his/her thinking is situated. For example, Skinner argues that by 'excavating' the alternative neo-Roman conception of freedom, as with analogous recoveries of earlier conceptions of political concepts and ideas that differ from those now regnant, the

> history of philosophy, and perhaps especially of moral, social and political philosophy, is there to prevent us from becoming too readily bewitched. The intellectual historian can help us to appreciate how far the values embodied in our present way of life, and our present ways of thinking about those values, reflect a series of choices made at different times between different possible worlds. This awareness can help to liberate us from the grip of any one hegemonal account of those values and how they should be interpreted and understood. Equipped with a broader sense of possibility, we can stand back from the intellectual commitments we have inherited and ask ourselves in a new spirit of enquiry what we should think of them.[23]

In the terms I used earlier, Skinner's position is that historical studies can widen and deepen thinking and acting in the here and now, including that mode of thinking/acting that is political theorizing. Although perhaps modest by comparison with the objectives of the canonical historians and with related but differently based views that I consider below, Skinner's defence against the charge that his studies are merely antiquarian does take it as uncontroversial that the commonalities between, say, liberal and neo-Roman conceptions of freedom are sufficient to allow us to compare and contrast them in ways not only intelligible but important to us. Once recovered, an understanding of the neo-Roman view of freedom can be brought into significant ideational and normative juxtapositions with liberal conceptions of freedom; whether effecting such juxtapositions leads us to reaffirm our commitment to the liberal view, to move our thinking in the direction of a neo-Roman understanding, or, say, to develop a hybrid view,[24] is a question that historical studies do not answer. But having the comparisons and contrasts in mind will help us to 'ruminate' in a more informed manner concerning the choices that we have made and continue to make.[25] (This is very much a Millian thought, although perhaps not one attended with the most soaring of Millian expectations or hopes.)

It is tempting to introduce at this juncture Rawls' distinction between concepts that are shared and conceptions concerning those concepts about which we are in disagreement.[26] Rawls' concern being with justice and right, his attempt to bring about reasoned agreement concerning them presupposes that we can understand and fruitfully engage with one another, do not simply and fruitlessly talk past one another, as we argue for particular conceptions of justice and right. He claims (somewhat abruptly in *A Theory of Justice*) that it is the fact that we share concepts of justice and right that makes this possible. As regards the concepts that Skinner is addressing in the work just cited, liberty or freedom, we can

Reflections concerning political theory 231

understand both liberal and neo-Roman conceptions, can fruitfully argue over their respective merits, because the concepts of freedom and liberty are salient features of our shared conceptual inheritance and experience.

There are, however, respects in which Skinner introduces and partly endorses positions substantially more general than Rawls' account of the particular concepts of justice and right (or, in the matter specifically at issue in the text under discussion, of liberty/freedom). In one of numerous references to the work of Donald Davidson, he says:

> There is unquestionably a deeper level of continuity underlying the dispute I have been examining over the understanding of individual liberty. The dispute revolves, in effect, around the questions of whether dependence should be recognized as a species of constraint; but both sides assume that the concept of liberty must basically be construed as absence of constraint on some interpretation of that term. The point of considering this example has not been to plead for the adoption of an alien value from a world we have lost; it has been to uncover a lost reading of a value common to us and to that valued world.[27]

These are welcome and effective responses to the charge that contextualist studies are merely antiquarian, that they are studies of the past past not the historical past. What bearing do they have on the distinction between the historical past and the practical past? Certainly the largest parts of Skinner's work are in the mode of the historical not the practical past and hence show the continuing value of that distinction. Certainly his works are importantly distinct from the works of students of the canonical persuasion. As with Oakeshott's 'ideal characters', however, these distinctions sort out predominant tendencies in a large body of writing that, happily in my view, also includes elements of a 'practical' character, elements that show a concern with the relevance of then and there to here and now (and maybe to the everywhere and always).[28]

By way of further exploring complexities within the contextualist school I turn to some writings of Richard Tuck, writings that shed light on the value but also the limitations of the distinctions I am using. There are passages in Tuck's writings in which he takes a position essentially the same as the one just discussed in Skinner. For example, in *The Rights of War and Peace: Political Thought and the International Order from Grotius to Kant* (1999) he asks whether 'the long tradition of political thought which has been the subject of this book is of relevance to us any more?' His answer is as follows:

> This tradition is the richest tradition we have for thinking about human freedom. It was historically contingent, and is as a consequence precarious – it presupposes a kind of agent whom we would not now much like to encounter. But it is important that we are clear about what autonomy meant in the days when it became a central virtue, so that we can also be clear about what we may be losing in our own time.[29]

232   *Opacity, liberalism, and individuality*

He is not *recommending* (although he gives his readers and conversational partners reason to think that he may be doing so) the kind of agential autonomy he
has recovered, but, in Skinner's terms, he thinks we can better ruminate concerning our own affairs if we have a clear understanding of it.

In partial contrast, in *Philosophy and Government, 1572–1651* (1993),[30] Tuck
reports his and James Tully's thinking in the following terms:

> Tully and I have discussed our work together ever since we were graduate
> students together in Cambridge, and despite our many differences of opinion
> and emphasis, we share two beliefs about how the history of political thought
> should be written. One of them [generically the same as the beliefs of Skinner
> and Pocock but perhaps with differences concerning, say, language,
> meaning(s) and intentions] is that to understand the political theories of any
> period we need to be historians, and we have been very keen to depict as far
> as possible the character of the actual life which those theorists were leading,
> and the specific political questions which engaged their attention. But the
> other is that a study of the reactions to these questions should not be *purely* a
> piece of historical writing. It should also be a contribution to our understand-
> ing of how people might cope with broadly similar issues in our time. The
> point of studying the seventeenth century, for both of us, is that many of the
> conflicts which marked its politics are also to be found in some form in the
> late twentieth century; and, indeed, the better our historical sense of what
> those conflicts were, the more often they seem to resemble modern ones.[31]

This is of course not to deny that historical studies may have the value
claimed for them by Skinner and by Tuck himself in *The Rights of War and
Peace*. Indeed recovering the tradition studied in the latter book is likely to have
that and only that value for present thinking. That tradition was 'contingent' and
'as a consequence precarious'; if, as Tuck seems to be saying, it has largely disappeared, it does not 'broadly resemble' the politics of our own time and recovering it will be valuable to our present thinking and acting primarily because it
helps us to see 'what we may be losing in our time'. Presumably the modes of
thought and action that emerged in the seventeenth century were also contingent
and could have disappeared. Also presumably, the politics of the twentieth and
twenty-first centuries were contingent, and could have been different. Thus the
claim that studying the seventeenth century will help people of the twentieth and
twenty-first centuries to cope with their conflicts depends on a conjunction of
two contingencies, both of which must be understood.

On the view Tuck advances in *Philosophy and Government*, the study of what
Oakeshott terms the 'historical past' and the 'practical past' converge. Of course
this is not to say that the distinction is invalidated or becomes useless. There not
only can be but have been quite 'pure' examples of both modes of study and
reflection. When other students assess Tuck's account of the seventeenth century
they will properly do so by the criteria of the historical not the practical past. If
they find the account convincing they can (if they are so disposed) ask themselves

Reflections concerning political theory 233

whether he also makes good on his claim that the policies of the three centuries resemble one another broadly enough to say that studying the earlier one helps us to cope with the conflicts of the later ones. As we have already seen, Tuck is confident on both counts. Here is how the book ends:

> The descriptions of modern policies we find both in the *ragion di stato* writers and in Grotius and Hobbes, with standing armies paid for out of taxation, with self-protective and potentially expansionist states, and with citizens very unsure of the moral principles they should live by, looks like an accurate description of a world still recognisable to us.[32]

Can we also say that here, and perhaps also in those aspects of Skinner's thinking discussed above, there is a convergence between the study of the history of political thought and political theory? Of course Tuck is making empirical claims about major characteristics of twentieth- and twenty-first-century policies. These can be viewed as historical claims about recent politics (a history of recent political developments), or as political scientific claims about them. But the claims are at a high level of both conceptual and empirical generalization. Much the same is true about Skinner's analyses of beliefs and intentions, claims that are not restricted to particular here's and now's or then's and there's. Given the emphasis that both thinkers place on contingency and the constancy of change, it would clearly be going too far to treat these as claims about the always and everywhere. But both present critical assessments of prevalent political and related concepts, ideas and practices. Do they attempt to imagine political ideals that would, if accepted, lead to a politics that is improved by normative standards? This too would be going too far, at least as regards the texts here discussed. Skinner does not 'imagine' (although an element of 'imagining' may be unavoidable here) neo-Roman and liberal conceptions of liberty; he recovers the former and says that the latter is not only dominant but effectively without rivals in modern thinking and practicing. And Tuck recovers the sceptical, neo-Stoic configuration about which he teaches us. But Skinner effects a juxtaposition between the two conceptions of liberty and argues that we can think ('ruminate') better about both if we think about them together. Tuck effects an alignment or convergence between seventeenth- and twentieth- and twenty-first-century politics and argues that we can think better about the latter if we give informed and considered attention to the former.

It is clear that these elements of their thinking are not fully congruent with the conception of political theory that I sketched above. Skinner is not recommending either the liberal or neo-Roman conceptions, he is not arguing more than that awareness of them will help us to think better about both. Similarly Tuck is recommending attention to seventeenth-century thinking only as an aid to thinking about twentieth- and twenty-first-century politics. Thus we cannot say that either is advancing an ideal which, if adopted and acted upon, would improve our policies by normative standards. But the conception of political theory that I sketched is an idealized conception. As with the two conceptions of the study/ writing of the history of political theory, and as with Oakeshott's distinctions,

234 *Opacity, liberalism, and individuality*

the conception can be useful not only in identifying 'pure' examples of political theorizing but also in distinguishing some elements in a theory that allow us to say that it is, in part, an example of political theorizing. My suggestion is no more than that the features of the texts of Skinner and Tuck discussed in this section warrant that identification.

A further, and final, identification is supplied by John Pocock. In a recent essay, he has distinguished 'history' from what he calls 'historiosophy'. 'History' is a name for events and processes that may be said to have happened and can be narrated and interpreted, possibly as still going on. By contrast, for historiosophers 'history' denotes a condition in which processes go on, and which may be (in part?) discussed independently of the narrative of what these processes have been. 'Historiosophy' is instead 'the attempt to make history a source of knowledge and wisdom'. Historiosophy is close to what I have identified as political theory and thus we might say that the features of Skinner's and Tuck's text that I have singled out should be regarded as historiosophical.[33]

V

To bring this primarily taxonomic chapter to a close I borrow once more from Wittgenstein. We can think of the three main modes of inquiry and reflection I have discussed – political theorizing, the canonical study of the history of political theory and the contextual study of the history of political theory (Oakeshott's distinctions cross-cut but do not conflict with these distinctions) – as Wittgensteinian 'language games'. As Wittgenstein uses this term of art, language games are characterized by a more or less integrated web or *Gestalt* of concepts, ideas, beliefs, intentions, rules and more or less rule-governed practices, all of these having a public as distinct from a logically private character. Language games form wholes that for many purposes can be and usually are understood and 'played' by their participants as related to but distinguishable from other games. Every language game, however, even those such as logic and mathematics, are also characterized by a greater or lesser degree of 'open texture', that is by respects in which the explicit rules as well as the less clearly formulated conventions and norms of thought and action do not entirely determine what should be thought, said or otherwise done in this or that circumstance. Practised participants in (players of) the games are 'guided' by the rules and conventions, but at the bottom of the language games is the thoughts and actions of the participants. Moreover and particularly relevant here, along with recognizing the open texture of all games, Wittgenstein speaks of situations in which we are 'as it were between the games'.[34]

There are rules and conventions – we might call them commonly understood and frequently satisfied expectations – among those who play the three language games in question and hence we can identify clear examples of the playing of each of them; and these rules and conventions also serve as criteria for assessing plays of the games. We are, however, sometimes 'between the games' and find ourselves either drawn to more than one designation of this or that performance and more than one criterion of assessment of the performances we are considering or uncertain as to

Reflections concerning political theory   235

which designation is the most perspicuous. This seems to me to be the situation that obtains as regards political theory and the study of the history of political theory. For the reasons given in the course of the chapter, it is not a situation to be regretted.

Notes

1 For example Sabine 1955; Carlyle and Carlyle 1936; Barker 1956; Mesnard 1936.
2 Cavell 1969.
3 Pocock 2004, pp. 537–8.
4 Skinner 1969.
5 See esp. Skinner 2002a.
6 Oakeshott 1933; Oakeshott 1983, chs 1–3; Oakeshott 1991. Note that a modest version of the notion of the always and everywhere has crept in here.
7 Oakeshott 1975, chs. 1, 3.
8 See especially Rawls 2000.
9 Sabine 1955.
10 Pocock 1971.
11 Taylor 1938; Warrender 1957.
12 Skinner 1996; Skinner 2002c.
13 Tuck 1989; Tuck 1993.
14 Shapin and Schaffer 1985.
15 Kavka 1986; Baumgold 1988.
16 Oakeshott 1955.
17 See Skinner 1996: Skinner 2002c: Tuck 1989; Tuck 1993; Malcolm 2002, among others.
18 See Laslett's introduction in Locke 1988; Tully 1979; Tully 1993a; Tully 1993b; Marshall 1994; Marshall 2005.
19 Oakeshott 1975, pp. 29–31.
20 Baron 1966; Hankins 2000.
21 As this criticism has been mounted by Gunnell 1979; Gunnell 1982; and Tarlton 1973. Skinner 1988 correctly says that the charge has a philistine quality. I would go further: Gunnell has argued that both contextual historians and various contemporary political theorists fail to address currently pressing political questions. But rather than addressing such questions himself, he devotes himself to criticizing the writings of others. Thus even if he is correct that those he critiques are at one remove from current political questions, he himself is at two removes from the issues he claims should be the subjects of political theorizing and of the history of political thought.
22 Skinner 1998, p. 116.
23 Skinner 1998, pp. 116–17; see also Skinner 2002a, pp. viii, 5–7.
24 Cf. Scheffler 1982, addressing a related issue.
25 In a welcome invocation, Skinner 1998, p. 118, favourably cites Nietzsche's example of the cow which has a separate organ that allows it to ruminate concerning materials that it has ingested: Nietzsche 1994, p. 10.
26 Rawls 1971, ch. 1.
27 Skinner 1998, pp. 117–18, n.29, referring to Davidson 1984, pp. 125–39, 183–98. Skinner 2002a, also endorses Davidson's view that

> unless we begin by assuming that the holding of true beliefs constitutes the norm among the peoples we study, we shall find ourselves unable to identify what they believe. If too many of their beliefs prove to be false, our capacity to give an account of the subject matter of those beliefs will begin to be undermined. Once this starts to happen, we shall find ourselves unable even to describe what we hope to explain. The implication, as Davidson himself puts it, is that 'if we want to understand others, we must count them right in most matters'.

236 *Opacity, liberalism, and individuality*

Skinner does have substantial disagreements with Davidson: see Skinner 2002a, pp. 47, 131, 139.
28 Skinner's discussions of Reinhardt Koselleck and the *Begriffigeschichte* school (e.g. Skinner 2002a, pp. 175–87) are also relevant here.
29 Tuck 1999, p. 234.
30 Tuck 1993.
31 Tuck 1993, pp. xi–xii.
32 Tuck 1993, p. 348.
33 Pocock 2004.
34 Wittgenstein 1958, p. 188e (II.ix).

References

Barker, Ernest (1956). *From Alexander to Constantine*, Oxford: Clarendon Press.
Baron, Hans (1966). *The Crisis of the Early Italian Renaissance: Civic Humanism and Republican Liberty in an Age of Classicism and Tyranny*, rev. edn, Princeton: Princeton University Press.
Baumgold, Deborah (1988). *Hobbes's Political Theory*, Cambridge: Cambridge University Press.
Carlyle, A. J. and R. W. Carlyle (1936). *A History of Medieval Political Theory in the West*, vol. 6: *Political Theory from 1300 to 1600*, London: William Blackwood and Sons.
Cavell, Stanley (1969). *Must We Mean What We Say?*, New York: Cambridge University Press.
Davidson, Donald (1984). *Inquiries into Truth and Knowledge*, Oxford: Clarendon Press.
Gunnell, John G. (1979). *Political Theory: Tradition and Interpretation*, Cambridge, MA: Winthrop Publishers.
Gunnell, John G. (1982). 'Interpretation and the History of Political Theory: Apology and Epistemology', *American Political Science Review* 76, pp. 317–27.
Hankins, James (ed.) (2000). *Renaissance Civic Humanism*, Cambridge: Cambridge University Press.
Kavka, Gregory S. (1986). *Hobbesian Moral and Political Theory*, Princeton: Princeton University Press.
Locke, John (1988). *Two Treatises of Government*, ed. Peter Laslett, rev. edn, Cambridge: Cambridge University Press.
Malcolm, Noel (2002). *Aspects of Hobbes*, Oxford: Clarendon Press.
Marshall, John (1994). *John Locke: Resistance, Religion and Responsibility*, Cambridge: Cambridge University Press.
Marshall, John (2005). *John Locke, Toleration and Early Enlightenment Culture*, Cambridge: Cambridge University Press.
Mesnard, Pierre (1936). *L'Essor de la philosophie politique au XVIe siècle*, Paris: Boivin.
Nietzsche, Friedrich (1994). *On the Genealogy of Morality*, ed. Keith Ansell-Pearson, trans. Carol Diethe, Cambridge: Cambridge University Press.
Oakeshott, Michael (1933). *Experience and its Modes*, Cambridge: Cambridge University Press.
Oakeshott, Michael (1955). 'Introduction', in Thomas Hobbes, *Leviathan*, ed. Michael Oakeshott, Oxford: Blackwell, pp. vii–xvi.
Oakeshott, Michael (1975). *On Human Conduct*, Oxford: Clarendon Press.
Oakeshott, Michael (1983). *On History*, Totowa: Barnes and Noble Books.
Oakeshott, Michael (1991). 'On the Activity of Being an Historian', in *Rationalism in Politics and other Essays*, ed. Timothy Fuller, Indianapolis: Liberty Fund, pp. 151–83.

Reflections concerning political theory 237

Pocock, J. G. A. (1971). *Politics, Language, and Time: Essays on Political Thought and History*, Chicago: University of Chicago Press.

Pocock, J. G. A. (1987). *The Ancient Constitution and the Feudal Law: A Study of English Historical Thought in the Seventeenth Century:A Reissue with Retrospect*, rev. edn, Cambridge: Cambridge University Press.

Pocock, J. G. A. (2004). 'Quentin Skinner: The History of Politics and the Politics of History', *Common Knowledge* 10, pp. 532–50.

Rawls, John (1971). *A Theory of Justice*, Cambridge, MA: Belknap Press.

Rawls, John (2000). *Lectures on the History of Moral Philosophy*, ed. Barbara Herman, Cambridge, MA: Harvard University Press.

Sabine, George (1955). *A History of Political Theory*, New York: Henry Holt.

Scheffler, Samuel (1982). *The Rejection of Consequentialism: A Philosophical Investigation of the Considerations Underlying Rival Moral Conceptions*, Oxford: Clarendon Press.

Shapin, Steven and Simon Schaffer (1985). *Leviathan and the Air-Pump: Hobbes, Boyle, and the Experimental Life*, Princeton: Princeton University Press.

Skinner, Quentin (1969). 'Meaning and Understanding in the History of Ideas', *History and Theory* 8, pp. 3–53.

Skinner, Quentin (1988). 'A Reply to My Critics', in *Meaning and Context: Quentin Skinner and his Critics*, ed. James Tully, Princeton: Princeton University Press, pp. 231–88.

Skinner, Quentin (1996). *Reason and Rhetoric in the Philosophy of Hobbes*, Cambridge: Cambridge University Press.

Skinner, Quentin (1998). *Liberty Before Liberalism*, Cambridge: Cambridge University Press.

Skinner, Quentin (2002a). *Visions of Politics*, vol. 1: *Regarding Method*, Cambridge: Cambridge University Press.

Skinner, Quentin (2002b). *Visions of Politics*, vol. 2: *Renaissance Virtues*, Cambridge: Cambridge University Press.

Skinner, Quentin (2002c). *Visions of Politics*, vol. 3: *Hobbes and Civil Science*, Cambridge: Cambridge University Press.

Tarlton, Charles D. (1973). 'Historicity, Meaning, and Revisionism in the Study of Political Thought', *History and Theory* 12, pp. 307–28.

Taylor, A.E. (1938). 'The Ethical Doctrine of Hobbes', *Philosophy* 13, pp. 406–24.

Tuck, Richard (1989). *Hobbes*, Oxford: Oxford University Press.

Tuck, Richard (1993). *Philosophy and Government, 1572–1651*, Cambridge: Cambridge University Press.

Tuck, Richard (1999). *The Rights of War and Peace: Political Thought and the International Order from Grotius to Kant*, Oxford: Clarendon Press.

Tully, James (1979). *A Discourse of Property: John Locke and His Adversaries*, Cambridge: Cambridge University Press.

Tully, James (1993a). 'Placing the *Two Treatises*', in *Political Discourse in Early Modern Britain*, ed. Nicholas Phillipson and Quentin Skinner, Cambridge: Cambridge University Press, pp. 253–80.

Tully, James (1993b). 'The *Two Treatises* and Aboriginal Rights', in *An Approach to Political Philosophy: Locke in Contexts*, Cambridge: Cambridge University Press, pp. 137–76.

Warrender, Howard (1957). *The Political Philosophy of Hobbes*, Oxford: Oxford University Press.

Wittgenstein, Ludwig (1958). *Philosophical Investigations*, trans. G.E.M. Anscombe, 2nd edn, London: Blackwell.

An interview with Richard E. Flathman

The following is from an interview given by Richard E. Flathman on July 7, 2014 at his home in San Rafael, California.

Questions from Paige E. Digeser

PED: You were an undergraduate at Macalester College (1956, History) and then went to graduate school at the University of California, Berkeley, in Political Science. You taught at Reed College from 1961 to 1964 and then at the University of Chicago from 1964 to 1972. From Chicago, you moved to the University of Washington-Seattle (where you served as Chair of the Department) from 1972 to 1975 and then to Johns Hopkins University, where you were Chair of the Department (1979–1985), and from which you retired as George Armstrong Kelly Professor in 2009.

At Berkeley, your doctoral dissertation was on "Leadership and Constitutionalism: The Original Conception of their Relationship" (1962). How did you get from an interest in constitutionalism and leadership to your work on political concepts and ordinary language philosophy?

REF: I decided against trying to publish my dissertation, which I didn't like, and I don't think anyone else liked it either. So I had to start all over. When I got to Reed, I decided that I wanted to do the kind of philosophizing that I had encountered in London and Oxford while researching my dissertation and that to a limited extent was practiced by colleagues at Reed. I had some philosophical training at Macalester, but nothing in the materials in which I had now become interested. I was going into new territory, because as a student at Berkeley I had very little involvement with the philosophy department. The one person there who was doing things that I later was going to be doing was Hanna Pitkin. We had some conversations together, but we never had a very personal relationship. So the time at Reed was extraordinarily busy, but also very productive. By the time we left Reed after three years, I had a completed draft of the book, *The Public Interest*.

It's important to remember that in the 1950s and 1960s, it seemed like that kind of philosophical work was no longer possible. It had been discredited. In order to do what I thought I wanted to do I had to somehow overcome that

An interview with Richard E. Flathman 239

sense that it was illegitimate, so I had to take up the logical positivists and the logical empiricists. I had to satisfy myself that something like reasoned discourse was possible concerning issues like the public interest, obligation, justice and so on. What I came up with initially, in *The Public Interest*, was a form of rule utilitarianism derived, more than from any other source, from Richard Hare. I was able to satisfy myself, that, yes, I could talk, I could teach, I could write about moral and political theoretical matters without embarrassment. It was a groundwork on which that kind of thinking and writing and teaching could be founded.

PED: After *The Public Interest* (1966), there were a number of books that followed in relatively quick succession: *Political Obligation* (1972), an edited collection on political concepts (1974), *The Practice of Rights* (1976), *The Practice of Political Authority* (1980) and then *The Politics and Philosophy of Freedom* (1987). In that body of work, did you initially see yourself a building a more comprehensive theoretical edifice?

REF: At that time, I was reading and teaching Hume, and I did have the ambition of creating a kind of architectonic, encompassing system. It's an oddity about Hume, because although he is known as a skeptic, he did foster in a number of people, including myself, the idea of an encompassing philosophical theory. The particular form of that theory was a kind of enlarged, expanded utilitarianism, which is what Hume offers us. Then I became less enchanted with it over time. Partly I suppose—although historically this may not be the right sequence—by reading Bernard Williams' critique of utilitarianism in his book with J. J. C. Smart. About that time, I got more interested in skepticism, and I read Montaigne, Sextus Empiricus, and Cicero. The spirit that you imbibe if you take those writers seriously is about as anti-system as you can get, so that, together with my disenchantment with utilitarianism, put an end to the ambition of an architectonic, utilitarian theory that covered law and politics.

PED: Throughout your career you have been close to John Pocock. At Hopkins, he sat in on your language and politics seminar, and you sat in on his historiography seminar. In addition you were close to the other members of the History Department at Hopkins (Orest Ranum, Louis Galambos, John Russell-Wood and Willie Lee Rose). You have also said that you admired and learned a great deal from the historian of art, Michael Fried, particularly from his book, *Absorption and Theatricality*. Yet, you never really did the history of political thought.

REF: You are absolutely right. Bill Connolly and I both had the idea, and even kind of prided ourselves in it, in setting out something of a Hopkins political theory stance, a distinctive stance. That is, we *worked with* the history of political thought and *with* the history of philosophy, and in Bill's case, the history of just about everything, but we had as our objective continuing, as best we could, what we thought made those people worth working with. So we didn't want to just comment on their work, or explain it, we wanted to continue it. Now that's a very sort of egotistical thing, not that we ever

240 *An interview with Richard E. Flathman*

thought we would continue it in the sense of [that in] years to come people would read us like we read Plato and Hobbes and so on. But that was our objective, and that is the way we tried to teach political theory – to teach it as something of an engagement. There developed, to me, a quite fascinating kind of emergent mindset that was an attempt, never of course entirely successful, to meld together the Wittgensteinian understanding of language with a Nietzschean understanding of cultural spirit. We [Bill and I] fed off one another in those ways. As time went on, students were working with both of us. That was very fruitful.

PED: Your later work carves out a distinctive understanding of liberalism that is tied to a difficult and soaring ideal of self-enacted individuality. Some of this comes from Michael Oakeshott, but you say that the work of Fried was also an influence. Could you say more about that? In addition, does this ideal of individuality differ from the notion of the self as a work of art or from a kind of self-insistence egotism?

REF: Although this may be something of a reconstruction, Michael Fried's *Absorption and Theatricality* played a role in my interest in self-orientation, self-development and also concepts like opacity and mysteriousness. Theatricality is being all you are from everyone else and absorption is being for everyone else by being for yourself. The point is to absorb yourself in yourself and to make yourself into something that, it would be almost be gaseous to say, proud of yourself. It is because you engaged in this activity of self-cultivation that you could walk with your head high into any seminar on your subject matter in the world and have something to say. Does this ideal differ from the notion of the self as a work of art or from a kind of self-insistence egotism? Yes, I think so because, in the first place, it has other-regarding dimensions built into it. We're talking about virtues of action and action involves doing things that involve other people or affect or can affect other people. The fact that the idea of virtue is built into it counters and defeats the idea of egotism because egotism is self-referential.

PED: Your ideal of individuality is also very much tied to a notion of opacity and the opalescent that you seek to celebrate.

REF: I remember being struck by the word opalescence. Nancy and I were in the Philadelphia Art Museum, and we came across this kind of diorama, and it had these objects that are sort of like rocks, sort of like glass balls, and sort of like ice peaks and they give off a light, but they also absorb light, so they don't shine. You could say they glow but it would be like a phosphorescent worm glows in the dark—a combination of things—interiority but also communicativity. I think that to me is the lodestone of teaching. That you are absorbing, taking in from the materials and from the students and other people in the room and you're also giving out. It's a constant interaction. I never thought about it before we started talking about this interview, but I now realize that Huntley Dupré at Macalester College had this combination of interiority and communicativeness. He was what I could never be—effervescent—he just glowed with enthusiasm about everything, but he was also the world's great listener. You would start talking, he would shut up, cock his ear and just listen to you. He wasn't an intellectual influence in the sense that there was any set of ideas or body of belief or methods that I took over from him. But I think it's a certainty that if it hadn't been for him, I wouldn't have gone to graduate school.

PED: There is a mysterious character associated with these notions of opacity and the will. You can't cash them out in terms of reasoned explanations and so forth. It seems that we are at the limits of what we can say, yet we want to say something about it.

REF: I see what you're struggling with, and I don't think I have much to help you with. One thing, almost a gadget, that comes to mind is Stanley Cavell's notion of *acknowledgment*. I have no knowledge of this, but I acknowledge it. I don't understand why you love that person, but I acknowledge that you do, and I will conduct myself differently because of that acknowledgment. The acknowledgment will show up in the ways that I will conduct myself other than I would have if I hadn't made the acknowledgment. I think you are onto something when you say [in the introductory chapter] that it is a matter of motivations or a matter of intention. If I ask about the intention with which you promise me to do this, haven't I, in a sense, spoiled it? We are very much on the periphery, on the margins of what we can talk about in this regard.

PED: Arendt seems to have a similar sort of position, particularly with regard the idea of digging into motivations. Bring this to the light—bringing it publicly has a kind of distorting quality to it.

REF: I tried to defend the idea that Arendt had a robust idea of the private. This idea of spoiling it – I like that idea. To ask, "Why did my wife give me a present for our anniversary?" Do I need an explanation from her? Is she somehow expected to give me an explanation for this?

PED: As I understand it, your position differs from Arendt's because you want to say that opacity is not only protective or defensive, but also a wonderful thing. Opacity, imagination, and willfulness are not merely something tolerated but to be celebrated.

REF: Yes, that's what I think. Maybe the project of defending it is misbegotten. So far, the best way I have thought of defending it is by imagining the alternative. Imagine entire transparency, where I know exactly why you are doing what you are doing and I can see into the depths of your soul. What is it that the person who is going to burn Joan of Arc after? What does that person want to know? What difference would it make to know that Joan of Arc did what she did for this reason or that reason? The act, so to speak, speaks for itself. It has to, because no one can speak for it.

PED: One of the themes that runs through much of your conceptual work is the degree to which any rule-governed practice has an open-ended or unsettled quality to it. Why doesn't the value of unsettlement and instability lead you to endorse a form of agonistic democracy? You appear to have no great trust of state institutions...

242 *An interview with Richard E. Flathman*

REF: When I was young, I thought if we all do it together and everyone is involved and supportive, then what's to be afraid of? Social democracy—democracy which involves everybody in the political process and maintains as much equality as possible in the capacity to participate—that's not something to be afraid of, that's something to look to as a way of solving our problems that have been with us from the earliest days of our history. That's the way that I thought then. Well, gradually my confidence in that diminished. It was partly experience. What happened when people tried to act on that kind of expectation or sentiment? The results seem to be going from bad to worse.

PED: Not even an agonistic conception of democracy?

REF: I think there was a time when I was so emphatic about this that I wouldn't even have even described myself as an agonistic democrat. I described myself as an anarchist, or, as I did, a would-be anarchist. From that perspective, the main thing that political theory has to do is keep reminding us of the dangers of power of one person being able to tell other persons what to do on penalty of punishment or harm or whatever. The idea of looking to the public for constructive, productive beneficial outcomes lost its hold on me. That's when I began quoting things from Nietzsche, like, "how could anything that is common, be good?" So communitarianism, and all those words that start with "comm," are troubling. I would go around giving talks in which I would use words like the "fucking state" on a platform, in a hotel. Of course, I was making a fool of myself, but I didn't feel that way. I thought, "This is something that was important for theorists to do." Well, I think I got some distance, not very far, past that. I started quoting E. M. Forster, "Two Cheers for Democracy." I became more enthusiastic about quoting Constant, who has a very similar sentiment about democracy.

PED: So that's Constant at the end of his essay on liberty on the liberty of ancients...

REF: Yes. As far as democracy is concerned, as a matter of commendation or condemnation, that is about where I've ended up. But at the same time, as a matter of optimism or pessimism, I've become much more pessimistic. Democracy doesn't seem to be settling anything. You remind me of this phrase, "impede the impediments" that comes from T. H. Green and Hobhouse and Bosanquet—those late nineteenth-century liberals or communitarian liberals. They all talked about that. I see the point, but if the impeders are as bad or worse than the impediments, what do you gain by giving them authority? You may have to acknowledge their presence and their power, but do you have to dress it up as something meritorious that we should be grateful for? That seems to me to be altogether wrong.

PED: Is there no productive place for the state to cultivate or encourage this great ideal of individuality? Can't the state provide certain conditions—education, health care? Aren't these all basic conditions for individuality?

REF: It would be pretty stupid of me to say no to that because it is in front of my face. I see the state doing that in a few, very fortunate, very blessed

An interview with Richard E. Flathman 243

circumstances. If you ask yourself where are these places, what accounts for their success in using the state or something like state authority to pursue these objectives? Well, there is no single answer. In every case there are a number of circumstances that can hardly be counted on. But it's hard to generalize over the conditions that are even so much as compatible with or even contributive to individuality.

PED: But that's a very different perspective than the one that you offer in which the state should be seen as no more than a *modus vivendi*. But what you are saying now is somewhat softer. As qualified as it is, perhaps even more hopeful...

REF: I don't know about hopeful. A somewhat bolstered sense of the state's abilities however the probabilities may be diminished. I'd like to feel a little good about the fact that in these particular respects my thinking has changed, fluctuated even, over time. You're confronted with different images. Different experiences. Different ideas. You have to form new responses to new combinations.

PED: Doesn't democracy provide a way to handle some of these issues through processes of deliberation?

REF: If we all deliberate, by which Fishkin and other proponents of deliberative democracy think of as some kind of combination of the rational and reasonable, then we would be able to resolve our problems. It is really almost a sort of technocratic ideal, except in a humanist dress. What do they do? They organize these meetings, and they invite people to come who are going to vote. And they invite themselves to come to give so-called informative, thoughtful lectures and so then the decisions will come out better. There is a woman at Berkeley, her name is Sarah Song, and she's one of these deliberative democrats. She came right out and said, "What do you think about deliberative democracy?" And I said, "I don't think very much of it all." So, I said, let's start with Hobbes. Hobbes talks about deliberation at some length. He parses it "de-liberation"—to take away from you a liberty that you otherwise would have had. That's exactly what these democrats want to do. Up until I plight my troth to them I can vote any way I please or not but now I've been instructed by the experts and I can vote, but I have to vote the right way. The idea that people would make mistakes in voting ... how could they possibly make mistakes if the experts told them what was the right thing to do in this case? Well, I'm exaggerating.

PED: It comes out of the conversation; it's not meant to be governed...

REF: Yes, but in the upshot or the outcome, either it's the way they say it's going to be or else the whole thing is a fiasco because if we don't get better by deliberating, why bother? I see no evidence whatsoever that we get better by deliberating. In this country [United States] and in many others we have campaigns that go on for months and months and huge numbers of words are exchanged and dollars are spent and images are broadcast; is there any reason to think that we get a better result because all of that? No, no, of course not. You and I may think it was better and we'll be pleased. But other

244   *An interview with Richard E. Flathman*

people won't think it was better and they'll be displeased. As Bernard Williams says, in politics, if the vote goes against you, it doesn't show that you were wrong, it shows that you lost. Period. And you can come back if you've got the guts to do it and try again. That distinction between losing and being wrong is a vital distinction in politics. If we didn't have that distinction we would be right back to where the Shia and the Sunnis are because they can't be wrong and nevertheless rational or reasonable or godly or whatever. It's a zero-sum game. That was exactly Bernard Williams' point: "Alright guys, you won the vote, you get your way. Do you want my heart and soul too? No, I'm going to stay right where I am, and if the issue comes up again, I'll be right back at you." It's a kind of a holocaust mentality—I'm putting it too dramatically—to get rid of the opposition.

PED: In that light, the Arendtian business about pushing truth out of politics makes more sense. It's a club...

REF: ...to beat you on the head. I've always had a lot of sympathy for that view. But she's a dramatist. She expresses it in overly dramatic terms because, obviously, there are truths that we've got to have in politics. They are not on a subject that she is thinking of—they are not about *the* good, *the* true and so on.

PED: You have written a great deal on freedom and have defended a conception of liberty, but you don't see yourself as a libertarian. Why not?

REF: First, because I am a liberal I share the libertarian concern with the abuse of power, particularly state power, but for me, corporate power, the power of lawyers, the power of school superintendents, whatever—wherever you have authority and you have some power to back it up, I want to be cautious. The libertarians are cautious about one locus of power—that is, the state. But even that is too simple. Because the ones who trumpet states' rights—they're wary of the federal government, but they're quite willing to let the states go their own way, even if that means school segregation or lynching or whatever.

Now, another reason is the one that I quote from Nietzsche that I am not interested in making a living; I am interested in making a life. It seems to me that the libertarians as we now know them from Ayn Rand forward are interested in making a living. They want to maximize their accumulation of income or wealth or property, whatever good materially they happen to fancy. Nietzsche's idea of making a life is a totally different idea. It is a matter of making oneself into a person, in the ways we talked earlier today such that an individual can accomplish something of value in his or her own eyes and can contribute something of value to the lives of other people. That's a sentiment that's writ large in Nietzsche, and I think it's not "writ" at all in people like the two Pauls [Rand and Ron] and other people who flaunt their libertarianism.

There is one more story, since I'm into stories, about libertarianism that I like to tell, which is from the civil libertarian Alan Barth. He tells the story of the Doukhobors—have you heard that story?

An interview with Richard E. Flathman 245

PED: No, I haven't.

REF: The Doukhobors are a religious sect that came from Russia and many moved to Vancouver, British Columbia. As Barth tells it, they have this peculiar custom which is at some stated interval—a year, a month, whatever—they have to expose themselves entirely to their God, which means that they have to go out of doors naked. So this Doukhobor is doing that, and a Mountie comes along and is going to arrest the Doukhobor for indecent exposure, and so the Doukhobor thinks that he can expose himself to God better running out here than in the jail cell. And so he runs. They chase, and, of course, the Doukhobor is unburdened by any clothes, and the mounted policeman is getting tired and falling behind, and is gradually stripping off his clothes so that he can catch up. He finally catches up, but now there is no difference between him and the Doukhobor. That's Alan Barth's way of talking about McCarthyism and the first amendment and related rights. That is, in the name of protecting various freedoms and rights people are prepared to use methods that were used by those who were most against those rights. I've always liked that little story. Anyway that's about all I can say about libertarianism.

PED: In your piece on abortion, it's interesting to think of how that essay fits in with the other things you say about the character of theory and theorizing.

REF: If there is any place in my published work where I ceased to be a theorist and became a theoretician, that's it. I'm prescribing. It's an essay in persuasion. But that doesn't mean I have abandoned Oakeshott's distinction between being a theorist and being a theoretician. This raises the distinction I wanted to mention between meta-theory, theory, and prescriptive theory or practical theory. Meta-theory is a theory about theory. It's about what theory can be expected to do, maybe about some of its protocols, maybe about what its limitations are. When I first encountered meta-theory in the English language, it was all to the effect that these are the things you cannot do. It was all negative, all negation. At the very same time, you mention that there was already some constructive theorists going in print, but if you crossed the channel there were tons of it going on, it's just that nobody on this side of the so-called pond was reading it or almost nobody.... Fred Dallmayr was reading it.

Theorizing on this view is an activity of trying to arrive at fairly large-scale generalizations both conceptual, and, to some extent, empirical, but more the former than the latter, and put them together in ways that they seem to be mutually supportive. That's what a theorist tries to be or tries to do.

A practitioner, an applied theorist, a prescriptive theorist tries to take a set of circumstances and say this is what ought to be done. Either more or less generally. For example, all kinds of Rawlsians take Rawls's general position and try to apply it to more particular cases, and indeed there is a considerable industry of people who were trying to do that; they are trying to write more increasingly detailed blueprints of what a just society should be like. I

246 *An interview with Richard E. Flathman*

would be with Oakeshott in saying that's completely ridiculous. It's risible. It would fall apart at the first touch of a wand if anyone chooses to take one out of their pocket. That tripartite distinction is what I wanted to mention and now we've done it.

PED: One last question, then, on freedom: Are there occasions in which freedom is not a good? There are those, such as Foucault and Marcuse, who think that freedom (e.g., the free market) can itself serve as an instrument of government and of discipline. Should individuals ever be suspicious of the idea/ideal of freedom?

REF: One thing about freedom that we can't be suspicious of is what I call its elemental character: it is just part of you as an agent that you are able to form beliefs, frame intentions, adopt purposes and act to pursue those purposes. That's just you being a human being and it may be even some other creatures being what they are. We have reason to think that chimpanzees do those things to a degree, etc. Freedom as elemental is not subject to question, that's why I call it elemental. You could say that it's elementary, but I think the idea of an element, as in an element of the universe, captures the idea better. So that kind of freedom you can't be in question of. If you think you are, then you're confused and need to be corrected and you can be corrected just by pointing out to you that you are asking the question.

PED: Like asking whether you can pretend to be conscious.

REF: Exactly, very good point. Okay. The ideal of freedom. If you mean by that what I call the liberal principle, that it's a *prima facie* good to have and satisfy desires and purposes, then as an ideal that seems to me, that it can be questioned, because it has been by all kinds of people, from Augustine to Eric Fromm, who say that freedom is our enemy. So it can be questioned. Then you might get into certain generalizations: can I question the ideal of freedom while at the same time acting on it? Suppose I say that I don't value freedom. Well, is that an act of freedom on my part? Can I generalize it? Can I say, "I deny the value of the ideal of freedom and so should you?" Now, on what grounds should we question the ideal of freedom? Then we get down to particulars. What does the ideal encompass and what's to be said for it? Because of the connection between being free and accomplishing anything, it's very hard to see how you could self-consistently question the ideal. You can question this or that representation of it and it happens every day all over the world. So there is no pretending that you can't do it. Will it ever be possible to refute or disarm that question? No, I don't think so because there are many things that people want to be free to do which we could never, in our right mind, think of letting them do and so we stop them, if we can.

When you get beyond the level of the ideal and get down to the particulars, then you got to get more empirical about it. You have to see what this freedom, that this person wants right here and now, will do to me or to other people. We've arrived, at least some of us, at some very general propositions about that. They're enshrined in the Magna Carta. They're enshrined in the Declaration of the Rights of Man. They're enshrined in the Declaration of Independence. They're enshrined in the UN Charter. If you look at those documents you see that most or all of them are at a quite general level. They're not at the level of only this property or that or giving this speech or that but at the level of some defensible generalization: it's a good thing that people can do or have want they want to do or have. Then you qualify them. For much of time as a practical, legal, political even moral matter, the work basically consists in the qualification. When it gets down to the idea of freedom as an actual characteristic of human interaction, then it gets down to where the cookie crumbles in its particularities. As a liberal, I would place giving freedom a very high priority. And if there was a question of whether there should be this freedom or its restriction, I am, in the beginning at least, going to be against restricting it. You can sometimes convince me otherwise.

It comes back to the distinction again between theorizing and being a practitioner. I'm not a constitution-writer. And theorists shouldn't be constitution writers. They shouldn't be legislation writers. They can work with constitution writers, but as constitution writers, and not as theorists. It's a hard division of labor to maintain. Every time some political theorist thinks he or she has gotten a bright idea they want to make it general and they want everyone to accept it. And, of course, that's quite appropriate in their little niche in the world, that's what they should do. But it's a very modest little niche. I can be accused of a lot of things, but I can't be accused of overestimating the significance of political theory. I can estimate pretty highly the value of an education in political theory. People who learn about it and learn to think in it are benefited from it. So I am willing to spend a good part of my life teaching it. But stop there please. With Michael Oakeshott, the distinction between being a theorist and a theoretician will always be important to me.

PED: Thank you so much.

Index

abortion 55–83; arguments against right to 65–76; as a liberty right 62–76; moral right to 76–7; powers and immunities and 79n3; as a right based on the liberal principle (LP) 61–4; as a right in the strict sense 77–8

Ackerman, Bruce 43, 51, 52, 209, 213n5

agency 3, 83n20, 93–4, 95n1, 99–101, 103, 105, 108–11; arts of 210; Nietzsche on 155; *see also* agency liberalism

agency liberalism 8, 203–7; equality and 206; freedom and 206; individuality and 204; reason and 204; and strong voluntarism 209–10

akrasia 103, 105–8, 114n3–114n4

anarchism: Flathman and 8, 242; Hobbes on 187; Nietzsche on 149; and willful liberalism 211

Anscombe, Elizabeth 132–3

Arendt, Hannah 105, 170, 179n20, 180n29, 180n31; on authority 32, 53n1; and freedom 89; on motivations 241; the past and 222; on truth 244

Aristotle 87, 89, 92, 103, 107, 156; Hobbes on 225

authority: absolute 186–7; difference between *in* and *an* 33, 36, 43–4, 47; Flathman's view of 48, 244; formal procedural (F-P) theories of 33–4, 37–40; Hobbes on 183–202; and liberalism 42–54; purpose of 189; theory of *an* 33–6, 43–9; theory of *in* 34–40, 43–4, 47–9, 53; *see also* the authoritative

authoritative, the 3, 43, 45–9, 54n5, 54n8, 88, 119; as a grounding for *an* authority 46–8; as a grounding for *in* authority 47–8, 53

autonomy 34, 88–9, 94, 101–2, 232; as an ideal 153–5; Nietzsche on 146–7, 152–6, 156n2; *see also* freedom as autonomy (freedom$_3$)

Benn, Stanley 90

Bentham, Jeremy 118, 199, 225

Berlin, Isaiah 96n2, 98, 114n1, 118, 180n25, 203, 206–7, 210, 213n8; Skinner's view of 229–30

Brest, Paul 114n3

Brody, Baruch A. 81n17

Cambridge (contextual) school of thought 227, 219–20, 224; and canonical approach 222, 226, 228–9; and Flathman's approach to teaching 227; as a language game 234; on relation of text to context 225; on relationship to present concerns 229–32, 235n21

Cassinelli, C.W. 36–8

Cavell, Stanley 218, 241

complementarism 159–60, 162–4, 170, 174–5, 177

Connolly, William E. 156n2, 210, 239–40

Constant, Benjamin 203, 205, 206, 207, 210, 225, 242

Dahl, Robert 2

democracy 5, 9, 48, 89, 213n6; Flathman's view of 211, 241–3; Nietzsche on 144, 149, 154–5; virtue liberalism's enthusiasm for 208; willful liberalism and 211

discipline: and formal procedural (F-P) theories of authority 39, 40, 184; as a condition for freedom 9, 91, 107, 141–56, 156n1; as a condition for strong voluntarism 4, 7, 211–12; of reason 207, 208, 209–10

Doukhobors 244–5

enslavement 4, 89, 93, 96n2, 99, 108–9, 113, 142, 150; *see also* unfreedom
Epictetus 141, 156n1
equality 13–22; agency liberalism and 206; defined 13; and Generalization Principle (GP) 13–21; formal character of 20–1; Hobbes on 182, 185, 198, 213n4; virtue liberalism and 206

Feinberg, Joel 89, 98–9, 109–10, 114n1
Flathman, Richard E.: and anarchism 8, 242; approach to teaching 227, 239–40; celebration of opacity 4–6, 241; conception of liberalism 240, 247; commitment to the liberal principle (LP) 246; criticism of deliberative democracy 243–4; critique of Oakeshott's concept of authority 47–8, 52–3; defense of formal view of equality 13–22; differences with libertarians 8–9, 244–5; and the distinction between theory and practice 245, 247; on the history of political thought 227, 233–4, 239–40; Hume's influence on 239; intellectual biography of 238–9; on *Leviathan* as a paper tiger 199; Nietzsche's influence on 148–56, 244; as a theorist of meaning and the limits of meaning 2–5; view of authority and the authoritative 48, 244; view of democracy 241–3; view of individuality 240–3; view of political theory 221, 227, 239–40, 242, 247; Wittgenstein's influence on 2–5, 9n1
freedom 3–4; as action (freedom$_2$), 88–9, 94, 95n1, 101–2, 117–18, 145, 153; agency as a condition for 99–103, 105–6, 108–11; and agency liberalism 8, 206–7; as autonomy (freedom$_3$) 88–9, 94, 101–2, 146–7, 152–6, 152n6; communal (freedom$_4$) 88, 95, 101–2, 110, 112; and discipline 9, 141–56; elemental character of 246; -evaluable 134, 138; fully virtuous (freedom$_5$) 88, 95, 101–2, 110, 112, 147; habitual conduct and 101, 103, 105–8, 110, 114n1, 115; Hobbes on 87–8, 93, 98, 114n1, 116–18, 123, 125, 183, 186, 191, 194–7; and internal constraints 100–9; liberal principle (LP) and 246; as movement (freedom$_1$) 88–9, 94, 101–3, 109–10, 112, 117–18; negative theory of 3–4, 8, 51, 89, 91, 93–4, 96n2, 98–9,

100, 113, 114n1, 118–19, 142, 145, 206; Nietzsche on 142–56; positive theory of 3–4, 89, 91, 93–4, 96n2, 98–15, 142–3, 147, 207; self-activated 87–8, 91, 94, 114n2; single concept of 99; situated character of 93–4, 99, 112, 116–40; rejection of freedom$_4$ and freedom$_5$ as forms of 111–14; *see also* agency; *akrasia*; autonomy; unfreedom
Fried, Michael 239–40
Friedman, Richard B. 32, 36, 43–4, 47
Friedrich, Carl J. 32
Fishkin, James 208, 243
Foucault, Michel 4, 6, 100, 101, 141, 151, 153, 156, 156n1, 160, 210, 246

Generalization Principle (GP), 13–21, 21n1
Gewirth, Alan 21n1
Gray, John 95n1
Gunnell, John 235n21

Habermas, Jürgen 4, 102, 171, 208, 209, 222
Hamphire, Stuart 7, 150, 156, 203, 205, 207
Hare, Richard 239
Hegel, G.W.F. 4, 94, 117, 171, 178n3, 184, 206, 208, 221, 227
history of political thought: as about the always and everywhere 220–2; canonical view of 218–19, 220, 224, 226–8, 229–31; contextual view of 219–20, 222, 224, 226–31; convergence with history of political theory 233–4; historical past and 221, 227, 231, 232–3; influence on Rawls 223; practical past and 228, 231–3; relation to political theory 217–35; *see also* Cambridge (contextual) school of thought
Hobbes, Thomas 8, 44, 47, 48, 180n21, 213n4; and absolute authority 186–8, 190–1; agency liberalism and 203–7; on authority 183–201; on commonwealth by acquisition 183–5, 195; on commonwealth by institution 183–4, 195; on freedom 87–8, 93, 98, 114n1, 116–18, 123, 125, 140n1, 151; historical interpretations of 225–6; on history 222; individuality and 182, 187; ironic reading of 193; on law 190–5, 201n7, 201n10; on the meaning of deliberation 243; on power 197–9; on the theory of temperate government 186, 188, 191, 192, 195; willful liberalism and 210, 211

250   *Index*

Hohfeld, Wesley N. 57–8
Hume, David 125–6, 176, 225; influence on Flathman 239

ideals 4, 7, 9; Flathman on 153–5; Nietzsche on 149, 150–1, 213n9; positive freedom and 104, 109, 147
individuality 1, 4, 6, 7–9; agency liberalism and 204–6; discipline and 7, 211–12; Flathman's view of 240, 242–3; Hobbes on 182, 187; and opacity 175–6; opalescent 7, 240; and plurality 159–60, 163–4, 166–7, 170–1, 174–5, 176–7, 180n26, 180n31, 210; self-enacted forms of 7; willful liberalism and 210–11

Kant, Immanuel 13, 51, 117, 180n24, 207, 208, 209, 221, 225, 226, 227
Kateb, George 207
Kenny, Anthony 124–5

Laing, R.D. 100, 101
Larmore, Charles 213n5
Levy, Jacob T. 1
Lewis, George Cornewall 33
liberal principle (LP): as a basis for the right to abortion 62–3, 78, 79; definition of 60–1, 206; as a foundation for rights 61–2; as an ideal 246
liberalism 8–9, 179n20, 203; Ackerman's tenets of 43; and authority 42–54; and certainty 53; and complementarism 159; as a family resemblance concept 203; Flathman's conception of 1, 240, 247; and generosity 179n14; interest group 213n5; Locke's version of 50–1; and opacity 177; the rational and 5–6; the reasonable and 5–6; suspicious of *an* authority 47, 49–50; suspicious of *in* authority 48–9; and toleration 167; and Wittgenstein 163, 167; *see also* agency liberalism; liberal principle (LP); virtue liberalism; virtuosity liberalism; willful liberalism
libertarianism 114n1, 211; Flathman's views of 8–9, 244–5
Locke, John 50–1, 121, 140n2, 170, 208, 226, 228
Lyotard, Jean-François 205, 207, 212

MacCallum, Gerald 89, 90, 96n2, 99
Madison, James 94
Marx, Karl 160, 170, 222
meaning 1, 2–6, 164; meaning in use 27–8,

120–6; and meaninglessness 2, 4, 121, 137, 173; and object-word theory 121–4, 126, 129; public character of 23–4, 29; situated character of 122–8, 133, 134–5; *see also* Wittgenstein
Mill, John Stuart 46, 114n1, 118, 170, 203, 205, 207, 208, 210; historical interpretations of 225–6
Miller, David 95n1
Montaigne, Michel de 7, 141, 148, 150, 151, 153, 156n1, 207, 211

Neumann, Franz 89
Nietzsche, Friedrich 4, 6, 7, 9, 160, 180n31, 213n8; on autonomy 146, 153–6; and discipline 144, 149–50, 151–2; Flathman's response to 148–56; on freedom 142–56; and fully virtuous freedom 147; on negative freedom 145–6; on political doctrines 143–4, 154–5; and positive freedom 147; and resistance 144–6, 148–50, 156; strong voluntarism and 210–11; weak voluntarism and 210

Oakeshott, Michael 7, 9, 179n20, 181n31, 210, 211; on adverbial rules 51, 53, 206; on authority 32–4, 39, 44, 51, 53n1, 54n8–54n9; and criticism of *an* authority 45, 49; and defense of *in* authority 47, 49; Flathman's critique of 47–8, 53; on the historical past 220–1, 227, 228; on ideal characters 221, 231; on the past past 221; on the practical past 220–2, 227, 228; on the present past 220, 222, 228; on rules 94; on self-enactment 204; and the theorist/theoretician distinction 227, 245, 247
opacity 4–5, 6, 9n1, 163, 165–6, 173; and Arendt 241; criticisms of 171, 174–5, 180n31; individuality, plurality and 171–2, 173–4, 240–1; responses to 175, 177
opalescence 1, 4, 7, 9, 163, 240; *see also* individuality
Ortega y Gasset, José 170, 179n14

perfectionism 7, 8, 147, 212, 213n9
philosophy 219, 224, 225, 230; role of 23–5, 26–7; as therapy 24–6; *see also* political philosophy; political theory
Pluhar, Werner J. 80n9
pluralities 4, 5, 6, 7–8; and individuality 159–60, 163–4, 166–7, 170–1, 174–5,

176–7, 180n26, 180n31, 210; *see also* complementarism; individuality

Pocock, J.G.A. 219, 224, 225, 229, 232, 239; on history versus historiosophy 234

political philosophy: role of 28–30, 230

political theory: death of 2, 238–9; definition of 217, 218, 227; convergence with history of political thought 233–4; Flathman's view of 221, 227, 239–40, 242, 247; as a language game 234–5; relation to the history of political thought 217–35; *see also* Cambridge (contextual) school of thought; history of political thought; political philosophy

rational, the 1, 5–6, 52, 208, 243

Rawls, John 5, 6, 32, 51, 52, 53, 206, 207; and distinction between concept and conception 230–1; influence of history of political thought on 223; perfectionism and 213n9; and virtue liberalism 208–9; and theory/practice distinction 245–6

Raz, Joseph 32, 35, 209, 210

reasonable, the 1, 5–6, 49–50, 90, 165, 206, 208, 243–4

Reynolds v. *Sims* 14–15, 16, 20–1, 21n2–21n5, 22n7

rights: to abortion on demand 55–83; and community 60; defined as warrants for action 56–7, 59, 75, 76; Hohfeld's typology of 57–8; and individuality 60; justification for 59–62; and the liberal principle (LP) 60–2; as power and immunities 79n3

Rorty, Amalie 106–7, 108

Rorty, Richard 170, 205

Rousseau, Jean-Jacques: and freedom 89, 118, 125–6; and the Generalization Principle 13, 22n8; and Hobbes 185; and individuality 160, 172; and opacity 180n26, 180n28; and sociality 116–18, 120, 140n2, 140n3; and virtue liberalism 208

rules and rule following 3–4, 39, 201; and criticisms of *in* authority 47–8; not a strict calculus 92; Wittgenstein on 23–4, 27–8, 129–31, 134–9

Sach, David 96n4

self-enactment 1, 7–9, 182, 204, 210–11, 240

Shklar, Judith 205

Simon, Yves 32

Singer, Marcus 13, 21n1

situatedness: and freedom 4, 94, 99, 112, 116–19, 135, 139, 152; and meaning 122–8, 133, 134–5; and the self 3, 7, 116–18, 125, 133, 134, 180n31

skepticism: Flathman and 1, 6, 8, 239; and Hobbes 185, 188, 190, 201n6; and liberalism 49, 52, 163, 204, 206, 207, 213n3; and opacity 172–3; Wittgenstein's response to 131, 161–2, 163, 172

Skinner, Quentin 96n3, 235n25; and the history of political thought 219, 224; on Hobbes 225; influence of Davidson on 236n27; influenced by present practical concerns 229–34; response to Gunnell 235n21

Starzinger, Vincent E. 21n6

Strauss, Leo 3, 170, 222

Szasz, Thomas 100, 101

Taylor, Charles 99, 103, 104, 109, 118, 125, 126, 128, 170, 171, 180n20; and virtue liberalism 208, 209

Thomson, Judith Jarvis 82n19

toleration 6, 167, 180n21

Tuck, Richard 1, 225–34

Tooley, Michael 79n4, 81n14

unfreedom 87–9, 94–5, 113, 132, 152–3; and autonomy 153; Hobbes on 114n1, 183; and Marxism 95n1; and negative freedom 91, 96n2; and Nietzsche 145–6; positive freedom and 4, 93, 114n1; and rule following 93, 137–9; situated character of 116–17, 126–8, 130, 134

utilitarianism: Flathman on 5, 239

virtue liberalism 8, 203, 207–9; role of reason in 208; voluntarism in 209

virtuosity liberalism 6, 9, 212; *see also* willful liberalism

voluntarism: strong 209, 211–12, 213n9; weak 209, 210

Warren, Mary Anne 82n19

Wertheimer, Alan 1

Wertheimer, Roger 69–70, 81n15

Williams, Bernard 103, 203, 239, 244

willful liberalism 1, 5–7, 9, 210–12; and agency liberalism 210; and individuality 210; as a perfectionism 212; and public policy 212; strong voluntarism and 211–12; *virtù* liberalism 212; *see also* liberalism; virtuosity liberalism

252 *Index*

Wittgenstein, Ludwig: against private language 4, 23, 29, 81n15, 122–6, 137, 180n27, 234; and the authoritative 46, 50, 54n5; on beliefs 161–2, 163, 168; on not commanding a clear view of our language 162–3; and competing theories of meaning 120–2; and complementarism 162, 163, 174, 176; and facts of nature 130–1, 133–4; and family resemblance concepts 72, 127, 137, 168, 203, 209; and forms of life 45, 165, 169, 170, 178n7, 179n16; and freedom 128–33; influence on Flathman 2–5, 9n1; language games and 23–5, 28–9, 30, 31n12, 119, 130, 164, 165, 168–9, 170, 179n16, 180n27, 234–5; and meaning in use 27–8, 120–6; and object-word theory 121–4, 140n4; and opacity 127, 165–6, 168, 175–6; philosophy of language of 23–31, 69, 140n5, 178n6; and politics 178n5, 179n12; and religion 165–9, 179n16; and rules and rule following 23–4, 27–8, 47–8, 94, 129–31, 134–9, 140n6, 140n7; and situatedness 119–34